Bob Evan

895

ON AMERICAN SOIL

ON AMERICAN SOIL

How Justice
Became a Casualty
of World War II

Jack Hamann

Happy Birthday, Dave!
All the best,
Jack Hamann

Algonquin Books of Chapel Hill
2005

Published by
ALGONQUIN BOOKS OF CHAPEL HILL
Post Office Box 2225
Chapel Hill, North Carolina 27515-2225

a division of
WORKMAN PUBLISHING
708 Broadway
New York, New York 10003

Printed in the United States of America.
Published simultaneously in Canada by Thomas Allen & Son Limited.
Design by Anne Winslow.
Map illustrations by Laura Williams.

Library of Congress Cataloging-in-Publication Data
Hamann, Jack, 1954–
On American soil : how justice became a casualty of World War II /
Jack Hamann.—1st ed.
p. cm.
Includes bibliographical references (p.   ).
ISBN-13: 978-1-56512-394-6
ISBN-10: 1-56512-394-8
1. World War, 1939–1945—Prisoners and prisons, American.
2. Prisoners of war—Violence against—Washington (State)—Seattle.
3. Prisoners of war—Washington (State)—Seattle.   4. Prisoners of war—
Italy.   5. Prisoners of war—United States.   6. Prison riots—Washington
(State)—Seattle.   7. Fort Lawton (Seattle, Wash.)—History.   I. Title.
D805.5.F66H36 2005
940.54'7279777—dc22   2004058563

10 9 8 7 6 5 4 3 2 1
First Edition

For Gerry and Julianna

No tears are shed when an enemy dies.
—PUBLILIUS SYRUS (A.D. 42)

CONTENTS

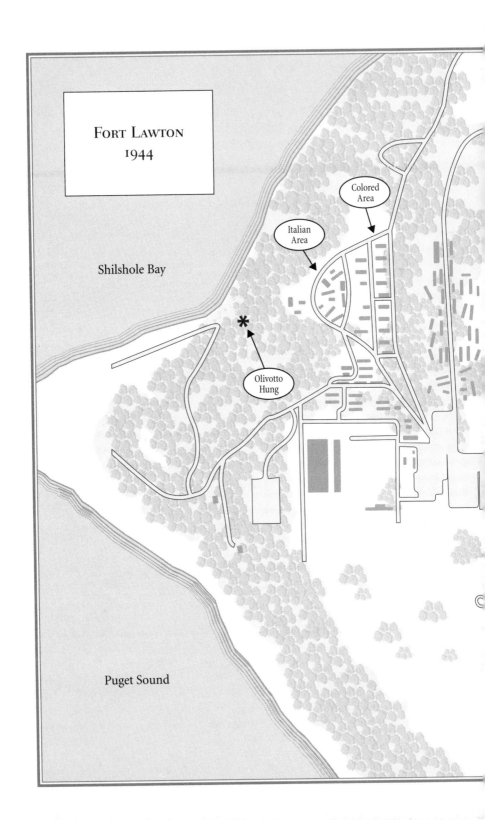

FORT LAWTON
1944

Shilshole Bay

Colored
Area

Italian
Area

*

Olivotto
Hung

Puget Sound

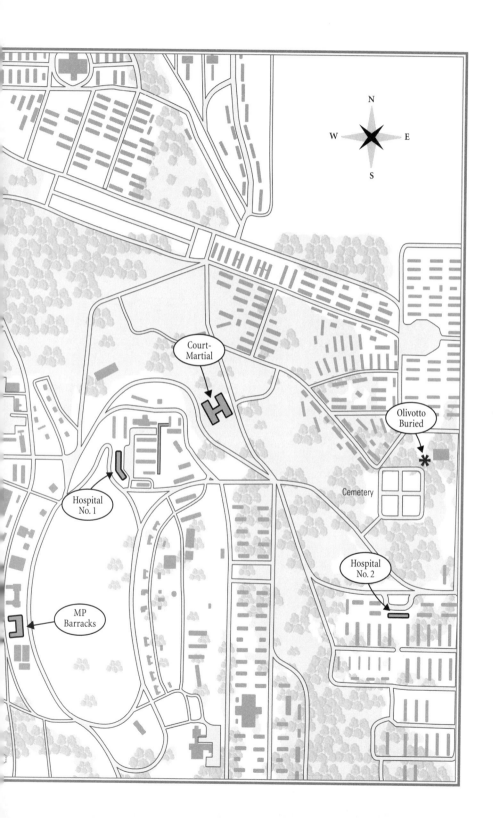

AUTHOR'S NOTE

YEARS AGO, WHEN I was still a young reporter, I began work on a story that has now taken me seventeen years to finish. Back in 1987, my assignment editor sent me to Seattle's Discovery Park, where bureaucrats were briefing the press about plans to expand a sewage treatment plant along the park's western boundary. The event was dull, and I soon found myself chatting with a park ranger.

Discovery Park occupied most of what used to be a U.S. Army base. The ranger told me that the site was sprinkled with unusual objects, many left over from past wars. "Like what?" I asked. "Well," she said, "there's this strange headstone in the old Fort Lawton Cemetery." She described it as a Roman-style column but with its top broken off. The grave had an inscription, but it wasn't in English. That's all she knew, except that whoever was buried there might have been some kind of prisoner and, she'd been told, he might have been murdered.

I visited the headstone, copied the inscription, then went back to the office to file my sewage story. Over the next several weeks, I poked around when I could, trying to learn more about the mysterious broken column. I went to the public library to check newspaper headlines against the date on the dead man's grave: 14 AGOSTO 1944. Sure enough, his death was reported on the front page of the August 16, 1944, *Seattle Post-Intelligencer*: an Italian prisoner of war had been lynched at Fort Lawton, and the prime suspects were members of a "mob" of African American soldiers. I was floored. I looked long and hard to find anyone who had ever heard about this incredible event. Even Seattle's leading citizens, and most if its historians, had no idea that the ensuing trial was the largest army court-martial of World War II or that the army prosecutor was Leon Jaworski, one of the most famous attorneys in American history. The death of a POW in U.S. custody, with military policemen among the suspects, had been an international scandal back in 1944. Yet the event was somehow conspicuously absent from history books and even from the collective memories of lawyers, soldiers, and journalists. I figured I was onto something.

At the time, I was a local television reporter, and managers in our newsroom were none too keen about me spending time on a forgotten episode in history. My benevolent assignment editor winked, however, as my photographer and I slipped out to conduct a few interviews on the sly. Another photographer joined our little conspiracy, followed by other colleagues who volunteered to help where they could. Eventually, management had no choice but to buy me a ticket to Texas, where many of the surviving defendants were still living.

With the help of nearly half the newsroom, we aired a one-hour program about the Fort Lawton murder and court-martial. Local media critics loved it, and it won some awards. I felt generally pretty smug about pulling the whole thing off.

But mostly, it was a lie.

Not an intentional lie, mind you, but the continuance of a falsehood that the army had foisted on the press in 1944, and the press had all too willingly passed along to the public. In the all-consuming chaos of world war, army censors had kept reporters on a tight leash, often hiding important facts in the name of national security or prohibiting the publication of telling details to protect the army's reputation. My television news report perpetuated many of those lies, because it relied too much on secondary sources and because I had been denied access to government documents that still remained classified. I had little reason to doubt that the newspapers had gotten it mostly right. Besides, the reporters who had bothered to sit through the monthlong trial never publicly expressed outrage about the eventual verdicts, and I wasn't sure whether I could either.

Years went by, and I traveled the world, filing hundreds of other stories, big and small. I often thought about the men I had visited in Texas and was dogged by a nagging sense that the full story hadn't been told. They had endured a trial beyond imagination, battling the immense legal resources of the most powerful army on Earth. Decades later, they still believed the army had resorted to rumor, innuendo, and prejudice to serve the personal ambitions of some and the political fortunes of others. Truth, it is often said, is the first casualty of war. Personal liberties and due process soon follow. All those American soldiers, sailors, and airmen had been fighting for democracy, but what is freedom if there's no justice for all?

For years, those who had worked with me on the Fort Lawton story often told me, "You ought to write a book about it." When our youngest child left home for college, my wife, Leslie, and I decided that the time might finally be right. Fifteen years older and—in some ways, perhaps—wiser, we headed this time for primary sources, those back rooms where musty boxes filled with thin yellowing papers are stored in archives and libraries and museums. We spent weeks at the National Archives in College Park, Maryland, almost always the first in line each morning and the last to leave each night. We poured through an endless stream of boxes crammed with files stuffed with papers, many of them poorly indexed. As we drew closer to the relevant materials, we discovered that the army had only recently declassified much of it for public viewing.

Finally, one hot afternoon, Leslie uncovered the treasure we had been digging for. From boxes indexed under an obscure subcategory of a now-defunct army department, she extracted three fat files. In those files was the army's formerly secret report about the Fort Lawton incident, prepared by an exceptionally interesting brigadier general for his boss, the army inspector general. There, among thousands of incriminating pages, was the story, more or less, of what *really* happened at Fort Lawton the night of August 14, 1944.

The unearthing of the general's report led us to hundreds of other documents, and kick-started several road trips across America. Visiting small towns and large, we drove thousands of miles, conducting interviews, gathering new evidence, and filling in large gaps. We tried to learn the whereabouts of almost four hundred people, many of them long dead. Fortunately, many of the key figures were still alive and willing to share their memories. In other cases, family members helped resurrect documents, photos, and family histories.

This is their story. All quotations have been verified; every important fact has multiple sources. Sometimes, of course, the truth hurts. There are heroes in this story but not very many.

There is an old saying: "Doctors bury their mistakes. Lawyers hang them. But journalists put theirs on the front page." In this case, some in the army managed to bury a mistake for more than sixty years, and dozens of journalists since—including me—helped keep it in the ground. The truth now emerges in no small part because of the American tradition of declassifying historical documents, albeit belatedly, even if they prove embarrassing. In this case, the truth also got a helping hand from several honorable men and women in the army itself—both in 1944 and more recently—who did not want the truth to be forever buried beneath that headstone. It is because of them that this story can now be told.

U.S. ARMY RANKS DURING WORLD WAR II

Officers	*Enlisted Men*
General of the Army	Master Sergeant
General	First Sergeant
Lieutenant General	Technical Sergeant
Major General	Staff Sergeant
Brigadier General	Technician Third Class (T/3)
Colonel	Sergeant
Lieutenant Colonel	Technician Fourth Class (T/4)
Major	Corporal
Captain	Technician Fifth Class (T/5)
First Lieutenant	Private First Class
Second Lieutenant	Private
Chief Warrant Officer	
Warrant Officer	

ON AMERICAN SOIL

PROLOGUE

August 15, 1944

JOHN PINKNEY BRACED AS his jeep pitched along rutted clay and gravel in the blackness before dawn. Beside him was Clyde Vernon Lomax, a skinny white kid from the bayou with long sideburns and an army six-shooter slapping his thigh. Although both men wore the black-and-white brassards of military policemen, Pinkney was a private first class and therefore outranked Lomax, if barely. Private Lomax, however, was in the driver's seat and in control.

Pinkney's wristwatch read four forty-five. To the west, the chilly wind-driven waters of Puget Sound flushed across shallow tideflats. Lomax downshifted, eased the jeep to a stuttering stop, but kept the engine idling; Pinkney stared vainly into the abyss. Although the vehicle's twin headlights illuminated perhaps thirty yards of sand and damp grass dead ahead, the eye-splitting glare rendered the rest of the world all but invisible.

Lomax tried to gaze beyond the lights to a point near the horizon where the headlands met water. He thought he'd seen a silhouette, or two or maybe three, or at least that's what he told Pinkney. The engine fell silent, headlights dissolved, and the two soldiers sat quietly, waiting for their eyes to adjust to the night. Peering toward the trees, they scanned for shapes in the shadows. Somewhere, tucked among the Oregon grape and red elderberry, or concealed behind trunks of madrone and bigleaf maple, scared soldiers might still be in hiding.

Five hours had passed since the first few frightened men scrambled into the woods and slid down slippery paths along the Magnolia Bluffs. It had been even longer since taps had signaled the end of the day at Fort Lawton, a sprawling army post just north of downtown Seattle. Wired on coffee but weary from lack of sleep, Pinkney and Lomax had tried all night to pick up the trail of soldiers still missing from their barracks, on orders to haul them back to their bunks now that the evening's excitement had ended.

As five o'clock approached, a chill pressed the back of Pinkney's neck and sunk between his shoulders. Sandpipers squeaked and scurried, while weathered fishing boats slid south, red beacons on bows, white lights trailing on sterns. As the night lifted, the bluffs gradually took form, tall cliffs dotted with bigleaf maples. Suddenly, Lomax snapped to attention: somehow, in this still-gray landscape, he had spotted a suspicious shadow up ahead.

Engine and headlights jumped to life, but the jeep slipped once and then twice on wet clay. The road was slick and the thought of getting stuck unappealing, so Lomax parked and both men stumbled out into the damp grass. Picking their way through ever-higher brush, they reached the base of the bluffs without speaking a word. Pinkney would later say that he never even learned Lomax's name. In turn, Lomax would report that his fellow soldier that early morning was simply "this nigger MP." Neither man could later be certain which of them first spotted the lifeless body of Private Olivotto.

As Pinkney drew nearer, the sight seemed less real. Strung between two massive maples above a trickling creek, a pair of steel cables stretched above a third. Suspended from the lowest cable was a thin rope, tautly strangling the limp body of a dead man. Pinkney's eyes widened, and for a moment he wondered, or even hoped, that the figure was an effigy, a dummy stuffed with straw. The steel cables were, after all, part of an obstacle course used by Fort Lawton's soldiers. It would have made sense that, there in Seattle, a body on a noose would be fake, part of some sort of training exercise for soldiers headed overseas. Of course, if Pinkney had been home, in Kansas City, a similar silhouette would have meant only one thing: another colored man had been strung up by a mob or the Klan.

But with each halting step, the light grew less gray, and the form now ten yards up the hill revealed itself as definitely human, definitely not a black man. He was barefoot, wearing only olive GI boxers, a white undershirt, and a khaki army shirt. On his left shoulder was a round green and white patch, bearing unmistakable bold letters that spelled out ITALY.

CHAPTER ONE

CAMP FLORENCE
May 1944

THE TOWN OF FLORENCE is just out of Tucson, past the Superstition Mountains and Picacho Peak, beyond the east riverbank of the Santa Cruz. The road to town drifts northwest across the flat bottom of an ancient inland sea, searing in summer and uncomfortably cold most winter nights. Green fields line both sides of the highway, thanks to a mix of soil, sun, and miles of manmade canals. Cotton farmers here grow some of the finest long fiber this side of Egypt.

Just beyond Florence is the Gila River and, past that, a spur for the Southern Pacific Railroad, its tracks dead-ending at what used to be the gates of Camp Florence. Back in 1944, twin fences topped with barbed wire protected the rest of the world from the restless men locked inside what was once the largest prisoner-of-war compound ever built on American soil.

On May 17, 1944, Guglielmo Olivotto and his best pals, Imo Nolgi and Bruno Patteri, sweltered in the stuffy heat of a two-story wood-frame barrack. The three Italian prisoners stayed busy at their bunks, fighting the anxiety of the uncertainty ahead. In less than twenty-four hours, they were to be loaded onto a troop train and shipped to an undisclosed U.S. army installation in yet another unfamiliar part of America. Although Camp Florence had its drawbacks, it had proved safe and familiar and much less daunting than the prospect of switching to another strange venue in this never-ending war.

Heaped atop each man's canvas cot was a mound of clothing and equipment, all newly issued for their one-way journey out of Arizona. Leather service shoes with new laces and refurbished soles, clean but needing a shine. One garrison cap and two cotton field hats, both a bit frayed. Socks and handkerchiefs, GI drawers and undershirts. Two pairs of pants, one web belt. A toothbrush, shaving brush, safety razor, and five blades. A meat can, canteen, canteen cup, fork, knife, and spoon. Dog tags stamped with name, rank, and prisoner-of-war serial number. Miscellaneous bivouac equipment.

Of all the gear spread across each cot, none looked more out of place than a matching pair of worn but clean khaki shirts. Olivotto had been in Arizona for nine months, and the only outer clothing he'd ever been issued was dark blue: surplus U.S. army suntans and olive drabs soaked in vats of indigo dye to distinguish Italian prisoners from their American captors. Until now, all his outer shirts, pants, and jackets had come stamped with the six-inch yellow letters PW on front and back. But this morning, he'd been handed the very same uniforms worn by the U.S. army; only the buttons were different, plain rather than metal. Each pile of clothing included a handful of oval cloth patches, with instructions to sew them on the left sleeves of all outer garments. The patches, green and white, were inscribed in bold letters: ITALY.

Guglielmo, Imo, and Bruno shared mixed feelings about their decision to accept a new assignment. There had been whispers from fellow Italians that it was all a trick and that the Americans intended to stick them back into battle, fighting Japanese and mosquitoes in some godforsaken jungle in the Pacific. There were other rumors too, enough to persuade some prisoners to take their chances in the withering oven of the upcoming Arizona summer rather than travel to an unknown new location, even if it meant missing out on the liberties and privileges promised to those who would be leaving with Olivotto and his buddies the next day.

But Guglielmo wasn't about to stay behind while his two closest friends went away. Eight days earlier, they had made the decision together, agreeing to be among the very first enlisted men to volunteer for a quartermaster company called the Twenty-eighth Italian Service Unit. Stuffing his canvas barracks bags with his newly issued gear, there was just enough room for rosaries, playing cards, cigarettes, hard candy, a small statue of the Virgin Mother, and a creased card bearing her image. The world was still at war; he would simply have to take his chances.

THROUGHOUT HISTORY, BEING a prisoner of war was a fate often barely better than being killed in battle. Capture usually meant humiliation, torture, or starvation; it sometimes meant being worked to death or being used as a human shield on the battlefield. In the uncertain aftermath of the First World War, diplomats from forty-seven nations gathered in Geneva, Switzerland, determined to inject a measure of humanity into the ugly business of caring for captured soldiers. A long list of requirements and restrictions were drafted, all meant to preserve prisoners' dignity and to minimize the inevitable resentment that had so often launched new wars of retribution. The Geneva Convention for the Treatment of Prisoners of War was a major diplomatic breakthrough, although some countries, including Japan and the Soviet Union, refused to go along.

Those nations that did sign the treaty promised to treat prisoners humanely and protect them from acts of violence, insults, or public curiosity. Prisoners of war had a right to clean, safe quarters and to food rations equal in quality and quantity to whatever was served to the detaining power's own troops at its base camps. They were to have access to books, games, and recreation and to be allowed to buy personal items, including tobacco, at military canteens. Captured enlisted men, but not their officers, could be put to work as long as there were adequate protections for health and safety. Prison jobs could never, however, have any direct relation to combat and could not involve the manufacture or movement of weapons or explosives. To ensure the rules were being followed, representatives from the International Committee of the Red Cross and from neutral nations like Switzerland were to be offered regular access to all prison camps.

Americans, however, were hardly experts in the care and feeding of war prisoners in their own backyards. Most battles since the end of the Civil War had been fought on foreign soil, where captured soldiers were usually corralled in large stockades not far from the front lines. During the First World War, only 1,346 enemy troops spent any time in captivity in the United States.

In World War II, the military got into the prisoner-of-war business right away when, in the chaotic aftermath of Pearl Harbor, a Japanese sailor accidentally beached his miniature submarine. A few more POWs trickled in during 1942, mostly Germans captured in North Africa by British forces, then redirected to the United States to relieve overcrowding in English prison camps. These first few enemy soldiers were an afterthought, treated as little more than a drain on military money and manpower.

The army was made responsible for the care of all foreign prisoners, no matter which branch of the military actually captured them, under the jurisdiction of a newly created post called the provost marshal general. Prison compounds, it was hoped, would be built where surplus barracks or obsolete Civilian Conservation Corps buildings were already available. All camps were to be located in rural areas, far from city dwellers who might be fearful of fugitives and particularly distant from military installations and factories, where the possibility of espionage was a relentless concern. Initial proposals penciled most prisons south of the fortieth parallel, where warmer weather meant lower costs for heating, insulation, and wintertime clothing.

Where surplus barracks were not available, Provost Marshal General Allen Gullion was authorized to order construction of entire compounds from the ground up. Early on, eyes turned to Florence, Arizona, a remote town in a sunny climate where a sizable state penitentiary was already part of the community. In January 1942, the army paid four million dollars for five hundred acres of pancake-flat land north of the Gila River. Blueprints were drafted for a sprawling complex, including barracks, a bakery, a 486-bed hospital, a swimming pool, twenty theaters, courts for volleyball and basketball, and guard towers all around.

If the United States was to stay true its Geneva Convention commitments, Camp Florence would be the War Department's shining model.

The thought of Nazis and Fascists lurking not far from schools and playgrounds did not sit well with town fathers in rural Arizona. On February 17, 1942, the men of the Rotary Club of nearby Superior, Arizona, gave U.S. senator Carl Hayden a piece of their collective minds. "The members of this club, who you know are the heads of businesses, unanimously protest the establishment of an internment camp at Florence, Arizona. We realize that such camps are essential and that selfishness might be [in] back of protests as to where they are located, but we assure you that it is not selfishness in this case." Arizona's unselfish Rotarians felt they were doing their country a huge service by warning Congress that the region's four large copper mines would be threatened by the presence of a POW camp. In a separate letter, E. D. Dentzer, general manager of the Magma Copper Company, explained that relatives and friends of Germans and Italians were certain to move near the prison compound in order to be close to loved ones. "I feel sure a lot of those people would be potential saboteurs and, therefore, a menace to any and all defense industries in this locality."

Small-town paranoia, however, was no match for a nationwide military machine demanding sacrifice from citizens and communities everywhere. By April, construction at Camp Florence was well under way, and by fall military police escort companies were living in the barracks, training for the day when Nazi, Fascist, and Japanese prisoners would find their way to the Arizona desert. Events in North Africa, however, soon accelerated their timetable.

At 3:40 P.M. on May 7, 1943, British tanks rolled into Tunis. Forty-five minutes later, Americans entered Bizerte, forty miles northwest. Exhausted Allied soldiers had finally conquered both major ports on Tunisia's northern coast, a hard-fought reward after six bloody months battling entrenched German and Italian forces in the mud-caked hills of northern Africa. During the last week of April and the first week of May, a quarter-million Axis soldiers trudged out with their hands up, roughly a hundred thousand Germans and the rest Italians. It would be the largest mass surrender of the war.

Almost overnight, Allied commanders around the world were forced to secure shelter for the unexpected swarm of new enemy prisoners. Tens of thousands were shipped to Britain and her colonies in India and South Africa, or as far away as Australia. Thousands more were placed in the ballast holds of vessels bound for the United States, where Pentagon officials scrambled to find somewhere to stow them on American soil. The new camp in Florence was soon filled to capacity.

The mass capitulation in Tunisia had been both poignant and surreal. German soldiers, still wearing the uniforms of proud, battle-hardened warriors, had been shocked by their defeat and remained defiant toward their captors. Most Italians, on the other hand, were fairly giddy with relief. Some had labored in Africa for as long as five years, pawns in Benito Mussolini's dream of a new Roman Empire. Ferruccio Umek, captured May 7, 1943, later told the *Chicago Tribune* that he had been conscripted into Italy's Africa campaign "without training, without uniforms, without weapons. Our shoes were full of holes; we were full of lice." The heat had been fierce; the sand blown by searing winds had sometimes swallowed them whole. Rations had been meager: a typical meal might have been little more than carrots, salted sardines, and moldy black bread.

Chased by British general Bernard Montgomery from the south and east, and by British general Kenneth Anderson and American general Omar Bradley from the west, the Italians had struggled for weeks without adequate food, water, sleep, or ammunition. The only thing Italian soldiers hated more than their German allies were their own Fascist officers, many of whom had earned rank through political favor rather than military skill. The favored greeting was "*Speriamo*," short for "*Speriamo che finisce questa guerra*" ("We hope that this war ends"). The prospect of laying down guns had been, for most Italians, a welcome and long-overdue deliverance.

Guglielmo Olivotto had been a speck in the teeming crowd of surrendering soldiers that week. Olivotto was no kid: he was thirty-one years old, born in Nervesa, a village sixty miles north of Venice. The town, on the south bank of the Piave River, squatted at the base of Montello Mountain, above a broad plain dotted with small vineyards and modest farms. Shops and cottages surrounded the central piazza, built of stone and old timber, washed with pastel paint every forty years or so, then left to peel until a patchwork of stone peeked through again. Guglielmo was barely six years old when Nervesa was reduced to rubble during one of World War I's bloodiest battles, as Austrian forces pushed south of the Piave, only to be driven back again a few days later. The town, when eventually rebuilt, was renamed Nervesa della Battaglia, in honor of its heroic defense of Italy.

Guglielmo grew up at a time when young men regularly fled rural Italy to chase dreams of decent wages and brighter futures, mostly in western Europe and America. By 1922, unemployment was so rampant—and inflation so out of control—that Benito Mussolini and his nationalist Fascists had little trouble bullying their way to power. Olivotto, still a teenager, packed his bags and headed west, spending the next seventeen years as a laborer in France. His expatriate life came to an abrupt end in 1940, however, when Hitler's panzers quickly overran French resistance. The Germans forced most Italian émigrés to return home, where they were immediately conscripted into the military.

Olivotto was a quiet man, well read and devoutly religious. He was lean, five feet ten inches and just 150 pounds. His eyes were dark; his hair was black and thick, except for a bald spot on the crown of his head; he wore a dark mustache. A thin scar slid down the right side of his scalp at hairline. He was never married and had no children. He didn't drink or gamble. He had no interest in being a soldier.

By 1942, Private Olivotto was an army truck driver, stuck in the miserable heat of the Libyan desert. Libya had been ceded by the Turks in 1912 after the collapse of the Ottoman Empire, and a brutal program of Italianization followed. By 1940, one hundred thousand Italians had been sent to Libya as settlers, hastening the death or dislocation of half the native Libyan population. In the meantime, the

North African beachhead provided Mussolini a base to invade Ethiopia, Sudan, and Somalia.

But Il Duce's ambitions were cut short. On a moonless night in November 1942, U.S. and British troops stormed the shoreline in Casablanca, Oran, and Algiers. Just three days later, the Allies controlled Morocco and Algeria, the entire western third of North Africa. Within weeks, the British Eighth army, surging from Egypt in the east, rolled into Tripoli, capital of Italian Libya. Olivotto and thousands of his fellow soldiers were forced to retreat west into Tunisia, where they were caught in a vice between advancing Americans, British, and French on one side and General Montgomery on the other.

War correspondent Ernie Pyle, who slept, ate, and marched with troops in Tunisia, was one of the few American reporters to write unabashedly about what he admiringly called the "God-damned infantry":

> I was sitting among clumps of sword grass on a steep and rocky hillside that we had just taken, looking out over a vast rolling country to the rear. A narrow path wound like a ribbon over another hill. All along the length of that ribbon there was a thin line of men. For four days and nights they had fought hard, eaten little, washed none, and slept hardly at all. Their nights had been violent with attack, fright, butchery, and their days sleepless and miserable with the crash of artillery . . . Their walk was slow, for they were dead weary, as a person could tell even when looking at them from behind. Every line and sag of their bodies spoke their inhuman exhaustion . . . Their faces were black and unshaved. They were young men, but the grime and whiskers and exhaustion made them look middle-aged. In their eyes as they passed was no hatred, no excitement, no despair, no tonic of their victory—there was just the simple expression of being there as if they had been there doing that forever, and nothing else.

One of those retreating from the American advance was John Apice, an Italian tank driver. "Our battles were tough. The heat in the tanks, and the lack of food and drinks, made it so hard to be able to drive those damn tanks for hours at a time. We moved around to fight. We usually never went more than a couple of days before another battle broke out. Our battles lasted a couple of hours, or several months. There was never any way to tell which one it would be . . . For every man we killed, there were another two behind him. For every tank we destroyed, there were two more on each side. We were outnumbered and tired and sick."

Little wonder that soldiers on both sides were glad when they ran out of land at the tip of Tunisia.

CAMP FLORENCE WELCOMED its first Italian prisoners of war on May 4, 1943. Within days, most were given a single printed sheet of stationery, with space for name, rank, and POW number and a rectangular box in the middle to compose a letter to a loved one in Italy.

Silvana:
    I am now altogether out of danger, in fact, one might almost say that I am on a pleasant vacation—believe me, I am really very comfortable, I am eating plenty of good food & because of this comfortable life I am putting on weight. —Rino

Carlo:
    We are being treated very well here—we sleep on cots with two quilts—whenever we want to we can bathe, even any time of the night. There are three meals a day and they are very good and plentiful. We are treated courteously, and we are really leading a life of fine gentlemen. The canteen has everything we need and there are plenty of cigarettes. We also have a movie theater. We are really well off! —Your brother, Ianici

Papa:
    Certainly I have no reason for complaining as I am situated now. You too will be astonished when you learn how I live here. I

am in a flourishing village of wooden cottages especially built for our use — our sleeping quarters are very clean and I enjoy all manner of comforts. —Your son, Ettore

Letters from POWs were not private; they were gathered each day and piled on desks of army censors. Any references deemed inappropriate or seditious or just plain too negative were either deleted or pulled from the mailbag. At Camp Florence, though, censors found little to edit.

Signa Tere:
I am very comfortable & well, Tere, so do not worry, just have faith . . . The voyage here was delightful and I find myself with many friends in Arizona, land of dreams and illusions! We are enjoying the utmost cleanliness and comfort. In addition, the food is really marvelous, just to give you an idea of what we eat, here is the menu for today's breakfast: chocolate, toast, butter & honey; dinner: spaghetti, potato salad, salami, cheese and dessert, or stewed fruit, and in the evening we eat at a table set with real dishes. We are given three dollars per month for "pin money"— there are plenty of cigarettes. Tere, you can write to me as often as you want to. —Your fiancé, Achille

On May 9, a new shipment of prisoners arrived in Arizona, most of them transferred from overcrowded British internment camps in South Africa. Some had watched comrades die of thirst on forced marches through the desert. Others had wasted on diets of stale bread and weak broth. Within hours, the new arrivals realized Camp Florence was miraculously different.

Mother:
I want you to know that I am no longer in South Africa—now I am in America, and I am so comfortable that it's like being in

Paradise—they treat us so well. This time, Mother, I am telling you the truth—here, nothing is lacking. —Armando

Papa:
I have had the pleasant surprise of finally being treated like a human being, that is, sleeping in a comfortable, well-aired cottage furnished with a comfortable cot. The climate is very warm, seemingly well-chosen. But after all, I am in America, the nation of dollars. —Grancesco

Many prisoners had not heard from family members for years and agonized whenever they heard occasional news of the war's progress in Europe. Patton and Montgomery were now barreling through Sicily, and Mussolini was on the run. Throughout Italy, war-weary citizens suffered from an endless drain of money, manpower, and hope. Some of the letters written at Camp Florence may have made their recipients' suffering seem even worse.

Primula:
The treatment we get in this camp is excellent. As to the food served us, I can almost say that it is even better and more plentiful than our meals at home were. Therefore, Primula, dear, cheer up, and think how lucky your husband is to be in America and how he wishes you could have the things to eat that he is enjoying. —Armando

Week after week, POWs poured in. New arrivals wore uniforms tattered by war, skin blistered by African sun, and hair infested with lice. Each was given a physical exam, a dental checkup, and an inoculation against smallpox. Personal items—watches, crucifixes, good-luck charms, photographs, even carpet slippers—were inventoried, then handed back. Foreign currency was confiscated and stored for safekeeping until the end of the war. Every POW was photographed, fingerprinted, and asked to fill out a form giving name, rank, and home address. Each was issued a prisoner of war serial number.

Although Mussolini had been running Italy, King Vittorio Emanuelle III remained nominally in power. Most foot soldiers were apolitical and would have preferred to sit out the war, but of those who did profess a loyalty, it was usually to king and not to the Fascists. The War Department viewed Fascist sympathizers as troublemakers or even worse, so almost every arriving prisoner was interviewed in private by an officer from army Intelligence. To probe a prisoner's allegiance, questions on the standard interrogation forms included "Do you think Italy, Germany and Japan can still win the war?" "Are German troops popular in Italy?" "Have you complete faith in the Fascist leaders?" Those who openly sympathized with Mussolini's Fascists were quickly segregated from soldiers who said they were members of the king's army. Sympathizers were kept in separate barracks under close guard. Where answers were ambiguous, a "watch list" was prepared to keep an eye on possible problem prisoners down the road.

The U.S. army's Psychological Operations branch also mined new arrivals for possible propaganda to use during the invasion of Italy. Their standard list of questions included "What are the latest political jokes?" "Have you heard any scandal about Mussolini?" "Have you seen any chain letters recently?" German prisoners, on the other hand, were specifically asked whether they'd heard any good jokes about the incompetence of Italian soldiers.

The glow of POW gratitude at Camp Florence was evident throughout the summer of 1943. Independent inspectors began touring the compound, filing reports with the International Committee of the Red Cross and the YMCA. From the very first visit, the inspectors' tone was as complimentary as the prisoners' letters home: "Camp is spotlessly clean and sanitary." "Prisoner morale is good." Florence "is the nearest to a model camp which we have seen in POW camps." The examiners snapped small black-and-white photos of rows of two-story wood barracks, each with broad eaves extending from both the upper and lower levels to provide shade from the broiling Arizona sun. Inside, they captured images of smiling Italians standing next to well-spaced cots beneath high ceilings supported by dozens of tall, square posts. Not visible were the pinup girls, torn from the pages of *Esquire* and *Life,* with fanciful names of Italian girls scribbled at the bottom. A snapshot taken at the camp entrance showed two men standing in the shade of an enormous cactus, a stately saguaro soaring at least twenty feet above them, extending more than a dozen fat, fleshy arms into the desert sky. Visible in the background were some of the twenty-six guard towers ringing the camp perimeter.

Newspapermen were equally enthusiastic. Chester Hanson of the *Los Angeles Times* was impressed that the Italians "have their own theater group and an 18-piece orchestra . . . The maestro is a bearded gentleman of ability. They have a stage in the recreation hall. This group worked diligently and has put together a variety show that even one who cannot understand Italian can enjoy . . . Costumes—remember these men came over here in prisoners' clothes—made themselves, even to the filmy long bloomers of the 'lady' oriental dancer, with a tied-on bust effect and the veil from the eyes down. And was 'she' some dancer!"

Hanson marveled at the resourcefulness of clever men filling idle time in prison. He wrote about a trio of opera singers wearing white jackets sewn from bed sheets and bow ties cut from cardboard. Hanson saw "suitcases made out of thin scrap lumber, and one, a remarkable piece of work, made out of tin cut from five-gallon cans. Beautiful cigarette cases made out of aluminum cut from canteens and polished with sand and dust rubbed on the metal with a piece of bacon rind." Inmates painted a fresco in the camp chapel and built an outdoor shell of adobe as an acoustic backdrop for evening concerts. A series of elaborate vegetable gardens sprung up between dusty barracks.

Long before the first prisoners arrived, a well-meaning official made sure the camp was equipped with sporting gear. The Camp Florence warehouse had been stuffed with enough bats, balls, gloves, rackets, helmets, and goals to outfit four full baseball teams, two football teams, four basketball teams, and enough tennis and badminton equipment to keep several courts hopping. Unfortunately, much of the gear gathered dust, as the Americans belatedly learned that Italians preferred soccer, volleyball, and bocce. Eventually, the best soccer players were permitted to play matches against local teams made up of Mexican migrant workers.

To Italian enlisted men, the Camp Florence amenities were all the sweeter because commissioned Italian officers were nowhere in sight. The Geneva Convention required roomier quarters and additional liberties for higher-ranking officers; Arizona was built for enlisted men only. Italian officers had their own camps in Utah, California, and Texas. As far as the men in Florence were concerned, the separation couldn't be wide enough.

BY THE TIME a train carrying Guglielmo Olivotto, Imo Nolgi, and Bruno Patteri pulled into Camp Florence in early September 1943, the prison had been transformed into a barbed-wire oasis. After Olivotto, Nolgi, and Patteri were each prodded by army Intelligence and probed by army doctors, they were given a pile of new clothing and directed toward the showers. Camp guards had grown accustomed to seeing men caked with months of grime return time and again the very same day to enjoy another round of soap and hot water. In a few cases, men had stretched out on the floor to let water pour over their grateful naked bodies for hours at a time.

When Olivotto first reached his bunk, he was greeted with another treat. Resting on the mattress was a one-page letter, translated into Italian, written by Colonel William A. Holden, the American camp commander:

To the Italian Prisoners of War, Florence Internment Camp, Florence, Arizona:
Permit me to welcome you to this camp. Due to the fortunes of war, you find yourselves detained by the Army of the United States of America. Your detention will be managed strictly in accordance with agreements made between the United States of America and the Kingdom of Italy.

You have my full assurance that you will at all times be humanely treated and protected, particularly against acts of violence, insults and public curiosity.

Colonel Holden was a soldier's soldier, a thin-faced, droopy-eyed man from Sparta, Wisconsin, who had earned a silver star and purple heart while an infantryman in France during World War I. His empathy for the grunts who shouldered the real burdens of war led him to view his current assignment as more like a headmaster at a boarding school for wayward boys than a warden at a wartime prison:

As a soldier and as a camp commander, I advise and urge you to preserve your morale. You can best do this by taking advantage of the opportunities afforded you to correspond with your family; by participating in athletics and other recreational programs; by keeping your person and your quarters scrupulously clean; by carefully obeying all orders and instructions of the American Army personnel on duty with you; by attending religious services, and, very important, by preserving a serene disposition at all times.

The colonel's words must have seemed either an unlikely deliverance or a cruel hoax. Soldiers like Olivotto had just emerged from an unforgiving world of kill-or-be-killed; suddenly they were being told they would be cradled in the bosom of a benevolent captor:

You are still soldiers of the Kingdom of Italy and your civil status is protected. You are not confined or detained as punishment. It is my duty to detain each of you until properly released. Outside of the detention features of your stay here, you will be cared for on a basis comparable to the care given to soldiers of the United States of America.

Within days, bookish Olivotto discovered he had access to a library with four hundred Italian titles. He could spend part of an evening watching subtitled Hollywood movies, films like *Tarzan Finds a Son*, *Ziegfeld Girl*, and *Out West with the Hardys* or cartoons like *Mickey Mouse* or *Popeye*. He could read Italian American newspapers, like *Il Progresso Italo-Americano*, *La Voce del Popolo*, and *Il Corriere del Popolo*, all bearing scraps of news about the war and the homeland. And he could even marvel at camp-sponsored newsletters written by fellow inmates, chock-full of stories and gossip and puzzles and drawings and excerpts from juicy novellas with names like *Notte di Nebbia* (Foggy Night) or *L'amante* (The Lover).

Perhaps most comforting to Olivotto were the three priests who took turns conducting mass and hearing confessions. Father Barbato was a U.S. Army chaplain, Father Daniele Dal Sasso a fellow prisoner of war. Father Jacques was a local Arizona priest who spoke Italian and went out of his way to spend time in the hospital or stockade or with men who were naturally shy or lonely, like Olivotto. Prayers became as much a part of Olivotto's camp routine as saluting.

At night, inmates lined up for a turn with the company barber, grateful for a posttrim dollop of scented hair oil; lilac was the favorite. Small tables crafted in the camp woodshop were crowded with soldiers playing checkers or chess or poker or *morra*, an Italian finger-guessing game. Some stayed on their cots, composing one of the two letters they were permitted to send each month. Sometimes, after taps sounded and lights were dimmed, guards could hear one or two Italians softly sobbing. Compared with Africa, Florence, Arizona, was a huge relief, but it still wasn't Florence, Italy.

Twenty months after Pearl Harbor, American soldiers, sailors, and airmen were spread from the South Pacific to the Aleutian Islands to the Mediterranean. At the Pentagon, generals and admirals secretly geared for the eventual invasion of France at Normandy. The U.S. Army was now six million strong and growing, swollen from its paltry prewar level of barely a hundred thousand. Young men enlisted or were drafted or worked in big-city factories churning out tanks, ships, fighter planes, and supplies. The exodus of able-bodied workers away from rural communities triggered a farm labor crisis throughout much of middle America. The nation still needed food, but no longer had enough hands to help gather the harvest.

Around Florence, the labor-intensive cotton crop was most often picked by Mexican braceros, migrant workers who traveled from Florida to Texas to California as crops and local labor pools dictated. But even braceros could not fill the growing labor vacuum, and farmers couldn't round up enough local women and children willing and able to toil in the sun. Soon enough, cotton growers' attention turned to Camp Florence.

The Geneva Convention clearly endorsed the use of POW labor for noncombat activities, particularly for cultivating and harvesting crops. Throughout America, tens of thousands of POWs—including German prisoners living in their own separate camps—were relocated near small towns in order to harvest crops of corn, wheat, and soybeans. By July, army officials in Florence began establishing prison side camps in arid towns between Phoenix and Tucson. In Eloy, tents and frame bunkhouses were erected under cottonwoods near the Santa Cruz River. At Mesa, the army took over a compound originally built to teach the manly skills of western ranch life to the sons of East Coast aristocrats, including Teddy Roosevelt's boys. A Red Cross inspector reported that morale in prison side camps was unexpectedly high: Italians enjoyed living in quarters not surrounded by barbed wire in places where military police guards rarely treated them like inmates.

Chopping cotton was hard work. Lower-grade snapping cotton was picked by plucking the entire boll, then slipping handfuls into a long bag strapped over one shoulder, trailing behind like a canvas bridal veil. Higher-grade long-staple and short-staple cotton had to be separated with the fingers, exhausting labor that left hands raw, backs sore, and shoulders aching as canvas bags grew heavier and hotter as the day wore on. For the month of November 1943, an average of 1,549 POWs per day picked roughly fifty-four pounds of cotton each, a grand total of just under two million pounds for the month.

When all the cotton was chopped, prisoners cleaned irrigation ditches, dug potatoes, picked fruit and vegetables, harvested alfalfa, and maintained roads. And while POW labor helped farmers save their crops, it didn't necessarily save them money. Labor leaders chafed at the prospect of underpaid workers diluting American wages, so the army agreed to charge farmers the competitive local hourly rate of forty cents an hour, minus expenses. Those wages were paid directly to the military, with the bulk of the money deposited in the U.S. Treasury. In 1944, the government earned twenty-two million dollars from the sweat and toil of its enemy soldiers, helping offset the considerable expense of housing and feeding more than fifty thousand Italians and two hundred thousand Germans.

At the camp itself, Italians were the primary workforce in the bakery, laundry, warehouse, and mess halls. All prisoners, whether they worked or not, earned ten cents a day, payable in coupons redeemable at camp canteens for cigarettes, beer, candy, postage stamps, and sundries. Those who held jobs were paid an additional seventy cents a day, a significant incentive in an environment where tobacco and other small luxuries went a long way to ease the heartache of homesickness. A stash of camp coupons brought a measure of control, even dignity, to men who had spent so much of their young lives having someone with a gun telling them what they could and could not do. Performers in the orchestra and theater ensemble so impressed Colonel Holden that he paid them for their practice time and performances, in violation of army regulations.

Guglielmo Olivotto spent most of his first four months at Camp Florence picking cotton. Each morning at dawn, his crew piled into the back of a farmer's pickup, tossing wolf whistles at young women who happened along the dusty roads (although Guglielmo was much too shy to join in). In the fields, a broad straw hat provided meager relief from the midday sun; temperatures were often unbearable until the calendar crept toward Thanksgiving.

As Christmas approached in 1943, life at Camp Florence began to lose a little of its luster. The Italian government had officially surrendered in September, but German soldiers still occupied most of northern Italy, and Guglielmo had to assume that his parents and younger brother were in constant danger. Now that Italy was no longer at war with America, many Italian prisoners openly longed to return home, either to help the Allies push Hitler out of their country or to simply feel their loved ones' embrace. Army censors found it harder to keep up with letters deemed too negative to be mailed abroad.

Rita:
They have the nerve to take us into the open to work under the broiling sun. —Giovanni

Pierina:
I'm in a desert that is worse than Sirte. They make us work in the sun and even the ground is hot. If I were free I would never again be captured alive. —Simone

Speranza:
There are some people who, to curry favors and benevolence from the Americans, covertly do the harassing act. We have, however, organized a strong-arm squad; anyone caught doing any harassing gets beaten up good and hard. One of our petty officers who forgot that he was an Italian was taken to the hospital yesterday with a broken shoulder. —Umberto

Prisoners who had once been grateful to sleep on cots now complained to the Red Cross inspector about the lack of pillows. They grew restless about the slow pace of mail and suspicious that American soldiers had pilfered personal items or cheated them out of camp coupons. The army required daily drilling—marching back and forth in formation—an activity that grew more unpopular as POWs put in longer work days. No one was firing guns at them, but most had never really wanted to be soldiers in the first place.

If Italians were no longer enemies, they were not yet allies. Officially, President Franklin Roosevelt classified Italy as a "co-belligerent." That cold-shoulder description caught the emerging post-Mussolini government by surprise, but with Germans still in Italy it was in no position to complain, since U.S. soldiers were still risking their lives to help liberate their homeland.

On December 14, 1943, Marshal Pietro Badoglio, Italy's provisional leader, issued a statement, to be read to all Italian prisoners of war in America. "In the new political-military situation," he wrote, "it is our intention to proffer the Allies all possible, active collaboration in order to achieve the common objective of ridding our country of the residue of German troops still occupying a large section of our nation. It is therefore our duty to help the Allies in every possible way, excepting in actual combat." Badoglio's declaration seemed simple, but it would profoundly affect U.S.-Italian relations throughout 1944 and change the lives of many of the men imprisoned in Arizona, including Private Olivotto.

Three weeks later, on January 6, 1944, the chief of staff of the War Department's Army Special Forces drafted a secret plan to take advantage of Badoglio's offer to "help the Allies in every possible way." The plan called for the formation of what would come to be called Italian Service Units, or ISUs. Qualified prisoners could volunteer to be included in military companies comprising 175–200 enlisted men and a handful of officers each, organized almost exactly the same as equivalent American units. Members of ISUs would be issued American army uniforms and wear appropriate Italian army rank insignias on their clothing. They would be quartered on or near American army forts, posts, and bases, and employed just as a noncombatant U.S. Army company might be. The pay would be about twenty-four dollars per month, the same as American GIs. Most important, Italians in the service units could expect increased privileges and freedom. "It will be the policy of the War Department," the chief of staff wrote, "to encourage unit pride among members of Italian Service Companies. As the loyalty and work efficiency of a company becomes apparent, reductions in guard personnel will be accomplished and additional privileges may be granted to the company personnel."

It was a risky proposition. On the one hand, the army was just as desperate for manpower as farmers were. The idea was to assign Italians to relatively menial but important tasks on domestic army installations, freeing American soldiers for duty overseas. But it also meant that some Italians would be living near sensitive military operations and interacting with residents of bigger cities and towns. The success of the plan depended on a fairly high level of loyalty and cooperation from men who had been captured at gunpoint and locked behind fences for much of the previous year.

Although the army had tried to segregate Fascist/Nazi sympathizers when they first arrived at Camp Florence, the intelligence safety net was full of holes. Almost every week, reports surfaced of prisoners being bullied by unrepentant Fascists. A cardboard sign in the Post Exchange, lettered in crayon, pleaded DO NOT BRING YOUR POLITICAL ARGUMENTS IN HERE. The War Department decided that all POWs would have to be screened once again, and that those with "Fascist tendencies" would be banned from joining ISUs. With more than seven thousand Italians now assigned to Florence and its dozen side camps, that task would prove difficult.

Colonel Holden got right to work. Of several thousand inmates interviewed for ISU suitability, 415 were deemed ineligible and the rest were cleared. Each qualified prisoner was handed an application form. "I promise," read the form, "that I will work on behalf of the United States of America at any place, on any duty, excepting in actual combat, and that I will assist the United States to the best of my ability in the prosecution of its cause against the common enemy, Germany." The form included an acknowledgment that unspecified special privileges would be granted those who signed, and it required applicants to promise they'd respect the implicit trust behind those privileges. The application would be valid once the POW signed, dated, and submitted the form to the camp commander.

Army brass expected a flood of forms; they were surprised when they received barely a trickle. It turned out that scores of Fascists had managed to evade detection, determined to undermine the ISUs. Fascist infiltrators bullied their compatriots, boasting that Germans were winning the war in northern Italy and threatening reprisals against soldiers and their families back home if they cooperated with Americans. A rumor circulated that the phrase "any place, on any duty" in the loyalty oaths meant ISUs would be sent overseas, probably to the Pacific. The phrase "excepting in actual combat" was viewed with suspicion: a noncombat assignment not far from the front lines could quickly turn deadly if an enemy lobbed artillery or dropped bombs or pushed through Allied lines.

Even those not intimidated by infiltrators were reluctant to sign. Many were content with life at Camp Florence, where friends, food, and entertainment were plentiful and where a comfortable daily rhythm provided considerable peace of mind. The prospect, however remote, of being forced to serve once again under the command of their own much-despised Italian officers was more than many could stand. Life was good, uncertainty was bad, and earning a few more dollars hardly seemed worth it.

The Pentagon grew alarmed by the paucity of ISU recruits out of Camp Florence. Officials in Washington ordered Colonel Holden to turn up the heat. The 415 Italians who had failed the recent screening examinations—including Daniele Dal Sasso, the POW chaplain—were loaded on a train and shipped to a high-security POW compound in Hereford, Texas. A few days later, the most adamant among the nonsigners were told they'd be banished to a distant side camp and deprived of privileges unless they cooperated. At the moment of departure, several gave in and agreed to sign. Everyone else was told that, despite the characterization of ISUs as voluntary, "the only conceivable excuse for not signing would be disloyalty to the Italian Government and pro-Nazi sentiments."

Still they resisted. Colonel Holden, running out of ideas, traveled to a side camp to personally address a thousand men who still had not signed up. He later reported that he "again offered every authorized inducement and intimated the authorized dire consequences for the nonsigners. Guard protection, security, and immediate transportation were offered those who would sign. This was announced as a final opportunity. The results were negative." Three weeks later, "the most eloquent and highest-ranking Italian Officer" made a pitch "and most particularly stressed the desires of the Italian Government and Marshal Badoglio's proclamation. The results were wholly negative." Undaunted, the same Italian officer sat down with 350 nonsigners, each one at a time, and offered to provide immediate transportation to a secret location and protection from those who might still be bullying. Only one Italian agreed.

Camp Florence had become a victim of its own success. Every inspector who toured the camp considered it among the very best examples of how POWs anywhere in the world should be housed, fed, employed, and treated. Yet even Italians who had grown attached to Florence could see the handwriting on the wall. Word spread that Camp Hereford in Texas was a hellhole, and that those who refused to "volunteer" for ISUs might end up locked up there with the worst soldiers the Italian army had to offer. There were also rumors—true, as it turned out—that Camp Florence would soon be converted to a compound exclusively for German POWs. By late April, several companies of ISUs began forming, as reluctant prisoners finally turned in their applications. On May 1, 1944, U.S. Army captain Francis Beckman of Seattle arrived to take charge of what would soon be known as the Twenty-eighth Italian Service Unit. Beckman was told that the unit would be based at Seattle's Fort Lawton, although the Italians would not learn their destination until they actually arrived.

In the original plan, companies were to be assembled by carefully combining soldiers with a mix of useful skills, like cooks, carpenters, plumbers, and mechanics. But with pressure mounting, the ISUs were thrown together with whichever men agreed to join. On May 9, Ernesto Cellentani, a captain, was transferred from Utah and assigned to be the ranking Italian officer of the Twenty-eighth ISU, assisted by Lieutenant Giovanni Lobianco. The next day, Wednesday, Guglielmo Olivotto, Imo Nolgi, and Bruno Patteri were among twenty-one who signed on. On Friday, another twenty-nine turned in their forms, the following Tuesday, one hundred forty more, and on Thursday, May 18, the final ten were added.

More than two hundred men, still thousands of miles from home, sick with worry about the fate of their families, drained after years of fruitless battle, somewhat rested after months of extraordinary treatment by their captors and clearly anxious about a future in an unknown location for an uncertain amount of time were leaving Florence. As the train pulled out along the Southern Pacific spur at 4:38 P.M. on May 18, they felt the warmth of the Arizona sun for the very last time. In three days, they would see the sun rise in Seattle.

CHAPTER TWO

FORT LAWTON
June 1944

ON JUNE 6, 1944, a full moon hung low in a cerulean Seattle sky just as the thin, brassy strain of reveille separated ten thousand Fort Lawton GIs from their sleep. Nine hours earlier, boatloads of American soldiers tossed in the surf off France watching that same moon slide into the Atlantic. Moonset marked the start of D-day, and for thousands of GIs storming the beach at Normandy, it was the last beautiful sight they'd ever see.

The soldiers in Seattle knew nothing about the invasion; June 6 was just another day in a long line of dull duty at one of the most bucolic military bases in America. Perched on a wooded bluff six miles northwest of downtown, Fort Lawton lorded over the frigid waters of Puget Sound. Bald eagles balanced in the tops of windblown snags; pods of black-and-white orcas chased salmon and sea lions below. The immense grassy parade grounds at the top of the Magnolia plateau opened to sweeping views of the snowcapped Olympic Mountains in the west, to the steely peaks of the Cascade Range in the east, and to regal Mount Rainier in the south, catching the first and last rays of cloudless days on its towering summit. Cloud-free days appeared with unexpected frequency, despite the region's rain-soaked reputation.

The fort was ringed with pockets of dense woodland: ferns and nettles at the base of Douglas fir, hemlock, western redcedar, and madrone. Most conspicuous were the bigleaf maples, *Acer macrophyllum*, great twisted muscular trunks wrapped in capes of spongy moss. The maples' veined leaves were broad enough to wrap a man's outspread hand and supple enough to whisper in a springtime breeze. Afternoon gusts from the bluffs below made branches creak and trunks groan beneath swaying canopies soaring fifty feet above the ground. Maples ensured that great swaths of the fort bathed in deep shade during the day, turning to black holes at night, even when the moon was full.

Bigleaf maples thrived because their competition had been largely stripped away. In 1898, tall stands of native evergreen trees were clear-cut from the Magnolia Bluffs to make way for the army's newest fort. The post's design was more elegant than utilitarian: officers' quarters, built on Chuckanut stone foundations, were carefully crafted in Victorian style, with large rooms, high ceilings, rounded windows, and hand-carved woodwork, all beneath roofs of Philadelphia slate. Grand porches supported by Tuscan columns offered views of broad boulevards leading to more modest housing for noncommissioned officers and barracks for enlisted men. Smaller avenues connected the hospital, commissary, fire station, stables, blacksmith, bakery, band house, and guard station. Few army posts, if any, could match the elegance and breathtaking beauty of this fort, all of which made it easier to overlook secrets settled in the shadows or half-truths hidden down the banks of maple-lined bluffs.

ON JUNE 6, 1944, Guglielmo Olivotto awoke to another day in what seemed like paradise. Gone were the deserts of Africa and Arizona; in their place was a dappled forest ringing with songbirds, an apparent Eden of clear air and cool temperatures. Home was now a bunk in a barracks tucked in a quiet grove near the edge of the bluffs; there were no armed guards, no barbed wire, no obvious signs that the members of the Twenty-eighth ISU were prisoners of war. His sixteen days in Seattle had been the best sixteen days since his conscription four years earlier. The threat of war and violence seemed far away.

The Italian Area appeared isolated, but was actually just down an embankment from what the fort called its Colored Area: three dozen buildings housing four companies of black soldiers. On the very day the Italians first arrived in Seattle, the black companies had departed for a weeklong bivouac sixty miles away. On June 6, the Negroes, as everyone called them, had been back at the fort just a couple of days and were largely unaware that their new neighbors down the hill were Italians.

Of all the black soldiers at Fort Lawton, one in particular would eventually regret that Guglielmo Olivotto had moved into the neighborhood. Luther Larkin was a corporal out of Arkansas. His unit had begun basic training back in February and in less than a week, the boys in his company would stand for inspection. If they passed, they'd earn a three-week furlough, their first in four months. It had been a year and a half since Luther had seen his parents, and with overseas orders due at any time, it could be his last visit home for a long while to come.

Home was West Helena, Arkansas. His parents, Cornelia and Luther Sr., owned a house just outside the city limits, near a pecan grove in the swampy hollow where West Helena's black families lived in wood houses and tar-paper shanties. An open sewer drained from the hospital at the top of the hill and trickled down the dirt road; residents threw wooden planks in the street to help avoid the mud. The Larkin's frame house, hot and humid much of the year, had a screened porch for air. Water was pumped by hand; an outhouse served its purpose around back. On cold autumn nights, a woodstove burned scrub oak and knotty pine. Although Helena had plenty of pipes carrying natural gas, those lines ran only to houses in the white parts of town.

Luther's father, Luther Larkin Sr., grew up in Searcy, a cotton country hamlet northeast of Little Rock, at the western edge of the Arkansas Delta. A god-fearing tenant farmer, his life revolved around the church, where he sang in the choir, filled baskets for the needy, and led Bible study as a Baptist deacon. His son was eight and his daughter, Lola Mae, nine when the Great Depression nearly put White County cotton out of business. A sawmill in West Helena, near the west bank of the Mississippi, offered a steady paycheck, so he moved his family to Valley Drive, not far from the mill at the end of

Sebastian Street. On Fridays—pay day—he'd bring home Moon Pies and Kool-Aid. Sunday evenings, the whole family sat around the radio, listening to Jack Benny and Flash Gordon while sucking pickles and peppermint candy.

Young Luther never went by the name Junior. His mother called him "Boy," and that's how all his family knew him. Cornelia Larkin had been raised in a Quaker boarding school, unheard of for a Southern black girl at the beginning of the twentieth century. In West Helena, she looked in vain for work in a bank or at the phone company, jobs usually reserved for whites. Her only option was to teach in a segregated school, a career that ended once the sawmill closed and Luther Sr. lost his job. Cornelia took work as a domestic, because cleaning and cooking for white families paid more than teaching reading and writing to black children.

There was always food on the table. Cornelia kept chickens, and her garden contributed corn, cucumbers, okra, and peas. Luther loved to fish; he'd roll old tires down soggy roads on the way to the pond, collecting green snakes to scare girls and gathering frogs and dragonflies to take home in jars. He'd take apart bugs or amphibians to see what was inside and, as he grew older, had little fear of blood and plenty of interest in anatomy. Cornelia made sure the family's bookshelves were filled with secondhand books—her only option in a town where the sign on the public library read NO COLOREDS. Luther read Socrates and Plato, Buck Rogers and Booker Washington; he later joined a book club so he could study volumes about medicine and the human body. When a neighbor's goose collapsed, he grabbed his surplus-store medical kit and opened the bird on his makeshift operating table.

In the 1930s, most black boys in the Deep South left school after fourth grade. Larkin persisted through the eleventh grade, making the best of what was then one of the nation's sorriest school systems, and segregated at that. By seventeen, he was strong-willed and unafraid to take risks. His mother's Quaker school sensibility had been drilled into him time and again. "Look up, child, look up, don't look down." She also warned, "Don't get too happy."

If Larkin dreamed of attending medical school, those dreams were tempered by the twin realities of poverty and race. There were several black colleges in the South, but most required a high school diploma and more money than Larkin could hope to save. Ten months after Pearl Harbor, he got his draft notice, so he turned his attention to the army. Thousands of blacks were heading off to war, and surely, he figured, Uncle Sam would need to train plenty of black medics to keep all those Negro soldiers patched up during battle.

As it turned out, very few black soldiers carried guns. Every army needs men and women to manage the myriad chores that make it possible for combat soldiers to do their jobs. By the time Luther Larkin was drafted in October 1942, black servicemen were commonplace but black infantrymen were rare. More than four hundred thousand African Americans had served in the First World War, yet only two infantry divisions—thirty thousand men—saw duty overseas, and fewer than fourteen hundred were commissioned officers. By World War II, the ratio of blacks to whites in the army was almost the same as the ratio in the country at large, thanks to a selective service system that conducted two separate drafts, one for whites, another for nonwhites. Each department within the army was urged to take its fair share of minorities, and although the overwhelming number of officers continued to be white, more than three thousand African Americans had reached the rank of second lieutenant or above by the start of 1943, including one brigadier general.

The army was changing in other ways. Before World War II, combat soldiers were largely responsible for their own housekeeping chores at army bases, tasks such as cooking, cleaning, maintenance, and supplies. But by 1942, the Pentagon needed more combat soldiers to concentrate on actual combat; those not carrying guns would do all the rest. A major reorganization gave birth to the Army Service Forces, a huge bureaucracy designed to ensure that fighting men were fed, clothed, trained, nurtured, supplied with weapons, and paid wages, no matter where in the world they were deployed. The ASF included lawyers and chaplains and bookkeepers and engineers; it took charge of purchasing and warehousing and shipping and maintenance. Soldiers in the Army Service Forces drove forklifts and slung hash and fixed engines and laundered hospital linens and dug graves. The ASF did everything but pull the trigger.

A disproportionate number of blacks were assigned to the Army Service Forces, many in menial jobs. On its face, the system was color-blind: inductees who scored lowest on aptitude tests were routed to repetitive jobs requiring more brawn than brains. But half of all black soldiers (compared with 8.5 percent of whites) graded out as Class V, the lowest of five categories on the military's standard intelligence exam. Three-quarters of all black recruits had grown up in the South, where most had little more than a primary grade education, usually in substandard schools.

The American military segregated its soldiers, so that army companies, each with approximately two hundred men, were designated either white or colored. Some black companies did see combat and many distinguished themselves in battle. But by 1942, when roughly 10 percent of army soldiers were black, 34 percent of quartermaster units and 42 percent of engineering units were African American. The segregation was even more pronounced in the Transportation Corps, where certain specialties, like port companies, were almost 80 percent black.

The Transportation Corps was in charge of shipping the army's troops and equipment by land, sea, or air. Eight ports of embarkation ringed the American coastline: Boston, New York, Hampton Roads, Charleston, New Orleans, Los Angeles, San Francisco, and Seattle. The Seattle Port of Embarkation serviced Alaska and parts of the Pacific, purchasing millions of dollars worth of food, supplies, ordnance, and equipment and storing it in warehouses up and down the coast. The port also included the Fort Lawton Staging Area, where soldiers were temporarily housed before forming into units and shipping off to war. Many of those units were Negro port companies.

WHITE ARMY OFFICERS were often baffled by black soldiers; some had never had a one-on-one conversation with a person of color before they entered the service. A War Department official observed, "White officers assigned to Negro troops are disgruntled, disinterested and willing to work only for another assignment. Negro soldiers feel this attitude. The result is poor discipline and lack of control."

In some training camps, a confidential memo circulated among officers titled "Certain Characteristics of the Negro which Affect Command of Negro Troops." The memo was a checklist of the presumed attributes of most, if not all, black soldiers:

> Gregarious, extrovertive [*sic*], strongly attached to group and family.
> Easy-going—line of least resistance. Not physically lazy.
> Loud in speech—argumentative.
> Keen sense of humor—quick to laughter, out loud.

The list included characteristics that could have easily come from a book about training puppies:

> Very sensitive: Resentful of correction. Takes same as highly personal. Easily hurt by criticism, esp. in public. Appreciative of praise, even the slightest. Reacts to tangible awards for good work.
> Has to be shown to be convinced—learns by experience.
> Loyal to death once loyalty has been inspired.

Other ascribed attributes were more overtly racist:

> Mentally lazy, not retentive, forgetful.
> Lacks mechanical sense—relatively poor "natural" mechanics and careless of detail.
> Ruled by instinct and emotion rather than reason.
> Has to be made to face facts, prone to escapism.

Some descriptions, while equally racist, revealed a certain fascination:

Physically strong regardless of size. Weak feet.

Conserves strength. Great endurance.

Superior at concealment, scouting.

Has a keen sense of rhythm which can be put to good advantage in drills of all kinds (marching, gun-crew).

Doesn't hold a grudge as a rule.

Shows respect for age and proven experience.

Others exposed a level of annoyance, if not fear:

Shows respect in rather "negative" fashion, strange at first.

Talks "own language," can be reached through same. Freely pokes fun at other Negroes, insults same, but hotly resentful of similar treatment by whites.

Stubborn [to] no end. Hard-headed as a Swede.

Proud, esp. of personal prowess and physical abilities.

Extremely jealous, esp. of women relations.

Increasingly aggressive, esp. in public (much more noticeable in Negro women than men).

Most generalizations, however, simply reinforced a prevailing notion that blacks were, for the most part, little more than children:

Quite imaginative in some respects.

Hot-tempered, to the point of physical reaction.

Competitive when rewards are at stake.

Will "show off" on every possible occasion.

More prone to want to be "popular" than respected by fellow soldiers.

Difficult to make assume responsibility.

LUTHER LARKIN LIVED in a Jim Crow world and had joined a Jim Crow army. The law of the land was separate but equal: blacks were entitled to equal facilities, accommodations, and opportunities as long as those privileges were in spaces not shared with whites. In practice, all-black segregated schools, restaurants, motels, and train cars were almost always smaller, poorer, less convenient, and last in line for public funding.

Although separate but equal was also the rule in the military, the army was an early leader in efforts to reduce some inequities. Those efforts, however, often met stiff resistance from civilians. Ulysses Lee, in his landmark book *The Employment of Negro Troops*, offers these examples:

> in 1942, protests about the location of Negro troops continued to pour into the War Department from all over the country. The state of Mississippi and Camp Wheeler, Georgia, wanted no Negro officers. The citizens of Rapid City, South Dakota, were afraid that their town could not offer the proper entertainment facilities for Negro troops. A "thunder of complaints" went up from all over the state when a Negro cavalry regiment was ordered to Fort Clark, Texas. [In] Albuquerque, New Mexico, and Spokane, Washington, citizens objected to stationing Negro Air Forces units at nearby fields, for they felt that their own Negro populations were too small to provide social contacts for Negro men. Las Vegas, Nevada, and Battle Creek, Michigan, objected to military police and field artillery units respectively. When the citizens of Morehead City, North Carolina, heard that a white coast artillery station at nearby Fort Mason was going overseas and would be replaced by a Negro unit, they asked their senators and congressmen to intervene.

Ignoring most objections, the army assigned colored units to posts throughout the United States, including the Deep South, where nerves were most raw. White residents of Southern communities became hypervigilant whenever groups of Negro soldiers came to town on a pass. Black enlisted men from large northern cities regularly flaunted local racist customs, refusing to step off the sidewalk when a white person passed or daring to look white women directly in the eye. Anger on both sides, often fueled by alcohol and easy access to guns, led to a number of violent confrontations.

At Fort Benning, Georgia, the body of a black army private named Felix Hall was found hanging in the woods. Black soldiers were convinced it was a lynching· Hall had been hung with a noose, and his hands had been tied behind his back. The army's white investigators, however, treated the case as a probable suicide. No one was ever prosecuted.

In Fayetteville, Arkansas, a white military policeman shot and killed a black soldier after a confrontation at a bus stop between a group of black GIs—many of them drunk—and an inexperienced detachment of white MPs. In the ensuing melee, a white MP was also shot dead. The Fort Bragg provost marshal ordered every black soldier on the post locked in the stockade overnight, and tensions between blacks and whites at the fort simmered for weeks.

At Camp Van Dorn in Mississippi, a black private from the 364th Infantry was shot while fleeing a local sheriff. When news of the soldier's death reached his regiment, a company of black soldiers grabbed rifles from their supply room and threatened to riot. The mob rushed a squad of Negro military policeman; one of the rioters took a bullet in the ensuing exchange.

As the war dragged on, the number of deadly racial incidents increased. Major confrontations erupted in Georgia (Camp Stewart), California (March Field and Camp San Luis Obispo), Texas (Fort Bliss), Kansas (Camp Phillips), Kentucky (Camp Breckinridge), and Pennsylvania (Camp Shenango). "Through all of these," reported Ulysses Lee,

> ran the common thread of friction between Negro soldiers and both city and military policemen. Where Negro military policemen were used, generally on a temporary basis in the Negro sections of towns, they were usually unarmed, increasing their difficulties in the control of troops. Most of the disturbances were followed by newspaper publicity, not always accurate. The papers

could not always get facts from local or other public relations officers and took what they could find to support what became, in the Negro press, a campaign for armed Negro military police and, at times, in the local white press, a campaign for the removal of Negro military police embracing, in some instances, the removal of all Negro soldiers.

In the state of Washington, the army intercepted a letter written at Fort Lewis by James Williams, a black army private from Providence, Rhode Island:

> The truth is that there isn't a Negro here who feels that his greatest enemy is Germany or Japan . . . The crimes committed by the Nazis and Japanese seem unreal and far away to them while the crimes committed by Southerners in this country are known to all of us. Many of the boys in my barrack who come from the South can tell stories of being run out of town, of being threatened, and being intimidated. For every story of Nazi cruelty which is related, they can counter with an equally gruesome, true story of Southern inhumanity. It is small wonder then that we have little desire to fight beside people whom we consider our aggressors . . . How many times have I heard the statement, "We might as well die over here [stateside] fighting for our rights as overseas fighting for the rights of [white] Southerners."

Black soldiers who served overseas were often amazed at the difference between the way they were treated by foreign civilians and by white soldiers in their own army. Army censors, reading letters written by American troops in Britain, noted that black enlisted men clearly preferred the way they were treated in England. Wrote one, "I've been here about 2 weeks, and find it very pleasant . . . Both colored & white [officers] are here together . . . Back at the other Post, conditions were just the opposite, which had colored & white troops and were kept separate with the colored boys living under very adverse conditions."

English civilians often treated black American soldiers as honored guests. One soldier reported, "The people are very nice to us. They worry us to death about coming to have tea with them . . . I have met a girl, and she is real nice. I might even bring home an English wife. How would you like that! She has a place of her own out in the country. We go horseback riding and swimming and play tennis every Sunday."

In a few instances, relationships between black Americans and white English girls grew complicated. "After I came over here," wrote one soldier, "I met a girl, her husband was killed in action. I have been going with her five months. Now she say she is going to have a child, and she is saying it's mine. Well, it could be mine. That's how I am standing. We don't have any of our race over here. She is a white girl, and she wants to come back home with me after the war."

Censors also intercepted letters from white soldiers, who, in these excerpts from three more letters, painted a decidedly different picture:

These English people never did see black civilize [sic] people before, that is why they like them. And these color boys, they pay these English girls a lot of money to get sex incourse [sic] and these girls really go for them in a big way.

The American Negro is the worst problem over here. They are running wild. They tell the English girls they are American Indians and go out with white girls all over. There are some queer babies being born over here now. Our cook was knifed by one negro last week and is now in a hospital. It's going to be bad when these negro soldiers come back and try to do the same in U.S. I'm afraid we'll be in a big race war like I predicted quite a while ago. It sure makes you feel sick to see a pretty blonde walking about and holding hands with some big grinning nigger.

The race situation doesn't sound good but after seeing it over here, I hope they kill every nigger within a radius of 500 miles. I guess I don't mean that, but something should be done.

Racial hatred and violence was nothing new to Luther Larkin; he had grown up in a time and region where blacks were expected to know their place, and where stepping across the established boundaries spelled certain trouble. The army, however, offered opportunity, and, at first, his love of medicine served him well. He was sent straight from his hometown army reception center in Arkansas to a medical unit at the Port of Seattle, skipping the usual requirement of six weeks of basic training. The U.S. Army Medical Department had been under fire from the Selective Service for failing to request its required quota of black recruits; Larkin was called up at a time when fewer than 3 percent of the department's enlisted men were nonwhite.

For eighteen months, Luther worked at an army dispensary south of downtown Seattle, assisting pharmacists and surgeons, driving ambulances, and filing medical records. Observant and eager to learn, he gradually mastered enough skills to become a medical corpsman, one of the proudest specialties in the U.S. Army. Corpsmen were considered among the bravest soldiers on the battlefield, tending to wounded comrades in the line of fire, often at great personal risk. Medical corpsmen were not doctors; they stopped bleeding, set bones, treated shock, and provided painkillers. Mostly, they saved lives, stabilizing wounded men until others could transport them to a bed or an operating table.

Larkin hoped to go overseas as a medic but for most of 1943 had to bide his time in Seattle. It was a tough place to be a young black soldier; African Americans were a tiny minority in Washington State, and the deep roots of a unique brand of Northwest racism nourished suspicion and hatred toward people with darker skin. In 1852, white settlers named their new town in honor of Sealth, an Indian chief of the Duwamish and Suquamish tribes who had greeted them warmly on their arrival. But just four years later, shots were fired and Indians were killed after refusing to move off their ancestral lands. In 1886, a mob herded 350 Chinese onto Seattle's docks and demanded their deportation. The Chinese had finished years of backbreaking labor building the Northern Pacific Railroad; Seattle's whites didn't want them competing for scarce jobs once the rail lines were running.

Early African Americans faced similar mistreatment. In 1879, when no more than one hundred of Seattle's thirty-five hundred residents were black, an editorial in the *Seattle Post-Intelligencer* warned that "there is room for only a limited number of colored people here. Overstep that limit, and there comes a clash in which the colored man must suffer. The experience of the Chinese on this coast indicates that beyond question." The newspaper acknowledged that institutional segregation in the Deep South harmed blacks but felt no shame arguing that "the South is essentially the home of the colored man. In it he can live easier, and in a manner more in accordance with his nature and desires. Until he is stronger and better able to protect himself, it will be wiser for him to give way."

Just twenty years later, in 1899, Seattle was a changed city. The Klondike gold rush in Alaska brought a swarm of new residents and a good measure of prosperity, as Seattle served as staging ground and supply center for tens of thousands of prospectors. Four hundred blacks now lived in a city of eighty thousand residents, although most African Americans struggled to get by on the meager wages of laborers and domestics. Once the gold was gone, others suffered too: immigrant Norwegian fishermen were forced to go farther out to sea to find coho and sockeye salmon; transplanted Swedish loggers had to travel higher into the mountains to cut fir and hemlock. City fathers pressed to find new industries willing to relocate to Seattle, preferably with reliable jobs and steady paychecks.

The army came to the rescue. As the century turned, a growing emphasis on military might in the Pacific meant new facilities were needed on the West Coast, inspiring city leaders to lobby for the construction of an army post, preferably near downtown Seattle. City boosters found a sympathetic ally in General Elwell Otis, the U.S. Army chief of operations for the Pacific. While Otis acknowledged Seattle's strategic military location, he had an unrelated motive for backing the city's bid. In a report to Secretary of War Russell Alger, Otis described the citizens of the fast-growing Northwest as "restless, demonstrative, and oftentimes turbulent upon fancied provocation."

Otis thought a fort could help keep locals in line, especially trouble-some labor unions, much to the glee of Seattle's emerging capitalists.

The chamber of commerce went to work, collecting enough land and money to assemble seven hundred acres of farm and timberland, which it donated to the city, which in turn gave it to the army. The new fort needed a name, so Elwell Otis decided to honor General Henry Lawton, the only white officer to command black troops during four conflicts: the Civil War, the Indian wars, the Spanish-American War, and the Philippine insurrection. Lawton, a bon vivant who had cap-tured the elusive Indian leader Geronimo in Mexico and led the in-vasion of Cuba during the Spanish-American War, had recently died during a battle in the Philippines while under Otis's command. Otis, suffering pangs of guilt about Lawton's death, made sure the new fort would be named after his friend.

The arrival of the army inevitably meant the eventual appearance of black soldiers in Seattle. It started quietly in August 1900, when a de-tachment of the all-black Ninth Cavalry pitched tents at Fort Lawton The Ninth Cavalry Buffalo Soldiers had been one of the most deco-rated regiments in the American West, at the forefront of many of the major battles in the Indian wars. At the outbreak of the Spanish-American War in 1898, black men had been heavily recruited by the army, after doctors noticed that many African Americans seemed to enjoy a natural resistance to malaria and other tropical diseases in Cuba and the Philippines. The Ninth Cavalry was again in the thick of action, fighting side by side with Teddy Roosevelt on San Juan Hill. At the end of the Cuban campaign, they were lauded as heroes, but their presence in Seattle was barely noted. After a few weeks at Fort Lawton, the Ninth shipped out to China, where they were thrust into the bloody Boxer Rebellion.

By 1910, Seattle was home to nearly a quarter-million people, in-cluding twenty-three hundred blacks. Another nine hundred African Americans were stationed at Fort Lawton, part of the infamous Twenty-fifth Infantry Regiment. The regiment had transferred to Seat-tle from Fort Brown, near the strictly segregated border town of

Brownsville, Texas. In Brownsville, rumors of an assault on a white woman led to a nighttime shooting rampage that took the life of a local bartender named Frank Natus. Local whites claimed the assailants were black men wearing army uniforms, even though the white commander of the Twenty-fifth Infantry insisted that every black soldier had been accounted for. On November 28, 1906, without a court-martial or civil trial, President Theodore Roosevelt ordered the dishonorable discharge of all 167 soldiers in the Twenty-fifth Infantry's First Battalion. The *New Orleans Picayune* celebrated the president's action but wanted him to go further: "Whatever may be the value of the Negro troops in time of war, the fact remains they are a curse to the country in time of peace." John "Cactus Jack" Garner, the congressman who represented Brownsville, introduced legislation that called for "elimination of all blacks currently in the military and barring black enlistment." The bill was defeated, but Garner went on to serve two terms as vice president under Theodore Roosevelt's cousin, Franklin Roosevelt. It wasn't until 1972 that President Richard Nixon signed a proclamation exonerating all the black Brownsville servicemen, but by then only one member of the regiment, eighty-six-year-old Dorsie Willis, was still alive.

In October 1909, a rumor began circulating in Seattle's Magnolia neighborhood: the colored soldiers from south Texas were headed to Fort Lawton. It didn't matter that all the Brownsville suspects had been kicked out of the army or that the black soldiers who replaced them had just completed a difficult and dangerous assignment in the Philippines; ever since the Brownsville incident, whites had begged the army not to bring black soldiers into Seattle. The rumor turned out true: the tarnished Twenty-fifth Infantry was indeed on its way, and an atmosphere of fear and mistrust settled around the fort like a fog.

Racism in Seattle was different from what Luther Larkin had known in Arkansas, where blacks were a much larger part of the population. Historian Paul de Barros observed that prior to World War II, "fewer blacks than Japanese Americans lived in Seattle. Between 1940 and 1950, Seattle's African-American population grew from 3,789 to

15,667. It was the promise of war work—in the aluminum plants, shipyards, and airplane and electrical power industries, plus the armed services—that drew these new immigrants. What they found, unfortunately, wasn't always as hospitable as the 'free air' they had hoped for."

Newcomers from the South were disappointed but not surprised to learn that the majority of well-paying defense jobs were offered only to whites, despite a 1941 presidential order outlawing discrimination by federal contractors. Labor unions weren't covered by the order, and most unions were openly hostile to blacks. "We resent that the war situation has been used to alter an old established custom," explained an official for the all-white International Association of Machinists, "and do not feel it will be helpful to war production." Although the Seattle-based Boeing Aircraft Company did hire a few African Americans, it assigned them to segregated bathrooms and lunchrooms and stood by as they were denied full union benefits and seniority. Sadly, some jobs outside the defense industry became available to blacks only because the Japanese Americans who had once held them had been locked away in internment camps.

Restaurants and motels in rural parts of Washington State still had signs that read WE CATER TO WHITES ONLY. In Seattle itself, movie theaters provided separate seating for black patrons, and a black family might find certain bathrooms, drinking fountains, or amusement parks off-limits. The biggest department store in town, Frederick & Nelson, ran a Christmastime help-wanted advertisement in the *Seattle Post-Intelligencer,* offering jobs to "whites only."

In 1943, real estate agents refused to sell houses to African Americans anywhere except the Central District, an area of older homes east of downtown. Five thousand were forced to live in a neighborhood that had been home to thirty-seven hundred only a few years earlier. The newest arrivals, primarily from the South, were generally poorer and less educated than those who had lived in Seattle before the war. Established blacks often looked down their noses at the rural transplants now renting rooms in their attics and basements; they mocked their grammar, laughed at their coveralls and bandannas, and were sometimes made nervous by their apparent crudeness and lack of manners. Seattle police filled the King County jail with African Americans, most of them Southerners, many of them accused of crimes committed against other black men and women.

Because Luther Larkin wore a uniform and was well read, he was able to move easily in Seattle's Negro neighborhoods. He loved music and kept his radio tuned to his favorite disc jockey, Bill Sawyer of KEVR. The Central District was home to a string of vibrant nightclubs, featuring young local performers like Quincy Jones, Ernestine Anderson, and Ray Charles. Throughout the war, all the giants of jazz—Count Basie, Duke Ellington, Ella Fitzgerald, Cab Calloway, Roy Eldridge—played regular dates in Seattle. Most of the big bookings were at the enormous and ornate Trianon Ballroom, a downtown landmark featuring a four-thousand-square-foot white maple dance floor beneath a huge sparkling ball suspended from a soaring ceiling. But while many of the faces performing on the Trianon's giant clamshell bandstand were black, the same was not true of the thousands of faces on the dance floor.

The Trianon owner, John Savage, barred his doors to black customers, on the excuse they were "bad for business." Savage also claimed that the city had an ordinance prohibiting "mixed dancing," but newspaper reporters never bothered to check that no such law ever actually existed. The "no coloreds" policy came to a head in 1940, when posters appeared promoting Lionel Hampton's upcoming date at the Trianon. Hampton was a huge star, and several members of his band had grown up in the Central District. Blacks wanted to see the show and grumbled loudly when the owner refused to lift his ban. Hoping to head off further trouble, the Trianon's manager approached the owners of the *Northwest Enterprise,* one of Seattle's two Negro newspapers. The manager offered to stage a blacks-only "Jim Crow Night," in mocking honor of the demeaning segregation policies of the Deep South. The newspaper owners were offended and rejected his suggestion that the *Enterprise* sponsor the event. He found other sponsors, and the Trianon began to hold "Colored Folks" dances on Monday nights (known, to blacks in the Central District, as "Spook Nights"). The other six nights, they were allowed on stage but not on the dance floor.

IN LATE 1943, the call went out for more battlefield medics, and soldiers in Larkin's small unit at the dispensary were asked to volunteer. Larkin was one of the first in line, but the army noted that he had not yet endured the standard six weeks of basic training. Every soldier, no matter what his job, had to get into the best physical shape he could while learning to defend himself and to destroy the enemy. From concealment and camouflage to field sanitation and first aid, GIs were taught how to read a map, fix a bayonet, fire a machine gun, and pitch a tent. Feet blistered from ten-mile hikes, and heads swam in the minutiae of army protocol and procedure. Soldiers marched back and forth so many times they grew to know every speck of gravel and blade of grass along the route, all the while swearing under their breaths about the drill sergeants screaming in their ears and corporals yapping at their heels. Night maneuvers made them homesick and cold; army food made them long for real meals from their mothers' kitchens.

For Larkin, six weeks of basic, plus a few more weeks of specialized training, was a relatively small price to pay for the chance to head overseas as a medic. In January 1944, he lugged his bags from the downtown Seattle dispensary to Fort Lawton's colored barracks, eager to begin. Within days, however, he came down with a fever and a swollen throat. It was the mumps, a mildly contagious illness that the army treated by sticking him in quarantine, in a hospital ward alongside soldiers with measles and chicken pox and tuberculosis.

Larkin regained his strength and fell in with a group of "casuals": inductees who'd arrived straight off the bus and were not yet assigned to a unit. The casuals were raw recruits, including many men who had little in common with Larkin. He was obviously educated, causing boys from the South to view him as somewhat uppity. A tough crowd from Texas didn't trust him because he didn't drink or gamble. And

Northerners, many from the big city, considered all Southerners dull and slow no matter what their schooling. For the most part, Larkin kept to himself, biding his time until his overseas orders came through.

But in late April, just as he completed his six weeks of basic training, Larkin received startling news: the army simply did not need any more black medical corpsman right then. Most of its combat soldiers were white, and a black man—even one trained to save lives—could not eat, sleep, and travel with a white unit. Although there was still a shortage of medics, Luther's unique talents were no longer in demand.

It was a tough blow. He had now endured two winters in Seattle, and during the endless weeks between Thanksgiving and Easter, Fort Lawton had been as dark, damp, and cold as any place he had ever been. There was little sun and plenty of drizzle, a steady drip from drab skies in a stubborn chill that left fingers numb and joints aching. Arkansas seemed a very long way away.

The fort's Colored Area, where Luther had been quartered, was a collection of long, tall whitewashed barracks tucked in Lawton's recessed northwest corner, somewhat hidden from white barracks and from the rest of the fort. The newest residents were the 650th and 651st Port Companies, soldiers from the South, mostly, mixed with a few city types from Chicago and Detroit. Some were as young as nineteen, including baby-faced, bull-necked John Hamilton of Houston; a strong, deep-throated young man from Austin named Les Stewart; and twenty-year-old Bill Jones of Decatur, a proud man with a large head and quick wit, who became Luther's friend. Many in the port companies were much older, like thirty-six-year-old Wallace Wooden, from the toughest part of Chicago, and Willie Basden of Miami, thirty-four and shy. They too had just completed basic training, but unlike Luther, they were all new to the army.

The fresh troops had entered the service at a difficult time. Earlier recruits like Larkin had come aboard when victory seemed plausible if not certain, like talk of a World Series during spring training. But as war dragged on, stories in the newspaper painted a more realistic picture: battles were lost, soldiers were maimed, neighborhood boys came home dead. By 1944, the buck privates at Fort Lawton had reason to be edgy: Hitler was still having his way in much of Europe, and tales of war out of the South Pacific were often horrifying. The prospect of stateside service as a manual laborer in a segregated unit was not entirely offensive to everyone.

Luther moved his bags into Barracks 719 to join the 650th Port Company as it started several weeks of specialized stevedore training. Men who had grown up on farms or in Midwestern cities were taught to be cargo checkers, crane operators, coopers, riggers, blacksmiths, welders, and mechanics. Luther, now a corporal, had to put aside his medical corpsman training and learn how to load and unload military cargo from ships.

On June 13, one week after D-day, members of the 650th and 651st stood for inspection. For days, they had washed windows, shined shoes, scrubbed garbage cans, and picked litter. Their sheets and blankets secured with army corners and stretched like drums, men in pressed khaki milled near the foot of bunks as a corporal stood watch at an open door, scouting the arrival of Major John McLachlan Jr. At 0800, the alarm sounded, and Arthur Kapitz, the second lieutenant, ordered Barracks 719 to attention. Moving double-time, Kapitz strode directly toward the approaching inspector, stopped six paces from the major, and saluted. "SIR! Second Lieutenant Kapitz, platoon commander, 650th Port Company reports! SIR, do you want to inspect the ranks at this time?"

The inspection took two hours. Major McLachlan, a stickler for detail, liked what he saw. In an earlier report, the 650th had earned his praise for its ability to follow orders and had been awarded better than average marks on overall basic and technical training. The company's rifle marksmanship had been outstanding, as was its talents on the obstacle course. Its members had scored poorly on knowledge of the Articles of War, and the company cooks were so inept that some had been sent to a special messing school for further instruction. Overall, though, McLachlan found little fault with the men of the 650th and on June 13 gave them passing marks on their final inspection. They were now soldiers in a full-fledged company of the United States Army. They had earned a three-week furlough, effective the very next morning. It meant they could finally head home for a visit, and when they returned on the Fourth of July, they would learn when, if not where, they would be loading and unloading ships. The odds were it would be somewhere overseas.

CHAPTER THREE

MOLLYCODDLING
July 1944

It HAD NOW BEEN more than a year since Guglielmo Olivotto and tens of thousands of his countrymen had surrendered in North Africa, but their presence was still felt by American GIs stationed throughout the Mediterranean. George Fordyce was a U.S. Army truck driver stationed in the Sahara. Letters from family and folks back in Kansas came about as often as desert rain, but when they did, the thirty-seven-year-old corporal broiled about the news he'd been getting from home. For some reason, he'd been told, the very Italians who'd been rounded up in Tunisia were now living the good life in the United States. Fed up, Fordyce sat down an army typewriter and banged out a letter to Arthur Capper, the U.S. senator from Kansas who had known his aunt's brother in Topeka:

North Africa

Dear Senator Capper:

I am writing in regard to the way, according to all newspaper and letters from home folks, as to the royal entertainment of P.O.W. in the States.

It was the hardest letdown the boys have received in many a moon.

I am in a limited service Quartermaster Truck Company, made up of boys who have been in the thick of it.

The thoughts of having our wives, sweethearts, and others doing that, and the thoughts of what goes on not mentioned, as we
know the folks are human, makes the boys' blood boil.

We are situated at a place that we pass one of the first ceme-
teries established and can see the crosses over our friends that
won't be coming home.

We wish you and your colleagues in Congress would do something to remedy the same.

Respectfully yours,
Cpl. Geo. F. Fordyce
3635 QM Truck Co.

Corporal Fordyce was just one of many. By July 1944, army in-boxes
were bulging with letters and clippings from soldiers, veterans, politicians, journalists, and commentators, all agitated about the government's decision to give Italians paying jobs and additional liberties.
Some letter writers, like Robert J. Miller of Milwaukee, were furious
that Italian Service Unit soldiers were allowed to wear American uniforms, even if those khakis and olive drabs were hand-me-downs:
"United States uniforms are still the SACRED POSSESSION of the AMER-
ICAN FIGHTING UNITS . . . I'll be darned if I can understand where you
or any other individual who is a member of our Army Service Forces
can issue instructions to clothe those men in such a prize possession."

Others, like M. C. Swope, the fiancée of a soldier stationed at Fort
Monmouth, New Jersey, hated the fact that Italians had the run of the
post: "They are free to 'clutter up' the P.X. and Service Club," she complained, "which has always been overcrowded with our own boys who
have a perfect right to be there, thus making it practically impossible
to get service and further necessitates the rubbing of elbows with men
who not many months ago would have destroyed our boys if given the
opportunity."

In New England, three soldiers laid up in the Fort Devens hospital
dashed off a sarcastic letter to the editor of a Boston newspaper: "It
was with great pleasure that we read of the Italian prisoners in Boston

being taken on sightseeing trips and visits while our gang gets all smashed up fighting for Italy over there. We suggest that the next thing to do is to get all the nice German prisoners and have them visit the homes of the boys whom they tried to kill in Tunisia, Salerno and Cassino . . . They wouldn't think we were soft or nutty, for that is the way they treated our airmen who were shot down over Germany . . ."

In Plainfield, New Jersey, the editors of the *Courier-News* were outraged that members of an ISU were given a whirlwind tour of Manhattan, including the Empire State Building, Radio City Music Hall, and St. Patrick's Cathedral: "We feel the Brass Hats of the War Department (or whoever is responsible) are carrying it too far when they give war prisoners the 'Key to the City' and permit them to be taken on sight-seeing tours and picnics . . . Why should former prisoners be molly-coddled? They killed or helped kill our boys. When they were defeated at the cost of our blood and sweat they threw up their hands and surrendered. Then we take them on picnics . . . The next thing we know, we'll have Mussolini, Hitler and Tojo touring the country as our guests."

National commentators quickly picked up the refrain. Bill Cunningham, writing in the *Boston Herald*, wondered if the Italians in U.S. prison camps were cowards: "Somebody dreamed up a new name for the status of a licked outfit and decided to call them co-belligerents . . . In this country co-belligerency has been extended to the former minions of Il Duce, all of whom were captured in the process of shooting and killing American boys . . . Have these fellows requested guns and the privilege of going back to help free their native land? If they even asked to go back and help move the gear of war I'd stand at full salute, but does co-belligerency mean that only American kids are fit to fight and die for Italy?"

Leland Stowe, Pulitzer Prize–winning war correspondent, figured the army was simply sending Italian POWs the wrong message. "Are our authorities spending as much effort to win Italian prisoners to democracy as they expend for their entertainment?" he questioned. "What is the Army doing to shape the political ideals of all Axis prisoners?" And popular gossip columnist Walter Winchell went right for the jugular, raising the specter of foreign enemies stalking American streets: "They are housed not far from shipping yards and naval reservations. These war prisoners are allowed to wander about town without guards. They are allowed to be overnight guests in nearby homes and they are treated as though they were returned war heroes. Only last week one father complained about his daughters being molested by them on the streets of Bayonne, N.J."

Many of the accusations were true, to a point. Men in the ISU *were* taken on field trips, and they were allowed liberal access to service clubs and other post recreation areas. John Eager, the general in charge of the Italian Service Unit program, believed that "any limited liberty they receive is for the purpose of maintaining or increasing their output of work." Provost Marshal General Archer Lerch admitted that "they are allowed to go about their work without armed guards, but under supervision. They are permitted to make visits to post exchanges, theaters, and chapels on the post, and occasional group recreational trips off military reservations under the supervision of American military personnel." Responding to beefs about the use of gasoline and tires at a time when both were strictly rationed, Lerch said, "If transportation is required on these trips, the men charter and pay for the bus out of their earnings."

By July 1944, there were 178 ISUs in communities across the country, employing nearly thirty-four thousand Italians. Army public affairs officers wavered back and forth between playing up the benefits of labor units on the one hand and enforcing a stoic silence about their very existence on the other. As criticism grew, the War Department decided to launch a major public relations campaign, highlighting what it called the "substantial contributions to the American war effort being made throughout the United States by members of Italian Service Units." The Pentagon hoped to blunt what General Eager described as "a wave of indignation and resentment which expressed itself in the form of scores of letters to President Roosevelt, members of Congress, the Secretary of War, the War Department, and to newspaper editors condemning this liberalized treatment and apparent coddling of prisoners of war."

Brigadier General John Eager, a forty-five-year-old career soldier, was a former military attaché to Rome who spoke fluent Italian. From ISU headquarters on Staten Island, the general tried to reassure reporters that "Italian members are all volunteers, have been screened by military intelligence, are subject to immediate return to prisoner of war camps for abuse of privileges, and are under the supervision of American personnel at all times." When he made those statements in July, he couldn't know that events at Fort Lawton in August would expose the fallacy of his assurances.

THE WAR DEPARTMENT's public relations offensive scored a few small victories, as reporters sympathetic to the army's point of view published upbeat stories. "I believe I have seen more prisoner-of-war camps in this country than any American civilian other than a representative of government or organizations such as the International Red Cross," boasted reporter Robert Devore in an article for *Colliers* magazine. "What I discovered convinced me that we are not coddling our war prisoners." But most journalists, to the army's continued frustration, disagreed. "These Italians have reached a captive's Utopia," declared *Business Week*, "enjoying all of military life's necessities and a few of the privileges denied their skulking comrades and their erstwhile allies from Germany."

Few things riled the public more than reports of Italian dalliances with American girls. Soldiers in Virginia Beach, according to the *Washington Post*, were "fed up with the Italians strolling along the boardwalk and flirting with the bathing beauties . . . Enlisted Italians serving in Army service units in this country are living up to the adage about Latins being romantically inclined by yelling 'Hello, Gorgeous' and walking away with the GI's girls on furlough." A War Department spokesman responded that "when these men go on furlough, 30 or 40 of them are accompanied by one American officer or enlisted man. Naturally, that escort cannot keep an eye on all the park benches and it is entirely possible for the Italians to yell 'hi-ya toots' to the American girls."

In England, where Italian prisoners were given an opportunity to be "cooperators"—the British term for ISUs—liaisons with English girls spurred similar outrage. A solicitor for the county council of Lanarkshire sent an angry telegram to Sir James Grigg, British war minister, insisting that "all Lanarkshire is up in arms. We will not rest until we get satisfaction . . . Last Sunday I traveled through a country road outside East Kilbride and counted eighty-four Italian prisoners of war in uniform. They were with girls aged between fifteen and seventeen. Most of them were conducting themselves in a disgraceful manner," he reported. A girl of fifteen "was drunk three times in one week and has learned to smoke twenty-five cigarettes a day." He went on, "These men are feeding on the fat of the land and thinking they have licked the world."

As the war wore on, stories about American girls becoming engaged to Italian POWs were front-page news. Nineteen-year-old Eva Caprari, daughter of a grocer in White Plains, New York, proudly announced she would marry Delfino Rosatti, a twenty-four-year-old corporal with the 321st ISU. The *New York Times* related this telling anecdote about Eva and her parents: "The mother, waiting on customers at the store, said she thought Rosatti was a 'fine young man' and that the marriage would be a good one. The father, wielding a meat cleaver on a chopping block, grunted concurrence."

The Geneva Convention, however, got in the lovesick couples' way. The treaty required warring nations to return prisoners to their homelands "in the same status as when captured" once the conflict was over. Congressman Vito Marcantonio of East Harlem, writing to General Eager on behalf of a constituent named Alfred Nicosia, wanted to know if "same status" included marital status: "Mr. Nicosia states that an Italian prisoner of war, Private Giorgio Genta, ran off with his daughter and had sex relations with her. Mr. Nicosia is desirous that this man marry his daughter and states that the prisoner of war has indicated his willingness to do so." General Eager stuck by the book:

"Members of Italian Service Units were captured as enemy prisoners of war and they still retain the status of prisoners of war, despite the fact that those who have joined these service units are given limited privileges which are not granted to other prisoners of war. War Department regulations prohibit the marriage of prisoners of war, including those in Italian service units, except by proxy with a person residing in the country which the prisoner was serving at the time of capture. This regulation has been applied consistently and without exception." Private Genta would be sent home after the war, still a single man. If Miss Nicosia wanted to follow him, that was her business.

THE NATIONAL FUSS over Italians during July 1944 largely bypassed the Twenty-eighth ISU at Fort Lawton. Mindful of the debate raging elsewhere, Colonel Harry Branson, the fort commander, restricted his new Italian charges to base for most of the month. To Branson, the ISU was simply an unwanted distraction at a time when he had plenty else on his mind.

Harry Branson was a beleaguered bureaucrat who looked the part: high forehead and sagging chin, oversized ears, and a substantial nose. Born the same year as Dwight Eisenhower and raised, like Ike, in Kansas, he was now fifty-four years old and unlikely to earn a general's star while commanding a post so very far from the hub of war. Since Branson had been given limited opportunity to shine, he figured the least he could do was avoid screwing up.

Branson's fort had been little more than an afterthought at the war's beginning, elbowed aside by politically connected ladder climbers running the show at the much bigger port down in San Francisco. At first, most soldiers passing through Lawton were headed for Alaska, assigned to the Aleutian Islands or to construct the fifteen-hundred-mile gravel road from Dawson Creek to Fairbanks that would later be known as the Alaska Highway. By 1943, the number of troops being shipped to stations in the South Pacific began to overwhelm the ports in San Francisco and Los Angeles. Fort Lawton was ordered to pick up much of the slack, forcing Colonel Branson to oversee the quick construction of dozens of new barracks and support buildings. Rather suddenly, his sleepy little outpost became a fairly substantial military base.

Included among thousands of new soldiers being processed through Fort Lawton were hundreds of Negro troops, which meant Branson had to find additional money and space to build segregated quarters for eating and sleeping. On top of everything, his Fort Lawton Staging Area remained an activation and training center. That job alone— turning raw recruits into battle-ready soldiers—would have been enough to give most fort commanders a sizeable headache.

By July, the mission of Fort Lawton was secretly changing. As the Allies advanced toward Paris, victory over Nazi Germany looked more promising, allowing war planners to shift greater attention to Japan. Orders were drafted to ship 120,000 a men a month into the Pacific war zone via the West Coast ports. With the atomic bomb still an uncertain experiment, the Pentagon prepared for an eventual all-out invasion of Japan. The assault was expected to generate a tidal wave of American casualties, creating unprecedented demand for hospitals and bed space. Fort Lawton was quietly tapped to supply much of that space.

The members of three Negro port companies—the 650th, 651st, and 578th—would be among the last soldiers to use Fort Lawton for basic training. Branson needed their barracks for the wave of transient troops heading through his fort and into the Pacific, but none of the three port companies was scheduled to ship out until August at the earliest. For the next month or so, the colonel had to find something for his black troops to do in Seattle. The two hundred Italians in his Twenty-eighth ISU were likewise in need of temporary work.

In many ways, black American soldiers and their Italian neighbors had simply been interchangeable parts in the Fort Lawton workforce. African Americans were often stuck working as waiters, porters, and valets in service clubs, messes, and barracks reserved for white officers. That practice, however, came to an abrupt end in late June when the secretary of war issued a terse presidential directive. The Roosevelt administration, said the memo, would no longer tolerate discrimination at military installations "with respect to race, sex, color, religion, creed, national origin, or political or other affiliation, except as may be required by law." While the edict seemed strong, it did not mean the army would be fully desegregated; that historic step was still years away. But the directive sent a signal to commanders like Branson that black soldiers could no longer be treated as "houseboys" for the convenience of army officers. Almost immediately, dozens of servile duties formerly assigned Fort Lawton's blacks were transferred to Italians from the ISU.

Guglielmo Olivotto became a janitor, sweeping floors, washing windows, and cleaning toilets in officers' barracks. He was diligent, rarely sick or absent, always on time for the daily eight fifteen fallout that marked the start of each day. After work, he attended English language classes, a requirement for all ISU soldiers. Shy, but eager to learn, he often headed down to the beach at the base of the bluffs after class to practice new words with his pals Imo Nolgi and Bruno Patteri. In July, the sun stayed above the horizon until well after eight; the evening glow lingered well past ten. The three men usually leaned against driftwood, talking about food and family and the girls they missed and the plans they'd made for that uncertain day when the Americans would allow them to return home. Of the three, Guglielmo was always quietest. Often he would simply turn away and read from a well-worn prayer book. As summer stretched on, Olivotto's friends began to notice that he'd grown even more withdrawn.

THERE WAS LITTLE chance, however, that news of an ISU soldier's ennui would reach the desk of Harry Branson. On July 1, the colonel opened his Saturday mail. The endless pile of memos, directives, orders, and counterorders included a letter stamped CONFIDENTIAL. Jim Kuttner, commander of the war prisoner camp in Monticello, Arkansas, had typed four terse paragraphs, reminding Branson about a shipment of Italians due to arrive at Fort Lawton in just five days. The shipment was huge—one thousand men—and Branson had already been scrambling to find some way to feed, house, and process so many prisoners in such a short time. The Italians, he had been told, were scheduled to stay at Fort Lawton for three or four days, then board a transport ship headed to Hawaii. Colonel Kuttner, however, wanted to make sure Branson fully understood what he'd be dealing with. "The prisoners supplied on this movement," said the letter, "are mostly Fascists."

Colonel Branson was not amused. It was bad enough he'd have to play nursemaid to POWs at a time when so much else was going on— he had assumed all along that these newcomers would be relatively docile, like Olivotto and the other Italians now in his ISU—but Kuttner's letter made it clear these soldiers weren't the kind of men he'd want to have waiting tables at his officers' club. "When they discover their ultimate [overseas] destination," Kuttner warned, "it is believed there may be numerous attempts at escape and possibly even a mass attempt. It is therefore suggested that maximum guarding be supplied by your station during the time this shipment is there."

Branson didn't have "maximum guarding." If anything, Fort Lawton had been chronically short of military policemen for months; his pleas for reinforcements had fallen on deaf ears. The army wanted its best soldiers on the front lines, so MPs were usually men who barely met the military's minimum standards or who had been kicked out of their combat unit for piling up too many demerits. The average MP rarely stuck around Fort Lawton for more than a month or two, and most were generally bored or unhappy or both. Military policing was a low-prestige assignment, and with the high turnover, most Fort Lawton MPs had little or no training in how to control unruly mobs.

Branson picked up the phone and called George McNay, the twenty-six-year-old whiz-kid army major who served as his post engineer. McNay was a can-do guy, someone who jumped at an order and got it done on time and under budget. The two men quickly agreed that building a temporary stockade large enough to hold a thousand prisoners in such a short a time was out of the question. McNay suggested turning a half-dozen existing barracks into a makeshift compound, even though the area available was only large enough to comfortably hold perhaps eight hundred men, give or take a hundred.

Branson knew it would be inadequate, but it was the best he could do. He told his young engineer to get going.

McNay wasted little time. In less than forty-eight hours, he and his crew had wrapped a barbed-wire fence around the barracks' perimeter, erected eight guard towers, and fired up thirty-two one-thousand-watt floodlights. They finished just hours before the first inmates arrived, on the Fourth of July. Major McNay had pulled off a small miracle. Colonel Branson would soon need several more.

The first Italians inside the compound were not, however, part of Kuttner's large contingent due in from Arkansas. Instead, they were ten prisoners who had been shipped from a compound in Texas, all of them officers, including two doctors and a chaplain. The ten newcomers were grateful to be in Seattle, a reward, they assumed, for their promise to swear allegiance to the Allies and to join an Italian Service Unit. For months, they'd been stuck in Camp Hereford, one of two prisons where openly ardent Fascists had been warehoused. As anti-Fascists, they had been tormented by Camp Hereford's inmates and had begged the camp commander to send them elsewhere. Fort Lawton was apparently going to be their new home.

But the ten officers would soon have company. At 6 A.M. on July 6, the first train from Colonel Kuttner's Arkansas camp pulled into Seattle. Five hundred Fascist prisoners disembarked under the heaviest guard Colonel Branson could muster, each POW clutching a barracks bag stuffed with whatever personal items he owned. Fourteen hours later, the second train rolled in, disgorging the remaining five hundred men. That night, the ten Italian officers from Camp Hereford found themselves with a thousand new companions, all crammed into McNay's makeshift stockade. Because wartime troop movements were always kept secret, none of the Italians had any idea they were to be shipped to Hawaii. The ten Italians from Texas had a sickening feeling that something might have gone terribly wrong.

The next morning after breakfast, all the newcomers were ordered to line up for physical exams. Each man was examined by an army doctor, then directed into a building staffed with American supply clerks. The first clerk guessed the size of each man's head, then handed him a gas mask and motioned to have him check for a snug fit. The next clerk distributed a handful of mosquito bars, and the third, a container of insect repellant. Within minutes, the line broke down as prisoners turned angry, cursing in Italian, clamoring to get the attention of a translator. A POW spokesman bolted to the head of the line and demanded that the processing stop immediately. Gas masks, he said, were only used in combat areas, and the Geneva Convention prohibited sending prisoners into battle. The mosquito bars appeared to offer proof that the army intended to move them to a malaria zone, and everyone knew that the South Pacific—a hot spot of warfare—was a haven for mosquitoes.

The objections grew louder; supply clerks slowly retreated. Doctors, hearing the commotion, put away their stethoscopes and evacuated behind the uncertain protection of wide-eyed MPs. The Americans withdrew to the gate and filed out of the compound, glancing back at jeering prisoners pressed against barbed wire. Fists in the air, the POWs chanted, defiantly crowing that they knew their rights and would not fight for America. The outnumbered GIs were in no position to argue.

When news of the uprising reached Colonel Branson, he grew livid. The prisoners, he told his officers, would be issued proper overseas equipment one way or another, whether they liked it or not. He ordered supply clerks to box the gas masks and insecticides and truck them to the Seattle waterfront on Elliott Bay. When the transport ship pulled out of Seattle in a day or two, Branson said, army escorts could figure a way to force the Fascists to take their equipment while en route to Hawaii. He then telephoned port-of-embarkation headquarters, hoping to talk to his boss, General Eley Denson, the port commander. Denson, though, was out of town; his assistant promised to have Colonel John Hood, the acting commander, call back as soon as possible.

At 3 P.M., the post chaplain burst into Branson's office with more bad news. One of the ten officers from Texas—the Italian chaplain—had just told him that the Arkansas prisoners were plotting to kill them. The ten officers, he said, were shocked to learn they'd been locked up with Fascists; the army was supposed to know they had agreed to collaborate with the United States and had come to Seattle assuming they'd be offered a spot in an ISU. Somehow, the Arkansas Fascists had discovered they were collaborators and had threatened to murder them. They were now begging to be removed from the stockade.

Harry Branson stood up, strapped on his service revolver, and ordered his assistant to find Bill Orem, the fort's provost marshal, and Milton Carter, the head of his military police detachment. He jumped in his staff car and wound through Fort Lawton's maze of streets, most of them named after states. Texas Way was big and broad; Utah Street wound down to the beach; Washington and Oregon Avenues circled the parade grounds.

Branson pulled up to the stockade; everything seemed calm. When Major Orem and Captain Carter arrived moments later, it seemed safe to send them in to extricate the Italian officers. Cautiously, they passed through the gate and walked up to the officers' barracks. They climbed the wooden steps, opened the door, and found themselves face to face with at least two hundred Italians. The Fascists had closed ranks, obviously expecting the Americans' arrival, and were certainly in no mood to cooperate. Captain Carter slammed the door, jumped back down the steps, then shouted, in English, to the Italian officers trapped inside, "Go to the rear of the barracks! Do it now! Stay there until we return!"

Carter and Orem retreated, Branson ordered all the MPs at the stockade to assemble. Draw your weapons, he told them, and corral these prisoners into the opposite end of the compound. Keep the ten Italian officers in their barracks. Don't take no for an answer. Reluctantly, the MPs waded in, creeping from barracks to barracks, rounding up small groups of defiant Italians, forcing them with pistols drawn into an open area between the barracks and the barbed wire. When the main yard was finally cleared, Orem and Carter raced back in and led the ten terrified officers to safety.

It had become clear to Colonel Branson that the prisoners' anger would only grow, putting his MPs and perhaps the rest of his fort in jeopardy. Although army rules prohibited him from telling POWs where they were being shipped, he decided that the misinformation about being sent into combat was far worse. The colonel collared an interpreter, entered the compound, and walked as forcefully as he knew how toward the assembled crowd of prisoners.

"Attention! I am Colonel Branson, camp commander here at Fort Lawton. In compliance with Article 26 of the Geneva Convention, you are being transferred to a new destination. You will be allowed to take with you your personal effects, your correspondence and packages and so on. You will be given the same accommodations and, insofar as possible, the same treatment as American soldiers making the same trip."

From the crowd, in broken English, some yelled, "Where do you mean to send us?"

"Your destination is American territory. You will not be exposed to the fire of the combat zone nor used to give protection from bombardment, in compliance with Article 9 of the Geneva Convention. Your destination is a spot that is ideal for a prisoner-of-war camp, and in the approximate location of Hawaii."

Hawaii! Pearl Harbor! This crowd knew darn well that the Americans had entered the war because the Japanese had destroyed much of the U.S. naval fleet at Pearl Harbor. The rumors, then, were true! The Americans *were* sending them into combat. The prisoners' spokesman shushed the crowd, turned to the interpreter, and told him to translate a message for the colonel: "If you think you will make us move, we will resist, we will resist with force. We will not move."

Branson was out of cards. He was sure the army had no intention of sending these men into combat—there really *was* a nice POW camp in Hawaii—and as far as he knew, the army used every prisoner of war it could get its hands on in Hawaii to help harvest sugarcane and pineapple. The gas masks were issued only for the prisoners' own protection, in the unlikely event their transport ship should be attacked. But these men were clearly in no mood to listen. As they grew louder and more restless, the MPs brandished their riot batons and Branson marched out of the compound.

IT WAS SURPRISINGLY easy to be stationed at Fort Lawton and not know that a thousand Fascist prisoners were creating an uproar. The sprawling fort was busier than it had ever been in the forty-six years since it first opened, and thousands of new faces were passing in and out of the staging area each month. Even the two hundred men in the Twenty-eighth ISU were completely unaware that any Fascists had come to town; their barracks were nowhere near the temporary stockade.

Life at Fort Lawton had begun to wear on several of the ISU Italians, including Guglielmo Olivotto. Each morning, Guglielmo and his fellow janitors walked to work along Lawton Road, passing next to the usually deserted Colored Area barracks on their way up the hill. On July 5, while strolling between Virginia and Florida Avenues, Guglielmo was shocked to see, for the very first time, hundreds of black soldiers. The members of the 650th and 651st Port Companies had just returned from their three-week furlough, and the black men seemed surprisingly loud as the Italians passed by their barracks. Guglielmo's fellow workers noticed how frightened he seemed; perhaps it was the noise. The Italians moved on.

On each of the next several days, the ISU janitors could see that Olivotto grew more anxious each time he passed the Negro quarters. Black soldiers never actually bothered them; most GIs at Fort Lawton simply ignored Italians, probably because they wore army uniforms and kept to themselves. But something about these soldiers made Guglielmo unusually uncomfortable, and word of his odd behavior started to spread.

A few other Italians had problems of their own. Luigi Canevari, a twenty-six-year-old private, spent most days curled in his bunk, often sobbing—worried, he said, about the fate of his family in Italy. Canevari had been ordered to visit Captain Charles Sturdevant, the Fort Lawton psychiatrist, and came back with a diagnosis of moderately severe depression and reactive psychoneurosis. Sturdevant also evaluated Stelvio Federici, a corporal who shared the same barracks as both Canevari and Olivotto. Federici had been driven to distraction by Canevari's crying; he too was deemed mentally unstable. Captain Sturdevant recommended that both men be shipped to Bushnell General Hospital in Brigham City, Utah, where each could receive round-the-clock care in the army's psychiatric unit.

On Saturday, July 8—the day after the Fascists had refused gas masks and mosquito bars—Private Canevari and Corporal Federici were loaded into coach class on a Union Pacific passenger train bound for Salt Lake City. Two MPs, Corporal Bob Camozzi and Private Dave Conte, were assigned to accompany them, taking care to keep the two men apart, lest Federici start a fight with his sobbing nemesis. It took all afternoon and throughout the night to reach the Idaho border and another eight hours to wind through the lava flats of the Snake River Plain.

At Pocatello, Corporal Camozzi and Private Conte took their prisoners to the dining car for supper. After the meal, they returned to the coach car, where Canevari asked if he could get a drink of water. Minutes later, the MPs noticed he was gone. Corporal Camozzi ran to the back of the car, checked the latrine, then looked into the passageway connecting to the next car. A side door in the vestibule was unlocked and hung open as if someone had jumped off the moving train.

In his formal report, Union Pacific conductor Bill Baugh was struck by how casually the two MPs reacted. They "did not seem concerned that they had lost this prisoner. When asked if they wanted to make a report of this escape to anyone, they told me that they would make their report when they arrived at Bushnell Hospital in Brigham. Special Agent Wakley and I spent most of the night searching for this escaped war prisoner."

The next morning, the engineer of another eastbound train spotted Canevari's body along the side of the tracks. His head was split open and his neck broken. Although his right foot was severed at the ankle, there was no blood; the county coroner figured it must have been amputated by another train in the middle of the night, long after Canevari's heart had stopped pumping. The MPs continued to Utah, where they left Federici in the psychiatric ward and instructions to bring Canevari to the Bushnell morgue.

SEVERAL DAYS PASSED before anyone told Colonel Branson about the Idaho suicide. On July 8, the day the train left Seattle, Branson had been preoccupied with the uncooperative Fascists in his stockade. Midmorning, he took a call from John Hood, the acting commander of the Seattle Port of Embarkation. Colonel Hood had good news, sort of: the chief of transportation in Washington, D.C., after hearing about the previous day's revolt, had decided to cancel the order to transport the prisoners to Hawaii. On the one hand, it might help keep them calm, but on the other, what was the army going to do with them?

For the moment, it didn't matter. Branson drove back down to the stockade and ordered MPs to assemble the prisoners. You won't be going overseas, he told them. We'll tell you as soon as we can what you'll be doing. The colonel returned to his office to study his options.

Those options soon evaporated. Late that same day, another call came, once again from the port. Colonel Hood warned Branson to brace himself: the top guns in Transportation Division had changed their minds, deciding that the POWs *would* be shipped to Hawaii after all. Their transport vessel would weigh anchor in two days, and all one thousand prisoners had to be on board. The best Hood could do was assign another small battalion of MPs to the fort to help lend a hand.

July 9 was a Sunday, but no one in Harry Branson's top command was sitting in church. That day's sermon was held in the colonel's conference room; the congregation included his staff, the commanders of the MP units, and officers from the four American battalions scheduled to share the transport ship to Hawaii the next day. Branson's scripture focused on the importance of getting a thousand angry men out of Lawton and down to the docks as quickly and as safely as possible. There was, he said, no room for excuses and little room for error.

On Monday morning, July 10, inmates were served breakfast at 6 A.M., as usual. At 7 A.M., MPs from the Prisoner of War Escort Company entered the compound to extract five men, identified over the weekend as agitators. When one of the five resisted, an MP clubbed him with his nightstick, then dragged him to the back of a waiting truck. A platoon of MPs took positions around the stockade while the remaining prisoners were once again assembled in the yard. At 7:45 A.M., Colonel Branson spoke. "I have orders from Washington, D.C., to move the men in this stockade to the docks, where you will be transported by ship to a prisoner-of-war camp on American soil, safe from harm and away from battle," he announced. "You are to go to your barracks, procure your baggage and personal belongings, and go peaceably to the transport trucks."

"You lied!" came a call in Italian. Branson didn't need a translator; the prisoners were seething. At the gate, American troops from an engineering battalion stood at the ready, riot batons in hand. Outside the compound, members of the Negro port companies waited in reserve as soldiers from another battalion unrolled fire hoses.

"You must proceed in an orderly manner! If you do not go of your own free will, the United States Army will use force to execute this order! It is in your own best interest to cooperate."

"Never!" came the cry. "If you will try to move us, you will have to kill us first!"

Any semblance of control faded fast. Branson stepped aside as Colonel Hood moved in and raised his voice. "Attention! I am Colonel John Hood, acting commander for the Seattle Port of Embarkation. I am the highest-ranking officer in this area, and it is my duty under the Articles of the Geneva Convention to tell you that you must comply with our orders! You have been ordered to move, and we need your cooperation."

"Never! We will die first!"

Colonel Hood looked past the barbed wire and signaled the battalion commander. As Hood and Branson backed away, fire hoses streamed full-force toward the Italians, knocking dozens to the dirt.

At the same moment, engineering troops rushed through the gate, clutching batons. The prisoners, already backed against barbed wire, were surrounded. One Italian broke from the crowd and raised his hands in surrender, then staggered toward the helmeted soldiers. Several others, dripping wet, quickly followed, cowering to avoid a thicket of raised nightsticks. Those who surrendered were promptly ushered into the backs of the waiting trucks.

Most of the prisoners, however, did not submit. As American troops closed ranks, the Italians struck back, rushing their captors and forcing soldiers outside the fence to redirect the hoses. The Americans swung their batons, cracking skulls and bruising bones. At the edges, troops dragged small groups of Fascists through the gates where they were hogtied and carried away. As more and more prisoners fell to the mud under the barrage of nightsticks, the tide turned decisively in favor of the Americans. Within twenty minutes, the last prisoner was subdued; in all, forty-three Italians had been injured. Every last one was thrown into a convoy truck, and a half hour later, all one thousand men were at the Elliott Bay pier.

There was no further resistance. Their bodies bloodied and their confidence shattered, the prisoners stumbled out of the trucks and ran a gauntlet of MPs, who shoved them into the hold of the transport ship. The injured were fitted with bandages and splints, though none were taken to hospitals. Colonel Branson ordered a squad of black port-company enlisted men to head back to the fort to gather the Italians' barracks bags from the stockade and bring them to the docks. At the last moment, he made one final decision. The ten Italian officers from Camp Hereford had been sequestered in Ward 8 of the Fort Lawton hospital. Branson ordered a detail of MPs to assemble the officers, bring them to the pier, and load them on the ship with their Fascist tormenters. As far as Branson was concerned, they could now be someone else's problem.

Two days later, Harry Branson filed a formal report, relishing the chance to vent his frustration. In his report, the colonel all but refused to receive any more Fascists convoys at Fort Lawton unless the army first made sure they were broken into smaller groups and kept under tight control by accompanying American guards. He demanded that he be given the time and money to erect a permanent stockade and pleaded that a permanent, well-trained POW escort company be stationed at Fort Lawton. The army's Transportation Division agreed to Branson's demands, but it took more than a month for a specialized escort company to reach Seattle. As it turned out, it would arrive several hours too late.

ONE WEEK AFTER the transport ship set sail, Guglielmo Olivotto had almost completely withdrawn from all daily activities. His Italian supervisor, Second Lieutenant Giovanni Lobianco, sat him down and asked for an explanation. Reluctantly, Olivotto admitted that he was terrified of Negro soldiers. None of the Fort Lawton blacks had actually come near him, he said, but he couldn't shake his fear. It was so bad, he couldn't bear to go to his janitor's job any longer, since it required him to walk past the colored barracks.

Lobianco was baffled. Most men in his unit were somewhat intrigued by their black American neighbors. Just like the Italians, black soldiers liked to sing, and their laughter was often loud and contagious. Sure, they raised the occasional ruckus, and it seemed they got into their share of fights. But even Italians who couldn't speak English understood that most of the hubbub from the Colored Area—often fueled by beer or bootleg whiskey—was harmless. In any event, the black Americans generally left the Italians alone.

Because Lieutenant Lobianco had a soft spot for the reclusive private, he continued to probe. At last, Olivotto came clean. It all started in Africa, he said, in the prisoner-of-war camps in French Morocco. His unit had surrendered at Cape Bon in Tunisia, only to be loaded into dank cattle cars for a nightmarish westward trip across North Africa. Days later, after being dislodged in Casablanca, they had been stripped of everything except their uniforms. Prisoners lived in tents, freezing at night beneath threadbare blankets, suffocating during the day with little shelter from the oppressive sun.

The stockade guards had been native Moroccans, primarily Muslim

Arabs and Berbers. Most were veteran guerillas, hardened by years of fighting for independence from France. Olivotto remembered that the guards were not inclined to show much sympathy for their new European captives. Fresh water—already scarce at the POW enclosures—had often been withheld as punishment or torture. In one camp, a visiting American aviator had been shocked to see that "prisoners lived like pigs in a pen. Their food and water were put into troughs, and their only shelter was a brush arbor at one end of the enclosure." In other camps, minefields were cleared by lining up Italian prisoners and marching them through.

Olivotto said he was haunted by the endless cries from those who had been wounded in battle, some suffering from gruesome burns over much of their bodies, getting little or no medical attention in the sprawling stockades. There were new wounds too, inflicted by guards who prodded or stabbed prisoners with bayonets or threatened to sodomize them. Most horrifically—and Olivotto swore it was true—he witnessed guards cutting arms and legs off living prisoners. It was terror he could not erase from his mind.

Lobianco, who had seen his share of atrocities, was sympathetic. But what, he wondered, did this have to do with the American Negroes at Fort Lawton? While most Moroccan Berbers had complexions worn and weathered by the desert sun and wind, the actual color of their skin ran the gamut from white to olive to black, thanks in part to a robust slave trade from sub-Saharan Africa in the nineteenth century. Was Olivotto confusing Americans with Moroccans?

Lieutenant Lobianco refused to stand by as his countryman slipped further into a shell. He went to his Italian commander, Captain Ernesto Cellentani, to ask for help. Cellentani agreed to approach Captain Francis Beckman, the American officer in charge of the Twenty-eighth ISU. Beckman, fully aware that one of the Italians had jumped to his death from a moving train just a few days before, agreed to send Olivotto to see Captain Sturdevant, the psychiatrist. With any luck, Beckman thought, Sturdevant might find a way to talk some sense into this odd Italian.

• • •

OLIVOTTO DID SIT down with Charlie Sturdevant on July 18, but few noticed. The port of embarkation was crawling with VIPs that day, as Major General Mervin Gross, top gun of the War Department's Transportation Division, was in town on a formal inspection tour. Colonel Branson, worn out from what seemed like weeks of nonstop crises, was once again in the hot seat. Not only did he have to make sure his bustling fort was spic-and-span; he'd been told to host a dinner in the general's honor, the kind of event that usually involved endless chitchat and a fair amount of booze. Officers' parties were not his strong suit: Branson had earned a reputation for getting a little too frisky with officers' wives—particularly the lookers like "Bee Gee" Walker, wife of Captain John Walker—and he wasn't looking forward to hearing his own spouse remind him to take it easy on the scotch.

As usual, however, nothing for Colonel Branson came easy. On the very day General Gross arrived, tragedy struck in San Francisco, distracting the general and sending shivers through ports up and down the West Coast. At 12:45 A.M. on July 18, soldiers in San Francisco's 749th Military Police Battalion had been roused from bed and told to head out to the Port Chicago Naval Munitions base in the East Bay. A massive explosion had obliterated two transport ships as they were being loaded with ammunition by black sailors. The MPs arrived to find smoke, flames, and body parts. Three hundred twenty men were dead, another 390 wounded, many seriously. Two hundred two of the dead and 233 of the wounded were African American. The 749th scurried to secure the perimeter and tend to the wounded. Little did they know that the explosion was the triggering event in what would eventually become the largest navy court-martial of the war. Nor could they know that they would soon be involved in what would become the largest *army* court-martial of the war, this one up in Seattle. In both cases, every one of the defendants would be enlisted men; every one of them would be black.

CHAPTER FOUR

THE LIFE OF REILLY
Early August 1944

THE SUMMER OF 1944 was a tough time to be fifteen. Joyce Langsted's mama finally allowed a touch of lipstick; and it was—at last—okay to curl her hair, if just a little. All Joyce's friends knew that if a girl wore her sweater a little tight and carried her skirt *just so* on her hips, she'd turn a few heads and maybe catch the eye of a boy who'd notice that she is no longer a little girl.

But Joyce was still in ninth grade, and the boys her age acted like little kids and the older ones had all headed off to war. Just when she'd reached the age when a girl loves to dance and hopes for a first kiss, all the guys in last year's senior class were off in Italy or the Pacific. Sure, she lived in Seattle, which was awash in sailors and crawling with GIs, and those trim bodies looked pretty good in those starched uniforms. But army boys and navy fellas were always from someplace else, headed for somewhere far away, and their idea of a good time seemed to be a home run when she was just getting comfortable with the idea of second base.

Joyce was not, however, prepared to let her pending young woman-hood pass her by. Her daddy, Carl Langsted, a Danish immigrant, worked in the Marine Division of the Army's Corps of Engineers, which is why her family—three boys and three girls—lived on Queen Anne Hill, just a few minutes from Fort Lawton. Joyce and her twin sister, Joan, attended Queen Anne High School, where everyone called them the "Gold Dust Twins." On school days, they pressed their foreheads to the windows of the bus as it drove around Queen Anne and passed near Interbay, where it seemed hundreds of uniformed men were busy with whatever it was soldiers on the homefront were supposed to do. As June approached, the twins dared each other to find a summer job within the gates of Fort Lawton's fortress of eligible young men.

You had to be sixteen to work at the post, so Joyce and Joan had to fudge a bit when they sat across from Oda Tooley, the lady in charge of hiring civilians to work the fort's half-dozen post exchanges. Mrs. Tooley wasn't easily fooled by these underaged applicants, but she was impressed with the girls' moxie and reassured by the fact that they lived in the neighborhood and had a father at the fort. Good workers were harder to find than ever, especially since older girls could get better wages filling in at factories while men were away at war. She hired the twins, and assigned them to PX No. 3, located in the farthest reach of the fort.

Duties at PX No. 3 were fairly straightforward: serving coffee and sandwiches and canned soup to hungry soldiers and selling cigarettes and toothpaste from the army canteen. With their blonde hair and blue-green Scandinavian eyes, the Langsteds earned a good share of tips from love-struck Iowa farm boys and smooth New Jersey Romeos. If some of the boys got a little too handy, one twin stepped in to rescue the other. Two heads, they told everyone, were better—and safer—than one.

PX No. 3 was different from other Fort Lawton post exchanges because half the American boys who hung out there were black soldiers from the 650th, 651st, and 578th Port Companies, and many of the rest were Italians from the Twenty-eighth ISU. To Joyce, the Italians seemed an exotic blend of broad shoulders, narrow waists, dark eyes, and wavy hair. Most spoke little English, but it seemed they all knew how to flirt; there was no mistaking the look in their eyes and the tone of their voices. In time, Joyce was less inclined to ask her sister for protection.

By August, one Italian in particular made sure he knew Joyce's work schedule at the PX. Roberto Pasquale Solombrino—everyone called him Pasquale, but Joyce used all three names—was a handsome young sergeant from Naples. He spoke more English than most and loved to sing—a gift from his mother, who had performed with the Neapolitan opera. He'd been captured in North Africa and now lived in ISU Barracks 710—adjacent to Olivotto's barracks—and worked nights as a waiter in the officers' club. During the day, he sipped coffee or soda at PX No. 3, making small talk with the blonde beauty and her bubbly twin. Joyce enjoyed the attention, even if Roberto Pasquale Solombrino was sometimes a bit too forward. She barely noticed when white GIs sipping beer along the other wall stewed at the attention she'd be giving that "slick-talking Italian bastard."

On Sundays, Italian American families from Seattle arrived at the fort in their Packards and Buicks, carting baskets of sausages, bread, cheese, and grapes to share with Italian prisoners. Most local visitors had emigrated from Italy before the war, leaving their families stranded in the homeland. Forays to Fort Lawton allowed them to glean shreds of news about life in the towns and villages they had left behind. The POWs helped where they could, even if they sometimes had to feign familiarity with people or place in order to curry continued favor.

After his bleak experience with the rebellious Fascist prisoners in July, Colonel Branson was in no mood to grant members of the Twenty-eighth any more latitude than necessary. But by August, he was under growing pressure from the Ninth Service Command to loosen the reins. Reluctantly, Branson followed the lead of other forts and authorized weekend visits to private homes. The rules were strict: hosts had to request their ISU guests by name; no more than four prisoners at a time could join a family at their house for dinner; each quartet had to be accompanied by an American escort, and everyone had to be back in barracks before taps sounded at 2300. The POWs, naturally, loved the idea, and the army hoped the program would cultivate support for the still-controversial ISU program among the Italian American community. American GIs, however, grew ever more unhappy as they watched prisoners head off base for evenings of food and fun.

When news of the visitation program reached the Langsted home, the reception was equally mixed. Carl Langsted wasn't keen on the idea, and his son Ole agreed. Ole was in the navy, and couldn't understand why anyone should allow Mussolini's men to set foot in their house. But Mary Langsted was sympathetic to her twin daughters' pleas. After all, these prisoners had mothers, and what would happen, God forbid, if Ole were ever taken captive overseas? Wouldn't she want to know that another family somewhere shared a meal with her boy? The girls were given permission to ask four men from the Twenty-eighth—including Roberto Pasquale Solombrino—to come to dinner on Saturday evening, August 5.

Colonel Branson's home visitation policy was not welcome news for the six white American soldiers assigned to supervise the Twenty-eighth ISU. Their ranking officer, Captain Francis Beckman, ran an extremely loose ship, demanding little more than minimal effort from his charges. The captain, a large man nearing fifty years old, had grown soft from years in government desk jobs. Born in Iowa, he had moved to Puget Sound to raise a family and built a cabin in the San Juan Islands for the retirement he hoped would come soon. Beckman's style was to lie low and pray the war passed quickly by without anyone paying much attention to him or the company he commanded.

Private Fred Perata was a perfect fit for Beckman's outfit. As one of three interpreters assigned to the ISU, Perata figured he was living the life of Reilly, all things considered. Born and raised in San Francisco's Portola District, Fred was an only child, a rare distinction among Italian families of the day. His father was in the junk business, incinerating the garbage collected by his immigrant neighbors. Fred was good with numbers, so when the army learned that its new recruit had a degree in accounting from the University of San Francisco, it put him to work in the bookkeeping office at Camp Roberts in central California. From his desk at battalion headquarters, Perata could glance out the window and see poor saps in the infantry slogging heavy packs in the rain as they drilled for overseas combat. Soon enough, he figured, the mounting manpower shortage would sweep up anyone who could carry a gun, and he'd be forced to trade his green eyeshades for a steel helmet. But just in time, he came across a poster inviting college grads to apply for army foreign-language school. He signed on and spent the next nine months basking in the sun at Stanford University, where he and his roommate flirted with California coeds and polished up on the Genovese dialect Fred's parents had spoken at home. Perata assumed he'd be shipped to Italy, where he'd be assigned to work as an interpreter for army interrogators as they tried to break down newly captured prisoners. But by the time he graduated from Stanford, Italy had surrendered, and orders came to report to Fort Lawton.

As an interpreter, Perata's quarters were in the Italian Area, but permanent housing was scarce. His cot, therefore, was inside a four-sided canvas pyramidal tent, supported in the middle and along the sides by wood poles secured with jute rope. His tent mate was fellow interpreter Mason Gould, a short, wiry athlete with sparkling eyes and an easy grin. Gould's friends called him "Mase," although his college baseball coach called him "Lefty"; Gould had been a star southpaw pitcher at the University of Michigan, leading the Wolverines to the 1941 Big Ten title with a 6–1 record.

Once in the army, Gould shared Perata's concern about slogging with the infantry. Although he could aim a baseball, Mase could barely point a gun. In the military, whenever a soldier on the rifle range completely misses his target, a man assigned as the target puller raises a red flag that vaguely resembles a woman's underwear. This signal of humiliation is known to GIs as "waving Maggie's drawers," and Gould endured more than his share of taunting. At the first opportunity, he too went off to foreign-language school. He ended up at the University of Iowa, where college girls flirted with him by waving their lingerie as he and his fellow uniformed students marched beneath their dorm windows. In Iowa, at least, the underwear had nothing to do with missed targets.

Although Gould, Perata, and a third interpreter, Al DiGiacomo, provided translations for all of the Italians, each had only minimal contact with Olivotto, who remained reclusive. None of the three were particularly interested in learning more about Olivotto's problems because they each happily embraced Captain Beckman's laid-back style, determined to keep heads down and noses clean for the duration. Six days a week, the ISU men awoke at reveille, ate breakfast, then headed out for work. That gave the American interpreters and supervisors most of the rest of the day to themselves, filling out forms or perhaps translating a few phrases for soldiers in sick call. Perata, with his accounting background, was the point man whenever anyone bitched about late paychecks or missing canteen coupons. It was not tough duty. There was little incentive for any of the Americans to complicate their lives by prying into the affairs of a melancholy prisoner.

As in any army, a more pressing concern was the quality of messhall food. Because ISU kitchens received essentially the same rations as American mess halls, the Italians could never get enough pasta or sweets. Perata, enlisting the help of the company supply sergeant, Edward Haskell, became a master at negotiating trades between American and Italian pantries: corn for spaghetti, butter for oil, eggs for sugar. To the Italians, cooking was high art, and each mealtime their company chefs painted a canvas fit for a king. Time and again, grateful prisoners told Perata, "*Si mangia bene come prigionieri*" ("We eat well as prisoners"). Italian cooks often rewarded Perata and Haskell for their trading skills, treating them to prime cuts of beef or to exotic cakes and pastries.

Sergeant Haskell was another San Francisco boy. Tall and skinny, he grew up in a flat at Hayes and Filmore, kitty-corner to the Catholic Sisters' Home. His mother worked for Mr. Muscowicz, looking after the apartments he owned across the street. Haskell's father sold Packards for a while, then drove a lumber truck when he wasn't sick with cancer. Early one morning, Haskell took the call from San Francisco Hospital telling him his dad had died. In 1938, he turned down a chance to attend West Point so he could take a job with Crocker Bank to help support his widowed mother and younger brother.

After Pearl Harbor, most of the young men in the bank applied for commissions in the reserves with Naval Intelligence. The navy accepted almost everyone except Haskell: at six foot one and 137 pounds, he was deemed underweight. The army, desperate for manpower, wasn't as picky. Soldiers with flat feet or bad eyesight or a too-thin frame qualified for "limited" service, and filled noncombat jobs stateside. Haskell's first assignment was in San Francisco, pushing papers at the army induction center at 444 Market Street. Three square meals a day and minimal drilling helped put on twenty much-needed pounds, and he was soon wooing girls with his Hollywood-handsome looks: thick wavy hair, strong chin, and electric smile. Within a year, he got orders to head to Florence, Arizona. Until the train pulled into the camp, he had no idea he'd be working with prisoners of war. He never remembered meeting Guglielmo Olivotto.

At the induction center, Haskell became friends with Grant Farr, a boy from Utah whose ticket to a limited-service assignment was poor eyesight. Farr was flat-out brilliant; he'd been drafted while in graduate school at Cal Berkeley and decades later would become a renowned economist. With a high forehead, narrow eyes, and long fingers, he was tightly wound, puffing furiously at the Chesterfields that perpetually hung from his thin lips. Although his family was Mormon, he drank, smoked, and swore as much as any soldier, and he never went to church. He loved to read and in his spare time deconstructed major-league baseball box scores as if they were advanced economic equations. When Haskell was dispatched to Florence, so was Farr. When they were both transferred to Fort Lawton, they ended up roommates.

Haskell and Farr bunked together in the Italian orderly room, just a few yards from the tent shared by Perata and Gould. The orderly room, neat as a pin, would be nearly destroyed during the chaos on the night of Guglielmo Olivotto's lynching, and its layout—and its American occupants—would become crucial to both the prosecution and defense of the massive trial that followed.

The building was little more than a small, one-story whitewashed wood-frame structure, thirty-six feet long and twenty feet wide. Visitors approached by climbing four wood steps on the east side, entering the front door into a twelve-by-twenty-foot reception room where

three Italian officers processed paperwork behind two parallel coun-
ters. A second door led to the main room, twelve by twenty-four feet,
where Farr reigned as company clerk. A coal stove kept the room warm
and dry in winter, while a bank of screened windows along the north
wall welcomed salt-air breezes during summer.

A third room, in the southwest corner, was an eight-by-eight-foot
warren, where Captain Beckman pushed papers at a mahogany desk
nestled beneath the south window. Like the interpreter DiGiacomo,
Beckman worked a day job at the fort but went home each night to his
wife in Seattle. The fourth and final room, adjacent to Beckman's and
nearly twice as large, was the sleeping quarters for Haskell and Farr.
Their beds were pushed against opposite corners, with a standing
closet against one wall, and a south-facing outside door next to the
window—the only way to enter or leave the building other than the
main entrance in the reception room.

The orderly room stood in the southwest corner of what everyone
called the Italian Area, a small clump of buildings in an isolated,
wooded glen near the fort's western perimeter. Four large wooden barracks, numbered 708 through 711, housed fifty enlisted men each.
Building 712 was the latrine, 713 the orderly room, 714 the Italian
mess hall, and 715 the barracks for the four Italian officers. Ernesto
Cellentani, the Italian company commander, paraded through the
compound like a bantam rooster, hands behind back, nose in air,
smoking Lucky Strikes from a slim cigarette holder. Like most Italian
officers, Cellentani was hated by his troops, their memories still fresh
from watching officers take showers in the North African desert while
they, the enlisted men, looked on, dying of thirst. Of the four officers
assigned to the Twenty-eighth, only Lieutenant Lobianco, Olivotto's
supervisor, earned the respect of his men; his calm demeanor and
keen sense of fairness won plenty of Italian and American friends.

The Italian Area was a bit bigger than a football field, and shaped
like a reverse letter D. On a map, the Italian Area's eastern boundary
was Wyoming Avenue, running north-south beneath an embankment
leading to the Colored Area above. The rest of the ISU was bordered

by a half-circle section of Lawton Road, curving from the south, bending west then bending east, until it intersected Wyoming Avenue again. West of the Lawton Road loop was dense woodland, save for a clearing that everyone called "Bocce Alley." The clearing was home to a small Catholic chapel and a large recreation hall—complete with a boxing ring out back—framed by a flat grassy spot the prisoners used for animated lawn bowling games called bocce ball.

From the recreation hall, small footpaths led farther west down the steep incline of the Magnolia Bluffs. Eighty feet below was a rocky beach marking high tide for the waters of Puget Sound. An obstacle course ran along the base of the cliffs and included a section with three heavy wire cables suspended across a ravine between two massive bigleaf maples. The cable portion of the obstacle course was 450 feet from the Italian barracks, through dense vegetation and down the precipitous bluff. To walk a fairly straight line between the two points would be difficult at best and all but impossible in the dark of night. The usual way to reach the water was to walk or drive three-quarters of a mile along West Utah Street, a gravel road that snaked south down the slope before turning north to a point on the beach. The end of the road was not far from where Clyde Lomax and John Pinkney would spot Olivotto's body on the morning of August 15.

ON AUGUST 2, Fred Perata climbed the steps leading up to the orderly room, passed through the reception area, and exchanged hellos with Grant Farr, stationed at his desk in the company room. Perata had been ordered to report to Captain Beckman, an unusually formal request in a company so relaxed that saluting a superior officer was usually considered optional. Beckman's little office was always open: it had a portal, but no door. The captain waved Perata in, invited him to take a seat, and got right down to business. Colonel Branson, Perata was told, had decided to allow small groups of Italians have dinner in the homes of local civilians. The first supper sorties would be in three days, Saturday, August 5, and Perata had been assigned to chaperone four Italians having a meal at the home of Carl and Mary Langsted.

The Langsteds, Perata was warned, had three daughters, two of them twins, whom he might recognize as soda jerks at PX No. 3. Perata's main assignment would be to act as interpreter, but it wouldn't stop there: he'd also have to babysit his hormone-charged POWs to keep them out of trouble with the girls.

This was not good news. For one thing, Perata feared his Saturday nights would no longer be free, and Beckman had warned the program might quickly spread to other nights if it proved popular. For another, the assignment could be tiring, since interpreters had to talk nonstop while Americans and Italians carried on conversations in different languages. Finally, he had a hunch that the babysitting duties would pose the biggest headache: a busy house filled with virile young men and lovestruck young ladies meant the odds were considerable that at least one couple might slip into a back room somewhere. If a girl got knocked up, the keister they'd run up a flagpole would belong to Perata.

On Saturday, as Pasquale Solombrino and three of his pals buttoned their best shirts and dabbed lilac-scented oil in their hair, it had been more than a year and a half since any of them had shared a meal at a table with young ladies, and no telling how much longer it might be before they might enjoy a home-cooked meal in their own mama's kitchen. In the company of Fred Perata, the four Italians were smart enough to remain on their best behavior, much to Perata's relief and to the surprise of the Gold Dust Twins. As expected, Colonel Branson waited just two days to announce that home visitations would be extended to three nights a week, Thursdays, Fridays, and Saturday. There, thought Perata, go my weekends. He couldn't know how quickly that lament was about to become the least of his worries.

CHAPTER FIVE

RIOT
August 14, 1944

HOT, HUMID DAYS ARE rare in Seattle, but August 14 dawned sticky and warm. A midsummer rainstorm over the weekend gave way to hazy Monday morning sunshine. Usually reliable Pacific breezes stayed offshore, hiding among the skirts of thunderstorms building for a brief assault later that evening. Fort Lawton thermometers tiptoed toward eighty degrees—hot for Seattle; even the deep shade of bigleaf maples offered little relief. Scattered among the wild nests of Himalayan blackberries, dark, sour fruit fermented in the stuffy warmth, emitting the heady aroma of rancid wine. The razor thorns on those vines shriveled ever sharper in the hothouse heat.

Windows in the orderly room were propped fully open, in a vain attempt to lure stray breezes. At his desk, Grant Farr flipped through the sixteen pages of the morning *Seattle Post-Intelligencer*. GERMAN DEBACLE IN FRANCE, screamed the headline; DEFEATED NAZIS FLEE FOR PARIS. The story—like most from the war—was a mix of truth, propaganda, and wishful thinking. Although the German army was in retreat, General Omar Bradley had allowed it to escape, a strategic move to protect General George Patton's XV Corps from an assault by Germans cornered in Argentan. Bradley's controversial decision, though, would be overshadowed by much bigger news just twenty-four hours later, as the Allies engineered an amphibious landing along the French Riviera, a massive operation second in size and scope only to the Normandy invasion on D-day.

The newspaper made no mention of the biggest local event of the weekend: President Franklin D. Roosevelt himself had made a brief visit to Seattle. On Saturday evening, FDR had completed the next-to-last last leg of a momentous, and largely secret, voyage that had taken him more than seventy-two hundred miles. Traveling from Washington, D.C., to San Diego to Honolulu to the Aleutian Islands, his ship had wound back down through Alaska's Inside Passage before docking near Seattle. On August 12, at 5:30 P.M., he appeared on the forecastle deck of the naval destroyer *Cummings,* docked at the Bremerton Naval Shipyard, across Puget Sound from Fort Lawton. Before a crowd of eight thousand sailors and naval yard civilians — and a national radio audience — the president described his conversations with General Douglas MacArthur and Admiral Chester Nimitz in Honolulu, hinting at preparations to reinvade the Philippines from MacArthur's base in New Guinea. His speech had been upbeat but ended with a note of caution: "More than a million of our troops are today overseas in the Pacific. The war is well in hand in this vast area, but I cannot tell you, if I knew, when the war will be over, either in Europe or in the Far East or the war against Japan itself."

The sun had just set as the *Cummings* slid into Pier 91, on the southern edge of Magnolia, just two miles from Fort Lawton. Secret Service men formed a protective corridor; the president's wheelchair was carried onto his private rail car attached to a waiting Great Northern train. The train slid past the front gate of Fort Lawton in the still of the night, just forty-eight hours before silence would be shattered in the fort's Italian Area. The president continued east for five days, on a route skirting the U.S.-Canadian border, with stops in Montana, North Dakota, Minnesota, Illinois, Indiana, Ohio, and Pennsylvania. By the time he reached the White House on August 17, the president's daily morning briefings would include dire reports that something had gone terribly wrong at the fort in Seattle.

EXCEPT FOR THE humidity, August 14 was a typical Monday in the orderly room. From his desk, Farr could hear the usual bustle in the reception room, where Italians lined up at the counter to deliver their daily list of concerns, complaints, requests, and requisitions. A few who showed up for sick bay—begging off work assignments for the day—had the bleary eyes, sour stomachs, and splitting headaches of a Monday morning hangover. The second weekend of home visitations had gone without incident, although Fred Perata had groused that it just wasn't right that the Italians should get such royal treatment. "If Italian Americans want to get news from the old country," Perata had said, "let 'em come to the fort on Sundays with a plate of cookies or something." It would be just a matter of time, he was sure, before some girl was going to get in trouble.

Several Italians had secured passes to go downtown over the weekend, although Sunday's showers and cooler temperatures had dampened much of the fun. Most had simply stayed on the post that Sabbath. Lieutenant Vito Melpignano, the Italian duty officer for the day, had ordered Guglielmo Olivotto to walk into each of the four barracks to remind men that mass would be conducted at ten that morning. Although Olivotto was shy, he was probably the most devout Catholic in the Twenty-eighth, and Melpignano figured he was the best man for the assignment. Still, it was no easy task: even Bruno Patteri and Imo Nolgi—Olivotto's two best friends in the company—had opted for extra sleep that day instead of another sermon.

On that rainy Sunday, men had written letters, played cards, sung songs, or sat for haircuts, venturing outside during breaks in the rain for games of bocce or a spar in the boxing ring. Others headed to the post theater, where all the films were in English, but glamorous women like Katharine Hepburn, Ingrid Bergman, and Maureen O'Sullivan provided all the translation they needed. Still others killed time at the post exchange, spending their canteen coupons on pitchers of low-alcohol beer.

As Farr glanced over the weekend incident report, he noticed that Sergeant Haskell had been called to break up a disturbance at PX No. 3 Sunday afternoon. A couple of Italians had been in some sort of scrape with white American GIs, but the duty officer, Lieutenant

James Ruel, had taken care of it. Haskell's report about the PX incident would languish unnoticed for weeks to come.

Late Monday afternoon, three Italians—Guiseppe Belle, Angelo Fumarola, and Antonio Pisciottano—came to the orderly room reception area to pick up passes for a night on the town. Although the rules required an American escort, many of the regulations around Fort Lawton's ISU were regularly overlooked or ignored. Italians, for example, were supposed to be drilled—essentially marched around in circles—every night after work, but the noncommissioned officers from both armies considered it a bother, so formation drills were few and far between. Similarly, roll calls were rare, and the nightly chorus of taps didn't necessarily mean that lights in the barracks were dimmed right away. None of the American noncoms—including Farr, Haskell, Perata, and Gould—carried a gun. Why would an Italian want to escape? And where would he go? Belle, Fumarola, and Pisciottano were handed their passes without any mention of an escort. Strict military discipline was for soldiers who faced the possibility of battle, and as the sun drew down on August 14, conflict seemed far away from Fort Lawton.

AT NINE TWENTY that evening, the Big Dipper hung low in the west. Grant Farr leaned on the railing of the orderly room porch, puffing a butt from his third pack of cigarettes that day. Distant steam whistles hissed, then wailed, then drifted away. Dry leaves clinging to the maple canopy chattered in the rising breeze. A single bulb burned at the entrance to the orderly room; similar lamps lit small spaces around the door of the latrine and the porch of each of the barracks. The rest of the compound was now so dark that an approaching face could not be recognized from more than a few feet away.

From the porch, Farr could hear bursts of laughter drifting down from the Colored Area. Growing up in Utah, he had never so much as talked with a Negro; here at Fort Lawton, he saw or heard black men only at a distance. Although they could be loud—more so than usual on this night—the areas reserved for blacks and Italians were well removed from the rest of the post. Farr twisted the embers of his spent

Chesterfield into a butt can nailed to a sawed-off pole salvaged from a pyramidal tent. A breeze carried away the last wisp of smoke, mixing it with the unmistakable scent of the approaching thunderstorm.

At ten o'clock, Italian sergeant Antonio Licciardelli dealt a hand of poker at a table in Barracks 708, the building closest to the Colored Area. Barracks 708, like most barracks, was filled with three long columns of double bunks. Overhead, two-hundred-watt bulbs hung beneath dome reflectors strung from high-beamed rafters. Men in Licciardelli's platoon gathered in clusters, gossiping or mending clothes or reading Italian-language American newspapers. Some stretched on bunks, enjoying the first cool relief from the day's muggy weather. A few wrote letters or read from the Bible. One or two were already asleep.

At 11 P.M., Corporal Andrew David dropped a needle in the grooves of a well-worn record. From his desk at the military police guardhouse near the center of the fort, Corporal David broadcast taps into a microphone connected to loudspeakers throughout the post. The familiar twenty-four-note lament was a recording of a bugle, without its rarely sung words:

> *Day is done, gone the sun,*
> *From the lake, from the hills, from the sky;*
> *All is well, safely rest, God is nigh.*

Sergeant Licciardelli gathered his playing cards as overhead lights snapped shut in slow, random sequence. Conversations continued in hushed tones; Private Nullo Beretta remained absorbed in a discussion with three other prisoners. With windows wide open, laughter and shouts continued to punctuate the night. At eleven ten, Beretta was startled to hear what sounded like a rock hitting the roof.

He slid off his bunk and walked out to the front stoop. To his right, he could hear shouting in the general direction of Building 700, the black mess hall just up the embankment. Suddenly, the three men who had been on a pass that evening in downtown Seattle barreled down the slope and tore past 708. Beretta called out, but the three Italians, all short of breath, raced by without a word. He glanced back

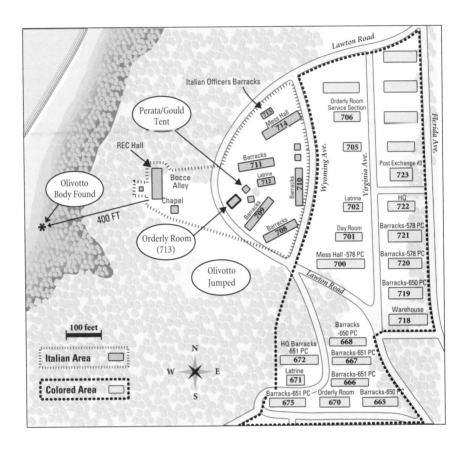

up the hill, saw nothing, and shrugged. He shuffled back inside his barracks, grabbed his towel and toothbrush, and headed out to the latrine.

By eleven twenty-five, many of the men in 708 had drifted into sleep. The thud of a brick slamming against shingles—followed by another, then a third, then a flurry—failed at first to register as impending danger. But the crash of shattering windows and screams of those impaled by glass shards triggered a gush of adrenaline that sent fifty hearts pounding. In near unison, they rose from their bunks, suddenly aware that they were under attack, without a single clue who was after them or why.

Victorio Bellieni, wearing nothing more than GI shorts and an undershirt, skittered to the nearest window and leaped into the void. As he hit the ground, the twenty-nine-year-old auto mechanic glanced up at the looming silhouette of an American soldier, unidentifiable except for a corporal's twin chevrons on a black steel helmet. The corporal shouted something in English, and others in the shadows barked replies. Bellieni, who had endured seven years in Mussolini's army— most of that in Africa—knew in a moment that he was quarry and that hounds were on his heels.

Bellieni sprinted west, toward the next barracks, ten yards away. Building 709 stood on short stilts, with three feet of crawl space beneath the floorboards. Running barefoot, the Italian stumbled, allowing his pursuers to make up lost ground. He dove for an opening between the tight web of vertical posts and cross-supports, but someone grabbed his leg. He shook free but heard a thud and felt a shock of pain convulse his lower back. Crawling on his belly, Bellieni glanced back to see a raised board in one man's hand and the glint of a knife in another. With panic overpowering pain, he grabbed a barracks piling and pulled, retracting his body underneath the building like a turtle in its shell.

Just a few yards north of Barracks 709, Fred Perata and Mason Gould were asleep in their tent. Perata jerked awake as Luigi Furlanelli, an ISU latrine orderly, tore open the tent flap and shouted, "*Aiuto!* Negroes! They everywhere! Help us! Please!" Perata leaped from his canvas cot, but Gould, a sound sleeper, had to be shaken awake.

Perata pulled his khakis and shoes from his footlocker. As he headed out the tent, he poked Gould once again, telling him to hurry. The nearest phone was in the orderly room, less than fifteen yards away. Furlanelli—whose bravery this night was just beginning—crawled out of the tent with Perata just as Gould finally sat up. A riff of shattering glass and muffled screams drifted into Gould's drowsy ears, inspiring him, at last, to pick up the pace.

Back in Barracks 708, twenty-three-year-old Private Nicola Corea stepped onto the porch and came face to face with a mustachioed man wearing sergeant's stripes. The sergeant flinched as a wooden club swung from elsewhere in the darkness and bounced off Corea's skull. Others jumped in, using poles and pieces of wooden fencing to batter the helpless Italian. As Corea crumpled to the ground, his attackers lifted his arms and legs and carried him from the porch. Feigning unconsciousness, Corea went limp. His struggling captors let him drop, had a quick discussion in English, then reached down to pick him up again. Sensing an opportunity, Corea thrashed his burly arms and kicked his legs, forcing his assailants to lose their grip. Blinded by blood pouring from his head, he broke for the latrine, forty yards to the north. A man waving a knife followed in pursuit.

Rosario Sidoti, a thickset Italian, cowered in the latrine portal. Peering out, he recognized the blood-soaked Italian running toward him as Corea; Sidoti, Corea, and Guglielmo Olivotto worked together daily, cleaning officers' barracks. Corea stumbled forward, dropped to his hands and knees, and cried, "Rosario, I am dying!" From the shadows, an American soldier lurched forward, a knife raised in his clenched fist. Sidoti, holding a scrap of lumber like a baseball bat, swung with all his might, cracking the invader on the back of his head. The knife flew away, and the American collapsed in a bed of flowers. Sidoti grabbed Corea's collar, dragged him to his feet, and retreated to a corner of the latrine, just as another Italian, Primo Bernabovi, made a break out the back door.

Private Bernabovi scampered in the dark toward the officers' quarters, nearly knocking over Captain Cellentani, who had been approaching from the north. The priggish captain, unaware until then that his men were under siege, brushed his jacket and demanded an explanation. A new burst of shouts and screams made a response unnecessary; he looked at Bernabovi and commanded him to go to the orderly room. The captain fled around the south side of the latrine, Bernabovi the north. Two black soldiers, however, blocked the private's path. "Take it easy, boy," said one, just before the other swatted him with a glancing blow to the head. Bernabovi raised his arms to deflect further injury, knocking the club—a length of wooden fencing—out of his assailant's hands. Looking up, he saw the second soldier lunge with a knife. Bernabovi spun like a matador; his attacker bulled past. As the American regained his balance, Bernabovi detected a cloud of stale beer and cigarettes. Seizing the chance, he made his escape, and dove among the pilings beneath Barracks 711.

Mason Gould was still pulling up his pants in his tent when he heard Augusto Todde holler his name. At age thirty-six, Todde was one of the oldest Italians in the ISU, and the ranking noncommissioned officer in Barracks 709, where Olivotto lived. Todde had been awakened by one of his men during the first wave of attacks on 708 and 710 and had rushed outside just in time to see Corea galloping toward the latrine screaming, "Help me!" Dashing back into 709, Todde ordered his men to dim the lights and barricade the doors, then ventured out to find Perata and Gould.

Todde, speaking Italian, told Gould that Negroes were running everywhere, attacking members of the Twenty-eighth. Gould, now hurrying with his socks and shoes, assured Todde that Perata had just left for the orderly room and was probably calling the guardhouse at that very moment. Todde withdrew, leaving Gould to tie his shoes after hearing him promise to join him in a moment. Gould stood up, pulled back the tent flap, and froze at the dimly lit sight of six, maybe seven, angry black soldiers. "Come on out!" a man in front growled. "Come on out or we're coming in!" Gould, a man not easily intimidated, stood just inside the tent threshold and shouted, "Hey! Listen, I am an American!" His voice, however, slipped beneath the surface of the rising din. Gould again peeled back the flap and demanded, "Hey! What's this all about?"

No one heard him. A hand grabbed his arm, another yanked his collar, and three or four others hauled him from the tent. A flurry of boards, bricks, stones, and fists rained from every direction, gashing his nose, bruising his skull, and striking him until the bones in both arms were shattered. Although the night was dark, it seemed to grow even darker as he slipped to the edge of consciousness. He refused to give in, managing to lift up and stagger a few steps from the tent. His attackers, surprised by his stubbornness, let him stumble away, quickly turning their attention to other potential targets.

Grant Farr had been dozing during the first several minutes of the raid. At eleven twenty, he thought he heard a distant crash but dismissed it as the usual clamor on this part of the post. He was almost asleep when Furlanelli—fresh from warning Perata—burst in. "Negro troops!" the latrine orderly shouted, "they are going through the barracks!" Furlanelli lunged over to Haskell, shaking him awake with the same broken-English alarm. Rocks and lumps of coal popped against siding, explosions of glass crashed like cymbals. Within seconds, Haskell was up and standing.

Augusto Todde barged in, followed closely by Fred Perata. Farr grabbed his pants and slippers, at the same time barking at Furlanelli and Todde to slow down, to get a grip. Todde begged Perata to help him push desks and chairs against the doors. "Relax!" Perata answered. "Let's try to take it easy, shall we?" The two Italians, worried that their warnings were being discounted, backed into the armoire, where they squatted among wool coats and leather boots, and closed the flimsy doors behind them.

Farr and Perata stepped out of the sleeping quarters into the main room, where a telephone sat on a desk outside Beckman's office. Farr flipped on the overhead lights and grabbed the post directory, running his forefinger down the page until he reached "Officer of the Day, Evening." The rotary dial spun, the line rang, and kept on ringing until it was obvious no one would answer. An Italian, clutching an injured arm, ran into the room. Two others followed, then three more. Farr swore under his breath, slammed the handset back on the receiver, and reached once again for the directory. This time he dialed the number listed for sergeant of the guard; the guardhouse picked up after just two rings. Andrew David, the corporal of the guard, took the call, and handed the phone to his sergeant, who said he'd send a patrol right away. Farr glanced over toward the reception room door; a stream of perhaps twenty Italians poured in, including Bellieni, Pisciottano, and Captain Cellentani. Many were in their underclothes, arms cradling their heads or limbs, most panting with shallow breaths. As Farr hung up the phone, a construction brick slammed into the wall directly above the desk, missing Farr's head by inches. He dropped his head between his shoulders and dove behind the coal stove in the middle of the room. Moments later, a window exploded in a shower of glass. The racket drew Haskell into the main room, still undressed; Perata yelled for everyone to get down and take cover.

Haskell retreated back through the sleeping room door to grab his pants and shoes. The back door of the orderly room was at the foot of his bed; its panels shook under a barrage of rocks and coal. The salvo sent Todde and Furlanelli bursting out of the armoire and back in the main room, where they were met with bricks and stones, pouring like hail. Hysterical Italians ran to Captain Beckman's tiny corner office, screaming as they dove for cover. Perata and Farr peeked out from the protection of the stove and caught the gaze of a half-dozen black soldiers noisily crowding the reception room doorway. Farr's eyes widened as a soldier flung a rock; he ducked just in time. From the doorway flew more missiles, including sticks and a stool that whizzed past Farr's head. A large black soldier, jostled from behind, stumbled into the main room. In his hand, he clenched a round stick with a pointed end; Perata immediately recognized it as one of the butt-can holders made from a sawed-off pyramidal tent pole. Squaring his shoulders, Perata stepped toward the intruder and, amid the uproar, shouted, "Hey! I am an American soldier! Stop this!" Dressed only his white undershirt and khaki pants, Perata wore no insignias that confirmed his rank, much less his nationality. The black soldier gripped the tent pole like an ax and launched a full swing from behind his right shoulder. Perata instinctively threw up his left arm; the pole ripped a nail from his finger. In the same split second, the stake bounced off his temple, above his left ear, and slammed into his left shoulder. Perata hit the floor like a sack. The ringing in his ear would stay with him the next sixty years.

Momentarily stunned by his own violence, Perata's assailant backpedaled, pushing his fellow intruders back out of the main room and into the reception room. Furlanelli sprung from beneath Farr's desk and slammed the door behind them. Pisciottano rushed to help Furlanelli drag a desk in front of the portal. Farr looked left and saw Bruno Bigatti on the floor, blood pouring from his right ear. He looked right and saw Perata slumped on the ground, a steady trickle of blood pooling under the left side of his head. Todde bulled in from behind, shouting at Pisciottano and Furlanelli to maintain their barricade. He cursed in Italian about the overhead lights, lunged for the wall switch, and plunged the main room into darkness.

By now, as many as fifteen Italians cowered in Beckman's tiny office; a half-dozen squeezed under the captain's desk. Victorio Bellieni hopped on top of the desk and tried to jump out the room's only window; he found his exit blocked by several soldiers standing just outside the window brandishing clubs and wooden planks. Captain Cellentani leaned toward the window and crowed, "Take it easy! No more!" His feeble effort had the opposite effect: he instantly became the target for a volley of rocks. A sharp stone slammed into his cheek, just below the eye, knocking him cold.

From the outside, the window into Beckman's office was almost six feet off the ground. Invaders stood on tiptoes or boosted each other up to see inside. Leaning in, they continued to club Captain Cellentani's limp body. One attacker banged an ax handle on the top of Beckman's desk, taunting those underneath with "Come on out, boys, come on out!" When his prey responded with terrified wails, the man with the ax screamed, "Shut up! Shut up!" The cries only grew louder.

The intruders seemed to be everywhere. Two men wearing American army helmets sat in a jeep, trying repeatedly to start the ignition. A third soldier jumped in and had more success; he fired up the engine, stomped the clutch, shoved the stick into gear, and lurched toward the corner of Gould and Perata's now-empty tent. The driver motored drunkenly back and forth, grinding gears and clipping the same corner over and over, without ever collapsing the center pole.

Of the dozens of men now converged in and around the orderly room, only the Italians had any substantial experience in actual combat. The American soldiers, both black and white, had primarily known only civilian life or the sheltered world of stateside military duty. By contrast, the wars in Tunisia and Libya had been numbingly brutal:

Italian soldiers had seen friends strafed by aircraft, incinerated in tanks, amputated by mines, and disemboweled by bayonets. Although the battlefield was now more than a year behind them, memories of the terror and confusion were never more than a loud noise away. In the blackness of August 14, all that fear came flooding back.

Their combat experience convinced most of the Italians to run and hide rather than stand and fight. Two exceptions that night were Furlanelli and Pisciottano, who leaned against the reception room door, even as it shook from repeated pounding on the other side. They held their ground against a thrust so strong it splintered wood, until a second shot drove the blade of an ax clear through the door, missing Pisciottano's skull by the width of a splinter. He fell to the floor, scooting on hands and knees to a nearby corner. Furlanelli jumped back, staring in disbelief as the door disintegrated with each swing of a double-bit blade. Standing in the darkness of the main room, all he could see of the intruders were silhouettes, backlit by the lights in the reception room behind them. Temporarily blinded, Furlanelli did not see the brick that shattered his cheek, just below his left eye.

It was now eleven forty. Fifteen minutes had passed since the sergeant of the guard had promised Farr help was on the way. Mason Gould, both arms broken, had dragged himself beneath Barracks 711, the only barracks the rioters seemed to have overlooked. In 709—Olivotto's barracks—and 710, rocks and coal continued to fly through shredded windows, but those still inside had managed to barricade the doorways with their bunks. An ax gouged holes in the front door of 710, but none of the invaders were able to break inside.

The Italians in 708 weren't so lucky. Antonio Licciardelli, the sergeant whose poker game had ended at the sound of taps, stayed in his bunk during the first rock barrage. He watched as members of his platoon fled out windows and doors; their subsequent screams convinced him to stay put. No one moved to barricade the doors; many dove beneath their bunks. Rocks and insults streamed in. The lights stayed off. Screams and shouts from the orderly room grew louder.

Just after eleven forty, the front door to 708 banged open. Licci-ardelli pulled his blanket up to his nose; he saw the outline of three men at the door. One panned a flashlight across the room, then aimed it underneath a bunk near the door. "Come on out!" the man with the flashlight commanded. The Italian, Private Guiseppe Magnasco, was the company plumber. "Come on out from under the bed!" Magnasco, shielding his eyes from the blinding beam, reluctantly slithered out. Looking up, he thought he saw an MP armband, and felt some of his fear slip away. But as he struggled to his feet, his shin burst in pain, kicked out from under him by a second intruder standing next to the man holding the flashlight. Magnasco screamed; a baton whipped across his head. His screams turned to cries and then to whimpers, as he tried to fend off blow after blow. In the darkened barracks, terrified Italians blurted Hail Marys; others sobbed in fear.

The flashlight fell next on Fernando Catenero, a mechanic in the motor pool. He too was ordered to come out from under his bunk and, like Magnasco, was rewarded with a smack across the skull. After be-ing kicked and punched repeatedly, Catenero feigned unconscious-ness until the attackers moved on. He rolled over to see a third figure standing at the door. Unlike the first two, this soldier was unmistake-ably a white man. "Go on!" Magnasco heard the white soldier say, "Get out of the barracks!" Both Catenero and Magnasco struggled to their feet; as they did, the white soldier cracked each of them with his ba-ton as they stumbled out the door.

Back in the orderly room, Haskell stood in the doorway between his sleeping quarters and the main room. Behind him, the back door fi-nally gave way. At nearly the same moment, black soldiers standing in the reception room were pushed into the main room by those from be-hind. They surged, brandishing knives, carrying entrenching shovels, and swinging the ubiquitous fence posts. Several ran toward the crowd of Italians in Beckman's office. Farr, stooped near the stove, picked a broom off the floor and came up swatting. To his right, an at-tacker swung a post; Farr wrestled it away, sending his foe scurrying.

Ten to twelve soldiers had now broken through the back door, filling the sleeping room and sandwiching Haskell between two waves of attackers. Looking into the crowd, he caught the sight of a light-skinned black soldier. Wing-eared and bushy-eyebrowed, the soldier stood with outstretched arms hooked to his sides, straining to hold others back in the sleeping quarters doorway. Sensing that this man might be a peacemaker, Haskell shouted, "I'm an American! Sergeant Perata's an American too! He's hurt; he needs help!" The light-skinned soldier barked back, "We don't want you!" Turning his head, the soldier tried to calm his surging companions, "Take it easy, now, just a minute!" Hearing this, Augusto Todde looked over Haskell's shoulder and shouted, "I am an American too!" The light-skinned soldier, noting Todde's Italian accent, shot back, "*You* shut up!"

Just then, a black soldier in the main room crept behind Haskell and raised a club. Todde, seeing the weapon, lowered his shoulder and shoved Haskell forward, thrusting him into the crowd of soldiers in the sleeping room door. The club missed its mark, harmlessly clipping Haskell's lower back. Todde spun around and lunged toward Haskell's attacker, but another black soldier intervened, waving a knife. Todde grabbed the second man's arm but loosened his grip when the first man clubbed him. The soldier with the knife slashed Todde's face; blood spurted from his forehead and from behind his right ear.

Farr looked back to see Haskell in the arms of black soldiers in the doorway. Stepping forward, with Ferrante now at his side, Farr again hollered that he, Haskell, and Perata were Americans and repeated his command that the intruders cease their attack. From a point behind the light-skinned soldier, a knife lunged toward Ferrante; the Italian ducked, and the blade plunged into Farr's upper arm. As Ferrante cringed, a wood plank slammed into his forehead above his left eye, and he dropped to the floor in a stream of blood. A soldier's boot buried his face, breaking his nose and sapping the last of his resistance.

Shocked and furious, Farr now feared for his life. He bolted forward, standing chest-to-chest with the light-skinned soldier. In the loudest voice he could muster, Farr roared, "*I . . . am . . . an . . . American . . . soldier!*" Those in the main room behind him took little notice; the din was too loud and the fighting too intense. But the rioters crowded in the sleeping quarters in front of him took a step back and fell silent. Farr's arm was bleeding badly; his blue eyes were wild and his face was draining pale. Pushing through the throng, a tall black soldier wearing the single stripe of a private first class stepped forward and took a hold of Farr's good arm. "You come with me," he said. "We're not after you." Dazed, Farr allowed his escort to lead him through the crowded sleeping room and out the back door.

After a step or two, Farr was again surrounded; the air reeked of booze and blood. Farr's guardian used a stiff, extended arm to shield him from a lurching soldier. "We DONE here now! This man, he is American. You let him be now, let him be, I say." Another man pitched forward; he too was repelled. Farr, still losing blood, struggled to keep his balance. His savior grabbed his uninjured arm once again and plowed through another crescent of soldiers, pulling Farr away from the orderly room and onto Lawton Road.

As he moved out of the melee, Farr saw that, for every black soldier carrying a stick, knife, or shovel, perhaps three others stood in the shadows, simply watching. Spectators lining the road and standing atop the berm above the Italian Area occasionally roared their approval; none attempted to intervene. Loud thuds and heart-wrenching cries spilled from 708; a war whoop and the crash of garbage cans echoed from behind the latrine. The orderly room was still the main attraction; overhead lights in the reception room projected shadow-puppet images of the violence inside. Whenever an Italian managed to escape, two or three rioters followed in pursuit. Attilio Vencato was tackled just as he reached the small stone chapel; he rolled twelve yards downhill into a pile of branches and trash. It was almost eleven fifty, and there were still no military policemen in sight.

Throughout the brawl, dozens of Italians managed to scurry across Lawton Road to take cover in the woods. Their decision took some nerve. The night was so black, they could barely see their own hand in front of their face. Those who ran too far risked sliding down the bluffs, still slick from the weekend rain. Barefoot and barely dressed, they tripped over downed logs, only to be clawed by blackberry brambles and speared by thistle. Once hidden, their arms and legs swelled with the burn of stinging nettles, a pain that cried to be scratched but then punished the scratching with insatiable itching.

Livio Petriccione hid behind a tree, gasping for breath. Somewhere in the void, a branch snapped. The hair stood on his neck; he felt as if he were radiating fear. A deep voice, speaking English, growled what sounded like a command. Like a cornered rabbit, Petriccione shrunk as small as he could, heart pounding and breath painfully on hold. A flashlight swept in his direction. Filled with alarm and adrenaline, he thought the hair on his head might turn completely white. Suddenly, he felt a poke. His racing heart felt as if it would burst. "*Psst!* It's me, Sfondrini!" Another Italian trying to hide. "Let's go down to the water!" he whispered. "NO!" Petriccione hissed, "They will grab us if we go down there!" Sfrondrini nodded. A moment later, the black soldiers lurching through the underbrush moved on. Sfrondrini crawled away.

Not far from the woods, beneath Barracks 711, Mason Gould slipped in and out of consciousness. Every minute or so, someone else dove for cover beneath the barracks; it was too dim to see, but he could hear men moaning. Dried blood caked in his eyes, but he couldn't lift his hands to wipe them. He longed for something to dull the pain in his shattered arms. In a moment of lucidity, he told himself to get out, to get away. Summoning every bit of resolve, he dragged out from under Barracks 711 and staggered in the direction opposite the uproar in the orderly room.

A few yards up the road, a rock ricocheted off Gould's already-sore ribs. A large black soldier, standing in the middle of the road, stooped to pick up another stone. "No!" Gould pleaded, desperately explaining that he was badly injured and needed a doctor. Words were his only defense; he couldn't possibly fend off another attack. The black soldier realized that this man was not an Italian. Not wanting to compound his mistake, he told Gould to get the hell away. Grateful, he stumbled on.

Reaching the northern intersection of Lawton Road and Wyoming Avenue, Gould saw a light burning inside Building 705. He limped down Wyoming until he came upon an Italian, a private named Voce. "Voce!" he pleaded. "It's Gould. I need help." The wary private edged closer. Recognizing that it was indeed Gould, Voce cradled his waist and steered him into Building 705, the orderly room for Negro service section soldiers. For a moment, Gould froze: all four men in the room were black. Corporal Roger Bradley, the charge of quarters, was equally struck: he had heard the reports of fighting between blacks and Italians, and now here was one Italian, maybe two, and one of them was covered in blood. Voce pleaded for an ambulance. Bradley glanced at his companions; as it turned out, all three were ambulance drivers. Bradley called the hospital, and minutes later, Gould was on his way.

By now, the only still-conscious Italians unable to hide were those trapped in Captain Beckman's office. Rioters remained outside the window, blocking any escape; fresh attackers barged through the doorway. Pisciottano, despite a deep V-shaped gouge in his left arm, tried to attend to the wounded, but was forced to retreat in the face of repeated blows. Unwilling to be beaten to death, he leaped to his feet and used the few English words he knew to let the obtruders know he too was a soldier, not an enemy. "We are Italian soldier! Please! Make stop!" He gestured frantically, mimicking a salute, pointing to nonexistent chevrons. It was to no avail. More black soldiers entered the packed room, and Pisciottano cowered on the floor, crying in utter frustration.

It was almost midnight. From the orderly room back door came a shout, then the halfhearted shrill of a whistle and a hesitant voice. "Hey! Break this up!" Then a second voice, this one with more authority. "Military police! *Military police!*" Thurman Jones of Meridian, Mississippi, a no-nonsense former tank commander with the Twelfth Armored Division, could hardly believe his eyes. Now a sergeant with the Fort Lawton Military Police, it seemed he had entered a room full of crazy people. Black soldiers holding white fence boards were swinging them like swords. Men in every state of dress and undress, from steel helmets to skivvies, were hollering or weeping or making some ungodly sound in between. The air was ripe with perspiration; the walls and floors were stained with blood.

A third soldier entered the room, John Pinkney of the 650th Port Company, the only black MP of the three now inside. As soldiers holding clubs fled from Farr and Haskell's quarters, Pinkney was stunned by the sight at his feet. At least a half-dozen Italians lay littered across the floor; many of them whimpering. Some were curled in fetal positions, blood pooling beneath their wounds, undershirts torn, bodies bruised. As Sergeant Jones pressed into the main room, Pinkney followed, fighting a wave of nausea as he contemplated what might be next.

The main room looked just as bad. To one side, an Italian covered his head and ears as a black soldier stood over him, repeatedly clubbing him with a butt-can holder. In his loudest voice, Jones barked an order for everyone to cease and to clear out immediately. Some soldiers jumped out the window; others skittered toward the reception room door. Sprawled near a desk, Bruno Bigatti's mutilated body shook with seizures. Jones turned to Pinkney and ordered him to stand guard at the back door.

Beckman's office was still in a lather, roiling with shrieks and sobs. Jones marched to the opening and began grabbing rioters by the backs of their shirts, pulling them into the main room and threatening them with his riot stick. Near the window, attackers were still using their clubs; one Italian seemed stuck at the ledge, a shuttlecock in a cruel game of badminton between black soldiers on the inside and the outside. All three MPs were now at work, grabbing assailants and shoving them out the office. For three minutes they tussled, until all that remained were the Italians, piled like sandbags beneath the desk and along the walls. One man with a gash in his abdomen was vomiting into a trash can. The Italian splayed on the window ledge had the empty sash pinned across his neck. In a corner, another Italian squeezed his eyes shut against blood sheeting down his forehead; still another rocked back and forth on his knees, praying wildly. Many were pretending to be unconscious. Others actually were.

Jones stormed back through the main room and sleeping quarters. Outside the back door, he saw two black soldiers who seemed to be spectators, one of them wearing stripes. "Sergeant!" he shouted at T/4 Robert Gresham, and ordered him to begin clearing his fellow black soldiers from the area. He then turned to Richard King, commanding him to get to a telephone to summon an ambulance or a doctor. Up Lawton Road, headlights signaled the belated arrival of more MPs, including Regis Callahan, the sergeant of the guard. Callahan leaped from his jeep, ran up the steps of Barracks 709, and pulled his revolver from its holster. "I will *shoot* the first man who comes up these steps!" he said. The black soldiers in the immediate area dropped their clubs and ran.

As Jones stepped back into the orderly room, he saw Haskell leaning over Perata, who was propped up in a chair. Perata was bare-chested; his blood-stained undershirt wrapped around his head. First aid had been administered by Furlanelli during the height of the battle, even though Furlanelli himself had by then been injured. Although his ISU job was a lowly latrine orderly, he had performed with more selfless heroism this night than men many steps above his rank. That selflessness would go unacknowledged in the months and years ahead.

Sergeant Jones surveyed the misery all around him. He turned to one of his MPs, Gasper DeVito, and told him he wanted wounded Americans to get first priority for the ambulances just then arriving. DeVito understood that what Jones actually meant were wounded white Americans.

Perata would land in the hospital for forty days. His fractured skull caused temporary facial paralysis. One rib was broken, and stab wounds penetrated his upper chest and the small of his back. A slashing cut on his groin severed nerves controlling some of the muscles in his right leg. He lost a pair of eyeglasses and an oblong Tavannes watch, a gift from his mother on his birthday.

Gould was hospitalized for sixteen months. His left arm was so splintered that doctors had to remove a slice of bone from his shin and screw it to his arm. The procedure, still somewhat experimental, required him to remain in bed for endless weeks. After several operations, the star pitcher known as "Lefty" had a left arm so atrophied it looked like a broom handle. His mother, worried sick, wrote to President Roosevelt. Perhaps because of that letter, Gould was transferred to a military hospital closer to home, on Staten Island.

Farr, after being escorted from the melee, had wandered aimlessly toward the barracks in the Colored Area. He regained his senses in time to return to the orderly room just as the injured were being evacuated. Haskell saw that Farr was himself wounded and found his friend a seat on the next ambulance. It was only at the hospital that Farr learned how much blood he had lost: in addition to the stab wound in his arm, he had been knifed in the left hip and in the groin. Until the medics pulled off his blood-soaked pants, Farr had assumed his lower extremities suffered nothing more than a bad bruise.

Haskell's wounds were superficial, undetected until the next day when, in the showers, another soldier asked him about a slice across his buttocks. Haskell spent much of the night helping Jones and the other MPs ferry three dozen injured Italians to the post hospital. Only later did he tally the other items he had lost: A pair of eyeglasses, a fountain pen, a wallet containing thirty dollars (nearly one month's pay), and a Ronson cigarette lighter, engraved with his initials, ESH.

As night wore into early morning, word of the riot spread up the Fort Lawton chain of command. White officers stormed through the Colored Area, turning off lights in the barracks and ordering men go to sleep. Military policemen were told to scour the woods for Italians, many of whom straggled out only after they sensed the coast had completely cleared. A halfhearted attempt to account for all 206 members of the Twenty-eighth ISU was abandoned in the confusion over who was in the hospital and who might be hiding in the woods. No one realized that Guglielmo Olivotto was missing until Pinkney and Clyde Lomax drove to the bottom of the bluffs several hours later, just before first light. The fort, unprepared for a riot, would soon prove even less prepared for a murder investigation.

CHAPTER SIX

BAD PRESS
Late August 1944

On Tuesday afternoon, August 15, a one-page memorandum slid across the Pentagon desk of Major General Wilhelm Styer, the chief of staff of the Army Service Forces. The memo, from his deputy, Colonel John Nash, described an incident at the Seattle Port of Embarkation, where "there were some Negro troops being staged right adjacent to the Italian Service Unit area. In the middle of the night (14–15 August) after everyone had gone to bed, the Negroes raided the adjacent area and beat up the Italians and stole some of their property. About thirty Italians were injured, none seriously. This morning, one of the Italians was found hanging from a tree. It has not been determined whether the Negroes did it or whether he committed suicide." Four hundred soldiers—every member of two Negro port companies—were now locked in a stockade "to prevent any further trouble." Nash's memo assured the general that "no information concerning this matter has yet reached the newspapers."

That final assurance was misleading. Fort Lawton was a tough place to keep a secret: hundreds of permanent army personnel and civilians lived off base, and word about two companies of black soldiers being in lockup spread like wildfire. Within hours, news of the attack and hanging made its way to reporters at Seattle's competing dailies, the morning *Seattle Post-Intelligencer* and the afternoon *Seattle Times*. The *Times* had the story first but lost its scoop when army censors ordered the paper not to print anything, pending approval out of

Washington, D.C. Late Tuesday evening, the Army Bureau of Public Relations authorized the Seattle Port of Embarkation to release a terse statement:

> At about midnight Monday, August 14, a number of Negro sol-
> diers raided the barracks of the Italian service unit at Fort Law-
> ton while members of the unit were sleeping. In the ensuing
> melee, which lasted only a few minutes, 24 Italians were injured
> and hospitalized.
>
> Several of the attacking soldiers were less seriously hurt. The
> attackers carried rocks which they picked up on the ground by
> the barracks.
>
> A short time following the fight the body of one of the Italian
> soldiers was found hanging from a nearby tree. He was identified
> as Gughielmo Olivanta [sic]. A phase of the investigation will be
> to determine whether this could have been a suicide.
>
> The post authorities placed the attacking soldiers under arrest
> and launched an immediate investigation. They promised disci-
> plinary action and said no further information would be available
> until the investigation was complete.
>
> The Italian service unit has been at Fort Lawton for several
> months, and there has been no previous trouble or appearance of
> ill will on the part of other military personnel at the post. The unit
> is made up of volunteers who have been carefully screened and
> found to be neither pro-Nazi nor pro-Fascist. They are used in
> various labor capacities at the fort.

The banner headline across the top of the Wednesday, August 16 *Post-Intelligencer* read, ONE DEAD IN LAWTON RIOT. Across the country, the *Washington Post* ran an Associated Press story under the headline ONE FOUND HANGED. Neither report elaborated beyond the information in the army press release. That afternoon, the *Seattle Times* tried to advance the story by reporting that black soldiers had snuck into the Italian Area. "Silently invading the Italians' barracks under cover of darkness, the attackers hurled stones at the sleepers." The *Times* also claimed that "an investigation of the Fort Lawton sentry system, which failed to prevent a midnight attack by Negro troops," was under way.

In the Fort Lawton hospital, Bruno Bigatti was clinging to life, his crushed skull the most serious trauma suffered by any of the surviving Italians. Pasquale Solombrino suffered lacerations and deep bruises, and repeatedly begged army nurses to let him see Joyce Langsted. Perata and Gould were both in considerable pain; their injuries were not yet made public by either the army or the newspapers.

In Washington, D.C., Major General Mervin Gross began to feel heat. As head of the War Department's Transportation Division, he knew that politicians and reporters would soon be all over him, demanding to know how things could get so out of hand at such an important port of embarkation under his command. General Gross read a dispatch from Major Irving Crawford, the port's director of Intelligence and Security, who had begun interviewing a few soldiers and officers at the fort. Crawford seemed to be working under the assumption that the riot was planned and premeditated. "From preliminary reports," Crawford wrote, "it appears that the colored units were quiet and in bed at the time that a check of the area was made by officer of the unit at Taps at 2300. Shortly thereafter, and apparently as a result of a preconceived plan, the rioters left their barracks and proceeded to the Italian inclosure [*sic*]." If Crawford was correct, then how were they able to keep such a plan secret? And if the port's Intelligence and Security Division couldn't uncover such a deadly plot before it was too late, how could it now be trusted to conduct the kind of investigation that would satisfy the War Department?

General Gross had good reason to worry about the Pentagon's reaction. The War Department was jam-packed with generals, and one of them, Archer Lerch, was already chafing about the way the matter had been handled by Gross's subordinate, Colonel Branson. As the army's provost marshal general, Lerch was not only commander of all army military policemen, he was also responsible for the welfare of all prisoners of war. Thirty-six hours on, Branson had been circumspect about the details of the disturbance, and slow to assign responsibility. If an American had died at the hands of another American, the Pentagon might have given only passing notice. But because the dead man was a prisoner of war, it had international implications, and General Lerch was getting phone calls from the State Department, asking questions he couldn't yet answer. Neither Gross nor Branson had been much help.

On Thursday, August 17, Lerch had even more reason to steam. Both the *Post-Intelligencer* and the *Times* broke stories that seemed to support Major Crawford's theory of a premeditated attack but with a significant twist. According to the *Post-Intelligencer*, the riot "was the climax of trouble which has been brewing for at least a month." "The cause of the trouble," wrote reporter R. B. Bermann, "was the dissatisfaction which soldiers who had seen battle service in Africa expressed over what they described as the 'pampering' of former enemies who had killed their buddies." What made this news was the fact that most of the American soldiers who had seen service in Africa were white, not black. Bermann went on:

What led immediately to Monday night's fatal riot was an altercation which took place Sunday night in the Fort Lawton post exchange when white American troops ejected a large number of Italians who, they charged, were monopolizing the seats. "The PX always does a lot of business on Sunday nights," a white American soldier explained, "and we were sort of burned up because the Italians got there first and we weren't able to get service. They were talking together in Italian and laughing a lot—and the boys got the impression they were laughing at them. I don't know if that was the case, but, anyway, the Americans got mad and chucked the lot of them out."

Both newspapers were quick to point out that—according to white soldiers—black soldiers felt the same way. "They were particularly sore," one white soldier told Bermann, "because the Negro troops were doing all the dirty work and the Italians were compelled to do so little." Another unnamed white soldier told the *Times*, "There was resentment because parties of Italians were taken to baseball games, and also because it was felt work given the Italians was not as arduous and unpleasant as that given the members of the Negro port battalion." No black soldiers were interviewed in either story; all members of the 650th and 651st Port Companies were still locked in the stockade.

Colonel Branson, under orders from Washington not to make any statements to the press, was enraged by this latest development. What business, he fretted, did soldiers under his command have offering personal opinions to newspaper reporters? And who thought up this wild story about the PX? After reading the story in the morning's *Post-Intelligencer*, Branson picked up the phone and dialed the *Times*, determined to make damn sure that at least one newspaper got the story straight. "Army authorities at Fort Lawton," the *Times* reported that afternoon, "said they were unaware of any altercation in the PX Sunday night, and that it could not have been sufficiently serious to attract official attention." The *Times* further endeared itself to Branson by concluding that Fort Lawton MPs "acted quickly to break up Monday night's riot." That, Branson knew, would be well-received by General Lerch.

At the Pentagon, however, the Fort Lawton mess was starting to feel like the first punch at a tar baby. Henry Stimson, the secretary of war, was trying to focus on the liberation of Paris, now less than a week away. Yet he was getting calls from Congress, demanding justice for a lynching in Seattle. Republican senator John Danaher of Connecticut passed along an angry letter from the Italian Central Council, "deplor(ing) the existence of conditions which permitted an attack by American Negro troops upon a group of Italian soldiers." "We urge," the council wrote, "an immediate and thorough investigation of the facts underlying the assault so that justice may be done in this instance and steps taken to prevent any possible recurrence of such unsoldierly and un-American tactics."

Stimson responded within days, telling Senator Danaher, "You may rest assured that as soon as the facts in the case have been established, proper disciplinary action will be taken with respect to the instigators as well as appropriate measures to prevent a recurrence."

The pressure intensified. *Time* magazine called the confrontation between Italians and U.S. troops at Fort Lawton "the worst yet." *Newsweek*, in a full-page article, reported that "it was apparent that the Negroes were bitter at the treatment afforded the Italians. There had been evidence that the Negroes felt they were being assigned more laborious duties than were their former enemies."

The New York–based *Il Progress Italo-Americano*, the country's most influential Italian language newspaper, headlined its editorial A DESPICABLE CRIME. The newspaper called the attack a "sad, ill-omened incident" that had come "just as we were observing, with deep satisfaction, a cessation of certain demonstrations of unjustified intolerance toward Italian prisoners." Accepting the official army line, the editorial concluded: "And the crime certainly puts in the worst light the Negro soldiers who planned it and carried it out with cynical barbarity . . . Let us hope that prompt, severe and just punishment of those who are guilty will serve as a salutary warning to all and will prevent the repetition of such atrocious offenses to the best traditions of highly civilized America."

A Seattle newspaper, *Gazetta Italiana*, complained that the military had failed to "enforce the strictest disciplinary measures," which might have prevented the assault: "It seems that the Italian soldiers at Fort Lawton have been the victims, for a long time, of innumerable provocations and insults against which they had strict orders not to react."

Copies of the editorials were immediately forwarded to the White House by DeWitt Poole, of the Office of Strategic Services. By then end of the week, the incident was included in formal military briefings, which noted, "White soldiers at Fort Lawton had been antagonistic toward the Italians. A member of the 28th Italian QM Company, working in the Fort Lawton Post Exchange, was slapped by a white soldier on the night of 13 August 1944."

Black newspapers were also quick to weigh in; they, too, sympathized with Italians and condemned the black suspects. The Seattle-based *Northwest Enterprise* titled its August 16 editorial RACE SOLDIERS SMEAR INTERRACIAL RELATIONS. The paper's editors complained that whatever the reasons for the attack, "none are sufficient to justify the end":

> The affray accomplished nothing of value to our Negro soldiers— if anything, they lost the ball.
>
> God, soldiers, are you aware of your responsibility? Did you think to escape by a conspiracy of silence? Straighten up. History has yet to record an ironclad conspiracy involving 35 to 50 Negroes.
>
> Soldiers, we are hurt. Lawlessness is the thing that is gnawing not only at our institutions, but at the very government itself.
>
> Daily we see strike leaders not only defy the government, but the U.S. Army. And when they have sufficiently abused its patience, somebody is going to get hurt. They are a poor pattern to follow.

The *Northwest Enterprise* was particularly incensed that Olivotto had been lynched:

> Of all people, it illy becomes our men in arms—or any members of our race—to dignify the rope, unless in self-defense.
>
> The most regrettable part of the entire foray is that the victims were innocent. Liberty and freedom is so sweet, no mortal is going to willingly dispense with it.

On Friday, August 18, General Gross received a second report from Irving Crawford. "There is a strong implication," Major Crawford began, "that the assault was instigated or encouraged by four white U.S. soldiers who have been buying colored soldiers beer at the Fort Lawton Exchanges. This matter is being intensively investigated today." The report also mentioned that "the Italian who was found hanging was considered by his fellow unit members to be a psychoneurotic," although the testimony Crawford had gathered so far had negated the possibility of suicide.

The Friday afternoon *Seattle Times* brought welcome news: U.S. TANKS REACH OUTSKIRTS OF PARIS; NAZIS RETREATING. Yet there was also this strange front-page headline: ITALIAN WAR PRISONERS, REVOLTING AT LAWTON, ARE QUELLED WITH CLUBS. The report was, in fact, the first public announcement of the July 10 uprising, when the company of Fascist Italian prisoners were beaten into submission before they boarded the transport ship to Hawaii. "Information on the revolt could not be printed earlier," explained the *Times*, "because of security reasons, although most of the details were known to newspapers." The newspaper's account of the official War Department explanation, five weeks after the fact, made the event seem fairly tame: "'The great majority of the prisoner group took no part in the demonstration,' the announcement said, 'but several leaders refused to board the trucks, compelling the use of some force.' Order was quickly restored. The War Department said Army authorities had been warned to expect trouble, and had sufficient force standing by, armed with night sticks, to subdue the 'mutineers' when they staged their uprising."

Army flacks took much the same approach when they spun the more recent events in an August 18 press release. The August 14 attack, they said, "was confined to one barracks and the orderly room in an adjoining building." The U.S. Army officers assigned to the ISU "were on the scene a few moments after the sentry had given the alarm. The fight lasted only a matter of minutes before guards and the Military Police had full command of the situation."

A private citizen trying to digest the news out of Fort Lawton could be forgiven for being confused. Was it black soldiers who resented Italians or was it white soldiers? Was the attack premeditated or was it haphazard? Was the melee quickly controlled or was the MP response a subject of investigation? Was the Italian hung or did he kill himself? The *Seattle Times*, tired of getting contradictory information from army spokesmen, sent its reporters to the bars and taverns where white GIs hung out. They found several GIs willing to carp, anonymously, about the official line coming out of the War Department. They painted a picture of long-simmering resentment at Fort Lawton. "Most of the articulate soldiers," said the *Times,* "agree that the Negro troops, vexed at the treatment accorded the Italians, which they thought was too 'soft,' got 'beered up in the PX (post exchange) and decided to clean out the Italians.' Others say that the Negroes were 'egged on' by white troops." One white soldier implied that blacks were more upset about Italians than whites were: "'They find themselves crowded out of the post exchange by these Italians. Not only that, but girls come out to service dances and make a big fuss over the Italians. They find 'em romantic. You know, speaking a foreign language and all that. What happens? The Negro soldiers see these guys—not even citizens—laughing and having a good time and they don't like it.'"

The Italians, meanwhile, remained terrified. Of the twenty-six who required medical treatment, all but a handful were back in their barracks by the end of the week. Colonel R. T. Arrington, sent to Seattle by ISU commanding general John Eager, reported that "the Italians are literally scared to death and Col. Branson has restricted them to their area (they accept this only too willingly) and has placed guards around them for their protection. He has wisely made no effort to work them since the incident as he does not have enough guards for them and feels that they would refuse to work unprotected. The consensus of opinion was that the usefulness of these troops here was at an end and the quicker they were moved the better." Colonel Arrington suggested that the Italians not be told about the proposed transfer "as it was not desired that such contemplated action make the newspapers."

Arrington was disgusted by the press, telling General Eager that "the local newspapers have taken up the incident and are continually hammering on it." He did not know that just a few hours before he wrote his dispatch, the War Department's Bureau of Public Relations had set in motion "a publicity campaign to counteract the effects of the criticism" that POWs had been pampered and coddled. "The incident at Fort Lawton indicates the need and presents an opportunity for additional constructive measures," the bureau concluded, including the release of "data as to the contribution which the Italian Service Units are making to this country's war effort." Among other things, the War Department had grown increasingly concerned about "repercussions which may result from the Fort Lawton incident in our relations with the Italian Government."

American diplomats echoed that concern. On August 16, an account of the melee had run in the *International Herald-Tribune* and had been read in capital cities throughout western Europe. On August 21, Secretary of State Cordell Hull received an angry cable from George Merrell, the president's personal representative to India. Merrell was incensed that a wire-service story about the Fort Lawton riot had been printed in the *Hindustan Times*. "It is most undesirable," Merrell wrote, "to have press items like the foregoing carried in the Indian press and it is unfortunate that they are permitted to reach India." Merrell informed the secretary of state that he had lodged a complaint with the Office of War Information.

Colonel Arrington's report included two other observations. After visiting the spot where Olivotto's body was found, he concluded, "I saw the place and it does not seem possible that it was a suicide." He also wanted General Eager to know that "the negroes involved were members of two port companies with an excellent reputation." It was the first positive statement written about the 650th and 651st Port Companies since the attack.

By Saturday, August 19, most of the black soldiers had been released from the barbed-wire stockade but remained confined to quarters. Thirty-year-old Pancho Jones, a member of the 651st sat down to type a letter to a friend in Washington, D.C. Jones, from Omaha, went by the nickname "Nebraska." His friend was a union man with the Committee for Industrial Organization (CIO). Before the war, Jones had been a union organizer, and a member of the National CIO Committee to Abolish Racial Discrimination.

Jones started by assuring his friend that although he was among the hundreds of soldiers whom the army arrested, he had no part in the riot. He wanted to "clear up any anxiety [this friend] might have had concerning my connection in the affair"; he had been off the post at the time. He also wanted to leak word of what his fellow soldiers thought of the allegations against them:

> The riot, contrary to what the authorities have released to the press, started four days before the Monday night incident. It started with white troops who had just returned from the Pacific theater. These guys beat up Italians for three days in the PX. They tried to get the colored troops to help them. It wasn't until Monday night after one of the Italians hit a soldier from our sister Company that our boys became involved. Unfortunately for us the Army has only involved the Negro troops. In this case, as usually, we are the "fall guys."
>
> There are many more factors in this case but I am sure they will not come out until after the war. The issues involved go deeper than those presented in the press. The white troops here were much more concerned by the presence of the Italians than we were. Certainly we resented the breaks they were getting, but there was nothing we could do about it. This was nothing new to us. To be charged with the whole thing, however, makes all of us rather sick.

DETAILS ABOUT THE Fort Lawton incident disappeared from newspapers as quickly as they had appeared. The world was still at war, and on Friday, August 25—eleven days after the riot—the U.S. army in Europe crossed the Seine River. Exhausted GIs fell into the arms of ecstatic French girls, celebrating, at last, the liberation of Paris. Back in Washington, D.C., Pentagon officials had little time for hoopla; it was still a long way to Berlin. And although hundreds of Allied and enemy soldiers were dying on battlefields every day, the death of a single Italian at a fort in Seattle continued to create political and diplomatic headaches. To the dismay of Major General Mervin Gross, reports out of Fort Lawton seemed increasingly convoluted and contradictory. It was time, Gross decided, to bring out the heavy artillery. He called in the best troubleshooter he knew, a no-nonsense brigadier general with little tolerance for bullshitters or bureaucrats. A man named Cookie would soon turn the murder and riot investigation on its head.

CHAPTER SEVEN

COOKIE
September 1944

ELLIOT COOKE'S EYES SHONE cornflower blue, except when he grew angry. As his temper rose, the sparkle vanished and liquid blue hardened to iron gray. In time, Brigadier General Elliot D. Cooke would see and hear enough about the events of August 14 and 15 to turn his gaze into full steel-eyed fury.

Cookie—as almost everyone of equal or greater rank called him—was a troubleshooter. As chief of the Overseas Inspection Division in the Office of the Inspector General, Cooke's job was to ferret out corruption and incompetence wherever it threatened to blemish the reputation of his beloved army. While many of his contemporaries commanded overseas divisions or brigades, Cooke trotted the globe as an army of one, defending the military's integrity and getting rid of those who dared sully it. Something about the mess in Seattle told him that the army's honor had been splattered with mud, if not stained with blood.

The Overseas Inspection Division had jurisdiction in Seattle because most men came to Fort Lawton to be shipped to the war in the Pacific. When Cooke arrived at the fort in mid-September, he was astonished to learn that all but sixty of the four hundred men of the 650th and 651st Port Companies—including Luther Larkin and many other leading suspects—had been sent to New Guinea. General McArthur's crusade to liberate the Philippines required a steady stream of supplies, most of which had to be unloaded by Negro port companies onto South Seas island beaches. Avenging an embarrassing murder in Seattle had to compete with the demands of prosecuting a worldwide war.

On Friday, September 15, General Cooke entered a building in the heart of what had been—just one month earlier—Fort Lawton's Colored Area. At his side was Lieutenant Colonel Curtis Williams, a former Arkansas district attorney, now an investigator with the Pentagon's Inspector General Office and Cooke's assistant. Piled on the table in front of them were stacks of reports and the transcripts of preliminary interviews with Farr, Haskell, Gould, Perata, a dozen Italians, and a handful of military policemen, all conducted by Williams before Cooke's arrival. Over the next five days, the general himself would interrogate another fifty-seven men, part of a sprawling investigation that would eventually include sworn testimony from 164 witnesses, ranging from buck privates to a brigadier general.

General Cooke's orders were to conduct an independent, classified inquiry into the riot and murder and to expose whom, if anyone, had been asleep at the switch while hostility and resentment had apparently been allowed to fester at the fort. He and Colonel Williams would investigate, not prosecute; a separate branch of the army—the Judge Advocate General's Corps—would independently oversee decisions to bring military criminal charges, if any. Cooke was to pass judgment on the performance of the fort's command and on its officers and on their fitness to continue their current assignments. If the fact warranted, Cooke would see that heads rolled in the officer corps, while the JAG prosecutor would seek justice in a separate court-martial against any enlisted men.

It soon became clear to Cooke why August 14 had been a pivotal date: that warm Monday was to have been the last full day in Seattle for the two port companies. Both had been scheduled to ship out Tuesday afternoon for their overseas assignment somewhere in the Pacific. Typical of wartime protocol, their eventual destination—New Guinea—had been kept secret, even from the soldiers themselves. They knew only that, after reveille the next morning, they'd have to stand for inspection with gear stenciled, shoes shined, and hearts ready for unknowable danger and/or adventure. They were undoubtedly anxious to be headed into a battle zone. It was a feeling that Cooke understood all too well.

ELLIOT COOKE WAS born on Staten Island on August 15, 1891, fifty-three years to the day before Guglielmo Olivotto's body was discovered at Fort Lawton. Cooke's father, Richard, was a stockbroker. His mother, Henrietta, doted on her eldest son, Richard Jr., which made it easier for free-spirited Elliot to drop out of school and run away from home at age fourteen with his buddy "Dunk" Harvey. They hopped a banana boat to Honduras, where the United Fruit Company taught Elliot to use a machine gun and gave him a job protecting plantations against anti-American agitators and displaced campesinos. Wounded in Tegucigalpa, he returned to the United States, making his way to a relative's home in Goldfield, Nevada. An amateur boxer and budding marksman, young Elliot lied about his age and hired on with a local sheriff's private militia, organized to intimidate striking miners. In 1910, he was drawn back south of the border, where he joined up with soldiers of fortune from around the world toting six-shooters in support of the Mexican Revolution.

Thoroughly enamored with life as a mercenary, he joined the foreign legion in Nicaragua, eventually making his way to Panama just as the First World War erupted in Europe. On November 16, 1914, he enlisted as a private in the U.S. Army, and by September 1917 he was in France, elevated to the rank of first lieutenant. Although still a member of the U.S. Army, Cooke was assigned to a Marine Corps battalion as company commander. On July 18, 1918, German troops engaged the marines in a fierce firefight in wheat fields near the village of Vierzy, east of Paris. Late that afternoon, Cooke watched in horror as his best friend, a lieutenant named Becker, was blown apart by German artillery. "He turned, grinned, and waved a greeting. He took one step towards me and then—disappeared," Cookie recalled. "The boy I had come to France with, bunked, eaten and played with, was gone. Hardly enough of his body remained for decent burial."

With every other officer in his unit dead or wounded, twenty-six-year-old Lieutenant Cooke continued to lead his men in battle for two hours, despite a serious leg wound. For his heroism, he was awarded three of the highest honors bestowed by the French military: the croix de guerre with palm, the croix de guerre with bronze star, and the fourragère. In years to come, Cooke prominently displayed the French citations on his dress uniform, proud to remind his peers that he was the only U.S. Army officer during World War I to earn all three (since the others in his unit were U.S. Marines).

As he buttoned his jacket before entering the Fort Lawton Colored Area, the decoration on Cooke's shoulder seemed eerily ironic. The fourragère is a braid, designed to commemorate the heroism of the Flemish troops who fought for the Spanish duke of Alva in the 1500s. The Flemish battled bravely, under threat of being hung if they dared retreat. The fourragère is therefore shaped like a hangman's noose, a fact that could not have escaped the attention of those who stared across the table at this imposing general as the Seattle interrogations got under way.

THE FIRST SEVERAL witnesses remembered August 14 for the most part as an utterly ordinary day. By evening chow, most black soldiers had finished packing their gear. Confined to base, some retreated soberly to their barracks, writing a letter to a wife or to a girlfriend—or to one of each—and reflecting on the fact that this might be their last night in America for a long time, perhaps forever. A few soldiers slipped through a hole in the perimeter fence to enjoy one last binge in downtown Seattle, often in the arms of a lady friend or a prostitute. A handful curled in bunks to page through their Bibles.

Many enlisted men headed to the PX, where a forty-ounce pitcher of beer cost thirty-five cents. Three soldiers—two of them black, one white—pulled MP duty in the PX that night. Military policemen were supposed to make sure no one got too drunk and that pitchers stayed inside the PX and women stayed out. But on their penultimate day on the post—and a payday, at that—rules were hard to enforce. By nine thirty, several had drained six glasses of beer or more, often fortified with sips from smuggled six-dollar pints of whiskey. Skin, stud, and other games of poker lured tipsy congregations to back corners of Barracks 667 and 675, while a GI blanket was spread on an upstairs floor for a craps game in Barracks 719. None of these details surprised Cooke; they were, after all, young men.

Cooke was, however, taken aback by testimony about what went on across the street from Barracks 719. Building 700 was the mess hall for the 578th, the only one of the three black port companies not scheduled to ship out the next day. In their interrogations, Cooke and Williams learned that the 578th had sponsored a noisy bon voyage bash in their mess hall for the benefit of the 650th and 651st. On August 14, the highest-ranking black soldier from the 578th was First Sergeant Wilbert Tanner, a large man with a dark, square face and an enormous belly. Cooke placed Tanner under oath and asked him straight out:

"What sort of party were you having there that night?"
"There wasn't any party there."
"There wasn't any party in your mess hall?"
"No, sir."

Tanner's mess sergeant and three company cooks all swore the same thing: the mess hall was quiet that night, they said, save for regular cleaning and a light meal for a late-arriving platoon. "A party? No, sir." But Cooke was a skilled inquisitor. He knew that young soldiers on the hot seat are unconvincing liars. Under pressure, their recollections begin to sound suspiciously practiced and their answers become much too literal. Droopy-eyed glances start to dance around the room, everywhere except the crosshairs of Cooke's blue-eyed glower. What might have seemed convincing during rehearsal quickly came apart once their made-up story hit the main stage.

Cooke's suspicions were confirmed by Addison George, a thirty-two-year-old corporal in the 650th. George, a Texan from oil-rich Brazoria County, had been drawn to Building 700 that night, he said, by the sound of loud music. He stuck his head in and saw Nelson Rice, a private with the 578th, cutting licks on an electric guitar.

"After you saw this man playing the guitar, did you observe what was going on in building 700, in the mess hall?"
"Yes, sir."
"What were they doing there?"
"They were dancing."

Under Cooke's questioning, others admitted that Building 700 was, in fact, hopping that night with music, women, and beer. Individually, each of those vices was strongly discouraged in army mess halls, but in combination, the party had clearly been out of bounds. When Sergeant Tanner was called back into the room to explain himself, Cooke could barely stifle his sarcasm.

"Sergeant, after reflection, have you had an opportunity to remember things that you were not so sure of when you first appeared here and testified?"
"Yes, sir, I did."

Realizing he was cornered, Tanner confessed he had indeed hosted a party for the benefit of his brethren heading overseas but claimed that the duty officer, a white captain named Alan Christensen, had given the okay. "In the early part of the night, I had asked him about a party," he recounted, "and could we have a party over there, since he was the Section Commander. And he told me there wasn't any objection." Dragged into the spotlight, an embarrassed Captain Christensen offered a slightly different spin: "I said to the sergeant, 'What about this business of having people over here?' 'Well,' he said. 'You know some of the boys are about to leave, and we want to have a little bit of a party for them.' And I don't mean to attempt to contradict somebody else's statement, but I am certain that I talked to Sergeant Tanner there and made a comment about whether or not it would be all right with his company commander to do that. I am certain of that."

But Tanner's company commander had gone into town that night. In fact, not a single white officer attached to any of the three black port companies was in the Colored Area after dinner on August 14. Several had slipped into Seattle for their own final fling before sailing; others retreated to the officers' club or to their own quarters, either location almost a mile away from the fort's isolated Negro barracks. By default, Captain Christensen was the only officer in charge.

Alan Christensen was thirty-nine, a high school English teacher from the town of La Grande in northeast Oregon. Raised on his parents' prune orchard, he joined the wrestling team and the ROTC while earning his teaching degree at the University of Oregon. As the depleted wartime army absorbed older reserves, Christensen was called to service in Seattle, where he was assigned to assist the provost marshal at Fort Lawton. On August 14, it was his turn to be duty officer for the section of the fort that included the Colored and Italian Areas.

As duty officer, Christensen was supposed to keep an eye out for trouble, checking up on his MPs and making sure the taverns closed on time. Christensen assured Cooke that he had been diligent that night, and that he had no hint of discord as he fell asleep at eleven ten in the duty officer's bunk in section headquarters. Manning the phones that night was Private First Class Glenn Pescatore; Christensen swore that Pescatore had never awakened him. No one involved in quelling the riot, it seemed, had thought to call section headquarters that night.

> "Here was a disturbance—and a very serious one—and you didn't even know it until you heard of it the next morning?"
>
> "That's right, sir."
>
> "Where is the missing link? What is wrong that you were not informed so that you could do something about it?"

Christensen had no answer. Cooke was incredulous. He dismissed Christensen and demanded to see Private Pescatore.

"How many times during the night did you see Captain Christensen?"

"I seen him from about four o'clock until about eleven o'clock that night."

"Where did he go then?"

"I don't know, sir. He never said. He just left."

"He left the building?"

"Yes, sir."

"He was not sleeping there?"

"Well, he came back around one o'clock, or somewhere in around there."

General Cooke seethed. He called Captain Christensen back in to the interrogation room.

"Am I to understand you went to bed in building 830?"

"Yes, sir. If that is the Fourth Section headquarters building."

"And you said an enlisted man was in there?"

"Yes, sir."

"Captain, he has sworn under oath that, between 11 and 12 P.M., you were not in that building."

"That is not true."

"He swore at twelve o'clock he went to see—to find you, to tell you about the relief of somebody, and you were not there."

"Between eleven and twelve o'clock?"

"At twelve o'clock sharp you were not there, and that you came in after twelve o'clock from somewhere."

"That is not true, sir."

Someone, of course, was hiding something. In disgust, Cooke complained, "We have so many people telling lies in this affair, it is hard to know who to believe." He had only been at Fort Lawton for two days, and already he was convinced that truth there was hard to come by.

During the two weeks before the general arrived in Seattle, Colonel

Williams had interviewed sixty-three witnesses. Williams told Cooke that he had been particularly disturbed by the testimony of the white military policemen on duty the night of August 14–15. Important events described by one MP often contradicted the recollections of another, and almost none were able or willing to identify specific perpetrators. One of the most exasperating cases was the testimony of Private Clyde Lomax.

Initially, Lomax looked to be a promising witness. Not only had he and John Pinkney been the first to discover Guglielmo Olivotto's body in the predawn darkness; Lomax was also one of the first white soldiers to realize that a riot was imminent the night before. That surprising coincidence led Williams to decide that Lomax should be first on the list of thirteen military policemen he planned to interview.

Lomax had arrived for his interrogation at Port of Seattle headquarters the morning of September 5 with an unusual military résumé. He was a lowly private, and therefore wore no stripes, but had been in the army for almost three years. Prior to his assignment at Fort Lawton, Lomax had seen duty on Attu Island in the Aleutians and been in the thick of combat in the Marshall Islands near the Equator, where he earned two bronze stars for bravery. It was no secret that military police battalions assigned to domestic bases were often a dumping ground for problem soldiers banished from overseas units, yet Lomax's lack of rank after so much service and so much apparent gallantry was conspicuously odd, even by those standards.

On the night of August 14, Private Lomax had been assigned a routine patrol, driving an MP jeep throughout the fort's northwestern quadrant. His job, as usual, was to enforce curfew and to collar drunk soldiers. Although he ordinarily drove alone, a staff sergeant from Texas named Charles Robinson was along that night for the ride. As they made their rounds, Lomax and Robinson were required to check in at the post guardhouse at the top of each hour, and they did so at 11 P.M. From there, they drove westward, in no particular hurry, toward the Colored and Italian Areas. Within minutes, Lomax told Colonel Williams, they approached Building 719, one of several barracks housing members of the 650th Port Company. "We found a colored man laying down at the front end of 719," Lomax said, "and in between 719 and 718 there was a gang of colored men around there. I stopped the jeep and we got out and I went over to take a look at him and see what was wrong and what all the racket was about."

The soldier on the ground was Willie Montgomery, a slightly built corporal from New York City. At forty years old, Montgomery was one of the oldest members of the 650th. Lomax continued:

> We talked to these colored soldiers who were surrounding Montgomery to see what was the matter with him. They said that two or three Italians hit him over the head with a stick or something, and knocked him out. I examined him and he wasn't cut at all. The colored soldiers, they didn't want to bring him to the hospital. I said we would take him to the hospital and one of them said, "We don't want him took to the hospital. We will keep him here." I said, "If he is hurt bad enough, we will take him to the hospital." They didn't say anything else, so me and Sergeant Robinson started up the jeep.

Clyde Vernon Lomax was a son of the Deep South, born on a farm in Hinds County, Mississippi. In the depths of the Great Depression, the Lomax family moved to Louisiana, where Clyde spent much of his boyhood in Melville, on the banks of the flood-prone Atchafalaya River. In Melville, white folks lived south of the railroad tracks, and colored folks lived to the north. In the center of town, Napoli's Furniture and Appliance store catered to coloreds and whites alike, but a black man could only expect service as long as all white people in the store were taken care of first. Boys like Clyde caught goatfish, using crawdads for bait, carrying the skinned fish home to be deep-fried and laid out over rice. When those same boys grew older, they used beagles to chase rabbits and hounds to hunt bear. Several times a day, freight train conductors hung from whistle straps as they roared across the rusted steel bridge spanning the Atchafalaya.

Lomax attended school through fifth grade. At age eighteen, only a few weeks before Pearl Harbor, he enlisted in the army at Camp Livingston, Louisiana. Until he arrived at Fort Lawton two years later, most of the men he had dealt with in the segregated army were white, like him. In his interview with Colonel Williams, he pointed out that he and Robinson felt surrounded by Negroes as they stood outside Barracks 719 on August 14:

At the present time, there was a colored man running diagonally across from where we are at 719, running down through the area toward 668 and 667, blowing [a whistle] as loud as he could. I don't know who that soldier was; it was dark and I couldn't make out the faces of them and all of them looked the same to me. I don't know exactly why he was blowing the whistle. It sounded like to me he was blowing it to get the whole company out. What come in my mind was that these Negroes, when they blew the whistle, I told Sergeant Robinson it looks like some trouble.

Before that, a few other things happened. When I heard one of those colored men say that "they got one of our boys and we are going to get them," I thought that meant the MPs at first. So I told Sergeant Robinson, I said, "Sergeant Robinson, we had better get the hell away from here before they gang us."

Lomax's professed fear of the men in the port companies caught Williams by surprise. He asked whether, prior to August 14, Lomax knew of any threats by colored soldiers toward white MPs:

No, sir, I didn't, but I had a rough guess that they were going to get after us. When I closed the PX up—that was on a Sunday, the 13th—a Lieutenant who I believe to be Lieutenant Ruel ordered me to close the place up. They were having trouble. The boys didn't want the Italians to come in the beer tavern at all—white boys and colored boys. They stood on the inside of the door and wouldn't let them come in, the white boys did.

I know one of them, T/5 Guy Stratton, they call him Tex. He was saying, "By God, they weren't going to come in there." I heard him say that. And he was going to beat the hell out of me on the inside there and I said, "If you want to fight, there isn't a damned thing keeping you from it." I would say they had been drinking, but I wouldn't say that he was drunk. After we closed the place up, Lieutenant Ruel took him and a couple of more boys and give them a good talking and took them up the road.

While all this was happening, there were colored troops standing in back of them, taking it all in. These boys in there, I don't know whether it was white boys or colored boys, but I am pretty sure it was a colored boy, they said, "We are going to beat the hell out of the MPs when we catch them alone." That was on the 13th.

Colonel Williams asked if he had reported the threat to his superiors; Lomax admitted he had not. He said he brought Sergeant Robinson with him on patrol the next night to guard against becoming a solo target. As tensions grew, he and Robinson threw Willie Montgomery in the back of their jeep, then hightailed out of the Colored Area, stopping first at the post hospital to drop Montgomery off for treatment, then at the guardhouse to alert the rest of the military policemen of the brewing trouble.

The more Lomax talked, the more agitated he became. He began to spin a tale that made him seem almost heroic, telling how he had gathered a carload of MPs and headed back to the Colored Area, where he saw dozens of black soldiers tear apart a white picket fence surrounding a small victory garden on the south side of the Building 700 mess hall. "They were all started toward the Italian Area, walking or running or whatever you want to call it," he said. "It was like they were doing both, walking and running. They said, 'We are going to mob them. They got one of our boys and we are going to mob them and get them.'"

Lomax told Williams that he parked his jeep and ran the twenty yards or so to Barracks 709 in the Italian Area, where he was confronted by a black soldier wielding a double-bit ax. Lomax was armed with a pistol but said he did not use it to defend himself: "I was too damn scared, and I think you would have been too. If I would have shot him—they knew damn well I didn't have more than six shots in the thing—if I had shot him they would have god damn sure have got me. I would have probably been in the hospital myself. I would have had that whole damn gang of them on me and I would have probably got it myself." Nonetheless, Lomax said, he tried to remain in control: "One other colored guy says—I was trying to get them to stop the racket—and one of them says, 'To hell with you, you goddamn MP.' I just told him, 'By God,' I said. 'Break this up before you get your ass in trouble.' There is one nigger MP that told them to break it up and I tried to tell them, but they wouldn't listen to me, but they listened to him, so he is the one that stopped the damn thing as far as I know."

Lomax remembered that military policemen had been quick, confident, and in control—-a far cry from what Williams had been told by Farr, Perata, Haskell, and Gould. To hear Lomax tell it, he and the other MPs had been Johnny-on-the-spot, nothing at all like the thirty-to forty-five-minute delay the others had reported.

But as Williams began interviewing other MPs, he found very little support for Lomax's version of events. Sergeant Robinson, a six-foot-tall Southerner who had just arrived at Fort Lawton in June, told Williams he was riding with Lomax that night so he could learn the layout of the post. Lomax, he said, never mentioned anything about threats from colored troops directed at MPs the night before. Robinson confirmed the story about finding Willie Montgomery sprawled on the ground in front of Barracks 719, but swore he never heard anyone blow a whistle, as Lomax had so clearly remembered. Although Robinson could not tell whether Montgomery's injuries were serious, he did not object when Lomax decided to drive right past the hospital closest to the Colored Area, taking Montgomery instead to the main hospital clear on the other side of the fort. He also could not explain why, on the way to the hospital, Lomax drove within a few yards of the guardhouse without stopping to tell anyone about a disturbance in the Colored Area. Robinson testified that he eventually returned to the Italian Area in the company of several other MPs, but Lomax was not with him. In fact, he never saw Lomax again that night.

Andrew David, the corporal of the guard on August 14, told Williams that Lomax and Robinson did not arrive at the guardhouse until just after eleven thirty, several minutes after David had already received a phone call from Grant Farr reporting a problem in the Italian Area. Although Lomax claimed Corporal David sent him to the barracks to wake the other MPs, David denied giving such an order. The sergeant of the guard, Regis Callahan, eventually dispatched about two dozen MPs, but none of the MPs interviewed by Williams recalled seeing Lomax in the area.

Williams grew irritated that none of the white MPs were willing to step forward to identify even a single one of the rioters. Sergeant Thurman Jones, who had done an otherwise admirable job leading the belated charge to clear the orderly room, nevertheless made no arrests, took down no names, and said he could not recall a single face. When pressed, Jones, born and raised in Mississippi, offered only, "One Negro looks like another one as far as I am concerned." Private Arthur Duncan, reared in Missouri, also claimed to have trouble distinguishing one Negro from another, explaining that he "never did live around them." To both Cooke and Williams, it smelled like a conspiracy of silence.

Regis Callahan, the sergeant of the guard, was particularly eager to close ranks. He vehemently rejected the contention of Farr, Perata, and Haskell that it took almost forty minutes after Farr's phone call for the first MP to arrive. "Either they were under an emotional strain due to the excitement of the circumstances they found themselves in," Callahan speculated, or their clocks and watches were off. As far as Callahan was concerned, his men had acted quickly and efficiently, quelling the riot within mere minutes of its inception. Although he was the MP in charge that night, he too declined to identify even one of the dozens of black soldiers he saw that night.

When Williams finished interviewing military policemen, he moved on to the Italians. His very first witness confirmed the tale about Willie Montgomery's injury. Guiseppe Belle had been one of the three Italians who spent the day on a pass in downtown Seattle. Returning to the fort just after 11 P.M., the trio ambled toward their barracks, passing near small groups of boisterous Americans in the Colored Area. Belle, a slightly built twenty-two-year-old who had been captured in Tunisia, told Williams that some of the black soldiers cursed him— "Goddamn Italians!"—as he walked past.

Belle, who spoke little English, turned to his compatriot Antonio Pisciottano for an interpretation. "Never mind, don't let it bother you, let's go to bed, let's go to sleep." Belle, however, knew just enough English curse words to realize that he'd been insulted. In his testimony, he related, "'God damn Italian son of a bitch shits,' they said. "Another soldier called, 'Hey, Italian,' and I stopped and turned around and he was almost on top of me and coming at me with a knife. I hit him with a left hook on the side of the jaw and he went down. The man must have been drunk, because I didn't hit him hard enough to knock down a sober person. I was scared and ran to my barracks and got in bed right away. I took off my clothes and went to bed."

Both Pisciottano and the third Italian, Angelo Fumarola, confirmed Belle's story. It was self-defense, they said, plain and simple. And the alleged attacker fit the description of Willie Montgomery. They knew nothing about getting revenge or about any supposed hostility toward MPs or black soldiers. The way they saw it, an agitated drunk had threatened their safety, and Guiseppe Belle had done what he had to do to protect himself.

As Cooke studied the transcript of Williams's interrogation, he brooded about the behavior of Private Lomax. The man is obviously a coward, he concluded, but worse, he might be hiding something. Why did he bypass the nearest hospital when seeking help for Montgomery? Why did he wait at least a half hour before letting anyone at the guardhouse know that trouble was brewing—and then lie, under oath, about the delay? And why wouldn't he identify the black soldier who allegedly blew a whistle, calling his fellow soldiers to fall out? Somehow a brief drunken fistfight had led to cold-blooded murder, and clearly someone knew more than they were saying under oath.

Looking for answers, Cooke climbed the chain of command. The captain in charge of Fort Lawton's MPs was Milton Carter, who readily admitted he had no military police training. He told Cooke he had not felt any need to investigate how his men had responded to the riot and hanging.

"How do you account for the fact that this Lomax, knowing the trouble was imminent, did not go to the guardhouse and so inform the sergeant of the guard in order that he might inform the officer of the day?"

"Some of the men, General, that they have assigned to my company in the three months prior to this time, should not even have been in the Army. I shouldn't make a statement like that."

"Who assigned these men?"

"They were replacements from overseas who were sent here and by whose order I do not know. They have had training in military police work and then they are assigned to my company as military policemen from the overseas stations. I would say that 50 percent of the men we received were not fit for MP duty. Now, that is not the fault of any individual or organization. It is a trend of trying to replace the men who are capable of doing overseas duty, with those who are not."

Carter reported to Major William Orem, Fort Lawton's provost marshal. Although in charge of post intelligence and security, forty-seven-year-old Bill Orem had no training or experience in either. He had been plucked by the army from a Civilian Conservation Corps camp, where he was director. Like many married officers, Major Orem lived off the post, near the University of Washington. By the time his phone rang at 12:10 A.M., the rioters had already been cleared from the Italian Area. The lieutenant on the other end of the phone line told him only that it was a "bloody mess." Orem threw on his uniform and navigated the nine miles to the fort as quickly as he could. He arrived around 12:30 A.M. to find guards already posted, and MPs scanning the woods for Italian stragglers. "I then proceeded to the Colored Area and found the lights on in a number of the barracks," he recounted. "I went in and a number of the men were up. I told them to get into bed immediately and turn out the lights. I aroused the first sergeant of each company, who appeared to be sound asleep, and told them to handle their companies and get them in order and asked them where their officers were, and they said they didn't know."

Under Cooke's withering gaze, Major Orem sheepishly confessed that not one of his MPs had bothered to detain or even try to identify any of the dozens of black soldiers raising hell among the Italians. Instead, they had simply ordered them back to barracks, in many cases still clutching bloody clubs or knives.

"Was any attempt made to search the barracks for bloodstained clothing and weapons, or men with blood on their hands?"

"No sir. I had a reason for that."

"What was it?"

"I felt it was best under the circumstances, in the middle of the night—and knowing what I do about the Colored soldier—to get them quiet and in bed without trying to stir them up any more. And I felt it would be detrimental, rather than an advantage."

"You were more concerned, then, with subduing the Colored men and getting them quiet, than to find out who might have engaged in some criminal action, is that it?"

"Yes, sir, that is correct."

Cooke was floored. This was an army base, for God's sake, home to hundreds of soldiers, most of them armed. A major with almost two hundred military policemen under his command lacked the instinct, if not the backbone, to order the quarantine and thorough search of a couple of companies of black soldiers. Orem, the officer responsible for conducting criminal investigations on the post, seemed to have distressingly little investigative sense.

Even as it had dawned on Major Orem that dozens of men were in the hospital, he delayed contacting Colonel Branson, the post commander, until after one o'clock.

"Did you tell him what had been told you, that it was a bloody mess, or didn't you think it was?"

"I did, sir, yes, sir."

"Didn't you tell him that everything was under control?"

"I did, sir. Colonel Branson may have asked me if I thought he should come down. If he did, I told him no, because I thought everything was under control and I thought there was nothing he could do. I am not sure exactly of what I told him because I was considerably upset, as you can appreciate."

As a result, Orem remained alone at the reins throughout the night. At one point, he ordered seven or eight men to comb the area but suggested they not venture too far into the dark woods because, he told Cooke, "it is rough ground. And I was just a little uncertain as to who might be down there, and, in other words, I didn't want my men getting into a lot of trouble down there, too." Instead, those men waited for terrified Italians to slip out from the trees, scratched, bruised, and occasionally bloodied. All but one Italian eventually returned, although none of Orem's MPs ever checked to see whether the names on the hospital roster fully matched the number of empty bunks in the barracks. Likewise, Orem never thought to order a head count for the black soldiers either.

"Did you make any attempt to put a guard to check the Colored soldiers that came in or attempted to come in their barracks?"

"No, sir."

"Could a party of Colored soldiers have come in and gotten in their barracks after you made your investigation here?"

"It is possible, by circling clear around. We had the whole area covered, but they could have."

By six thirty in the morning on August 15, the sun had risen but the sky was overcast. Major Orem had remained awake and was understandably exhausted. He was gathering himself, he said, in the MP orderly room when Private Lomax appeared at the door. The major might want to come down to the beach, Lomax had said, because it sure enough looked like there was a dead Italian hanging from the end of a rope. Orem, by then too tired to be surprised, had been called yet again to press his limited detective skills into action.

Major Orem told General Cooke that he headed down to the beach, saw Olivotto's body, and finally realized he was in over his head. He sent for an ambulance, posted a guard, and drove back up the hill to call Colonel Branson once again, this time to report the hanging and ask for help. The colonel, taken aback both by the news of the lynching and by his provost marshal's anxious demeanor, began to regret his decision to stay in bed after the first phone call. Weeks later, Branson found himself in front of General Cooke, trying to explain, under oath, that late-night conversation with Bill Orem.

"I asked him this question very distinctly—because I was much perturbed afterwards that he hadn't told me more fully—I said, 'Shall I come down?' and his answer was, 'No, sir, there is no need. Everything is in control and everybody is in bed and it is all quiet.'"

"Did he tell you the number of persons who had been injured?"

"No, sir."

"Did he tell you that some were fatally injured?"

"No, sir."

"In other words, he did not in any way indicate to you the seriousness of the condition of some of these people?"

"No, sir; if he had, I would have immediately gone down, because I was available."

To General Cooke, the colonel's limp explanation was crap, little more than cover-your-ass bullshit. At best, Branson had displayed an alarming lack of curiosity during that late-night phone call, especially given the circumstances being reported. In Cooke's way of thinking, any commander worth a damn would have erred on the side of overreacting and at least pulled his butt out of bed for an inspection of the area. At worst, Colonel Branson was lying, since Orem had sworn under oath that he *did* tell Branson during that phone call that dozens of soldiers had been injured. In any event, either the colonel or a major under his command was massaging the truth, and it was enough to drain the last drop of blue from Cooke's ever-narrowing eyes. No wonder sergeants were throwing unauthorized beer parties and duty officers were missing from their bunks and MPs were telling tall tales: the fort was under the command of officers who seemed unfit for their positions.

Branson's behavior only got worse. He finally made his way to the Italian Area at nine thirty Tuesday morning. The sun had burned through the salt-air fog, dispersing morning dew from the broad leaves of shiny salal. White military policemen, fitted with white lanyards and leggings, barked useless orders at tightly drawn clusters of Italians. Branson recalled that he had huddled with a clutch of his colonels, captains, and majors. Unhappy with Orem's performance under pressure, Branson decided to transfer responsibility for the criminal investigation to Lieutenant Colonel Henry Kleinhen, and to put post security in the hands of Colonel Alfred Baylies. At the same time, he assigned Baylies to head a small team of officers responsible for investigating how well the fort had handled the riot and murder, a team that also included—of all people—Captain Christensen, the young duty officer who had been unaccountably absent from his quarters the night of the riot. Finally, Branson told Cooke that he ordered the post engineer, Major George McNay, to begin immediate repairs to the Italian barracks to make them "livable" again.

Once again, Cooke was taken aback. Did Branson mean to tell him that he ordered a crime scene cleaned up *before* anyone had a chance to collect fingerprints or footprints or any other sort of usable evidence?

Yes, Branson admitted, he did. "On one side of me," he said, "I had two companies of colored troops who had just rioted. And I had a company of Italians who were very unstable, who had just been through a riot and were milling around. And my sole thought at that time was to prevent a further riot and to get everybody quieted down so that there wouldn't be any further trouble. I wasn't—or a thought never occurred to my mind—until right now, as a matter of fact—that anything of that character was doing away with evidence."

Cooke was hardly surprised when Major Orem admitted that, well, no, he had not spoken up when Colonel Branson ordered the cleanup.

"But you knew that the window sills and window glass that had been knocked out, might have had fingerprints on them, didn't you?"

"If I thought of that phase of it, I might say yes."

"But did you think of it then?"

"No, sir, I didn't."

"So then, you didn't think there was any more evidence available in the Italian Area, so you let the order for the cleanup go ahead without any more protest?"

"No, sir, that is not the point."

"What was the reason you didn't protest that then, if you thought there was evidence there?"

"I didn't protest the commanding officer's orders because I figured he knew what he was doing."

A man was dead and dozens of American GIs had apparently rioted. How was an army prosecutor going to put together a case if so much evidence had been destroyed? As Cooke contemplated that embarrassing possibility, Branson dropped yet another bombshell.

On August 15, as Branson was meeting with his officers in the Italian Area, a young white second lieutenant named Arthur Kapitz was up the hill in Barracks 719, laying into the men of the 650th. Kapitz told the two hundred men in his company that they had disgraced themselves, that in a matter of hours, they had torn down a reputation that had taken months to build. It was 10 A.M., and a troop train was set to leave the fort at 5 P.M., with both the 650th and 651st Port Companies on board. Kapitz told his men they had seven hours to clean up and move out.

To Colonel Branson, however, those seven hours loomed like an eternity. As long as colored soldiers were staged within a stone's throw of the Italians, he worried that another uprising was still possible. Many other black soldiers were billeted on the post that day, a thousand or so who had not been involved in the riot. What would happen, wondered Branson, when *they* caught wind of the overnight uprising? Branson told Cooke he "didn't want to cause any commotion or have any intermingling or any rumors to get out that might arouse" the rest of the black soldiers in the fort.

As Branson scanned the faces of the officers gathered around him, he knew he had to be decisive. He ordered that every member of the 650th and 651st be trucked immediately to another part of the fort, to a holding area as far as reasonably possible from the Italians. Since the two companies were leaving for their overseas assignment—New Guinea by way of San Francisco—anyway, he ordered Colonel Baylies to move up the scheduled departure by four hours, to 1 P.M. He then told Colonel Kleinhen, the port's inspector general, to assign someone from his staff to ride along on that transport train, conducting interrogations on the way to California. The task of smoking out the "ringleaders, participants and accomplices" in the riot and murder would fall on the shoulders of that lone officer.

> "Of course, you knew at the time there were some murderers in that group of Colored troops. You had found a dead body and you knew there was a murderer there?"
>
> "That goes without saying, but that wasn't the thing I was thinking of."

Henry Kleinhen had hurried to his office at the Port of Embarkation headquarters on the Seattle waterfront. Following Branson's orders, he told Captain S. K. Tyson to start packing: he'd be boarding the troop train headed to Camp Stoneman in San Francisco, grilling witnesses and possible suspects along the way. But Kleinhen's guts were churning; he had detected uncertainty in Branson's voice and sniffed a whiff of panic in his orders. Kleinhen told General Cooke that he walked across the hall and rapped on the door of Colonel Fred Teague, the port's chief of staff. "I remonstrated on the advisability of sending an inspector general along with the shipment, and in general about the futility of such an action, and suggested that it would be hard to explain later why these units were sent on to Stoneman without giving proper time for the preliminary investigation and identifications and other necessary proceedings, while all personnel of both sides were present," he said.

The two colonels, Kleinhen remembered, speculated that the murder of a prisoner of war might have international repercussions and agreed that shipping the perpetrators out so soon might look like a cover-up. Unfortunately, Branson was not just the *post* commander that day—he was also the ranking officer for the entire *port;* General Eley Denson, the port commander, happened to be 260 miles away, speaking to the Spokane Chamber of Commerce about the pressing need for Women's Army Corps recruits. Colonel Teague figured it was an appointment that he could safely interrupt. After several phone calls, he finally reached the general.

"You questioned the advisability of getting rid of those troops?"

"I questioned the desirability of their leaving at that time, yes, sir."

"That presupposes—I am not trying to catch you now, Colonel—that presupposes a lack of judgment on the Post Commander [Branson], does it not?"

"It means that, at that time, I did not think his judgment was good on that particular point. I had, and still have, confidence in his judgment. I feel that he has exercised good judgment. I will say this in justification of that statement: he was quite excited, and he was very, very nervous, and very, very much disturbed, and his mental attitude was, of course, affected accordingly, and his judgment was affected accordingly."

After all he'd heard, Cooke was not surprised to hear a Fort Lawton officer described as excited, nervous, and disturbed. Under pressure, men up and down the chain of command seemed to have lost
judgment and perspective—assuming they had those qualities to begin with. General Denson, at least, had the good sense to counter-
mand Branson's orders and had quickly convinced the War Department
to delay the port companies' departure by at least three days, even
though it would affect the resources available to General MacArthur
in the Pacific.

If Colonel Branson and Major Orem had displayed little aptitude
for detective work, two of the enlisted men under Orem's command
seemed, at least, to have sufficient credentials for such a task. In civilian life, Private First Class George Durel had been a Louisiana state
trooper. His partner, Sergeant Carl Johnsen had been a police officer
in Kansas City. The morning after the riot, the two investigators, at
Orem's orders, combed the Italian barracks for a half hour, stopping
only when post engineers began sweeping broken glass and removing
damaged furniture. Carl Johnsen came to his interview with Cooke
carrying a short list of the evidence they had collected: "We found one
hatchet, one double-bladed axe, one golf club, three steel bed posts,
approximately four 2×4s about 2½ feet long, five cigarette post
stands—2×2 stands they are—a various assortment of rocks and
bricks, one round pointed shovel, one broom stick—three feet long
with a nail in the end—a fatigue hat and pack shovel." There were
also two tree limbs three feet long. Most of the evidence was found inside the Italians' buildings.

None of it, though, had been properly tagged, cataloged, or stored.
In fact, admitted Johnsen, most of the so-called evidence had simply
been gathered by the Italians themselves, who carried blood-stained
debris to their ravaged orderly room and dumped it in a pile.

"Do you have fingerprint apparatus?"
"Yes, sir."
"Did you all take any fingerprint impressions on them?"

"No, sir."

"Why was that?"

"We didn't have time. We had so many things to do there. We were receiving orders from everybody and we didn't know who was the boss of the thing."

Colonel Baylies told Cooke that he too was confused. Colonel Branson had expected him to lead some sort of investigation into how the whole mess had been allowed to happen, while at the same time being in charge of babysitting nearly four hundred black soldiers, some of whom were surely criminals. Was he supposed to be a detective or a jail guard? And what was he supposed to do with Major Orem, by now deprived of sleep, authority, and self-confidence? Just before noon, as members of the two port companies were marched to a mess hall to eat lunch, Baylies was shocked to see several of them carrying knives. Beside himself, he barreled over to Orem and demanded an explanation.

"I told the Provost Marshal, 'These men going around with knives hanging on their belts, what is the idea? Take them away!' Which he did, and he handled their property. I don't know anything further on that."

"As far as you know, the motivation behind this was fear of further disturbance, is that correct?"

"I will go further than that. In my experience in handling Colored troops, I always kept knives away from them at all times."

Major Orem confiscated a half-dozen hunting knives and switchblades yet failed once again to treat it as criminal evidence.

"Were any tags put on each of those knives to know who they belonged to?"

"No, sir."

"What was the reason for the search, if you didn't identify to whom they belonged?"

"The idea, as I understood it, was to take the knives so that they would cause no further trouble."

"Again, we are just trying to prevent further trouble instead of trying to apprehend culprits or murderers?"

"That was my idea."

"Then whatever evidence was found could not be used for evidence because nobody knows where they found them?"

"That's right."

To conduct the search, Orem had enlisted the help of soldiers from a newly arrived military police unit, the 749th Military Police Battalion, just up from San Francisco. In a strange twist, this was the very unit which had been called out in the middle of the night just a few weeks earlier to corral black sailors angered by the deadly explosions at Port Chicago. The 749th had since been transferred to Seattle at Colonel Branson's insistence, to help guard any future shipments of unrepentant Fascist Italian soldiers, like those who had rebelled at Fort Lawton on July 10. Amazingly, all 144 MPs and their five officers had been in their Lawton barracks throughout the night of August 14–15, yet no one at the post guardhouse knew they were on the post. To Cooke, it was somehow fitting that Major Orem had been so out of the loop that he too had no idea that men specially trained to handle just this kind of disturbance had been at his disposal but were never called.

By noon on August 15, Colonel Branson's initial battle plan had begun unraveling. First, Colonel Baylies begged off his assignment to head up the officers' board, telling Branson he simply did not have time to both ensure post security and to lead an investigation into how the post had responded. Soon after, Colonel Teague—the port's chief of staff—called to break the news that General Denson had overruled Branson's decision to ship the two companies out early and that Branson would in fact have to keep them safely locked up on his post for at least the next seventy-two hours, maybe longer. Denson had also overturned Branson's appointment of Colonel Kleinhen as chief of the criminal investigation. That job would go instead to Major Irving Crawford, head of the port's Military Intelligence Division.

One portion of Branson's agenda actually did go as planned. Working nonstop, Post Engineer George McNay's crew managed to erase all signs of disturbance in the Italian Area. Twelve carpenters, three electricians, a plumber, and a handful of painters and Italian laborers had replaced trim, panes, plasterboard, putty, and paint so that by 4 P.M. on August 15, all three barracks and the orderly room were in better shape than they had been just seventeen hours earlier.

Over at the post hospital, army doctors were still assessing the human damage. Of the thirty-two men admitted during the night—including twenty-six Italians and three black Americans, plus Farr, Perata, and Gould—more than a dozen were still in bad shape. Two had penetrating knife wounds, three others had fractured skulls; Italian sergeant Bruno Bigatti was barely clinging to life.

At 4:15 P.M., Durel and Johnsen, the post's criminal investigators, were ordered to report to Major Orem's office. Major Robert Manchester, Irving Crawford's chief assistant in the port's Military Intelligence Division, was introduced as the latest officer in charge of the criminal investigation. The good news was that Manchester had lots of civilian experience in law enforcement: he had been a police detective in Long Beach, California, for seventeen years. The bad news for Johnsen and Durel was that they were being pulled from the case. Manchester told them to hand over whatever evidence they had already collected and followed them to the basement of the provost marshal's office, where unlabeled sticks, shovels, axes, and rocks were stored in a haphazard pile. As Manchester told Cooke, the evidence had been handled so poorly that it was of absolutely no value in court.

"You have had experience in criminal investigations of this nature, have you not?"

"Yes, sir, I engaged in this type of work, of criminal investigation, for a period of over 20 years."

"From your experience, can you tell me any part of this criminal investigation that was conducted properly?"

"With the General's permission, I would like to contend that the part I have conducted was conducted properly, unless you are referring to the part before that."

"I am referring to the part which pertains to the protection and preservation of vital evidence?"

"In answer to that statement, sir, I would say that there was no part of the investigation, insofar as it deals with the preservation of the recognition of evidence, or the apprehension or identity of the offenders—I would say no part of it was handled correctly."

By the time taps sounded on August 15, hundreds of Fort Lawton soldiers and officers had gone almost two days with little or no sleep. Members of the 650th and 651st were crowded into the same temporary stockade built for the Fascist Italian prisoners who had refused to board the transit ship to Hawaii two months earlier. Confused and angry, they feared that they were all potential murder suspects, until proven otherwise. A few blocks away, on officers' row, General Denson, exhausted after a ten-hour drive from Spokane, sat up with Colonel Branson well past midnight, trying to figure the next move.

It was clear to General Cooke that the appalling incompetence of Colonel Branson and his officer corps might jeopardize the prosecution of suspected rioters. He was even more concerned that those same officers may have botched the murder investigation as well. Major Orem, for one, had continued his pattern of investigatory ineptitude with his decision making as he arrived at the crime scene beneath Olivotto's still-swaying corpse.

"Was any effort made to take pictures of the body while it was suspended by a rope?"

"No, sir."

"Was there any attempt made to look for car tracks in the road or footprints around the body?"

"Yes, sir."

"Was any attempt made to get impressions of the footprints and make plaster casts of them?"

"I protected those footprints until the investigators from the Port could see them."

"How many days or hours later was that?"

"It must have been one or two days later."

Olivotto's dead body had been barefoot, so a pair of prints in the damp leaves and twigs below his body caught everyone's eye. It had looked to Orem as if the prints were made by shoes, with the toes pointed uphill, facing the body. Yet Orem's "protection" of that crucial bit of evidence amounted to nothing more than covering it with a spare piece of cardboard torn from a box. His crime-scene sloppiness would quickly prove damaging.

Ten thousand troops had been stationed at Fort Lawton that day, and wartime routines had continued uninterrupted for most of them. Those routines included daily training exercises requiring soldiers to negotiate the obstacle course. Within hours of the discovery of Olivotto's body, more than one hundred soldiers had scrambled straight through the area where the Italian had been hung, effectively obliterating any last chance to find footprints, tire tracks, or signs of struggle near the scene of the lynching. Lieutenant Colonel Leo Beckley, the director of operations, blamed Section Commander Major Jesse Haire, who blamed Colonel Branson, who pointed fingers back at Beckley. General Cooke blamed them all.

Even so, crime scene evidence would have been important only if an actual crime had been committed. What if Olivotto had committed suicide? What if, during the riot, he had managed to locate a rope and find his way barefoot through the blackness of the bramble-strewn woods, all the way to the obstacle course at the base of the cliffs? Might the frightened, paranoid Italian have climbed the wooden planks attached to the tree trunk, walked out onto the cable, tied one end of the rope to the wire, slipped a noose around his neck, and jumped?

Both Carl Johnsen and George Durel thought such a scenario unlikely. Both investigators were with Major Orem when he first viewed the body still dangling by a noose. As law enforcement officers from the South, Johnsen and Durel each had plenty of experience investigating the aftermath of lynchings. In Johnsen's opinion, Olivotto had first been strangled elsewhere, then dragged to the obstacle course and strung up to make it look like a lynching. "The Italian's tongue wasn't hanging out when he was taken down," he observed. "We noticed that. And if he had been pulled up here by the rope and the weight of his body and all, in the majority of cases his tongue will come out, and it wasn't. I was under the impression that perhaps he was dead before he was taken up there, or he was partially unconscious."

Durel came to the same conclusion. One other detail caught his attention.

"I have seen a few, and the man's face wasn't blue."

"You mean from strangulation?"

"Yes, sir."

But a Fort Lawton doctor had conducted a complete autopsy later that same morning. Dr. John Walker told General Cooke that the two Southern cops were just plain wrong: "He was extremely blue in the face, marked plethora of the face. And when I examined the body before it was taken to the mortuary—as soon as it was received at the hospital—the rope was still around the neck, and there was marked blueness of the entire area above the rope-line and none below."

Captain John Walker was smart but young, just four years out of the University of Michigan medical school. Despite his tender age, he was the doctor in charge of three departments at Fort Lawton's spartan hospital: radiology, laboratory, and pathology. By 1944, he had already conducted nearly fifty military autopsies, an astonishing number considering none had been combat related. An army officer had been electrocuted after touching a power line while climbing on top of a railroad car. An enlisted black soldier had disappeared while swimming in Puget Sound; his bloated and partially decomposed body had washed ashore ten days later. Olivotto was Walker's first criminal autopsy.

> "Captain, from the mark under the rope, was there anything to indicate the manner in which he was hanged; for instance, did it appear that he was pulled up off the ground; that he was lifted up and the noose put around his neck and left to strangle; or, was he pushed off a high place and the rope was left to crack his neck?"
>
> "My own personal deduction would be he was lifted from the ground by the rope slung over a branch or a cable, or whatever it happened to be; since there was no evidence of fracture of the spine, nor dislocation, as it might be, not always but occasionally or usually happens when a man is pushed off a height."

The neck is one of the most delicate areas of the human body. A "broken" neck usually occurs only if a hanging victim jumps or is pushed from a sufficient height, creating enough force to pull the spinal cord apart. Whenever a rope is used, asphyxia, not spinal trauma, is a far more common cause of death. Once a noose tightens, the carotid arteries on either side of the neck are pinched, depriving the brain of oxygen and creating the equivalent of a stroke. Gray matter nerve endings begin dying right away, triggering a biochemical cascade that causes the brain to swell and sends the rest of the body into paralysis. It only takes about ten seconds to lose consciousness and two to three minutes for all organs to cease working. Although a pinched windpipe can contribute to the brain's suffocation, it takes only about fifteen pounds of pressure to stop the flow of life-giving blood in the carotids.

To Cooke, many signs pointed to suicide. Most men, he assumed, would put up a terrific resistance if they were about to be hung. When a strangulation victim struggles, veins in the whites of his eyes usually hemorrhage, leaving conspicuous dark spots. Dr. Walker did not observe such a condition during the autopsy and in fact found very few marks on Olivotto's body. The Italian was wearing only an undershirt and boxer shorts, yet there were no bruises anywhere, no broken bones, only a bit of dried mud on his bare feet and a few superficial scratches on the front of his legs. That Olivotto's hands were not tied behind his back was an indication of suicide.

Yet other evidence suggested murder. Of all the places Olivotto might have chosen to kill himself, the obstacle course seemed among the least likely. The site was a long, difficult distance from the Italian barracks. The obstacle course cable itself was a mere ten feet off the ground at the point of the hanging; the rope was fourteen feet long. In the black of night, Olivotto would have had to be able to secure the rope to the cable tightly enough to support the full weight of his 155-pound body and to measure it at a precise length so that after jumping, his feet would not reach the ground. The rope had been tied a mere three feet away from the top rung of the wooden ladder planks nailed to the trunk of the southern maple, a convenient distance for a murderer who might have put the noose around Olivotto's neck, then thrown the other end of the rope over the cable and lifted Olivotto from the ground, as Dr. Walker had surmised. Once Olivotto was dead, his assailant could have climbed the rungs to secure the rope, trying to make it look like a suicide. Cooke pursued the possibility further with Walker.

"Did you remove the rope from his neck?"

"Yes, sir."

"In what manner was it tied?"

"The rope was spliced, a small noose, I would say, 2 inches in diameter and the other end of the rope was brought through this small loop, to make a complete noose. There was no knot tied, except a splice; a loop splice, two inches in diameter and the free end brought through the loop, which gives an ordinary slip knot, but not actually the kind of slip knot you would tie."

"That part of the loop that was spliced, was it a hasty splice?"

"No, sir, it was well-spliced."

"Was it a manufactured splice, or a hand splice?"

"It was a hand splice."

"Was it well done?"

"As I recall, it was fairly well done. I don't think it was an expert's job, but someone who knew how to splice."

"Would it have been possible to splice such a rope in the dark, within 5 or 10 minutes?"

"No, sir, not unless the man was an extremely expert splicer."

Several Italians had reported watching Olivotto leap in terror out of the window next to his bunk as rioters closed in on Barracks 709. None saw him carrying a rope, and he was not someone known to have any interest or skill in splicing. Captain Sturdevant, the fort psychiatrist, told Cooke that despite Olivotto's professed fear of black men, a methodical suicide in the heat of an attack was an extremely unlikely reaction to that kind of assault.

Cooke struggled with several other conundrums. Durel, Johnsen, Orem, and Robinson had all observed footprints in the mud beneath the body; none had been made by bare feet. Although Olivotto's hands were not tied, it was possible that he had passed out before being strung up or that his arms had been bound behind him with something soft, like a shirt, then untied after he died to make it look like suicide. That scenario wouldn't explain, of course, why the murderer might have wanted the death to seem unrelated to the riot; wouldn't he have wanted his murderous act to send some sort of message? Maybe, after lynching Olivotto, the killer suddenly realized the seriousness of his crime and thought it better to make the death seem self-inflicted.

There were other questions too. If black soldiers had wanted to injure or even kill Olivotto, why hadn't they used sticks and knives, as they had against all the other Italians? If they had wanted to hang someone, why go all the way to the base of the bluffs to do it? If they had carried Olivotto to the obstacle course, why were there no bruises on his body? If they dragged him, why were there only superficial abrasions on his legs? Perhaps Olivotto somehow made his way, barefoot, all the way to the beach by himself and happened across the rioters there. In that case, what were black soldiers doing so far from the riot, and why did they have a rope, and why was he the only Italian injured someplace other than the immediate vicinity of the barracks and orderly room? Finally, did it make sense that black men—the traditional victims of vigilante hangings—would, for the first time in American history, be the perpetrators of a mob lynching?

Was it possible that someone else did it, hoping it would be blamed on the rioters? Did Olivotto willingly hide in the woods with someone he assumed was his friend, only to be betrayed once they reached the obstacle course? Or what if Olivotto had been driven down to the base of the cliffs by someone he thought he could trust? That at least would explain the lack of bruises and scratches on his body. And Private Lomax, if he could be believed, testified that he had been on the lookout for a missing jeep when he discovered Olivotto's body.

They were all good questions, but Cooke didn't need to answer them in order to complete his mission. On balance, he concluded that the evidence pointed to murder, not suicide. The guilt or innocence of any suspects would be determined by a court-martial, assuming an army prosecutor could collect enough evidence to file charges and bring them to trial. Considering the mess made by Branson, Orem, and the rest, that prosecutor would have his work cut out.

AFTER TWO WEEKS of interrogations, General Cooke returned to the Pentagon, where he sat down at his typewriter and tried to sort out the merely negligent from the grossly incompetent. In any other setting, he might have been more upset with Captain Christensen, the duty officer who had clearly turned a blind eye toward Sergeant Tanner's unauthorized party and who may have been AWOL between eleven and twelve that night, then lied about it under oath. "However," Cooke wrote, "the whereabouts of Captain Christensen, while questionable in itself, has no direct bearing upon the riot which subsequently took place, since no information was received at headquarters regarding the disorder in question, and Captain Christensen did not know that such disturbance had taken place until the following morning." Cooke noted that it had been unusual, if not downright inappropriate, for Colonel Branson to appoint Christensen to serve on the original three-man Board of Officers charged with investigating the cause of riot, especially since Christensen hid the fact that he had been the duty officer that night from his two fellow officers on the board. Overall, Cooke viewed the board's minimal effort as little more than a dog-and-pony show, designed to make it appear the fort was taking action. "In a rather brief report," wrote Cooke, "this Board found the 650th and 651st Port Companies responsible for the damage done to the various buildings, and recommended that the cost of repairs [$218.16] be collected from members of those two organizations [roughly fifty-four cents each], without, however, having determined just which members had participated in the disturbance." Although Cooke might have recommended discipline for Christensen, he decided there were other—and in many cases bigger—fish to fry.

He was thoroughly disgusted with Lomax and Robinson. "The conduct of the two MPs, Sgt. Robinson and Pvt. Lomax, who first saw the riot forming, yet failed to take immediate steps toward the quelling of that disturbance, reflects, if not cowardice, a decided lack of proper training and a clear violation of the 96th Article of War. Despite these facts, neither of these men have been censored [sic] nor punished in any way." The Ninety-sixth Article of War was a catch-all statute that included "Conduct to the Prejudice of Good Order and Military Discipline." Cooke suggested that both soldiers, "not only by allowing a riot to form in their presence without attempting to prevent it, but also by not immediately informing their superiors of what was taking place, deserved to be court-martialed." He did not, however, specifically raise the possibility that Lomax himself might be a plausible murder suspect.

Collectively, all the other military policemen on duty August 14 suffered Cooke's wrath. "None of these MPs could or would identify a single Negro as having participated in the riot, although Sgt. Jones and his companions were in a fully-lighted orderly room for from 15 to 20 minutes with a large number of rioters. Because of this, the investigating officers cannot help but believe that the white MPs had, for some undetermined reason, agreed amongst themselves not to identify any of the rioters." Perhaps the white MPs had been pleased that black soldiers were doing the "dirty work" against Italians the whites so resented for being granted so much relative freedom. If so, Cooke couldn't say.

There was no equivocation about Major Orem. "The failure to secure identifications, which might reasonably be expected as a necessary requisite for subsequent disciplinary action, is considered particularly reprehensible," Cooke wrote, "because it rendered the final detection of the participants more difficult and certainly contributed to some of the guilty persons escaping justice. Furthermore, Major Orem's decision to tell Colonel Branson that 'everything was under control,' when from 20 to 30 persons lay seriously (some critically) injured, with not a single one of their attackers either apprehended or identified, constituted such an incomplete presentation of the facts and reflected such a decided lack of discernment for an officer of his grade, or such a complete failure to appreciate his duties and responsibilities under the circumstances, or both, as to raise question as to his qualifications for his grade and present assignment." In other words, General Cooke wanted Orem fired from his post and the army major's oak cluster removed from his shoulder.

The ranking officer at Fort Lawton that night was, of course, Colonel Branson. "The actions of Colonel Branson with relation to this entire affair can scarcely be construed as those of a competent commander when confronted with an emergency," Cooke lashed. While conceding that Major Orem had not been forthcoming during the late night phone call, "it is believed that Colonel Branson should have immediately determined the proportions and seriousness of the disturbance which had been reported to him." General Cooke warned that, if it turned out that Branson actually understood the extent and seriousness of what was occurring on his post, "yet failed to instigate an immediate investigation looking toward the administration of justice, such act of omission would be deemed extremely reprehensible." Branson's order to repair the Italian barracks before detectives could look for clues "contributed greatly to the confusion of subsequent investigations and also to the difficulty of administering justice." His aborted attempt to ship the two companies on an earlier train "clearly indicated a failure to appreciate the gravity of the situation confronting him in connection with the maintenance of proper discipline and the administration of military justice." Finally, Cooke was appalled that neither Branson nor those under his command took reasonable steps after the riot to personally determine who had dropped the ball. That failure to seek accountability, he concluded, "evidences such laxity as to raise question as to his ability to command."

On September 20, Major Orem was relieved of his duties as provost marshal and was replaced by Captain Christensen. Eight days later, Captain Beckman was dismissed as commander of the Twenty-eighth ISU. At the same time, secret plans were being discussed to relieve Colonel Branson of his command of Fort Lawton.

Guglielmo Olivotto, Italian Private

Corporal Luther Larkin   Sergeant Aurthur Hurks   Private William G. Jones

Staff Sergeant Grant Farr (l)
and Staff Sergeant Fred Perata (r),
28th Italian Service Unit,
Fort Lawton

Camp Florence,
Arizona

Fort Lawton,
Washington

Brigadier General Elliot D.
"Cookie" Cooke, Army Inspector
General, Overseas Division

Lieutenant Colonel Leon Jaworski,
Trial Judge Advocate

Major William Beeks, Defense Attorney

Broken column marking grave of Guglielmo Olivotto, on perimeter of Fort Lawton Cemetery

CHAPTER EIGHT

JAWORSKI
October 1944

EARLY-MORNING FOG ROSE through Seattle's steep downtown streets, carrying a whiff of creosote and a pinch of salt, muffling the rumble of the delivery trucks along Fourth Avenue. From his window at the Olympic Hotel, Lieutenant Colonel Leon Jaworski gazed down at the intersection of Fourth and University, where ghostly figures in gray fedoras and pale cloth coats waited for the light to change. With each traffic signal circuit, streams of office workers poured into crosswalks, circling the sidewalks before draining into the grand entrances of office buildings and shops for another day behind a desk or at a counter.

Jaworski felt miserable. The train trip from Dallas had seemed endless, made all the more unbearable after his rail car's air conditioner seized up and quit working. Sweltering in the stale air of his first-class berth, Jaworski had to step outside at each station stop for a cool breath, even in the middle of the night. Soon enough, his throat had tightened and his head grew heavy, sure signs that a cold would be his companion during his first few days in Seattle.

A pile of papers on the polished hotel desk included an envelope that had been waiting for his arrival. Jeannette, his wife of thirteen years, had wanted her husband to keep his family in mind as he began what would apparently be another ambiguously long assignment. The war had taken her Leon away from home for more than two years and counting, leaving Jeannette to care for three young children and a new house in Houston, all on a substantially smaller paycheck than what he had been earning as an up-and-coming trial lawyer. In the letter, Jeannette wrote of how Joanie, Claire, and Joe were all settling in at school and how the house was slowly getting into order. She was thrilled to report that a man from the telephone company had finally come by to install a telephone, although she was mighty unhappy to learn that the phone directory listing would be in her name only, a rather embarrassing circumstance for a respectable married woman. But having a telephone meant Leon had fewer excuses for not staying in touch, since his family would be just a long-distance call away.

Washing down two sulfa pills with a bottle of Dr Pepper, Jaworski, instead of phoning, pulled out a fresh sheet of Olympic Hotel stationery.

Dear Sweetie:

Thanks so much for writing me—so that I had a letter waiting for me at the Port when I reported there. It gave me a lift—and the news—especially about the phone—was so good. You and the children must write me all the news you can think of and as often as possible—because from the looks of things, I will not only be here for a long time but in addition, I will have my hands "plenty full."

In truth, Jaworski had been ecstatic about the assignment. He knew Jeannette did not fully appreciate what prosecuting this murder case at Fort Lawton might mean to his army career:

Honey, this is really a big job I am on. It's being watched closely in Washington. Yesterday and to-day (this morning) I spent conferring, and Monday I will start rolling up my sleeves.

Since joining the army in 1942, most of Jaworski's postings had been within a few hundred miles of his Houston home. Born and raised in Texas, he had never quite seen a place like Seattle:

This city is most uniquely situated. Actually it is on top of mountains—which overlook the water. Ships come and go and the sights are interesting. As time goes on, I will probably get to do some water traveling in these parts. The last two mornings have been foggy—by noon the sun was out. When I walk from the bus line to my Hotel I climb a *steep* hill—*plenty steep!* I huff and I puff.

He told Jeannette about his cold, but assured her he would drink plenty of liquids and get lots of rest, scaling back on his only two vices, scotch and cigars. He reluctantly asked her to mail his heavy winter coat, realizing it might set off alarms about just how long this assignment might last. To soften the sting, he turned the topic to their children:

Well, I didn't think Joanie would lose much time getting oriented in school. Has she taken flowers already? Just wait till Daddy's camellias cut loose. Am so glad the boy is getting going on his Cub work. Honey, is his football on? He was doing so well kicking and throwing last year. And Claire is stepping out! Tell her to be sure to write me if Charles is a good dancer. I hope that some way the children's dancing can be kept up—even if they can't go very often. But remember, one of these days your gas coupons will be gone and your car will be largely grounded. So try to find a place they can reach by bus.

Knowing money was tight, Jaworski offered advice about how to conserve ration coupons—a skill Jeannette had undoubtedly mastered long ago. Because he had grown up poor, it pained him to realize that his army paycheck was so miserly, yet the war was pinching everyone, and he knew Jeannette was not one to complain. In any event, he didn't plan to waste much money on long-distance phone charges:

Well I must sign off and drop down to eat. Eating prices are high here. Glad the Gov't is giving me $7.00 per day.—
Better buy you some air-mail stamps and always keep some on hand. Regular mail takes much too long. The time in Houston is

two hours later than it is here. I am so glad you have the phone—
About that listing, hope people don't think we are on a marital
vacation.

Well here goes all my love again to each of you—don't forget
to write. —Affectionately, Leon

No other lawyer in America may have been better suited to prosecute the Fort Lawton court-martial than Leon Jaworski. At thirty-nine,
Jaworski had been a hard-charging litigator for nearly two decades,
tackling high-profile topics like racial discrimination, organized crime,
and corporate fraud. His civilian résumé included time as a criminal
defense attorney; his military experience included prosecution of soldiers charged with murdering prisoners of war. He would eventually
earn worldwide notoriety for his prosecution of Nazi war criminals in
Europe and for his role in both the Warren Commission's investigation of President John Kennedy's assassination and as the special prosecutor who helped expose President Richard Nixon's complicity in the
Watergate scandal. But those prestigious assignments would not have
come his way unless he had managed to impress his superiors with the
way he handled the huge case he now faced in Seattle.

He was christened Leonidas Jaworski, named after an ancient war-
rior king of Sparta. His father, Joseph Jaworski, was born in Crakow,
Poland, later moving to Germany to become an evangelical pastor.
There Joseph met Marie, an émigré from Austria, and the couple had
two sons, Joe Jr. and Hannibal, the latter fancifully named for yet another ancient gladiator. In 1903, the family boarded a steamship for
America, drawn to the flat plains of central Texas where hundreds of
German immigrants had already settled. Leonidas—his family called
him "Nidi"—was born in Waco in 1905; a younger sister, Mary, followed one year later. Soon after, their mother became ill and died.

Young Leon did not mix easily with boys and girls his own age. He
was short, not particularly athletic, and had a squat, square head that
gave him what he liked to call a "muffin face." Other children teased
him about his thick German accent, the product of a home where few

books or conversations were in English. When America entered World
War I in 1917, Germans were fair game for taunts and scorn. Even in
Waco, proud home to dozens of churches and to Baptist-run Baylor
University, prejudice was rampant. Leon later remembered that Wa-
coans called sauerkraut "liberty cabbage," and streets such as Wagner
Avenue and Beethoven Drive were renamed Pershing Avenue and Wilson Drive. Joseph Jaworski, pastor of Evangelical Zion Church, coun-
seled his children to turn the other cheek and infused a deep sense
of humorless dedication to God, church, family, and community.
Joseph remarried, to a German-speaking neighbor in his congregation
and, like many immigrant parents, was strict about schoolwork. Joe Jr.
became an engineer, Hannibal a physician, and Leon, who loved to
talk and argue, entered Baylor's fledgling law school.

With neither girls nor football to distract him, Leon graduated with
a law degree at age nineteen. A state rule prohibited him from taking
the bar exam until he turned twenty-one, but in 1925 Jaworski became the youngest lawyer in Texas history after successfully petition-
ing for an exception. He loved being a lawyer and buried himself in
his work, leaving home before the sun rose each day and returning
long after dark. No Renaissance man, he ignored most pursuits not directly tied to becoming a better, more successful litigator, something
he later commented on in his autobiography: "I have no patience with
minutiae. I have spent my life cutting through trivia, getting to the
core of a story. Maybe this is why I have read, from beginning to end,
only two long novels in my lifetime: *Gone with the Wind* and *Dr.
Zhivago*."

Early on, Jaworski earned most of his money defending wealthy
Texas bootleggers arrested for running whiskey across the Mexican
border. His first highly publicized case, however, came as the court-
appointed lawyer for Jordan Scott, an illiterate black tenant farmer on
trial for his life. Scott was charged with the murders of Mamie and
Robert Pedigo, a young white couple for whom he had recently
worked. At the time, Jaworski considered the death penalty barbaric
and eagerly believed his client's story that someone else had killed

the Pedigos. He was also moved by Scott's grim recollections about the abuse and intimidation he suffered at the hands of police in the Pedigo investigation, including an alleged threat to turn him over to a lynch mob if he failed to put his X on a written confession.

The Waco newspapers had all but convicted Scott, and Jaworski was targeted with jeers and anonymous threats, including demands that he stop defending a "murdering Nigger." Waco, like many Southern towns in the 1920s, was controlled by the Ku Klux Klan. By Jaworski's count, all but one judge and one or two other lawyers in Waco and McLennan counties were members of the Klan. The mayor and city police chief were high-ranking KKK officials, as was the publisher of the local newspaper. On one occasion, Jaworski stood slack-jawed as a hooded posse appeared in broad daylight and tackled a man suspected of being a pimp, beating him with fists and clubs, and stripping off his clothes. He lamented about how otherwise good, God-fearing people could be so easily swept up by a movement that blamed minorities, immigrants, and non-Protestants for every social and economic ill—a human failing that would haunt him years later during his prosecution of war criminals.

He was given little time to investigate facts in Jordan Scott's defense; the judge feared a midnight lynching party might raid the jailhouse if a trial were delayed. In court, Jaworski faced a prosecutor willing to use invective and innuendo, and the all-white, all-male jury took just one hour to return a verdict of guilty and a sentence of death. Undaunted, Jaworski won a new trial, based on prosecutorial misconduct. With more time for research, he finally tracked down the man whom his client had accused of being the real killer. But to Jaworski's horror, the other man had an ironclad alibi, and Scott was forced to confide that he had in fact killed the Pedigos, allegedly in self-defense. A second trial followed, with the same result. Jordan Scott would be the first and only client Leon Jaworski ever lost to the electric chair.

Jaworski continued to bury himself in his work, eventually catching the eye of well-regarded law firms in Houston. There he built a successful practice from the wallets of a goodly share of "perfect" clients:

men with lots of money who made lots of mistakes. In particular, Houston was crawling with wildcat oilmen who learned to trust Jaworski's courtroom skills whenever they broke something, like a contract or another oilman's jaw.

Pearl Harbor changed everything. Jaworski was then a thirty-seven-year-old father of three with high blood pressure and an elevated pulse. He could have avoided service on medical grounds but felt compelled to heed the army's call for much-needed military lawyers. As the army ballooned to include almost ten million men and women, the number of crimes within the military rose accordingly; during 1944 alone, some eighteen thousand soldiers were convicted by general courts-martial. Men with Jaworski's trial skills were offered all the work they could handle. "My wife accepted my decision quietly," he later wrote. "She was the one who would have to manage the children, and our home, on my army pay and whatever savings we had. Jeannette never uttered a negative thought. It was not until months after the war that she told me she had spent sleepless nights, worrying about my leaving my family and law practice to join a young man's war."

He was assigned to the Eighth Service Command, based in Dallas, and quickly earned assignments prosecuting some of the toughest military cases in the Southwest. In one instance, three black soldiers were accused of raping a twenty-year-old white woman at Camp Claiborne, Louisiana. The soldiers claimed they had paid the woman for sex and that their liaison had been consensual. The defense team included future Supreme Court Justice Thurgood Marshall, representing the NAACP Legal Defense Fund. Nonetheless, Jaworski won a conviction, and the three men were sentenced to death by hanging. His earlier objection to the death penalty had softened: "No matter how serious the charge, there is often sympathy for anyone who has been called to serve his country. I find such sympathy misplaced. I felt regret, but mostly anger, at the creative ways these men dishonored their uniform. Soldiers, like law officers and politicians, are figures of authority whose actions are essential to the public order. They must be held accountable, swiftly and fully, for their misdeeds."

In December 1943, Jaworski was promoted from the rank of major to lieutenant colonel and selected to lead a series of particularly sensitive murder prosecutions. German prisoners of war were often ruthless whenever they caught one of their own cooperating with American captors; suspected collaborators were sometimes killed. The POW murder trials were conducted in absolute secrecy, in part to keep nearby American civilians in the dark about the Nazis in their neighborhood but also to avoid giving Hitler a further excuse to mistreat American airmen in German custody.

With his flair for investigation and his fluency in German, Jaworski rose to the challenge. Key witnesses, despite fears of retaliation, fell under Jaworski's spell and agreed to testify against the killers. In one case at Camp Chaffee, Arkansas, an unrepentant Nazi received the death penalty, although his sentence was later reduced to twenty years in prison. In another case at Camp Tonkawa, Texas, five men were convicted and, although authorities waited to enforce the sentence until after Germany surrendered, became the first World War II POWs on American soil to hang from the gallows.

Jaworski was a rising star in the Judge Advocate General's Corps. When the War Department needed someone who wouldn't botch the Fort Lawton prosecution, word went out that Jaworski was their man.

GENERAL COOKE HAD already departed Seattle by the time Leon Jaworski arrived, but Cooke's assistant, Curtis Williams, continued to interrogate witnesses, and Jaworski was invited to sit in. The prosecutor was briefed about how Colonel Branson and his subordinates had botched the initial investigation and was told from the start that much of the physical evidence had been misplaced or destroyed. True to form, Jaworski was determined to press ahead, using his own interrogation skills to try to persuade other witnesses to plug gaps in the evidence.

Jaworski soon learned that nearly all of Fort Lawton's military policemen remained stubbornly unable or unwilling to identify any of the rioters. He also confirmed that most of the Italians could not finger specific black soldiers; it had been too dark and chaotic, and the faces of the attacking soldiers had been too unfamiliar to leave clear, reliable impressions.

One Italian, however, mysteriously stood out from the rest. Augusto Todde, the sergeant major, was one of three ranking noncommissioned officers in the Twenty-eighth ISU. Todde told Jaworski what he had told Cooke and Williams, that he had played a huge role the night of the riot. Todde swore that he had tried to awaken both Gould in his tent and Farr in the orderly room, and he took credit for shoving Haskell out of harm's way during the height of the melee. Some of Todde's behavior had clearly been less than heroic, including hiding for several minutes in Farr's armoire as attackers threw rocks at Building 713 and later flipping the light switch off in the main room, making it harder for victims to identify their assailants. On the other hand, he had suffered injury—slashed with a knife across his forehead—and he had known the murder victim; he had been the highest-ranking NCO in Guglielmo Olivotto's barrack.

What most attracted Jaworski, though, was Todde's willingness to pinpoint individual American soldiers. One week after the riot, Todde was among twenty Italians transported to Camp George Jordan, a small army facility south of downtown Seattle, where all members of the 650th and 651st Port Companies had been temporarily sequestered. Four hundred black soldiers were ordered to walk past in single file as Todde and nineteen other members of his ISU studied their faces. While most Italians drew a complete blank, and a few others said they recognized one or two each, Todde had somehow been able to pick out nine men whom he said had unquestionably been in the Italian Area, most armed with clubs, several doing violence. To Jaworski, Todde seemed confident and articulate, shedding light in places where none of his fellow Italians could.

While the memories of other Italians seemed to fade, Todde's only grew sharper. Weeks after the attack, he confidently identified three additional men, then two more, then yet another two. In time, he was willing to pick out a total of sixteen men whom he swore had been in or around the fighting. As Jaworski looked on, Colonel Williams handed Todde a stack of mug shots.

"Todde, you realize the importance of being positive in this identification, as upon your word may depend the freedom or imprisonment of the man?"

"I understand that."

"You are still positive this is the man you saw in the orderly room of the Italian Area?"

"Yes, sir."

Augusto Todde was thirty-six years old. Born in Italy, he moved to Tripoli at age nineteen, where he found work as a radio dispatcher for a tour bus company. He spent seven years in the Italian military during Mussolini's initial African campaign, then was recalled into the army at age thirty-one, just as Il Duce joined forces with Adolf Hitler. Before being taken prisoner at Cape Bon, Todde had been assigned to the Signal Corps, setting up radio stations and coordinating radio intelligence. He was among the smartest and most experienced men in the Twenty-eighth ISU.

But there were other things in Todde's background that Jaworski did not know. During his time at Camp Florence in Arizona, Todde had been among those identified by U.S. army Intelligence as potential fascist infiltrators. Although he signed a standard loyalty oath as a prerequisite to acceptance into the service unit, an army screening team had labeled Todde a prisoner to be watched. A handwritten notation on the prison roster warned that Todde was "described as being sly and probably still pro-Nazi." His application into an ISU was accepted only because the screeners considered Todde "willing to work." He had originally been assigned to a unit headed for Camp Roberts in California but happened to be in the hospital the day his transport departed. Officials later reassigned him to the Twenty-eighth just as it left for Fort Lawton.

Within three weeks of the unit's arrival at Fort Lawton, two other

Italians on the To Be Watched list were taken away, banished to the segregation camp in Monticello, Arkansas. At the time, the Pentagon's in-box overflowed with reports of Fascist cliques operating inside ISUs, despite public reassurances that unrepentant troublemakers had been filtered out and locked away. In some service units, Italians who cooperated with Americans were openly bullied by Fascist Italian officers, compromising discipline and morale. There were no such reports of intimidation, however, at Fort Lawton.

Another Italian was an even more problematic witness: the man who may have helped start the entire riot. Guiseppe Belle was the POW who held his ground as Willie Montgomery hurled drunken slurs toward him and the two other Italians returning from their August 14 night on the town. When Montgomery bulled toward the trio, it was Belle who struck him in the jaw, claiming later that he thought he saw the flash of a knife blade in Montgomery's hand.

If army bureaucrats had done their paperwork properly, Belle would have never set foot in Fort Lawton. Early on, he had been identified by officials at Camp Florence as stridently pro-Fascist and/or pro-Nazi. On February 26, 1944, Belle's name was included on a list of prisoners to be transferred, not merely watched. Orders were drafted to ship Belle immediately to Camp Hereford, Texas, the heavily guarded compound holding only the most dangerous Italians. Belle, however, had been picking cotton at one of Florence's remote side camps in California and managed to slip through cracks during the initial segregation of known Fascists. A notation next to his name on the camp roster read "Condemned by G-2; fascist and revolutionary element." G-2, the Army Intelligence branch, had reached its conclusions by infiltrating the POW work camps and by interrogating Italian prisoners. A "condemned" designation was the most severe, indicating a POW posed an immediate and serious threat.

Belle, however, continued to duck under the radar, sliding unnoticed onto the list of those cleared in May for shipment to Fort Lawton. If Belle had been properly diverted to Camp Hereford, the spark for what became a riot may have been quickly extinguished. As it was, the army's mistake was never brought to Jaworski's attention, and Belle joined Todde on Jaworski's list of key cooperating witnesses.

With Belle and Todde in hand, Jaworski turned his attention to Private First Class Roy Montgomery. Roy—no relation to Willie Montgomery—had been singled out by more than a dozen men, white and Italian, as the one black soldier they were sure they had seen in the Italian Area during the riot. But Montgomery had also been definitively identified by Farr and others as a man who had bravely helped calm other rioters inside the Italian orderly room. Jaworski knew that Private Montgomery was a central figure and was determined to have him in his corner at trial.

Roy stood out because he was light-skinned. Three of his four grandparents were black, but his maternal grandfather was part Irish and part Cherokee. Roy grew up on his grandfather's farm in Leflore County, Mississippi, but after completing eighth grade he fled the poverty and segregation of the Mississippi Delta. He found work stenciling crates in a Detroit airplane factory and, later, making caskets. Drafted in 1943, he was shipped to Fort Lawton for basic training and assigned to the 651st Port Company as a hatch tender—a dockworker who signals a winch operator as slings of cargo are loaded and unloaded onto ships. He had a few close friends, but not many: the color of his skin had earned him the derogatory nickname "Mulatto."

Facing his interrogators, Montgomery had readily admitted heading into the Italian Area on August 14 with a fence post in his hand. He confessed to entering the orderly room and even to hitting a fleeing Italian on the back of the head but agreed with Farr's recollection that he, Roy, had been a peacemaker. He saw Sergeant Farr, "the one who wears the glasses," and Farr said, "We are Americans." He also saw Perata over in the corner. He had been hit on the head and was bleeding. "I don't know whether he had been stabbed or not," Montgomery said. Farr "just said, 'We are Americans,' and I said, 'We won't bother you all,' and I held up my hand to the guys that was coming in and the fight ceased. They stopped when I held up my hand."

Jaworski was baffled by this soft-spoken twenty-three-year-old.

With his eighth-grade education, Roy was sharper than many; he was religious and his demeanor was polite. Jaworski was encouraged when Montgomery quietly offered up the names of a few of the black soldiers who were with him in the orderly room, including two of his friends, Slick Curry of Shreveport and Johnnie Ceaser of Chicago. Because so many had sworn they'd seen a light-skinned Negro in the Italian Area, Jaworski figured he had Montgomery cornered, and that he'd be willing to cut a deal. But to his surprise, his offer of immunity in exchange for Roy's testimony went nowhere. Montgomery, it turned out, was indignant about the way he and other suspects had been treated. For weeks, he'd been stuck in the stockade, pulled in and out of interrogations, first by Orem's men, then by detectives and officers from the port, and finally by Williams and Jaworski. As days passed, word got out that certain men in the company had been ratting out fellow black soldiers, and Roy—because he was gone so often—was a prime suspect. On four separate occasions, Roy provided his interrogators with written statements, but each time army investigators demanded more names and details than he could honestly give. Even worse, Roy's inquisitors repeatedly reneged on what he took to be specific promises to move him out of the stockade, away from threats of retaliation. By the time Jaworski suggested that he become a prosecution witness, he'd had enough and refused to cooperate any further. It was an unexpected blow to a lawyer whose ability to charm potential turncoats rarely failed him.

Burned by Montgomery's rejection, Jaworski doubled his efforts to find black soldiers willing to take the stand on behalf of the army. Some, he assumed, might be motivated to save their own skins, hoping to trade testimony for a reduced sentence or outright immunity. Others, he suspected, would want to settle old scores, offering incriminating tidbits to get back at rivals. Still others might be inspired simply by a moral duty to obey orders and tell the truth, even if it meant implicating themselves and others. Jaworski grilled dozens of suspects from the 650th and 651st for hours on end, probing for details and searching for vulnerabilities. During several days of interrogations, only ten to twelve black soldiers were willing to name names. Jaworski soon discovered, however, that those with ulterior motives—immunity, revenge, and so on—showed more promise as witnesses, because they were more willing to reduce complicated events into black-and-white explanations. On the other hand, those who felt bound to tell the unvarnished truth tended to acknowledge shades of gray, a potential problem for a prosecutor seeking the death penalty. In the end, he settled on five black soldiers to provide the core of his case in chief.

The first was nineteen-year-old Dan Roy Daymond, a private from Houston, one of the youngest soldiers in the 650th. Daymond told Jaworski that on the night of August 14, he had been excited and anxious about heading overseas and had tried to calm his nerves by taking in a movie at the post theater. Afterward, as he strolled back to his barracks, a rowdy din echoed throughout the Colored Area, a jittery mix of drunken songs, loud laughter, and the shrill howls of excited gamblers. As he approached Sergeant Tanner's party in the mess hall, Luther Larkin burst out the door, with his buddy William Jones beside him. Willie Montgomery, clearly drunk, staggered behind them. Related Daymond, "And about that time, Montgomery said, 'All those other boys in the company 578th have been raising sand, because we have been working, and those Italians haven't been doing anything. Let's go down there and fool with those Italians.' And I said, 'No, we are leaving here, and there is no sense staying and bothering those Italians.'"

Just at that moment, the Italians Belle, Pisciottano, and Fumarola appeared on Lawton Road. "Montgomery asked them to 'hush up all that God-damned noise,'" Daymond said. "One of them spoke something in their language and Montgomery ran back there where they were walking and that was when he was hit."

Daymond told Jaworski that he ran forward, scooping rocks from the berm and hurling them in the direction of the fleeing Italians. Willie Montgomery had collapsed on the asphalt, eyes shut and breathing labored. Daymond, a strapping Texas teenager, scooped the skinny thirty-nine-year-old from New York in his arms and began carrying him up the road toward Barracks 719. Luther Larkin approached, he said, and shared the load by grabbing Willie's legs. As they drew closer to the light outside 719, Larkin looked at Willie's face—it seemed he was no longer breathing. Corporal Larkin ordered Daymond to lay Willie on the sidewalk, then searched in vain for a pulse. Daymond told Jaworski that Willie's foolishness had angered both him and Luther: "We tried to bring him to, but I wasn't successful. I just stood over there and looked at him and told him, 'It is a good thing—you ought to get hit. I would have let them alone.'"

As a crowd gathered, Daymond helped Luther roll Willie onto his stomach, stretching the unconscious soldier's arms above his head. Luther, he said, straddled Willie's thighs and began artificial respiration, pushing the heels of his hands into Willie's rib cage, just below his shoulder blades. For more than a minute, he rocked back and forth, lifting Willie's elbows to open his lungs, then pushing his middle back to expel the air. Finally, the drunken soldier began to cough.

Daymond remembered feeling relieved. The growing crowd of soldiers had been peppering him with questions; William Jones, he said, told everyone that Willie had been attacked by Italians. Moments later, Private Lomax and Sergeant Robinson pulled up in their MP jeep. As soon as Willie was carted away, Luther turned to go inside the barracks. Luther, remembered Daymond, said something about sounding an alarm, alerting the company that one of their fellow soldiers had been wounded: "He asked me did I have a whistle and I told him, yes. I didn't see him with a whistle. I later heard a whistle blown in the vicinity of 700, but I don't know who was blowing the whistle."

Jaworski knew Daymond's testimony would be crucial to his case. At a minimum, Daymond could help establish that black soldiers provoked the attack, apparently in misguided retaliation on behalf of Willie Montgomery, who had brought it all on in the first place with his drunken tirade. Daymond, though young, was streetwise, carrying a rap sheet from a youth spent running with a tough crowd in a part of Houston so destitute that only a few homes even had electricity. Jaworski, whose family lived on the decidedly wealthier side of

Houston's tracks, recognized in Daymond a certain charm, a matter-of-fact manner that might play well in court. He offered Daymond total immunity in exchange for his testimony. Daymond snapped it up.

A second Texan seemed even more valuable. Private Jesse Sims was a tall thirty-two-year-old who had grown up on a farm in Corrigan, near Austin. Sims spent most of his life as a manual laborer; he could neither read nor write. He could match drinks with anyone and loved to gamble. Sims told Jaworski that he had been inside Barracks 719 when Luther's friend, William Jones, ran upstairs. "He just said, 'Let's go! The Italians knocked out one of our boys!'"

After hearing a commotion, Sims said he went outside, where he saw Willie Montgomery sprawled on the ground. A few men had already made their own way down to the Italian barracks; he could hear them "chunking" and breaking windows. Luther Larkin, he said, blew a whistle, the signal for soldiers to fall out in formation. Sims told Jaworski that his own sergeant, Arthur Hurks, began urging men to take up arms: "He hollered, 'Come on, let's go!' And he was the first man that grabbed a club, he was the first one that tore the fence down. And the rest behind him grabbed pieces of board."

According to Sims, each man—Hurks, Larkin, and Jones—led a separate group down to the Italian Area. He admitted that he too tore a piece off the fence—to protect himself, he said—and headed down the hill to the orderly room.

"Who did you see inside the building right then you recognized?"

"I would be scared to say."

"There is no use being scared to say. All I want are the boys you saw."

"That is what I am trying to get now, trying to be sure. It seems like Willie Ellis went in there."

One by one, Sims gave up the names of men in his company whom he said he had seen: Roy Montgomery holding a club . . . Robert Sanders driving a jeep into Perata and Gould's tent . . . David Walton wielding a two-by-four . . . John Hamilton entering the orderly room . . . C. W. Spencer chunking someone . . . Freddie Simmons, Robert Gresham, Nathaniel Spencer, Johnnie Ceaser, James Chandler, Dan Roy Daymond, Emanuel Ford, Riley Buckner, Arthur Stone, Loary Moore . . . The list went on and on. Sims claimed that Booker Thornton had bragged that he'd "knocked the hell out of two of 'em," while Richard Barber admitted he'd "knocked the devil out of" another Italian. Although he wasn't particularly articulate, Sims was a gold mine of incrimination. Perhaps he knew something about the death of Olivotto too.

"Who did this hanging?"

"I don't know, sir."

"Do you have any idea?"

"No, sir."

"Did you hear anybody talking about it?"

"Not until the next morning, I heard Pinkney say he found a man hung."

"What did the boys say?"

"I ain't heard none say nothing."

"You didn't hear them say anything?"

"No, sir."

"Now, since you have been in the guard house, haven't you heard them talking about it?"

"No, sir, I don't know who could have did it. Some of them figure it was suicide, and some figure—I heard an Italian, he was in the guard house, and I heard him say, how come they didn't get the white boys in there?"

Sadly, Jaworski concluded, Sims knew nothing about the lynching. But here was a man who willing to swear that three men—Luther Larkin, Arthur Hurks, and Williams Jones—were in effect the ringleaders of the riot that led to Olivotto's death. The fact that Sims was illiterate might make him vulnerable to tough questioning by a good defense lawyer, but his plainspoken manner might also make him a sympathetic witness to the court. Jaworski offered complete immunity from prosecution for rioting, and Sims quickly agreed to testify at the court-martial.

Three other black soldiers agreed to be part of Jaworski's case in chief. Thomas Battle, a twenty-three-year-old private in the 651st Port Company from Edwards, Mississippi, was a jailhouse snitch, willing to pass along incriminating conversations he'd said he'd overheard in the stockade. Battle, a big talker, had a tendency to confuse facts, but Jaworski figured he could help corroborate the testimony of other more straightforward witnesses. Battle had no hesitation trading testimony for his freedom.

Private Alvin Clarke was another very young soldier, just nineteen years old, from South Haven, Michigan. He too was willing to swear that Luther Larkin led a group of men down to the Italian Area. Larkin, he said, blew a whistle and yelled, "Let's go down and beat up the Italians!" Clarke waited a few minutes before deciding to go down with a different group, whose leader he could not identify. Along the way, he saw Sammy Snow of the 650th knocked unconscious but did not stop to help him. Soon enough, he too was hit on the head but not before he recognized about a dozen of his fellow port company soldiers. Clarke was willing to give those names to Jaworski in exchange for immunity.

Jaworski offered one final deal to Willie Ellis. Corporal Ellis, also of Houston, had plenty of baggage of his own. During his initial interrogation, Ellis flatly denied ever going into the Italian Area. He said he knew nothing, recognized no one, and couldn't help with the investigation. But several soldiers, including Jesse Sims, had unequivocally placed Ellis in the orderly room, and the more Ellis was questioned, the more he stumbled. Realizing his excuse wouldn't sell, he abruptly asked Jaworski and Colonel Williams if he could start the interrogation over. "I might be guilty," he said, "but I am going to tell you the right story now."

Like the others before him, Ellis unleashed a cascade of names, implicating a dozen of his comrades. Although he had only recently joined the company, Ellis claimed he could specifically remember the names and faces of those who, like him, had rushed down to retaliate for Willie Montgomery's injuries. He remembered that a muscular soldier named Arthur Stone had taunted that "all the men that didn't go down there were yellow." Most important to Jaworski, he too agreed that Luther Larkin had played a key role in organizing the raid. "When I first seen Luther Larkin," Ellis recounted, "he came upstairs and he told about the Italians jumping him and he was hunting a whistle. He asked who had a whistle and didn't no one say anything. Someone over there was shooting dice and someone said, 'What the hell do you want with a whistle?' He said, 'These Italians jumped our boys.' He stood around downstairs. He found a whistle. He came back halfway up the stair steps and he blew the whistle. I later heard a whistle blow outside."

Ellis was also willing to implicate William Jones and Arthur Hurks. When the riot ended, he said, he saw Hurks standing outside Barracks 719, talking with two white MPs sitting in a jeep. Ellis told Colonel Williams that he thought he overheard one of the MPs compliment Hurks for a job well done, telling him, "You done a damn good job and saved us a job."

> "Could you identify either of the MPs if you saw them again?"
> "No, sir, I couldn't tell much about them because they was sitting in the jeep and Sergeant Hurks was standing in the front door by them."
> "Do you know Private Lomax of the MPs?"
> "No, sir, I don't know any MP."

Nonetheless, Ellis knew enough to convince Jaworski that he too deserved a spot in the prosecutorial lineup.

Jaworski now had a list of about fifty suspects, some of whom had been identified only once, others several times. He was particularly determined to discover who had jumped into the jeep and repeatedly driven it into Perata and Gould's tent. Sims had accused a soldier named Robert Sanders, a twenty-one-year-old private from South Chicago, but no one else seemed sure. The answer finally came from a talkative twenty-year-old from Louisiana.

His name was Willie Curry, but everyone called him Slick. He had six years of formal schooling, then worked as a delivery boy until he was old enough to join the navy. His hitch lasted just one month and a day before a hand injury forced him out on a medical discharge. The army, all but desperate for warm bodies, took him in, sending him to Alaska for six months of port duty. In July 1944, Curry was loading ships in New Orleans when he and a half-dozen others, including Sammy Snow, got orders to take a train to Seattle to join the 651st as it prepared to head overseas. Slick's quick humor and easy charm made him an instant hit with his new unit.

At first, Corporal Curry seemed as if he too might make another good witness for the prosecution. He was willing to name a few names but had trouble identifying others, because he was so new to the company. Eventually, without much prompting, he admitted coming across Robert Sanders and Richard Barber, two soldiers in the 650th who had been boyhood buddies in South Chicago. He said he saw Sanders and Barber in the commandeered jeep, trying without success to get the engine started. Slick admitted that he then walked up and offered to give it a try and within moments had the engine running. He put the jeep in gear and drove into Gould and Perata's tent.

"You took the jeep and drove it into the corner of the tent. Did you see anyone in there?"

"Yes, sir."

"Did you knock the tent down?"

"No, sir."

"Did you break the side of the tent down?"

"No, sir. I mean, Yes, sir, just one post."

"You broke one post?"

"Yes, sir."

"Did you drive the jeep into the tent so the wheels were on the tent floor?"

"No, sir."

"How many times did you drive the jeep against the tents?"

"Two or three times."

It was a clear admission of assault, if not attempted murder. Several witnesses had seen the tent being battered, but both Perata and Gould had already evacuated, and the identity of the person still inside—if any—remained a mystery. Curry also admitted that he hit an Italian with a fence board as the man ran from the orderly room. The more he talked, the more it seemed to Jaworski that Curry was better suited as a defendant than as a witness.

"Over by barracks 711," Curry went on, "someone says, 'Let's burn the barracks down.' They didn't burn it down. They was going to, and somebody in 708 was hollering, 'Here's some in this room!'"

Curry's information about Italian Barracks 708 broke important new ground. He told Jaworski and Colonel Williams that a white MP walked up to Herman Johnson, a black corporal from the 651st, as Johnson stood outside the barracks' back door. "He said, 'Go in and bring them out,'" Curry remembered, "Herman took the flashlight, ran around to the front door." Curry and Elby Murray came in the back way. Once inside Curry said he saw Herman Johnson hitting Italians with something that looked like a GI entrenching shovel. Elby Murray, he said, was beating them first with a shoe, then with his fist. Slick ran over as Johnson moved from bunk to bunk, shouting as he went.

"How many did you see Herman flash the light on under the beds and tell to get out from under there?"

"They was under the beds and under the covers everywhere."

"And you hit everyone you saw?"

"When he had one in the flashlight, I did."

"And Herman hit them, too?"

"Yes, sir."

"Were the Italians hollering?"

"I don't know, they was hollering, 'Mama!'"

Curry figured the three of them were inside the barracks for seven or eight minutes. They found fifteen to twenty Italians. "And we hit every one that we found. We wasn't trying to kill them, we were trying to hit them."

"Some were on the floor. Some got up and ran out if they could run past us, the ones that was lucky. If they got by one, the next man would catch him."

"With the fifteen Italians in there, weren't you afraid they would gang up and beat you up?"

"No, sir, I wasn't scared myself. They was running and—I guess they wanted to fight."

"They weren't fighting very hard?"

"They were battling a little bit."

"You were doing most of the pounding on them?"

"Yes, sir."

Eventually, Curry said, the three Americans left through the front door, where the same white military policeman was waiting. Herman Johnson returned the flashlight just as a carload of MPs drove down Lawton Road. The newly arrived MPs were led, he said, by Regis Callahan who, as Callahan had earlier testified, pulled out his revolver and threatened to shoot the first man to come up the steps. But if Slick was to be believed, Sergeant Callahan had apparently arrived seven or eight minutes too late.

Curry had nothing to offer about Larkin, Hurks, or Jones but admitted that he had also been in the middle of the orderly room chaos, where he confirmed Roy Montgomery's efforts to protect Farr, Perata, and Haskell. All in all, Curry was a wealth of new information and, between the jeep, the barracks beatings, and the orderly room melee, seemed to be at the center of most of the action. Jaworski knew that he had hooked a big fish and that a man like this might even know something about Olivotto's hanging, but he wasn't quite sure how to land him. While Curry had implicated others, he had also implicated himself. If he decided to indict Curry instead of offering him immunity, he might lose his chance to nail Herman Johnson and Elby Murray for their alleged vile behavior in Barracks 708. And Curry's confessions during interrogation meant little unless he could be convinced to put it down on paper; once in court, none of the defendants could be forced to testify against themselves.

Jaworski's gut feeling told him that despite his candor, Slick just was too culpable to justify letting him simply walk away, and he decided to focus instead on getting a written statement. But just when Jaworski thought he might reel in a confession, Curry asked to go off the record. By the time the court reporter resumed his shorthand, Slick had slipped the hook.

"Now, while we have been talking off the record, you state you don't want to talk any more?"

"Yes, sir."

"Why?"

"Because if the guys that did the hanging aren't found, then they are going to put it on somebody, somebody is going to do time."

"You are willing to do time for what you did?"

"I can't do no better if they give me time. I can't run off, I ain't going to try."

"Why don't you want to tell me, as investigating officer, the other persons present that night so that we can find out those and turn loose those persons who are not implicated in this case?"

"Well, I done told you."

"But there were fellows you knew that were down there. Why do you refuse to tell me the names of them?"

"I don't know all the guys."

Despite everything else he had admitted, Curry seemed convincingly emphatic that he had nothing to do with the lynching. But what about Herman Johnson and Elby Murray? Johnson, a thirty-two-year-old corporal from Detroit, had insisted he had never even gone down to the Italian Area, staying inside his barracks at the ironing board, pressing clothes for other men in his company. Johnson was a large man, tall and muscular, and his imposing physique stood out in the minds of several other witnesses who insisted he had, indeed, been in the thick of the riot. On a hunch, Williams and Jaworski decided to bring one of those men, Thomas Battle—the jailhouse snitch who had already been granted immunity—into the interrogation room to face Johnson.

"Thomas, in your testimony a while ago, you testified that Herman Johnson told you after the fight between the Italians and the Colored soldiers on the night of August 14, that while he was in the Italian Area the MP took a flashlight from his hands; is that right?"

"He told me that on the 15th. We was in the stockade."

"That is the next day after the fight he told you what I have just repeated?"

"Now, he wasn't talking to me, I walked up at the time he was speaking it. And that MP asked for the light, and he gave it to him."

"You also testified that Herman said he was in the Italian Area the night of the fight?"

"I did."

"Herman, what do you say to that testimony?"

"He is lying."

Despite his size, Johnson was soft-spoken. Married and the father of a fourteen-year-old boy, Johnson had worked before the war as an assistant foreman at the Packard Motor Car Company plant in Detroit. He was now a crane operator with the 651st, and pulled duty as the barracks orderly for Barracks 672. One of his jobs as orderly had been to distribute equipment for the pending overseas assignment. Rather meticulously, he had stenciled all of his own gear and clothing with J1145—J for Johnson and 1145 for the last four numbers of his eight-digit army service number. One piece of equipment, his trench shovel, had rounded surfaces that proved difficult to mark. Johnson had tried again and again to make a clear stencil, eventually imprinting his stamp in five different places. A trench shovel stenciled with five J1145 marks was one of the most conspicuous pieces of evidence collected in the Italian Area on August 15 by Orem's investigators.

"Did you lose a spade that was found in the Italian Area?"
"I missed my spade that night."
"Where were you when you first missed it?"
"At my bed."
"That night?"
"That night."
"Did you report it to anyone?"
"No, sir, it wasn't reported."
"Was the spade later found?"
"Yes, sir."
"Do you know where it was found?"
"No, sir, I had no real good answer where it was found."

Even without Curry's testimony, Jaworski figured, Johnson's story seemed fairly slippery, and he might be able to convict him based on the shovel and on Battle's testimony.

Curry had also implicated Elby Murray, but Murray was no longer in custody: he was now overseas. In fact, 340 of the 400 soldiers in the two port companies had been shipped to New Guinea, including at least two dozen men—like Luther Larkin, Arthur Hurks, and Robert Sanders—whom Jaworski's witnesses had named as key participants in the riot. Although General Denson had tried to postpone their transport until at least August 29, the Pentagon would have none of it. The war in the Southwest Pacific was at a crucial juncture, as General McArthur had recently secured dozens of ports south of the Philippines, at a cost of thousands of lives. Fresh port companies were absolutely necessary if McArthur was to maintain his supply chain leading to his momentous return to Manila. Denson was given until only August 23—just nine days after the riot—to identify suspects, pull them from the two companies, replace those suspects with fresh troops, and get the whole lot of them on a train for San Francisco, where they were loaded on a ship bound for New Guinea.

Of the sixty men left behind in Seattle, five were given immunity, and several others were set free. Private Herman Gentry was able to prove that he had been AWOL that night, slipping into Seattle to spend one last night with his girlfriend. Private First Class Samuel Thomas had snuck off in a car with another girl, returning long after the riot ended. Both young women were willing to vouch for their respective boyfriends, even when it turned out that both men had wives in Detroit.

Overall, Jaworski thought he had collected enough evidence to charge twenty-two of the men still in Seattle with rioting. Communiqués were sent via secret cable, ordering the immediate return another twenty-five men to Fort Lawton from the Pacific, including Luther Larkin and Arthur Hurks. Given the enormity of the pending prosecution, Jaworski figured he couldn't handle much more than that.

There were other considerations as well. In Rome, Allied diplomats were sending cables warning of dangerous instability within the emerging postwar Italian government. With the Italian economy in shambles and several northern provinces still under German occupation, American-backed moderates were being assailed by extremists on both the right and the left, including Communists. On August 16, the United States had relinquished military control of Rome and surrounding provinces. Within days, Alexander Kirk, the American ambassador to Rome, had received a sternly worded letter from the new Italian foreign affairs minister, reacting to news of the incident at Fort Lawton. "You will certainly appreciate," it read, "the grave concern that the recent news has caused us, and the negative reactions it is bound to have on Italian public opinion if the facts, as is probable, find their way in the press or be distorted by enemy propaganda. It would be extremely useful, in consequence, if the exact details could be known, together with an official indication of the steps taken by the competent Authorities to punish this brutal and, apparently, uncalled for aggression."

Three weeks later, Italy's high commissioner for prisoners of war, General Pietro Gazzera, sent a formal protest to the U.S. Army's Allied Control Commission, or ACC: "The tremendous injury suffered by our unarmed prisoners from American coloured military occurred only because no protection whatsoever was given to them by the Forces in charge of the Camp," the letter began. "I beg, therefore, the ACC to ask the Allied Authorities concerned to assure that the culprits of the incident are identified, and that orders may be given so as to protect life and safety of our soldiers from danger."

Olivotto's death had become an international embarrassment, made even more so as Allied troops advanced into Germany and discovered the often-deplorable conditions imposed on American, British, and Russian prisoners of war. Although Leon Jaworski was preparing to prosecute a murder and riot, he was also being asked to show the world that the American military was capable of protecting its prisoners and seeking justice, even when suspects were American soldiers and victims were former enemies.

A lesser attorney than Leon Jaworski might have cringed at the enormity of the task. By the end of October, it was clear that most of the physical evidence—even the original list of the names of the men who had been identified at Camp George Jordan—had been hopelessly lost or compromised. Despite weeks of interrogation, only four suspects had agreed to submit signed confessions. Jaworski had assembled a full slate of witnesses, but none of them were saints and many might prove vulnerable during cross-examination. Testimony about the riot was plentiful, but not a single witness or informant had come forward with evidence about the hanging. To make matters

worse, Colonel Branson, at General Cooke's insistence, was uncere-
moniously relieved of his command, an embarrassing development
that might open a Pandora's box of suspicion if the newspapers managed to put two and two together. Even the weather, which had been
balmy and beautiful, had finally started to turn. The days were darker,
the storm clouds more frequent, and the winds off Puget Sound cold
enough for Jaworski to start wearing his winter coat.

Despite everything, Jaworski was buoyant. He knew the Fort Lawton
case was being watched carefully in Washington, and a successful
prosecution could very well help him land the biggest prize of all: a
chance to prosecute war criminals in Europe. In his memoirs, he remembered the autumn of 1944 as a heady time. "Career men know
that, in wartime, where you serve is nearly important as how. I was just
another temporary soldier who would be going home, and returning
to civil law," he wrote. "But there were historic cases coming in Europe. I didn't plan to make the Army my life, but I wanted in on them.
You may not believe in beauty contests, but if you enter one you want
to be voted pretty."

He had been lobbying behind the scenes for months, knowing that
the Pentagon brass might prefer a West Point blueblood to a West
Texas trial lawyer. This Seattle assignment could make all the difference. His excitement was evident in a letter to his brother-in-law,
"Boots" Trautschold:

> Boots, I am up to my ears here in the biggest job I ever tackled.
> I hope I can prove equal to it. It will be the biggest trial the War
> Department has had in this war. Can't say much more about it
> now, but I believe the matter will be released to the press in a few
> days. If so, the chances are that the national press will carry it all
> over the country.
>
> I haven't told Jeannette yet—but I doubt that I will be back in
> dear old Texas before the middle of December. Will take me some
> leave then—the good Lord knows I will need it.

Under personal pressure to be home before Christmas—to mollify his wife and make himself available for war crimes trials in Europe—Jaworski anxiously awaited the arrival of the two dozen members of the 650th and 651st being shipped back from the Pacific. His investigation was running out of leads, and he hoped the prodigal soldiers in New Guinea would include one or more plausible murder suspects.

CHAPTER NINE

BEEKS
Early November 1944

AT THE EQUATOR, THE sun rose exactly at six and set twelve hours later; at noon it burned precisely overhead. Compared with Seattle, where the sun drifted in wide arcs during summer and barely sneaked through the southern sky in winter, the seasons in New Guinea were tedious and unvarying, as if engineered by the army itself.

Luther Larkin and the soldiers of the 650th and 651st Port Companies were detailed to a narrow stretch of beach along the northern New Guinea coast, squeezed between churning surf on one side and oppressive jungle on the other. Ungainly LSTs—landing ship tanks—flopped ashore, vulnerable as beached whales as they waited for Negro port companies to disgorge piles of cargo, equipment, and machinery onto the sand. The pace was hectic, the work never ending, and the rain showers relentless: pouring, sopping rain, three hundred inches a year, ten-minute bucket dumps every few hours down the necks and into the boots of soldiers already sweltering in ninety-degree heat and humidity. Passing storms packed so much moisture that tropical fungi crawled into body cavities, and wide swaths of skin seared with jungle rot. Mosquitoes injected malaria and dengue fever; rats carried mites swollen with scrub typhus, which spread high fever and hideous rashes. The world smelled dank and clammy; canned rations never seemed so rancid. It was hell.

For Luther Larkin, the irony was thicker than steam rising from the rain forest. Here on the supply lines, the army needed medics; but because he was black, he languished as a longshoreman, his brawn valued more than his brain. Even as men around him suffered in the swelter and died of disease, Larkin was little more than a mule, hauling the heavy armaments of war from pallet to sling to sand to storehouse. But just as it seemed no one cared if he lived or died, he got orders to return to Seattle.

All told, twenty-four men made the long trip back to Fort Lawton, in two unescorted groups. After marathon flights from the Southwest Pacific, followed by long train and bus trips from California to Seattle, the men in Larkin's group were led almost immediately to an office at the port, where one by one they were introduced to Colonel Jaworski.

At first, no one mentioned murder; Larkin willingly came clean and carefully spelled out his role in the riot. Yes, he had sipped a beer or two that night, first in the PX, then at Sergeant Tanner's party in the 578th mess hall. Sure, he could tell that Willie Montgomery was tanked; so were several other soldiers. Yes, he had helped carry Willie to the sidewalk outside Barracks 719 after the Italian slugged him. "Willie looked stiff as a wedge; he might even be dead." While others lit matches to make it easier for him to see, Larkin said he performed artificial respiration, which took quite a bit of time, maybe ten minutes. Before he knew it, Larkin remembered, they brought another boy who'd been hurt, Sammy Snow. Snow had a nasty cut on his head; it took time and plenty of bandages to get the bleeding to stop. All the while, a crowd had gathered. "While I was giving first aid to Montgomery," Larkin said, "I heard someone say we should blow out the entire company and go down there and show them that they should not come up here and jump on any of our men. I said that's the thing to do."

Larkin denied any direct involvement in the riot itself; he told Jaworski that he had not, in fact, even gone down to the Italian Area at all that night. And, like all the other suspects, he claimed to have no information about Olivotto's hanging. But three men who lived in Larkin's own barracks—Jesse Sims, Alvin Clarke, and Willie Ellis— were prepared to testify that otherwise disinterested soldiers had emerged from their barracks only because Larkin had blown a whistle.

In Jaworski's mind, the Good Samaritan alibi told only part of the story: Larkin, he had already decided, was a ringleader of the riot.

On November 2, fifteen more men, including Arthur Hurks, returned from New Guinea and were examined by Jaworski. Like Corporal Larkin, Sergeant Hurks appeared calm and confident, denying the claims of Sims and Ellis that he had ordered men to follow him into the Italian Area. Hurks remained cool despite the fact that, like Larkin before him, he did not have his own lawyer at his side. That wasn't unusual in 1944; values of discipline, honesty, and obedience were considered paramount during military criminal investigations, especially during wartime, and it was generally understood that a soldier who told the truth during a criminal interrogation should not need a lawyer. Although Hurks denied entering the Italian Area and offered nothing about Olivotto's death, he was one of the ranking noncommissioned officers in Barracks 719 that night, and was clearly in the crosshairs of two of Jaworski's star witnesses. With that, but little else to go on, Jaworski decided that Hurks too had been a riot ringleader.

By November 6, Jaworski had run out of time and out of leads. His key witnesses, particularly Augusto Todde and Jesse Sims, were willing to swear under oath that they could identify a combined forty-three men as participants in the riot. Jaworski decided to formally charge those forty-three with rioting, a criminal misdemeanor under the military's Articles of War.

Guglielmo Olivotto's death was more problematic. Although no one had yet come forward with any concrete leads about the lynching, Jaworski knew that the Pentagon and State Department would not tolerate a prosecution that failed to seek justice for the apparent murder of a prisoner in American custody. To secure a murder conviction, he'd have to convince a court that someone had intended to kill the Italian and had acted with malice in doing so. Naturally, he'd have to offer some sort of physical evidence, like footprints, fingerprints, blood or hair, or he'd have to come up with an eyewitness to the murder or an actual confession. So far, none of that had surfaced.

Under the Articles of War, Jaworski had another option: He could charge one or more suspects with a felony, like assault, then make a separate charge of felony murder, a legal theory that holds someone liable for a death occurring during the commission of a related felony. In the classic example, the driver of a getaway car can be charged with felony murder if one of his co-conspirators kills someone while robbing a bank, even if the driver never saw nor knew about the killing. If Jaworski could prove that one of the Americans had committed a felony during the course of the riot, and if he could show that Olivotto was killed during that riot, he might get one or more murder convictions.

Perhaps out of bravado, or perhaps hoping that more evidence would surface, Jaworski chose not to allege felony murder. Instead, he charged Luther Larkin, Arthur Hurks, and William Jones with the *actual* murder of Guglielmo Olivotto, which meant that he thought he could produce evidence that each of the three personally participated in the lynching. All three were also among the forty-three charged with rioting, but that at most was a misdemeanor. On November 6, the date the charges were announced, Jaworski still had no direct evidence that anyone had hung Olivotto but perhaps hoped that the fear of the death penalty might convince someone to come forward with more information.

The news stunned Luther Larkin. It was one thing to be fingered for rioting—Larkin had certainly been in the thick of the action August 14—but Larkin found the murder charge shocking. None of the Italians had picked him out of the lineup at Camp George Jordan, freeing him to join his unit as it headed to New Guinea. Who had since come forward to claim he was a killer? What possible reason could anyone have to tie the lynching to him? When, where, and how would he get an opportunity to proclaim his absolute and total innocence? Could it be that he would have been better off taking his chances on the beaches of New Guinea than in the stockade at Fort Lawton?

The next day, November 7, was Election Day; Franklin Roosevelt swept to a fourth term in office with 53 percent of the popular vote and the lion's share of the electoral college. In Europe, American troops pressed toward Germany; the Battle of the Bulge was just six weeks away. In the Philippines, General MacArthur, having established a beachhead in Leyte, pointed his troops toward his promised return to Manila. At Fort Lawton, Post Engineer George McNay brought his camera to the base of the Magnolia bluffs and took photos of the scene where Olivotto had been hung.

The responsibility for convening a court-martial fell on the shoulders of General Denson. As head of the Seattle Port of Embarkation, Denson was designated as the court-martial's "convening authority," which meant he was responsible for deciding where and when the trial would take place, who the judges would be, and whether or not to accept the final judgment of those judges once they reached their court-martial verdict. His first order of business, however, was to figure out who would represent the accused in court. General Denson decided that the entire job of defending all forty-three men would fall on the shoulders of just two army lawyers: Major William Beeks and his young assistant, Captain Howard Noyd.

Beeks grew up wanting to sail ships; he instead became a renowned expert on the law of the sea. Born in the Oklahoma Territory eighteen months before it became a state, he was twenty-four years old and living in Seattle when he made up his mind to enter the merchant marines. His young wife objected, insisting that a man with such a gift for words belonged on dry land. Beeks relented and instead attended the University of Washington law school before building a successful practice with one of Seattle's top law firms. But in 1942, he heeded the same call as Leon Jaworski and joined the military. Beeks started as a judge advocate for the Port of Seattle with the rank of captain, but he was soon promoted to major. He was posted to the Prince Rupert Port of Embarkation—six hundred miles north of Seattle on the western coastline of British Columbia—and charged with overseeing the legal affairs of thousands of soldiers on their way to and from Alaska and the Aleutian Islands.

Beeks was short and stocky with an enormous square head and

emerging jowls that made him look something like a bulldog. His looks fit his personality: he was blunt, gruff, and impatient. His wavy hair formed a sharp widow's peak atop his broad forehead; he could lower his chin, squint his eyes, and snarl questions in a way that dared a man to challenge his small stature or large intellect; you messed with Beeks at your own peril. When General Denson needed someone to defend the accused Fort Lawton rioters and murderers, Major William Trulock Beeks was his first choice.

Beeks returned home to Seattle with Captain Noyd in tow. Howard Noyd, just twenty-nine, had been Beeks's strapping but studious assistant in Prince Rupert. Raised among Swedish immigrants on a northwestern Iowa farm, Noyd earned a football scholarship to Morningside College before working his way through Drake Law School as an assistant football coach. Like Beeks, Noyd had met very few blacks before entering the army. Once, while in law school, he and several classmates—including the school's only two black students—had entered a café in downtown Des Moines. Having grown up in a small but tolerant Lutheran town, Noyd was stunned when the owner refused to serve nonwhites, and quickly joined his friends as they all left the café in protest, never to return. Drafted in 1942, he had never even heard of British Columbia before getting his orders to report there to work under William Beeks.

The short major and tall captain had no time to waste. It was not the army's custom to delay criminal trials once charges were announced, especially since trained manpower was in such short supply, and any soldiers who might be acquitted were needed on the front lines. General Denson elected to give the two lawyers just ten days to prepare their defense for all forty-three soldiers. The short time frame shocked Beeks, who had never before defended men on trial for their lives. He complained loudly, but it did him little good: the army's job was to win a world war, not spin its wheels. Thousands of other soldiers were asked every day to do what might otherwise seem impossible; it was now Beeks's and Noyd's turn to meet that same request.

It took the two lawyers three days just to meet and briefly interview each of their new clients. There was little opportunity to build trust or respect; those who might have been falsely accused barely got a chance to make their case, while those who knew they were guilty weren't quite sure how much they should come clean to two white strangers, who were officers to boot. Thirty-five-year-old Private Willie Basden struck Howard Noyd as utterly credulous to the point of being child-like. Soldiers from northern cities, like Wallace Wooden, David Walton, Johnnie Ceaser, and Booker Thornton came off as defensive, even angry. Those from rural towns in the Deep South like Roy Montgomery, James Chandler, and Freddie Simmons tended to be shy and well mannered, using "Yes, sir" and "No, sir" more as signs of respect than as military protocol. The lawyers and their clients seemed to have little in common; each was alternately confused or suspicious about the other's slang or jargon or attempts at humor, some of it, fittingly, of the gallows kind.

Privately, Beeks and Noyd admitted to having a hard time distinguishing so many black men one from another. It was even tougher because so many had similar names. For some reason, Jaworski had decided not to charge the Montgomery who started the fight, Willie, but did charge Roy, the Montgomery who helped stop it. Two defendants were Booker T's: Booker Townsell and Booker Thornton, both from Barracks 719. Also from Barracks 719 were two Spencers—Corporal Nathaniel T. and Sergeant C. W.; three Sanders, Private Robert, Private Edward, and Corporal Johnnie; and two corporals named Ellis—Willie and Russell. There were even two John Browns: Sergeant John S. Brown, the only defendant from the 578th Port Company, and Private John R. Brown, one of six defendants from the 651st. The other thirty-six were all members of the 650th, twenty-six of whom had lived in Barracks 719.

Major Beeks soon determined that Colonel Jaworski had made a mistake charging John R. Brown. From the start, Private Brown had insisted he'd spent the night of August 14 in a Seattle hotel with a girl he'd been dating named Melva Williams and with a sergeant named Herbert Evans. He told Beeks that Melva had rented Room 5 at the Coast Hotel, using the alias "Mr. & Mrs. Steward"; the two soldiers stayed with her until five thirty the next morning. Beeks ordered army investigators to track down Melva in the King County Jail, where she confirmed Brown's story, and gave a sample of her handwriting to compare with the Coast Hotel ledger. It was an ironclad alibi and all but assured Beeks that he'd be able to open the trial with a stinging rebuke to Jaworski's investigative aptitude and perhaps cast doubt on other indictments as well.

As Beeks studied the names of the five black soldiers granted immunity by Jaworski, he pondered their significance. Why would these soldiers speak out against men in their own company? All five accusers had admitted being down in the Italian Area, and some had even been spotted swatting POWs with sections of fence. Jaworski planned to call Alvin Clarke, but Private Clarke had been knocked cold, dragged to safety by some of the very men he now fingered as rioters. Dan Roy Daymond was also on the list, but many of Beeks's clients counted Daymond as a friend, and he had clearly worked side by side with Larkin to help resuscitate Willie Montgomery. Why had these two men turned their backs on their buddies?

Jesse Sims was another matter. Almost none of Beeks's clients had a good word to say about Jesse; he was, like most everyone else, a drinker and a gambler, but he got nasty when he drank and grew sore if the cards or dice didn't go his way. Sims's favorite game was craps, and he was always looking for action. It wasn't hard to find a game; just about any night, someone would spread an olive army blanket and fetch a few pairs of dice. Players placed their bets with a man willing to be banker and cheered as shooters tried to roll a seven or eleven or at least not crap out by throwing a three, twelve, or snake eyes. Any other score counted as a point and allowed a shooter to keep rolling, trying to hit that same point without throwing a seven. Everyone around the blanket rode bets with the man throwing dice, which meant the games got louder as the stakes grew higher. A soldier's army paycheck amounted to just a buck or two a day, so getting ahead by five or ten dollars in a single night could really mean something. Of course, losing that amount often caused hard feelings.

Because August 14 was both a payday and the port companies' last full day at the Fort, Beeks learned that money had flowed freely at the PX. By evening chow, some soldiers' wallets were already empty, spent on one last fling fueled by beer, cigarettes, and bootleg whiskey. A few, including Sims, hit up fellow soldiers for loans, hoping to win it back at the craps blanket. The biggest game that night was to be in Barracks 719, at the top of the stairs, in a space four feet from the upper landing. Arthur Hurks ran the game; it was his blanket, his dice, and he was the banker.

Arthur Hurks was twenty-two years old, born in Louisiana bayou country and raised in Houston by his mother, whom everyone called "Aunt Sweet." Arthur, an only child, was known to all his cousins, aunts, and uncles simply as "Brother." He grew to be six feet tall, a fit, trim and handsome football star. Before being drafted in December 1943, he worked as a rigger for the Houston Shipbuilding Company. Once in the army, he was promoted from private to private first class to corporal to sergeant in a dizzyingly few short months.

Around nine o'clock, Hurks told Willie Ellis—another of Jaworski's star witnesses—to push his bunk back a few feet to make enough room for the expected crowd. Ellis reluctantly agreed, but declined Hurks's invitation to join in; he had just come off KP duty and wanted to sleep. Once the game got going, sleep was out of the question, with as many as a dozen increasingly rowdy soldiers looking on or placing bets, usually risking about twenty-five cents per player per roll. Hurks told Beeks that as both sergeant and banker, he paid careful attention to anyone who seemed to get out of hand. "I remember Sims very well," he said, "because of the argument that he kept up in the game. The reason why he kept up so much argument, I imagine, to begin with, he wasn't his normal self. That is, he seemed to have been drinking. Then again, he was angry because he seemed to be losing his money every time he bet."

The lights had not been dimmed at the sound of taps; there had been too much noise, too much anxiety about the next day's scheduled departure, and absolutely no sign that any of the companies' officers were around to enforce curfew. A few minutes after eleven, some of the men in Hurks's game thought they heard shouting outside, but their money was down and the shooter was hot; he wouldn't crap out for another five minutes or so. According to Hurks, the game finally broke up once someone blew a whistle; as banker, he was the last to leave. Once downstairs, he walked out to where Willie Montgomery lay on the sidewalk, a group of men pressed around him. Someone, Hurks swore, had yelled, "The Italians killed one of our boys!" Across the street, he heard shouts, and from the Italian Area came the sounds of screams and shattered glass. Wilbert Tanner, the 578th first sergeant, bulled out of the mess hall brandishing a baseball bat, daring anyone to disobey his orders to return to barracks. Alvin Clarke, his bloody hands covering his head, staggered to the front porch of Barracks 719. Minutes later, John Hamilton appeared, his arm around the shoulder of a tall, slender white soldier. It was Grant Farr, clearly dazed, certainly uncomfortable about being escorted toward a barracks full of black men. Hurks said Hamilton asked him to help take Farr farther up the road, where he could be safer and get medical attention.

Sims, however, had told Jaworski that Hurks led a group of men down into the Italian Area. Sims had admitted going down himself, with a club in his hand, where he said he saw Hurks in the thick of it. Ellis had also confessed to being down there and had moreover told Jaworski that Hurks was a key perpetrator: "Sergeant Hurks was all up and down this thing, going from one room to another. I will be frank, I didn't see him hit anyone. He did have a club, kind of short. He seemed to be one of the participants in the fight."

Hurks swore otherwise, and plenty of other men backed his story. Hurks told Beeks he helped bring Farr to safety, then returned to Barracks 719, where his first sergeant, Robert Aubry, had just arrived. "He ran up and asked me what was going on and said for the fellows to get back in the barracks and told me to put them back in," Hurks reported. "He explained to me that if the MPs came down with machine guns that they could kill any of those fellows they wanted and nothing could be done about it."

Eventually, the first carload of MPs did pull up, led by Thurman Jones. He spotted the sergeant's stripes on Hurks's sleeve, and Hurks said Jones ordered him to stand guard to stop any more men from going into the Italian Area. "I bluffed the fellows by cussing them and talking loud and telling them the MPs were going to have to do a whole lot of shooting, and like that, and to stay back," said Hurks. "These fellows hesitated a few minutes and I continued to talk with them."

Hurks's story—that he stood his ground and held back the surging crowd—was confirmed by several other soldiers. Beeks became convinced that Hurks was telling the truth. Only two men had claimed to see him in the Italian orderly room, and one of them, Sims, likely held a grudge—bitter, perhaps, about his bad luck in the craps game and willing to strike out at a man who held a higher rank and most of that night's winnings. The other man, Ellis, may have been unhappy about being ordered to move his bunk, but that seemed fairly trivial. Beeks pressed Hurks for ideas about Ellis, and was surprised to learn that the two men had known each other in high school in Houston:

> I went to Yates School which was in the third ward, and Willie Ellis went to the Wheatley High, in the fifth ward. And those two schools are always rivals, especially when it comes to any sports, and especially football. I played on the football team for Yates High School, and, naturally, I took up everything that had to do with Yates High School . . . Regardless of who would win the football game, there was always going to be a fight, regardless of what happened. If Wheatley won, they was going to have a fight with Yates, and if Yates won they were going to have to settle with the Wheatley students.

In fact, the Yates-Wheatley rivalry was so renowned that their annual Thanksgiving Day football game drew crowds in excess of thirty thousand and was considered the most important noncollege football game in the country. Hurks had been part of the popular crowd; on

May Day, he was crowned king and his future wife, Sidney, was queen. By itself, a high school rivalry seemed another trivial reason, but it may have made it easier for Ellis to lump Hurks together with the eleven other men he had fingered.

Larkin had also had differences with his accusers, particularly Sims, who frequently mocked Larkin for being educated and for showing no interest in craps games. During his interrogations, Sims repeatedly revised his story until Larkin, initially a minor player, emerged as a central figure. At first, Sims said he wasn't sure who had blown a whistle: "I wasn't paying much attention." Eventually, he claimed that Larkin had indeed whistled, signaling everyone to fall-out into formation. He also swore he saw Larkin brandishing a knife in the orderly room.

But Sims was not alone. Three or four of Jaworski's witnesses claimed they saw Luther blowing a whistle or rampaging in Building 713. During his own brief ten-day investigation, Beeks found others who stood behind Larkin's story, willing to testify that he had heroically attended to Willie Montgomery, Sammy Snow, and Alvin Clarke. Beeks figured it would have been difficult, though not impossible, for Luther to be so many different places that night, but he found himself impressed by how calmly and eloquently Larkin expressed himself. Larkin was confident and focused and appeared unafraid to face the prosecutor or his accusers. He did not act like a man with something to hide.

The third man facing the death penalty was far less convincing. Private William Jones was twenty years old, from Decatur, Illinois. His father had been a maître d' at Decatur's stately Hotel Orlando on Water Street; Jones left school after ninth grade to work as a waiter and a porter. He was loud, talkative, and opinionated, a smarter-than-average young man easily drawn into arguments and occasional fights. Jones had sleepy eyes, a muscular build, and others tended to notice that he had an unusually large head.

Jones had been among those picked out by Italians in the lineup at Camp George Jordan and was therefore left behind when his company went overseas. During his initial interview with Jaworski and Colonel Williams, he denied any involvement in the riot. But, much like Willie

Ellis, the interrogators got the best of him, and he asked to go off the record. When he came back, he "promised to tell the truth."

Under oath, and before being charged with murder, Jones had admitted to Jaworski and Williams that he had been in the thick of the revelry during Sergeant Tanner's party. He told them he had been in the company of a young woman, Miss Brooks, but female visitors had to be off the post by eleven. Although soldiers were expected to escort their lady friends to the bus stop outside the main gate, Miss Brooks had lost interest in Jones and started to leave with another soldier. Standing outside the mess hall in Building 700, Jones said that Luther Larkin had offered to help defend his honor by intercepting his wayward companion, but Jones waved him off, dryly dismissing her. "No, that's all right, let her go along." Jones said he and Larkin hung back at the intersection of Lawton Road and Virginia Avenue with Willie Montgomery and Roy Daymond. Moments later, three Italians walked down the road, and Montgomery began swearing.

Several soldiers told Beeks they distinctly remembered seeing Jones in the circle of men surrounding Montgomery as Larkin tried to revive him. As a stream of curious soldiers converged, Jones apparently stoked the fire by telling everyone that the Italians had attacked and that Montgomery's injuries were proof. Jones admitted walking toward the Italian Area but said he stopped on the top of the embankment to sling lumps of coal at the roof and windows of Barracks 708 and 710 below. Standing with him, he said, was his platoon sergeant, Robert Gresham. Suddenly, two Italians bolted from their barracks, with a white MP on their heels. Gresham, Jones had told Jaworski, joined the chase.

> "Why was the MP chasing the Italians?"
> "He was going to bust his skull."
> "What did he say?"
> "'God damn, I am going to catch him and bust his skull.' Gresham said, 'Let's go.'"
> "Why was Gresham chasing him?"

"Gresham said he would help catch him."

"He wanted to help catch him and help bust him?"

"Yes, sir."

"This MP was a tall slim fellow?"

"That is right."

"He had a club?"

"Yes, sir."

"If you could see the MP again, could you recognize him?"

"No, sir, I don't know him."

"But you are sure, Jones, it was a white MP?"

"Yes, sir."

"Do you know Private Lomax, an MP at Fort Lawton?"

"I don't know Private Lomax."

Jones told Beeks that he did not join the chase, but wandered down the embankment and peered into the broken windows of Barracks 708. He denied going near the orderly room and said he never hit an Italian or anyone else. But Beeks wasn't so sure. Several soldiers described Jones as an instigator; Johnnie Ceaser said he had been startled when Jones burst into his barracks. "He said, 'Everybody out, there is a fight down there!'" A few thought they saw Jones outside the orderly room, pitching rocks through the broken windows. Private Jack Chapman said Jones bragged about having an ax that night. Daymond said he saw him brandishing a stick.

Even more intriguing was Jones's willingness to point the finger at twenty-five of his fellow soldiers during his interrogation with Jaworski and Williams. Fourteen of them were now defendants, including Larkin, Hurks, Frank Hughes, David Walton, Sammy Snow, and Henry Jupiter; five others—including Daymond, Sims, and Clarke—were prepared to testify for the prosecution. In some ways, Jones might have made an ideal witness for Jaworski. Among other things, he had unequivocally accused his two fellow murder defendants of the very behaviors Jaworski had alleged: "Luther blew the whistle and the 651st boys came out. They all came around Building 700. About twenty-five or thirty came out. When Sergeant Hurks blew the whistle, about fifty came out. After they had assembled in the vicinity of Building 700, Larkin and Hurks led them into the Italian Area."

But Jaworski had decided to make Jones a defendant, not a witness, even if Jones had been willing to implicate dozens of others. Beeks concluded that Larkin and Hurks were believable but decided that Private William Jones couldn't be trusted much farther than he could spit.

As the trial drew closer, Beeks considered other explanations for the murder and mayhem. On August 12—just two days before the riot—the enlisted men of the 650th and 651st had been detailed to the post theater to watch several army training films. Government movies were a routine teaching tool, spanning such diverse topics as the proper way to salute and the importance of using condoms. Soldiers preparing to head into combat sat through an endless lineup of movies about digging foxholes and starting fires and dressing wounds and capturing prisoners. Of interest to Beeks were films that stereotyped or denigrated enemy soldiers, designed to make it easier for inexperienced troops to kill without remorse. Men in units just days from departure were shown *Baptism of Fire,* a no-nonsense appeal to the importance of taking violent revenge whenever your buddies are attacked. In the film, a GI on the eve of his first battle is worried sick about his loved ones back home. A second soldier, already combat hardened, warns the nervous novice that the more he stews about death, the more likely he is to die. A fierce battle ensues; the rookie watches as his best pal, Bill, is badly wounded. Eyes widen, and anger overwhelms fear. "I'd like to get the bastard that got Bill!" He leaps from his foxhole, rifle in hand. "Here it comes . . . This is it . . . Kill or be killed!" An unlucky Nazi stands in the way, and the newly emboldened GI plunges his bayonet into the enemy's guts. "I never thought I could do that . . . Of course, I never thought anybody would try and kill me . . . Well, I've got it licked now, now I can fight!" One bad guy after another rushes forward, only to be speared by the young hero. "You're damn right I can fight!" he boasts. As the film ends, the soldier is in a French tavern, raising a frosty toast to his war-wizened buddies as they belt out the words to "You Are My Sunshine, My Only Sunshine." "Good guys," he says, "you sure find out what guys are made of!" Fade to black.

To Beeks, it seemed at least plausible that the training films had their intended effect and that his clients had done precisely as they had been instructed: coming to the defense of a seriously injured comrade with decisive and unmerciful force. Sure, many of them were beered up, and the Italians hadn't shown any previous signs of trouble, but these men, after all, were about to head into the Pacific war, where "kill or be killed" might be more than a line in a training film.

As evidence, Beeks considered the case of Private Edward Sanders—no relation to defendant Robert Sanders—who agonized over his decision to stay inside his barracks instead of joining the fight. As the battle raged, Sanders's buddy Herman Gentry tried to tell him he had a duty to support the boys in his company.

> "He kept asking me, 'Why are you afraid?,' and he said, 'These fellows that don't go out now and defend themselves are the men that are going to draw back and not help any of the boys overseas.'"
>
> "Did that make you feel bad?"
>
> "The Italians have never done anything to me, and I don't want to go out. I wouldn't want to go out on such a mission as that."

Sure enough, many who stayed near their own bunks suffered the wrath of soldiers returning from the fray. Defendant Booker Townsell reported that "I heard a fellow, I don't know who it was, he came in after everything was over and he said some yellow dogs lived in the barracks and they wouldn't get out and help." Witness Harvey Banks said he heard defendant Nelson Alston "say that all boys that stayed there were yellow, that didn't go down there with them."

One black enlisted man who had gone down to the Italian Area found himself ostracized for another reason. Private John Pinkney, a member of the 650th, lived in Barracks 665. The commotion outside

Barracks 719 escaped his notice until almost eleven thirty, not quite a half hour after the first assault on Farr, Haskell, Perata, and Gould. Private Pinkney ran outside and then into the orderly room for the 650th Port Company to grab a billy club and an MP brassard. "I was not an MP," Pinkney said. "At that time I didn't know whether the white MPs had been notified or not. I put that on so that I could maintain order until the white MPs came to take it over."

Most enlisted men, black or white, occasionally had to pull part-time MP duty. Pinkney himself had been pressed into service in July, when the transport of Fascist Italian POWs through Fort Lawton had gone awry. When it became clear on August 14 that something ugly was well under way, he figured it was his military duty to don an MP brassard and help where he could. "I went in front of barracks 718 and 719 on Virginia Avenue. The vicinity was crowded with Colored soldiers. They were talking and arguing. One of these boys that was hurt was being carried out of the vicinity. It was mentioned, 'Let's go down and bring those Italians out of there.'"

A simple man, thirty-one-year-old Private Pinkney had been a butcher in Kansas City before the war. In the army, he was trained to be a bull driver, a waterfront term for someone who operates heavy machinery at the docks. As Pinkney stood among the crowd outside Building 700, a carload of white MPs arrived, led by Thurman Jones. "The white MPs said for the Colored boys to stay around in this vicinity of 718 and 719 and they would go down and see what had been going on," Pinkney continued. "Then I said, 'No, I will go down with you,' and at that time they got out of the command car and we proceeded down Lawton Road. When I got on Lawton Road opposite 700, I made a remark to Sergeant Hurks of the 650th to keep all the men back until the MPs and myself ventured on down into the Italian Area. Sergeant Hurks kept the men from following us."

Pinkney was the only black man wearing an MP brassard in the Italian Area that night, and he testified that he was able to convince more than a dozen black soldiers to drop their rocks, sticks, and other weapons and return to their own barracks. Although the night was so dark "you couldn't see your hand before you," he said that both Luther Larkin and Arthur Hurks had tried to contain the crowd back up the road. About an hour after the riot ended, Thurman Jones assigned Pinkney to ride patrol with Clyde Lomax; he was with Lomax when they discovered Guglielmo Olivotto's body. To some in his unit, that made Pinkney a minor celebrity. "I made the remark, 'I am the one that found him hung, another MP and myself.' They asked me how he looked, how a hung man looks. No one said they had been there or had chased an Italian there."

But many others treated Pinkney as a traitor. "When I got back to my barracks the next morning, most of the boys were in the barracks because they didn't go to work that day," he said. "They made fun of me; I don't recall who it was. They said I takes MP on myself and I went down and run those guys out. As near as I recall they said, 'There is old MP Pinkney himself' and I said it didn't make a damn whether I did or not, it was all over with me and I hoped those that didn't like me taking up MP would start a fight with me. Sergeant Aubry just said, 'That's enough of that.'"

Beeks thought it odd that Pinkney was not on Jaworski's list of potential prosecution witnesses; he was, after all, one of two men who had discovered Olivotto's body. Beeks himself wasn't sure what to do with him; if he put him on the stand, he might help Hurks and Larkin, but he could hurt other defendants whom he saw near the orderly room. It was hard to guess how the court-martial might view his decision to become the only black MP that night, and Beeks had to wonder if Pinkney might be a bit of a loose cannon on the stand. Perhaps, Beeks decided, it was best to wait and see.

Beeks's forty-two defendants could be grouped into four distinct categories. In the first group were those who claimed they never left their own barracks or even their own bunks; in two or three cases, that may have been strictly true. Most, however, fell into the second category: men who had clearly gone outside, perhaps even down to the Italian Area, but had simply looked on, little more than curious spectators. A third group included those bystanders who eventually crossed the line, deciding to toss rocks or chase an Italian or two. Finally, there was the hard-core group—perhaps a dozen or so—who likely did the lion's share of the damage. While some of his clients undeniably belonged in the fourth group, Beeks was amazed that Jaworski had never charged Willie Montgomery with anything. Willie, after all, had started the whole fracas. What was Jaworski up to?

With but ten days to prepare, Beeks had a difficult time sorting out just which of his clients belonged in which of the four categories. Jaworski, of course, had charged all the men as if they had been equally culpable, issuing the ultimate accusation of murder at the three alleged ringleaders. Beeks scrambled to subpoena additional alibi witnesses, but most were overseas. He was none too happy when his initial efforts to merely locate Willie Montgomery came up empty.

But there was good news too. Beeks knew that four of his clients—Sammy Snow, Willie Prevost, Nathaniel Spencer, and Roy Montgomery—had each agreed to give Jaworski written statements that seemed to admit at least partial guilt in the riot. But once Beeks reviewed those confessions, he was pleased and somewhat surprised at how harmless those confessions really were.

Private Sammy Snow had unabashedly bragged about being the very first American to run down the embankment and into the Italian Area. Snow was hardly in a position to deny his involvement: like Alvin Clarke, he had been hit over the head almost as soon as he reached the Italian barracks. He said, "I didn't see who hit me. He must have been waiting by the barracks, squatting down when I came around the corner. He kind of ambushed me. I was running right into it."

But Snow insisted that no one—not Larkin, not Hurks, not Jones—had told him what to do. He had seen Willie Montgomery lying on the sidewalk and decided on his own that members of his company had to avenge the attack. "No one stood and gave a speech telling everyone to go . . . I heard a whistle, but I was already on my way down . . . There were about fifteen of us; we all pooled together going down there. It was dark; I don't know who else was with me."

Sammy Snow was age nineteen, the son of a Florida sharecropper.

He had arrived at Fort Lawton just two weeks earlier, one of several soldiers transferred in at the last moment from the Port of New Orleans to fill the remaining slots in the 650th before it headed overseas. Muscular but very short, Snow was outgoing and popular with his new unit. They were shocked when, at the outset of the riot, they saw blood pouring from a large gash above his ear. "A bunch of them came and crowded around me, they asked what they did," he stated. "I said, 'They done hit me.' They asked me who hit me and I told them the Italians hit me. They was cussing and going on—I don't want to use some of the language—going to 'beat the hell out of those mother fuckers,' and like that, cursing and carrying on."

At the end of his interrogation with Jaworski, Snow had agreed to write out a one-paragraph statement that began, "I went down in the Italian Area to fight them . . ." He did not name any other soldiers. So, though he had implicated himself, he had also undercut Jaworski's central thesis that the riot might not have started without Larkin, Hurks, and Jones leading the way.

The written confession of Willie Prevost mentioned just three men: Robert Sanders, David Walton, and Wallace Wooden. Prevost wrote that he "started into the area where the fight was going on" and that "on my way, I picked up a board." He claimed he saw Sanders driving a jeep into Perata and Gould's tent and saw Walton and Wooden in the orderly room. During Prevost's interrogation, Jaworski and Williams had decided to bring Wooden into the room to confront his accuser.

"Where did you see me? You know you didn't see me down there."

"You was standing in the orderly room."

"You didn't see me, you know you didn't. Do you want to get you a medal for it?"

"No, I don't want no medal."

By then, however, Wooden had been named by at least a half-dozen witnesses, both black soldiers and Italians. David Walton also seemed to be on everyone's list. As with Snow, Prevost's written confession shed little new light.

Nathaniel Spencer signed the third confession. A thirty-three-year-old corporal from Mississippi by way of Detroit, Spencer had been playing poker in Barracks 719 when the game was interrupted by a noise outside. "I ran downstairs and saw men running down to the Italian Area from all directions. I heard that our buddies were down there and needed help. So I ran down there." In his statement, Spencer admitted he was about to hit someone with a tree branch when defendant John Hamilton intervened "and said this is an American soldier." That soldier, presumably, was Grant Farr. If anything, Spencer's confession boosted Hamilton's credibility.

The final confession was submitted by Roy Montgomery, the light-skinned soldier who had helped calm the fighting in the orderly room. Montgomery wrote, "I picked up a 2-by-4 and went into the Italian Area, where I heard the noise." Once inside the orderly room, "an Italian soldier ran by me and I hit him with the 2-by-4." Montgomery identified Wooden, Ceaser, Curry, and Herman Johnson, but no one else.

All told, the four written statements didn't seem to Beeks to amount to much. Taken together, the admissions even threatened to weaken Jaworski's contention that Larkin, Hurks, and Jones should be blamed for inciting the riot since all four confessors claimed they went into the Italian Area on their own. Snow had been knocked cold before he could do much damage. Roy Montgomery, no matter what else he did, helped save Farr and others from further harm. Spencer and Prevost admitted to being little more than spectators armed with pieces of wood. Jaworski's case was beginning to look somewhat weak.

Later in life, Jaworski reflected on his time as a military lawyer and wrote that "the earnest lawyer often enters a case with the zeal of a missionary. Truth and protection are the fish he peddles." Rather self-servingly, he claimed that "I wouldn't try a prisoner of war nor any accused without the conviction that he was guilty. I just wouldn't do it! I either had the goods on him, or else I wouldn't try him." But after six weeks of preparations, and knowing what he knew about General

Cooke's scathing investigation, saying he had the "goods" on all forty-three defendants would have been a stretch.

Jaworski did enjoy one substantial advantage: he had access to Cooke's investigation, and Beeks did not. Cooke's report had been marked classified, ostensibly to protect "war secrets." Clearly, the real secret was the incompetent conduct of Colonel Branson, Major Orem, and their subordinates, including the fort's white MPs. And if Jaworski was bothered by Clyde Lomax's suspicious behavior, he certainly wasn't willing to share it with Beeks. As a matter of fact, he intended to call Lomax and Orem as witnesses for the prosecution.

ON THE EVE of the trial, Luther Larkin felt increasingly uncertain and alone. He sat down and penned a letter to Minnie Carr, his mother's sister in Chicago:

> I guess you've seen it in the papers already. It's a lie because they know we didn't do what they are trying us for. Two other soldiers and I are being accused of the hanging of an Italian prisoner of war. We are going to be court martialed and can expect nothing less than life imprisonment or death, all for a crime we did not commit.
>
> I feel so helpless in this frameup, and I know nothing about it at all. You see now, why I haven't written you in so long. I've been so downhearted I haven't written home and I'm not going to write mother any more until I get out of this dirty situation, if that is possible. The fact remains that we are not guilty and whether or not the truth will have any effect on our jurors or not is yet to be seen. We feel at the mercy of these people who, it seems, will do what they want to with us. I know, however, that God will make someone suffer for the injustice that is being done us here.

CHAPTER TEN

PROSECUTION
Late November 1944

LUTHER LARKIN CLOSED HIS eyes and took a long pull from his Chesterfield. The cramped bed of the two-ton army convoy truck, enclosed by a musty canvas canopy, smelled of shoe polish and hair oil and stale tobacco. Although forty-three black defendants and six white guards were sardined hip to hip along splintered benches in this and in two other trucks, almost no one said a word. Heads bowed, their chins bobbed in unison as the truck navigated the bumpy ten-mile route from Camp George Jordan to the gates of Fort Lawton. Larkin exhaled; all the oxygen in the back of the crammed truck seemed to escape with each stream of cigarette smoke.

The convoy slowly squealed to a stop on a gravel parking strip off Utah Street. The MPs hopped out, lowered the tailgates, stepped back from the truck, and squared their shoulders, right hands atop their service revolver holsters. Forty-three men, each sharply dressed in their best olive drabs, stiffly disembarked two by two onto the icy gravel, straightening their garrison caps as the MPs herded them through a back door. They entered a cavernous building, ringed with soaring divided-light windows above fir-paneled walls. Thick old-growth wood posts set into concrete floors supported heavy beams far overhead. The room looked like the inside of a huge barn with greenhouse-style windows above, but the building was as cold as a meat locker.

Larkin fell into a line leading to three long rows of folding wooden chairs, fifteen to a row. He removed his cap, tucked it in his belt, and followed his way down the second aisle. As he stood at attention, he noticed that his fellow black soldiers looked sharp in their dress jackets, with polished buttons, ribbons, and medals—some for good conduct and bravery—proudly displayed. To the left, an oversized American flag hung on a wall above a long elevated bench, with enough room to seat eleven judges. Below the bench sat a wooden witness chair, a small court reporter table, and larger tables for defense counsel on the left, the judge advocate on the right. A table for the press was positioned along the opposite wall, just in front of another section of folding chairs reserved for observers, four rows, eight chairs to a row. This was Fort Lawton Building 1128, adjacent to the hospital, newly built to process large groups of soldiers transiting to or from the Pacific. For the next thirty-three days, this spacious hangar would be a courtroom, the only venue on the sprawling fort large enough to accommodate so many people.

The spectator seating area was noticeably vacant, save for a few men in suits or in uniform and two ladies wrapped in scarves, wool coats, and mittens. Sadie Hughes and Jeanne Barber had come all the way from Chicago to support Sadie's son, Robert Sanders, and Jeanne's husband, Richard Barber, during their trial. Sadie and Jeanne lived in the same South Side neighborhood, just east of the El, not far from Comiskey Park. Jeanne had known her husband since she was nine years old; their families had been next-door neighbors on Wabash Avenue. Before he was drafted, twenty-two-year-old Richard had been a dining car waiter for the Pennsylvania Railway Company. Robert Sanders, one year younger, worked in a meat packing house. They entered the army within weeks of each other, and became inseparable after they both landed in the 650th Port Company. When Richard came home on furlough in June, he and Jeanne got married at the Shiloh Baptist Church. Both Jeanne and Sadie had been uneasy when their loved ones shipped overseas and stunned when the news came about their abrupt return to Seattle. When Robert sent a letter saying he and Richard faced charges that could land them in prison the rest of their lives, Sadie rushed to comfort nineteen-year-old Jeanne, who had no idea her husband had returned from New Guinea. Jeanne was sick about the news, and Sadie was determined to learn more. "I went to the Red Cross at once and got them to see if he was really back," she later wrote. "And they said he asked me to come to him, if it was any way possible. He had never been in any trouble before and he was frightened. The Red Cross and the Traveling Aide was wonderful and friends in every way to me."

Sadie and Jeanne rode the train together, leaving Chicago on November 8, the day after the presidential election. The Seattle Red Cross helped them find housing and arranged two or three meetings with Richard and Robert. Both women were determined to stay until the end of the trial.

Also in the courtroom audience were George Wood of the National Association for the Advancement of Colored People, and two Seattle attorneys, Charles Stokes and John Caughlan. Stokes was one of only two black lawyers in Seattle, and Caughlan, a white man, represented the International Labor Defense Committee and the Seattle Council of Minority Rights. All three men told the newspapers that black soldiers might have a hard time getting a fair trial in the segregated army. Caughlan was particularly incensed that more than forty defendants would have to share just two attorneys.

William Beeks had no time to fret about why there weren't more lawyers sitting with him at his defense table. He did, however, share the apprehension about getting a fair trial. At precisely nine o'clock, eleven white army officers filed into the room and took their places on the elevated dais. After a preliminary discussion to determine who should serve as interpreter for Italian witnesses, Beeks rose to address the panel of judges: "The defense would, if the court please, like to have each member of the court sworn to answer questions. I deem it my duty, in view of the seriousness of this case, to examine each member of the court at some length for the purpose of determining whether or not there is any possible prejudice that any member might have and of which the particular member might not be conscious."

It was a bold, if not presumptuous, move. Beeks was raising the specter of racism, questioning whether any of these eleven white men, each handpicked by General Denson, might have a hard time seeing beyond the color of the defendants' skin. Although the raised platform made the men look like judges, they were all regular army officers whose primary task was to act as a jury. One panelist, Colonel Wilmar Dewitt, had been designated as president. As required by the Articles of War, another member was an officer with legal training, referred to as the law member. For this case, Lieutenant Colonel Gerald O'Connor, a lawyer from New York, had drawn that assignment, and it was his duty to address all the lawyers' motions, including the one just posed by Beeks. "The procedure is unusual," he responded, "but in the interests of fairness to the accused, it will be permitted."

Beeks turned to Jaworski and asked that he issue an oath to the members of the court. Someone asked the court reporter to stop taking notes while Beeks asked his questions. R. B. Bermann of the *Seattle Post-Intelligencer* summarized the forty-minute exchange: "Major Beeks asked every member where he was born and reared, his occupation in civil life, whether he had ever belonged to any organization interested in Negro rights, whether he or any member of his family had ever had any experience which prejudiced him against Negroes, whether he would be embarrassed by returning a verdict of not guilty or by accepting the word of a Negro as against that of a white soldier and, finally, whether he would be willing to be tried, if he were accused, by a court with the same attitude as his."

These were uncomfortable questions, particularly for the five officers who held military ranks higher than Major Beeks. The oldest man on the panel was fifty-five-year-old Major Hector Carpenter, a druggist in civilian life. The youngest was Major George Crocker, a thirty-eight-year-old from San Francisco. The forty-four-year-old panel president, Colonel Wilmar Dewitt, was also from San Francisco. In all, there were four Californians; two New Yorkers; two men from Washington State; and one each from Hawaii, Maryland, and Virginia. When Beeks finished his questioning, both he and Jaworski were each entitled to have one judge dismissed, without giving a reason. Jaworski let go forty-six-year-old Lieutenant Colonel Martin Fennell of Hawaii, and Beeks booted the only true Southerner, forty-nine-year-old Colonel Paxton Campbell of Lynchburg, Virginia. That left two captains from Washington, forty-four-year-old George Atkinson of Spokane and forty-three-year-old Kenneth Weller of Seattle. Major Samuel Mac-Lennan, a forty-one-year-old postal inspector from New York City remained, as did fifty-three-year-old Major Milton Kimball of Monterey Park, California. The ninth officer was Lieutenant Colonel Anthony Stecher, forty-nine, of Baltimore. Stecher's regular job in the army was head of troop movement for the Seattle Port of Embarkation. He was an odd choice as a panelist, since he had testified extensively during General Cooke's investigation and had helped derail Colonel Branson's attempts to move up the shipment of the two port companies after the riot. Either Jaworski or Beeks was entitled to challenge any judge for cause; neither challenged Stecher. Since he hadn't seen Cooke's report, Beeks may have been unaware of Stecher's involvement. Even so, Beeks had put the court on notice that race was an issue, and the opposing lawyers agreed to let the trial continue with the remaining nine officers.

Law Member O'Connor read the name, rank, and company of each defendant, followed by the prima facie elements of rioting under the Eighty-ninth Article of War. A separate charge was read under the Ninety-second Article of War accusing Larkin, Jones, and Hurks of first-degree murder: ". . . acting jointly and in pursuance of a common intent, together with certain other persons whose names are unknown, did at Fort Lawton, Washington, on or about 14 August 1944, with malice aforethought, willfully, deliberately, feloniously, unlawfully, and with premeditation, kill one Guglielmo Olivotto, a human being, by hanging him with a rope by the neck."

Beeks entered a plea of not guilty for all defendants on all charges. Unexpectedly, he then asked to stop the proceedings, to continue the trial at a later date: "I have had ten days to adequately prepare—well, actually nine days to prepare—from the time the charges were served on the defense and to interview witnesses for forty-three men. I have been busy all of the time. I have interviewed over one hundred people, one hundred thirty-two, to be exact. I just haven't had time, even though I have employed all the diligence within my power, to properly prepare and thoroughly investigate and confer with my clients." He asked the court for a four-day continuance. Jaworski acquiesced but only after complaining, "I do have here in attendance witnesses who have been brought from distant places." Less than two hours after the opening gavel, the first day of trial had ended.

THERE HAD BEEN little sunshine over the weekend, and by the time the trial reconvened on Monday, November 20, radiators along the walls of the makeshift courtroom were clanking at their highest settings. The indoor air was lip-cracking dry, and as heat rose toward the vaulted ceiling, a chill settled around everyone's ankles. To Luther Larkin, New Guinea almost seemed a warm memory.

Thursday's brief session had given Jaworski his first real look at William Beeks, and he was impressed with what he saw. Beeks did not pretend to be charming; he could, on occasion, seem indignant and even a little angry. The stocky major had jumped at every opportunity to mark his territory, demanding that potential witnesses be excluded from the courtroom and insisting in open court that the five black soldiers who were given immunity be segregated from each other until after the trial. During several preliminary motions, Beeks repeatedly reminded the court that the night of August 14 had been dark and chaotic, planting the suggestion that identification of individual suspects might be all but impossible.

For several days, Jaworski had pondered how he might blunt Beeks's tactics. He began Monday morning by distributing notebooks to each of the nine judges. Inside each notebook were about two dozen pages, most of them blank except for the defendants' names, arranged in alphabetical order, two names per page. In the back, he told the jurists, was an index. "In this manner the Court will be enabled to, by turning to the index and seeing what page the particular accused is, jot down any notes that pertain to that particular accused as the testimony develops, and we hope it will be of some value and some benefit to the Court."

The gambit caught Beeks by surprise. With so many defendants, Jaworski could not possibly build his case one defendant at a time. He planned instead to present his version of the facts in roughly chronological order. If all went as he hoped, the judges would make a notation each time one of his witnesses mentioned a defendant's name. In the end, he hoped each notebook would be filled with blunt indictments of every defendant, written in each judge's own handwriting.

Beeks recognized it as a brilliant move but could think of no grounds to object. Clearly, the court was entitled to make notes, whether or not they used Jaworski's handy booklets. In fact, Beeks might be able to turn the notebooks to his own advantage, since he felt certain that the evidence against a sizable number of his clients was shaky at best and that the entries next to those names might be sparse. In his wildest dreams, he could never expect acquittal for all forty-three defendants, but he could try his damnedest to fight for those who were either innocent or the least guilty. The notebooks would stay.

The next order of business was a small victory for Beeks, as Jaworski announced that he was dropping all charges against Private John R. Brown, the soldier who had spent the night in a Seattle motel. No explanation was offered, but as judge advocate, Jaworski had the authority to dismiss charges against any defendant at any time. It was all Private Brown could do to suppress a grin as he was allowed to stand up, squeeze past his glum comrades, and walk out of the building a free man.

Jaworski abruptly called his first witness, matter-of-factly skipping an opening statement. Giuseppe Belle, the Italian who struck Willie Montgomery in the jaw, was sworn in and instructed to sit in the wooden witness chair, facing the panel of judges, his back to the gallery. Through an interpreter, Belle related how he and his two friends were returning from their soirée in Seattle when they came across Montgomery and three others. Jaworski asked what, if anything, the American soldiers said; his reply in Italian momentarily staggered the court interpreter.

"Shall I say it?"

"Yes, it is necessary for you to interpret it just as he is saying it."

"He said, 'God damn Italian son-of-a-bitch shit.'"

During his September interrogation by Colonel Williams, Belle had testified that just one soldier attacked him. In court, however, he swore that four men rushed him, one holding a knife in his right hand. In court, Belle said a flash of light reflected off the blade of the knife from the streetlight overhead. But his story in September had been that he was blinded by the streetlight because it was behind his attacker, turning the assailant and what might have been a knife into a hard-to-see silhouette. To Beeks, of course, these important contradictions would have been like blood in the water—if only he had access to Williams's interrogations and Cooke's report. But at this point, November 20, Beeks still knew nothing about the content of that investigation, except that he had been told that it was not available to either attorney. He was also not aware that Jaworski's very first witness was the man that army intelligence had identified as an unrepentant Fascist who should have been locked up in Texas.

Belle's testimony continued, painstakingly, as the interpreter had to repeat each question in Italian and each reply in English. Whenever Beeks found anything objectionable, his interruption usually meant the previous question had to be asked, answered, and interpreted all over again. The process soon grew tedious. For long stretches, Beeks and Jaworski bickered about Belle's tendency to go off onto long tangents when answering what Beeks thought were yes or no queries. When it came time for Beeks to cross-examine, Belle grew argumentative. Beeks asked for estimates about time, location, and distance, to which Belle repeatedly answered, "I don't know." The testier Beeks grew, the more obstinate Belle became. As the clock reached ten thirty, court-martial President Dewitt intervened:

Dewitt: How much longer are you going to be with this witness, Counsel?

Beeks: Well, I wouldn't be very long if he would answer my questions.

Jaworski: Now just a minute!

O'Connor: Now Counsel, let's don't have comments like that. We don't like to have those remarks and you don't want to forget he is speaking through an interpreter, and he is in a strange land, and I think under the circumstances he is doing the best he can and so are all of us.

Beeks: Well my only answer to that would be that I would be perfectly agreeable to have a recess taken at any time.

Dewitt: The court will take a fifteen minute recess.

Roy Daymond, the first of Jaworski's five black witnesses, was next. Daymond told how he helped Larkin drag Willie Montgomery back to the barracks but now claimed that Larkin, instead of giving artificial respiration, ran into Barracks 719 to get a whistle and came out blowing the company into formation. Daymond admitted going down to the Italian Area and rattled off the names of several defendants he said he saw there: Elva Shelton hitting an Italian with a stick, Frank Hughes carrying a knife, and David Walton holding a stick. He said that after the riot, James Coverson told him he had beaten an Italian unmercifully.

As he listened to Jaworski's line of questioning, Beeks began to suspect that the prosecutor was hiding something. At one point, Jaworski made reference to an interrogation where Larkin allegedly agreed with Daymond's version of events. Beeks shot up from his desk. "I want to demand at this time that the Trial Judge Advocate produce and have available the statements of this witness which is a basis or part of the investigating officer's report. I understand you have those, Colonel."

Jaworski tried to sidestep the request. His investigating officer was Major Robert Manchester, who reported to General Denson at the port of embarkation. Denson had been given a copy of General Cooke's report and also had access to the complete transcripts of Cooke's and Williams's interrogations. In addition, Manchester had interrogated dozens of suspects on Denson's behalf. Technically, Jaworski reasoned, those items were not in his "possession" as long as they remained in

Manchester's files. "I am very certain that I do not have any such thing as you have in mind that would fit the description you speak of," he countered. "I would be glad to bring the investigating officer's report but I am sure I have not any statement like that which you speak of."

Jaworski had no intention of turning investigative material over to the defense unless he absolutely had to. Although Law Member O'Connor could have instructed Jaworski to cooperate more fully, he did not. It would not be the only time O'Connor sided with the prosecution on evidence crucial to the defense.

When it came Beeks's turn to examine Daymond, he tried to establish that the private had been part of Sergeant Tanner's unauthorized get-together in Building 700.

> "Were you over at a party going on in the 578th mess hall?"
> "No, sir, I wasn't."
> "You weren't over there at all?"
> "No, sir."

But back on September 17, Daymond had readily admitted to General Cooke that he had been at Tanner's party:

> "Did you go across the street and into the mess hall at any time?"
> "Yes, sir, I did."
> "What was going on in the mess hall?"
> "When I came out and went into the mess hall, there was an Italian in there."
> "What was he doing?"
> "He was playing the guitar."
> "Did you see any beer on the table?"
> "Yes, I saw beer bottles."

Once again, Beeks had no idea that Daymond had just impeached himself. Beeks produced a transcript of his own pretrial interview with Daymond, in which Daymond swore he had never gone into the Italian

Area, the opposite of what he had just testified when Jaworski asked about Shelton, Hughes, and Walton. Beeks dug in.

"Now which is the truth, Daymond: were you in your barracks all the time or did you go down to the Italian Area?"

"I went down to the Italian Area."

"What did you go down for, to participate in the attack or see what was going on?"

"Just to go down there, sir."

"Just to go down there and see what was going on?"

"Yes."

"Quite a number of other men went down there to see what was going on, didn't they?"

"I don't know about them."

When Beeks was finished, Jaworski was allowed another turn. He hoped to diffuse Beeks's insinuations, but things quickly turned nasty.

Jaworski: Now, you have talked with me about your testimony in this case, have you not?

Daymond: Yes, sir.

Jaworski: I have asked you questions about it?

Daymond: Yes, sir.

Beeks: I object to Counsel leading the witness. He has already denied—

Jaworski: I thought you were interested in it.

Beeks: I am interested in your proceeding in a proper manner. You know the way as well as I do to proceed in these cases.

Jaworski: Now, if it please the court, I don't propose to take a lecture from Counsel as to whether I proceed correctly or not. If he has an objection to make I suggest he make it to the court.

O'Connor: I think in the future you should address your remarks to the court, Major.

Beeks: I should be glad to do that, but I submit the first off-the-record remark was made by Counsel.

If Belle and Daymond had come off as less than candid, Jaworski was sure he had a sympathetic witness in Grant Farr. Unlike Belle, Farr was an American, and unlike Daymond, he answered questions without hesitation or qualification. Jaworski led Farr through the horror of his night, beginning with when he awoke to find his orderly room quarters under attack. In somber detail, Farr described the noise and the blood and the pain all around him. He described his assailants the same way he might depict a park of wild dogs.

"The faces of the men I saw in the doorways and in the room were faces that were distorted, bloodshot eyes, lips drawn back over their teeth, and a general appearance of frenzy and hate."

"Now, Sergeant, did you notice anything about the nostrils of any of them?"

"Yes, sir, the nostrils were dilated."

His knife wounds, he said, had eventually dulled his senses, leaving only hazy recollections of the faces of the black soldiers who had led him to safety. Sergeant Farr knew someone in the orderly room had belatedly recognized he was an American soldier but could not say whether or not it was Roy Montgomery. During a series of lineups, he couldn't distinguish whether it was John Hamilton who had escorted him outside or whether Arthur Hurks had joined Hamilton to help lead him to the upper road. Several weeks after the attack, he picked out Richard Sutliff as a soldier who had just missed hitting him with a construction brick. On cross-examination, he told Beeks he remembered Les Stewart had been in the orderly room, brandishing a long knife.

"What particular physical characteristic is there about his makeup that is different than the other colored soldiers back here by which you are able to pick him out and say it was Stewart rather than some other individual?"

"Well, sir, one characteristic was the upright hair on the front of the head."

"You think that is peculiar to him and none of the other colored soldiers here have that?"

"No, sir, but that was one of the things I remember."

"Any other?"

"Well, he was of medium complexion. He wasn't as dark as some nor as light as some."

"Anything else, Sergeant?"

"No, sir."

Court-martial protocol allowed any of the judges to question witnesses. Lieutenant Colonel Stecher was struck by Farr's recurring inability to distinguish one black soldier from another.

"Have you been around Colored personnel before?"

"No, sir."

"Have you had any experience with them at all?"

"No, sir, not in the army. I was born and raised in Utah and I have never had a great deal of contact with the Colored people."

Jaworski's three Monday witnesses had helped describe the events of August 14, but their collective identifications of a handful of soldiers had been tepid at best. On Tuesday, he put Fred Perata and Edward Haskell on the stand to corroborate Farr's dramatic description of the attack; Sergeant Haskell could pick out only Roy Montgomery and Willie Basden, and Sergeant Perata—badly injured—recognized no one. Both were sympathetic characters, however, and Beeks did not attempt to minimize their version of the ordeal.

It was time for Jaworski to turn up the heat. His star witnesses were next: Willie Ellis, Jesse Sims, and Alvin Clarke, plus the Italian POW, Augusto Todde. Corporal Ellis was first; he implicated one soldier after another, a dozen in all. With the mention of each new name, Ellis was asked to stand up and walk over to the three rows of defendants, where he held his finger over the head of whichever man he was identifying.

During pretrial interrogations Ellis had sworn he had watched Luther Larkin blow a whistle and had later seen him in the Italian Area. During his time in the witness chair, however, Jaworski never asked Ellis a single question about Larkin. Ellis did lump Hurks and Jones with the crowd of soldiers he said he'd seen in the orderly room but never said a thing about seeing Hurks speaking with the MP, Private Lomax, after the riot. Most telling, each of the twelve men he identified had, in his recollection, been simply "standing around" somewhere. Beeks jumped on that point during cross-examination.

"You never saw any man, any colored soldier in the Italian Area, strike anybody?"

"No, sir, I didn't."

"You didn't see anybody damage any Government property?"

"No more than the jeep running into the tent."

Jesse Sims, the private who could neither read nor write, was next; he had plenty to say about all three murder suspects. Jaworski asked him to describe how his craps game was interrupted by William Jones. Sims remembered that Jones came upstairs shouting, "'The Italians have knocked one of your boys out out there.' He said, 'You Texas boys always talking about what you will do.' He say, 'All right, now let's go!'" Jones, he testified, led a group of soldiers down to the Italian Area. Sims said he did not follow but headed outside on his own, where he heard a whistle.

"Did you see who blew that whistle?"

"Yes, sir."

"Who blew it?"

"Luther Larkin."

Larkin, he testified, led a second group down to the Italian Area; a third group followed.

"Did anyone lead that group?"

"Yes, sir."

"Who?"

"Arthur Hurks."

Sims said he trailed behind Hurks's group, grabbing a one-by-four cedar picket from the broken fence along the way. He too said he saw Robert Sanders driving across the tent with a jeep and confirmed that Roy Montgomery had stepped in to protect Grant Farr. Sims agreed with Ellis that Barber, Stone, Simmons, and Nathaniel Spencer were all in the Italian Area, and he added the names of seven other soldiers—sixteen men in all. He reported watching William Jones smash a lightbulb above the porch of Italian Barracks 708.

Beeks knew this was an important cross-examination. Sims, whose street smarts made up for much of his lack of formal learning, forced Beeks to work for every answer. Even preliminary questions became a test of wills.

"About what time was it that the Italian Service Companies first occupied the area adjacent to the Colored Area at Fort Lawton?"

"That, sir, I don't know."

"Well, about what time was it, Sims, that you first saw them?"

"Sir, I couldn't exactly tell you."

"Well, I don't expect, Sims, for you to give the very exact day, but what is your best recollection of about when it was?"

"I can't remember that, sir."

"Well, they had been there a period of several months anyhow, hadn't they?"

"I don't know, sir."

Beeks asked about Sims's deal with Jaworski for immunity; Sims claimed not to understand. A question about what Sims ate for dinner turned into a five-minute debate about whether he had eaten anything at all. Sims claimed to remember which men had gone into the Italian

Area but drew a blank when asked to remember the names of those he knew had stayed behind. Either Sims was completely clueless or he had figured out that playing dumb might be a clever way to blunt Beeks's increasingly pointed attack.

Beeks refused to give up. Sims, he knew, was a heavy drinker and gambler, and those vices may help explain who he was or was not willing to finger.

"As a matter fact, weren't you down there at the PX celebrating a little bit because you were leaving the next day for an overseas destination?"

"Sir, any time I got hold of any money I would go down there and celebrate. There wasn't anything special on that day."

"You like to celebrate when you get a little money, do you?"

"Yes, sir."

Beeks had his opening. He moved to the craps game.

"Who was it in that crap game that had money that you thought you would like to get your hands on?"

"Sir, I didn't have no special one."

"You didn't care from whom you got the money?"

"No, sir."

There were plenty of men willing to testify that the dice had not rolled Sims's way that night, and that he chafed as he watched the last of his quarters slide into the banker's pile in front of Sergeant Hurks.

"Now, as a matter of fact, Sims, you were losing that evening, weren't you?"

"No, sir, I didn't lose that evening."

"Weren't you doing a lot of beefing around there about losing your money?"

"No, sir, not me, because I didn't have but a dollar and a half when I come in there."

"Didn't you lose that dollar and a half and beef about it?"

"No, sir. When I got out of there I have five dollars."

Although Sims had identified sixteen men, he said he could not re member how a single one of them was dressed that night or whether any of those whose faces he recognized were wearing helmets, garrison caps, or any other kind of head covering. After an hour and forty-five minutes of cat-and-mouse maneuvering, Beeks hoped the court would agree that the only details Sims seemed to remember about the night of August 14 were the names of sixteen men. And, like Ellis, he never said a word about anyone actually striking an Italian.

Jaworski's fourth black witness, Alvin Clarke, added little, except when it came to Luther Larkin. Clarke said he saw Larkin in the center of a group of thirty men, giving first aid to Willie Montgomery. At one point, he said, Larkin walked into the barracks.

"What did he do?"

"A few minutes later, sir, I seen him come out into the company street and blow a whistle."

"Corporal Luther Larkin blew the whistle?"

"Yes, sir."

"All right. And what, if anything, did you see happen after that?"

"A group of men gathered around him, sir, and he told them to follow him."

Clarke's story was that Larkin led the first group down; Sims had said Larkin led the second group. Neither man knew whether Larkin had also administered first aid to Sammy Snow. Clarke admitted he went down with the second group, but was almost immediately hit on the head, then rescued by Riley Buckner. Nonetheless, he claimed to have seen Henry Jupiter and Nelson Alston down in the Italian Area, each with a club. He also testified that Booker Townsell and Johnnie Ceaser both later bragged about hitting Italians. On cross-examination, Beeks—as he had with Sims—pointed out that Clarke's memory of the riot seemed to have been erased, except for those details that helped the prosecution.

Among them, Daymond, Ellis, Sims, and Clarke had singled out twenty-seven of the forty-two defendants. On the fourth day of trial— the day before Thanksgiving—it was Augusto Todde's turn. As others had before him, Todde walked up and down the aisle between each row of defendants, studying their faces until he paused to point accusing finger after accusing finger. When he picked out Johnnie Ceaser, he admitted he couldn't be sure when or where he saw him, only that he was "in the orderly room." Other accusations were similarly vague.

Jaworski understood that Todde's testimony strained credibility: How could he have recognized so many men with such certainty when the orderly room had been so dark and the scene so chaotic? Farr, Haskell, Perata, and Gould had all struggled to identify even one or two of their attackers, and most of the Italians had a hard time doing even that. In 1944, it was common for Caucasians to insist that they couldn't distinguish one black American from another, as Haskell confided many years later: "I remember seeing all the black soldiers in the courtroom. When I was there, they all looked alike. You know, you put them all together, same uniform and everything, you can't hardly tell the difference."

Jaworski attacked the skepticism straight on. He pointed out that Todde had lived in Tripoli since 1927.

"Did you at any time have occasion to see Ethiopians?"
"Yes."
"Well, tell us where you saw Ethiopians, and what your experience in seeing them was."
"I have seen them in Tripoli; in Libya."
"During what years?"
"During the years 1928, 1929 and 1930."

"And what was the nature of those contacts with Ethiopians during those years?"

"In that period, on the reoccupation of Libya, I was assigned with a company of Ethiopians and Libyans, and in that period I had occasion to be together with these Colored people."

And that, Jaworski maintained, was enough to remove any difficulty sorting one black American from another fourteen years later. Beeks was incredulous, but his animated objections to the relevance of Jaworski's questions were repeatedly overruled by O'Connor.

Beeks went home that night churning with frustration. In his years as a trial attorney, he had never quite come across someone like Jaworski. In many ways, the man at the prosecution table was his mirror image, another brainy, argumentative showman, a know-it-all accustomed to using his intellect to bully the less-gifted around him. Somehow, Jaworski found a way to stay charming, while Beeks came off as angry or even petulant. In Beeks's mind, Jaworski was leading all his witnesses, coaching their testimony as they went along. Time and again, Beeks jumped up to object, and time and again, Law Member O'Connor struck him down. Howard Noyd began to feel as if Jaworski had gotten under Beeks's skin. During one recess, Noyd even suggested that Beeks let him handle the cross-examinations for a while. Beeks would have none of it; allowing a young captain to go up against this swaggering colonel would smell of weakness. And Beeks was not weak.

Newspaper reporters found it all very entertaining. The *Seattle Times* declared that "exchanges between Colonel Jaworski and Major Beeks have been one of the high lights of the trial" and described Jaworski as "suave and hard-hitting." The *New York Times* called Beeks "a bulldog kind of man who shakes his witnesses until there is no more evidence to be drawn from them. He works with all his mental energy every minute of the trial."

THANKSGIVING DAY WAS not a holiday for the Fort Lawton court-martial, so Beeks showed up for the fifth day of trial determined to roast Todde on cross-examination. Beeks asked the stocky, black-haired sergeant to describe as many details as he could of each man he had identified—height, build, clothing, and alleged behavior. The process dragged, since every exchange had to be translated from English to Italian and back again. Todde, though, was unflappable, smoothly offering opinions that may or may not have been consistent with what he had said during pretrial interviews; Beeks still had no way to know the difference. In the end, Todde appeared to maintain the upper hand.

For Beeks, the day grew worse. Jaworski called Italian private Nicola Corea, who had been stabbed in the back; he testified that Sergeant John S. Brown had split his head with a rifle wrapped in brown paper. Several Negro soldiers, he said, picked him up and tried to drag him into the woods before he managed to wriggle free. It was dramatic testimony, and Corea told his story with the flair and body language of a seasoned performer. Beeks, however, soured Corea's mood by appearing to be unimpressed with the trauma the Italian had suffered. Corea steamed when the lawyer asked him to describe the man who had stabbed him. At one point, Beeks ordered him to stand up and walk over to a pole marked off with feet and inches.

"Now, I wish you would show us over on this pole how tall was this man?"

"I did not pick up a ruler to measure him."

"You saw the man, didn't you, through the door?"

"Yes, I saw him."

"All right. You give us your recollection of how tall he was."

"He is right here, if you want to measure him. I don't know why you want me to show you."

"It just shows this witness is a smart-aleck."

Beeks then asked for an estimate of John Brown's weight. The question was translated, and when Corea muttered something under his breath, all those in the court who could understand Italian started to laugh.

Beeks: If the Court please, there seems to be considerable merriment going on here.

O'Connor: The trouble is, the interpreters are the only ones that get it.

Interpreter: He said, "Blessed God, how the hell do I know?"

Beeks: Well, I think, if the Court please . . . I think by laughing at this witness we are only encouraging him in this sort of thing.

Jaworski: No, I don't think so, Major. He has, I think, been very informative, tried to do everything he possibly can. I don't think you can find fault with his efforts.

Beeks: I know very well you didn't have near the difficulty getting information I am having.

Jaworski: Major, I didn't ask some of the questions you are asking, either.

Beeks had no comeback. When Colonel Dewitt announced that in honor of Thanksgiving, court would recess at three, Beeks readily acquiesced.

Two competing local newspapers served Seattle's black community, and each provided stories about the trial to black-owned newspapers around the country. The *Northwest Herald* tended to be sympathetic to the defendants and their lawyers, commending Beeks for persisting in the face of what the *Herald* assumed was a stacked deck. The *Northwest Enterprise*, however, took the view that the defendants were generally an embarrassment to their country and to their race. Its editors were particularly critical of the defendants raised in the South, whom they condescendingly viewed as uneducated rubes and bumpkins. Summarizing the first week of the trial, an *Enterprise* reporter ended with a personal note. "One of the most interesting points in the trial as an observer, is the display of ignorance on the part of the accused rioters. As serious as is the case, we are forced to laugh when certain statements and questions are asked the Negro defendants." The note continued, "We hope that our white America, after associ-

ating with the migrants here from the southern states, will fully realize the sad mistake of allowing any Americans of any creed or race to
be subjected to unfair dealing by the more fortunate citizens of our
many communities."

The article was published November 24, well *before* any defendant
had taken the stand. The reporter, then, was presumably describing
Daymond, Ellis, Sims, and Clarke—all *Jaworski's* witnesses—when
he complained about the "display of ignorance."

As terrible as Thanksgiving had been for Beeks, the day after Thanksgiving brought a measure of redemption. Jaworski called Thomas Battle, the fifth black soldier protected by immunity. By the time Jaworski
finished Battle's direct examination, his prosecution witnesses had identified forty-one of the forty-two defendants at least once.

Thomas Battle and Bill Beeks had crossed paths a few days earlier
when Beeks was interviewing witnesses in preparation for trial. As
Beeks began cross-examination, Battle was visibly nervous, stumbling
through preliminary questions.

> "You are married aren't you?"
> "Sir, I am."
> "And how long have you been married?"
> "I was married on the 19th of—I believe it was February."
> "Of this year?"
> "Yes, sir—No, sir."
> "Last year?"
> "Sorry to disappoint you, it was this year."
> "You are not disappointing me, Battle."

Instead, Beeks could sense Battle's fear. He asked the young private
whether his wife had been with him the night of August 14; he said
she had not. Beeks read back Battle's earlier answer to the same question during Beeks's investigation: Battle had then sworn he and his
wife had been drinking and dancing at Sergeant Tanner's party. Rattled, Battle began to experience the same selective memory loss that

others had during cross; he couldn't remember what he ate, where he went, or who he was with.

"Your memory of that evening isn't too good at this time, is that right?"
"No, sir."

Beeks drilled in. Battle had just told Colonel Jaworski that he had seen Johnnie Ceaser breaking windows. But one week earlier, he had told Beeks under oath that Ceaser had done nothing.

"Sir, I must have been frustrated at that time."
"You think you were probably frustrated at that time?"
"It must have been a misstatement made at the time."

Then what about Ernest Graham? Was he still sure about where he had seen him?

"Sir, I am afraid to say that."
"Well, when Colonel Jaworski was questioning you here a few moments ago, didn't you tell Colonel Jaworski where it was you saw Ernest Graham?"
"Sir, so much passed through my head since then I do not remember."

Beeks felt ten inches taller. Just as so many of Jaworski's witnesses had ticked off names of men they thought had been part of the riot, he now had cornered a man who was ticking off reasons why he may have been mistaken—if not lying. Battle had even sworn that he saw Private John R. Brown, whom everyone now knew had been in a Seattle hotel that night.

"Battle, as a matter of fact, you were never down there yourself that night, were you?"
"Sir, I was."

Battle was toast. Beeks was ecstatic. The next day, the *New York Times* reported that "Beeks scored Friday when Pvt. Thomas Battle, Negro witness for the prosecution, broke apart under the Major's cross examining." The *Tacoma Times* said Beeks "scored heavily" for the first time in the trial when he "ripped into" Battle "with a rapier-sharp cross examination." That night, as he had done all week, Beeks took a pair of sharp scissors and carefully cut out the glowing articles to paste into his scrapbook.

Just as Thanksgiving was not a trial holiday, Saturday was not treated as a weekend. The court-martial continued on November 25 with testimony from several more Italians, each detailing the horrors they had endured August 14. Some talked of being dragged from beneath their bunks; others spoke of being chased down like rabbits, then beaten and stabbed. One testified about hiding in the woods, while others relayed the panic of being trapped in the orderly room. Unlike Todde, these Italians admitted it was all but impossible to identify their assailants. For the most part, the black men in the dark of night were a blur.

After lunch, the defendants were loaded into the backs of three trucks; everyone else climbed into jeeps or staff cars. The convoy drove to the Colored Area, where all forty-two defendants stood in line as the nine judges walked through Barracks 719, upstairs and down. From there, everyone walked to the Italian Area, where they toured the orderly room, tents, latrine, recreation hall, chapel, and Barracks 708 and 709. The only sounds during the excursion were idling engines and heavy boots on wooden floors; Colonel Dewitt had ordered everyone to remain silent. A steady drizzle softly drummed on the roof, but it soon turned into a torrential downpour. A November storm with warm, gusty winds and sheets of rain soon soaked through parkas and poured into shoes. After forty-five minutes, the fort was a quagmire, and Colonel Dewitt ordered everyone back to the courtroom. Surveying the sopping mess, he took it as a sign, and canceled proceedings for the rest of the weekend.

Leon Jaworski opened the second week of trial with seven black soldiers, one from the 651st and the rest from the 650th. Most had initially been suspects, but all seven were eventually released. Several spent time in the stockade with the defendants, where they testified overhearing men bragging about being in the Italian Area during the riot. Much of Monday's testimony covered similar secondhand conversations.

It proved to be another challenging day for Major Beeks. Two of Luther Larkin's fellow corporals in Barracks 719—Willie Cunningham and Addison George—each testified that Larkin had come looking for a whistle. Both men were from Texas, and the local press had a field day with Addison George, making fun of what they took to be his simple mind and rural grammar. The *Post-Intelligencer* reported that Addison "had the court in stitches" during Beeks's cross-examination.

"Beeks asked him, 'Do you remember the other day when I came down to Camp George Jordan to see you?'

"'No, sir,' replied George, 'I can't remember faces. One looks just like another to me.'

"'Well, do you remember this officer?' pursued Major Beeks, pointing to his assistant, Capt. Howard D.E. Noyd.

"'I remember some fellow like that,' was the reply.

"'Well, you remember that some officers were talking to you and asking you questions and a lady was taking down your answers,' Major Beeks queried. 'You were telling the truth then, weren't you?'

"'Yes, sir,' said George. 'You must have been there, sir.'"

Although the courtroom erupted with laughter, Beeks wasn't smiling. During his pretrial interrogation, Corporal George had said he wasn't exactly sure who had asked for a whistle. As far as Beeks was concerned, the admission that "one looks just like another to me" was grounds for the court to ignore George's additional identifications of Hughes, Walton, and Sanders. Yet again, another of Jaworski's witnesses seemed to have conveniently changed his story just in time for trial.

Richard King continued the pattern. A slightly built nineteen-year-old corporal from Colorado, King claimed to be a curious bystander, saying he had simply walked down Lawton Road to watch all the excitement. He hadn't gone far, he said, when the first carload of MPs arrived, led by Sergeant Thurman Jones, and including John Pinkney. King testified that Pinkney and Sergeant Jones told Hurks to keep the rest of the soldiers at bay, then commandeered King and Sergeant Robert Gresham to help restore order in the Italian Area. King identified seven men he said he saw in the area that night, including Larkin, Curry, Wooden, and Walton. Wooden, he said, had scolded him for helping the MPs. Booker Thornton had gone so far as to threaten him once they returned to their barracks. Thurman Jones, the white MP, confirmed that he had stationed both King and Gresham outside the orderly room to maintain order.

King's testimony seemed devastating, but once again Beeks was able to pull out earlier sworn statements during his own interrogation of King, statements contradicting many of King's trial recollections, including his identification of Larkin. King's eyes widened when Beeks asked him about his bunk.

> "Who slept over you?"
> "I slept on top."
> "Who slept under you?"
> "Sergeant Veeder."
> "As a matter of fact, you took Sergeant Veeder's field jacket and walked down there and you got some blood on it that night? And you permitted them to arrest him, didn't you?"
> "Yes."

Sergeant Harry Veeder, it turned out, drove a supply truck and had borrowed money from Pinkney that night so he could sneak into town to buy whiskey. Corporal King admitted he had stood silently by as Veeder was thrown into the stockade, even though he knew Veeder was implicated only because King had taken his jacket. Sergeant

Veeder gained his release only after admitting he had been AWOL that night.

Jaworski called Sergeant Robert Gresham to the stand to confirm that he and Corporal King had been conscripted by Thurman Jones of the MPs. Speaking so softly that he had to be constantly admonished to raise his voice, Gresham listed eleven men whom he said had been in or around the orderly room, including Larkin, Hurks, Barber, and Wooden. A twenty-one-year-old from Chicago, Gresham was a large man who had been singled out by many others—including several of Jaworski's own witnesses—as an active participant in the riot himself. For a time, he was even locked in the stockade but allowed to go to New Guinea when none of the Italians recognized him. Several defendants had warned Beeks that Gresham was not a man they trusted.

Beeks, however, was glad to see Gresham in the witness chair. As far as Beeks was concerned, Jaworski had opened a door by calling Gresham—a door into another issue that might throw the prosecutor's case into disarray. Gresham, Beeks knew, had been in the PX two days before the riot.

> "A number of colored soldiers were in there at that time?"
> "There were quite a few."
> "What occurred there that evening, if anything?"
> "Well, sir, an incident between white soldiers and one of the Italian soldiers."
> "What happened?"

At that, Jaworski jumped out of his chair. Anything that happened before August 14, he protested, was entirely irrelevant and immaterial. Not so, countered Beeks. In fact, he intended to produce a series of witnesses to testify that there had been a number of confrontations between white soldiers and Italians in the PX and elsewhere, and that in several cases, it had been black soldiers who had stepped in as peacemakers. It would, he asserted, help the court understand the general state of mind of the soldiers in the port companies on the night of August 14.

Jaworski knew from General Cooke's report that the Saturday and Sunday skirmishes in the PX could spell trouble for his prosecution, especially since the omnipresent Private Lomax had popped up there too. He told the court he objected to Beeks's line of questioning because it seemed to imply that provocation could be a proper defense for rioting, something, he said, the law clearly disallowed. No, replied Beeks, he was simply trying to shed light on the workings of the minds of his clients the night of the riot: "I believe the Court realizes that they are a very impressionable group, there isn't any doubt but what these Colored boys are impressionable. And for the purpose of considering punishment, I think that evidence is admissible, if for nothing else."

Jaworski could see that Beeks didn't fully realize the explosive potential of what he was asking, no doubt because Jaworski knew much more about what had happened in the PX on August 12 and 13 than Beeks did. The law member, O'Connor, couldn't grasp the significance either. He wanted to know more from Beeks.

"Have you any identification of the white man that was involved in this incident?"

"No, sir."

"Or have you any identification of the Italian prisoner of war that was involved in this incident you speak of?"

"No, sir."

"Well, then, in what way do you consider this evidence is material, Major?"

It was painfully obvious Beeks was not prepared to make a determined stand. In the meager time he had been given to prepare for trial, the persistent whispers about white hostility toward Italians had taken a back seat to the effort to save the lives of Larkin, Hurks, and Jones. Beeks did not realize that the white soldier who had started the PX fight was Tex Stratton or that the MP who had responded was Stratton's friend, Clyde Lomax. He certainly did not know that Cooke had insisted Private Lomax be court-martialed for mysteriously disappearing during the time Olivotto was murdered. He did not, therefore, consider that the white MP whom William Jones thought he saw chasing Italians around the barracks might be the same soldier who handed Herman Johnson a flashlight during the attack on Italians in Barracks 708. In each case, every MP was accounted for, except Clyde Lomax.

Jaworski smelled triumph. He implored O'Connor to slam the door on any testimony about skirmishes in the PX, contending they were red herrings, utterly unrelated to the riot. Although he knew that Stratton had twice threatened the Italians, and that Stratton and Clyde Lomax had talked about it afterward, he did not feel compelled to share that fact with the court or with Beeks. O'Connor, hearing nothing else from Beeks, slammed the door. "Now," he stated, "the testimony was there was an incident on the Saturday night, and that may stand. But any testimony as to the incidents and of what happened two nights before this last incident occurred, I hold that is irrelevant and immaterial."

The altercations in the PX were never mentioned again. In the next edition of the weekly *Northwest Enterprise*, the editor felt compelled to comment: "We wonder if the real evidence leading up to the fight between the Negro soldiers and the Italians, former prisoners of war, will be allowed to enter this trial? Or would this implicate our government and the heads of our Army? It's one hell of a mess if you ask me."

TUESDAY, NOVEMBER 28, was the ninth day of the trial, and for the very first time, one of Jaworski's witnesses mentioned the name of the murder victim. Imo Nolgi told how his best friend, Guglielmo Olivotto, panicked when Barracks 709 came under attack.

"He jumped out of the window."
"Before he jumped out of the window, state whether or not he said anything to you?"
"He said, 'Imo, are you coming, too?'"

Antonio Urbano, Olivotto's work supervisor, testified that as he was looking out the window of Barracks 710 during the height of the riot, he saw someone jump from Barracks 709.

"Did the person that jumped make any outcry at the time?"

"He was shouting, calling on his Mother to help him. He said, 'Mother, please—Mother, help me, they are going to kill me, help, help.'"

"Who was he attempting to get away from?"

"From the Negroes."

"What, if anything, did you see the Negroes trying to do?"

"To grab him. Seize him."

"About how many Negroes did you see attempt to seize him?"

"Four or five men."

"Did you recognize the voice that you heard calling out, that you have described to the Court, calling on his Mother to help, did you recognize that voice?"

"Certainly."

"Who's voice was it?"

"Olivotto."

Another Italian, Gennero Iodice, had been standing outside. He told the court that he saw Olivotto for a split second as he was running away from four or five black soldiers. Rosario Sidoti remembered seeing five men drag someone who had jumped out of Barracks 709 toward the direction of the woods. Mario Marcelli said that while hiding in those woods, he heard voices and a car heading down the bluff. After a long cross-examination, Beeks got Marcelli to concede that it would have been impossible for a vehicle to negotiate the footpath near where he had been hiding. Nonetheless, Jaworski hoped the court would agree that Sidoti and Marcelli provided circumstantial proof that Olivotto had been caught and somehow carried down to the obstacle course.

Jaworski's next witness was Charles Robinson, the white MP who had been riding with Lomax when they first came across Willie Montgomery lying in the street. Jaworski, inadvertently or otherwise, phrased his questions as if Robinson, not Lomax, had been the first to discover Olivotto's corpse the next morning. Robinson seemed confused by the error but never corrected Jaworski since he had in fact helped take down the body later that day, at Major Orem's direction. He testified that Olivotto's lifeless body was barefoot.

> "Now, I wish you would tell the court whether or not you inspected the ground for the purpose of finding any footprints or shoe prints?"
>
> "I did. I was looking for all kinds of clues, anything that might be around."
>
> "All right. State whether or not you found any bare footprints?"
>
> "I didn't see any, no, sir."

He did, however, find shoe prints facing uphill, directly beneath the body, and covered them with a piece of cardboard. All told, Jaworski hoped the lack of bare footprints proved that Olivotto did not commit suicide.

Beeks, of course, might have had a field day with Sergeant Robinson and Major Orem if he had known that General Cooke had demanded that Robinson be court-martialed and that Orem be demoted to a lower rank. As it was, Beeks hadn't even been told that General Denson had fired Orem as provost marshal and that one of the reasons cited was Orem's failure to preserve the shoeprints found beneath Olivotto's body. Beeks wasn't even aware that an entire company of soldiers had been allowed to run through the obstacle course within hours of the discovery of the murder scene. As such, Beeks asked Orem only a few harmless questions before allowing him to step down; Orem was undoubtedly grateful that General Cooke had not been given any role in the criminal proceedings.

As the tenth day of trial dawned, Jaworski confided to a reporter that he expected to wrap up his case in another day, maybe two. He planned to introduce the written confessions of Nathaniel Spencer, Roy Montgomery, Willie Prevost, and Sammy Snow, tie up a few loose ends, then let the defense take its best shot. Beeks, however, had something else in mind. When Major Robert Manchester, the port's criminal investigator, took the stand to swear that each of the four confessions had been given voluntarily, Beeks struck back. One by one, he called the four defendants to testify that their statements had, in fact, been coerced. Nathaniel Spencer said he was told "the Court would be much harder against you" if it concluded he had been in the Italian Area and hadn't first admitted it in writing. Called back on the stand under oath, Manchester denied making such a threat.

Roy Montgomery followed, saying he was first read his rights, including his right to remain silent, but was told his case would be referred to a "higher authority" if he refused to write out a confession. Montgomery said he complied only after Manchester promised to move him out of the stockade, where he worried that other defendants might treat him as a snitch. That promise, he said, was repeatedly broken, even after he rewrote his statement three different times. Finally, he stopped cooperating. Manchester admitted making the promise to relocate Montgomery but denied threatening Montgomery with a "higher authority."

The most incendiary accusations came from Willie Prevost. Manchester employed several criminal investigators, including Sergeants Ralph Young and Robert Fiske, plus two civilians, Jack Freeman and Benjamin Glasgow. Prevost said he wrote out a statement but was told it didn't include enough details, including the name of the soldier who had chopped down the door of the orderly room. Sitting on a table in the interrogation room was rope, which Prevost was led to believe had been used to hang Olivotto. Jack Freeman, he said, picked the rope off the table: "He throw the rope in my lap so I could see it, and he said I could have hung that man. He told me, he said, 'I could lay the hanging on you.' I told him, 'No, sir, he couldn't.'"

Prevost had continued to insist to his interrogators that he had admitted all he could, but Freeman persisted. After a long stalemate, Prevost said, he was told to leave the interrogation room, accompanied by Sergeant Young, a beefy twenty-eight-year-old redhead who, in civilian life, was an interior decorator in Chicago. Prevost recounted, "He walked up to me and said, 'Well, I hate to see you get messed up like that, because there is an Italian that has already identified you and they'll take his word, and if you don't admit the thing, his word will be used against you in court in a case,' and so he says, 'You better go in there and change those statements.'" Prevost said he stood firm. Sergeant Young, he said, picked up the rope and glowered.

> "He said I would know more about the case when that rope was around my damn neck."
> "You say that Sergeant Young said you would know more about the case when you were hanging by the neck by that rope?"
> "Yes, sir."

Only then, testified Prevost, did he agree to rewrite his confession, implicating Wooden, Walton, and Sanders.

Jaworski was not amused. Instead of wrapping up his case as planned, he had to use all of Thursday—the final day of November—eliciting a barrage of denials from everyone who had come in contact with Prevost. Freeman agreed that a rope was in the interrogation room but swore it was never laid on Prevost's lap. Young testified that the rope was handed to Prevost so he could try to identify it but denied making any threats.

> "After we had our break and had had a chance to have our coffee, and smoke our cigarettes, I returned and asked Prevost how he was feeling, and he said he was feeling all right. And then he asked if he could change his statement."
> "Nothing was said during that recess?"
> "No, sir."
> "But he came out of the room and said he wanted to tell all?"
> "Yes, sir."
> "Do you know what changed his mind?"
> "No, sir. He mentioned he wanted to get it all over with."

Jaworski pulled out all the stops. A total of seven people had been in the interrogation room that day, including two stenographers, Corporal Ernestyne Morgan and Lu Henderson, a civilian. All of them told slightly different stories but collectively seemed to agree that Prevost, after insisting at length he had nothing else to add, came back from a simple coffee break with Sergeant Young suddenly eager to tell all. At the end of the day, O'Connor was faced with a decision whether or not Prevost's confession was admissible. He decided to sleep on it, and adjourned for the evening.

WITH THE TRIAL now sliding into December, Jaworski found it difficult to keep his promise to Jeannette to telephone regularly. Long-distance lines were in high demand during wartime, often causing delays of three to four hours between the time he first placed a call and when an operator finally rang back to say a line was available. Trial days were long, and by the time he got back to the Olympic Hotel, the two-hour time difference between Seattle and Houston usually made it too late to pick up the phone. Although mail took a week, he tried to write when he could.

He also remained a faithful correspondent to his wife's sister, Wilma, and her husband, Boots. As the second week of trial drew toward a close, he was eager to tell his in-laws that the *Post-Intelligencer* had been sending artist Henry Roth to the trial almost every day and that he had often been the subject of Roth's drawings:

Am sending a clipping and a sketch that will give you some idea of it. It happens to be the Army's largest military trial of the present war. But what a headache it has been at times! Now as to the sketch! Don't let the artist fool you. It has been a h__l of a long time since I have been able to be as complacent as he pictures me.

Jaworski claimed that he was eager to get home, despite the national notoriety he was gaining at Fort Lawton. As it turned out, other things were on his mind:

If present plans materialize, I expect to be in Houston during the Holidays. It simply must not be otherwise . . . You see, unless there is some unexpected change in plans, I will be headed for overseas soon after that. That is as much as I can say about it just now. There is a very fine assignment in store for me—altho', of course, there is sometimes "many a slip between the cup and the lip."

He concluded with best wishes for the approaching holidays and another promise to see his family soon:

Write again, if you find time—please. —Leon
P.S.: Please send the clippings on to Jeannette at your convenience. I want her to send them on to Dad—will you please tell her to do so?

CHAPTER ELEVEN

DEFENSE
Early December 1944

WILLIAM BEEKS AND HIS wife, Florence, owned a home just a few blocks from Fort Lawton, in the starched Seattle neighborhood of Magnolia. Howard Noyd stayed downtown, at the posh Olympic Hotel, the same place the army quartered Leon Jaworski. Every Monday through Saturday, a big black army staff car pulled into the hotel's grand circular driveway to chauffeur Jaworski and Noyd to the fort, seven miles to the north. Although the two officers were opponents in the courtroom, they both worked for the same boss—the army judge advocate general—and generally enjoyed each other's company. Noyd, the Iowa farm boy, and Jaworski, the Texas preacher's son, shared a love for Scripture, football, and good food. Jaworski also liked to sing and was thrilled about a tune at the top of the charts, a Cole Porter number recorded by Bing himself, called "Don't Fence Me In." Its lyrics made Jaworski both proud to be a Texan and homesick for Waco. To Noyd's surprise and glee, Jaworski would sometimes fill the fifteen-minute commute with refrains from that popular song.

If Jaworski had felt fenced in by Willie Prevost's accusations that his written confession had been coerced, he felt even more corralled by Sammy Snow. On December 1, Beeks called Snow to the witness chair to contend that he too had been browbeaten into writing out a confession. Snow, who had been more willing than any other defendant to admit he had gone without hesitation into the Italian Area to avenge the attack on Willie Montgomery, now claimed his interrogators had pledged to pin Olivotto's murder on him if he didn't tell them even more:

> Sergeant Young, he threatened me by pulling off his coat and telling me he had a good mind to sock me if I didn't tell the truth and tell what went on down in that Italian Area . . . Mr. Freeman, he set on one end of the table and I was sitting on the opposite end, and he told me to look him right dead in the eyes and then he began to make some remarks, saying that he knew I didn't go to the hospital until three in the morning and that he was going to lay the murder rap on me of killing the Italian. He also stated—asked me—where my father and mother lived, and asked me if I had a sweetheart, and I said, yes, sir, and he stated if I didn't tell him the truth I would be a four-year loser and I would never see my mother and father again.

Snow, like Prevost, insisted that he had come as clean as he could but that it was never enough to satisfy the port detectives. After one interrogation, he was not allowed to return to the stockade but was instead locked for five days in solitary confinement in a windowless room. "I was carried down to the guard house and I was put in a cell," he said, "a cell that had only a little ventilation—opening in there. I didn't have anything to read, wasn't allowed to see anyone. When I was carried out I always had an MP with me. Wasn't allowed to speak to no one at no time."

As with Prevost, Jaworski was forced to produce a parade of denials from those who had been in the room with Snow during his five separate interrogations. They all agreed that Snow had been more talkative than most but insisted he had been read his rights and treated fairly. Manchester conceded that he had ordered Snow segregated from the other suspects, "because I was not satisfied with the first story he told me and I did not want him in a position, if he was so inclined, to support or build up an alibi." But Manchester disputed the use of the term "solitary confinement," because, he said, that only applied to situations where military prisoners were restricted to rations of "bread and water." In Jaworski's opinion, Snow was embellishing his story because he was upset he had not been offered immunity.

To Jaworski's chagrin, Beeks continued to hammer away at the confessions throughout Friday and into Saturday, December 2. It was some consolation, however, that O'Connor once again sided with the prosecution. He ruled that neither Prevost nor Snow had been threatened by anyone, and that their signed statements had been entirely voluntary. It was a point Jaworski had hoped would have been settled days earlier.

Finally ready to wrap up his case in chief, Jaworski called witnesses who testified to finding John Hamilton's dog tags in the orderly room and Herman Johnson's shovel in Italian Barracks 708. When Elby Murray told how Johnson had later asked him for another shovel, Beeks grew openly upset. On cross-examination, Beeks read back Murray's initial sworn statement, an account that contradicted much of what he had just said to Jaworski in open court: "If that testimony isn't impeaching, I might just as well fold up my briefcase and go home."

Jaworski *was* ready to go home. To prove the dead Italian was in fact Guglielmo Olivotto, he called Giovanni Prinzi, the Italian chief warrant officer, who had viewed the body at the Bleitz Funeral Home. To establish that Olivotto had died by hanging rather than some other way—and died during the riot rather than some other time—he called Captain John Walker, the young doctor who had conducted the autopsy. It was Dr. Walker's opinion, based on the rigor mortis in Olivotto's body, that the Italian had died between 11 P.M. and 1 A.M., perhaps a little later. Finally, to prove that the hanging had occurred on the Fort Lawton obstacle course, he called Clyde Lomax.

Jaworski knew that General Cooke had demanded Lomax be court-martialed. He knew that none of the other MPs could account for Lomax's whereabouts much of the night. He knew that Lomax was prone to use racist language. But most important, he knew that Beeks had no idea how much baggage Lomax carried. Even so, he might have avoided calling Lomax altogether except for one very embarrassing hole in his case: army investigators had somehow misplaced the rope, and Jaworski could not produce the murder weapon!

Lomax proved a difficult witness. He mumbled his answers to the first few questions, prompting O'Connor to admonish him to look directly at the members of the court and speak up. While describing the events of August 14–15, he repeatedly used the term "Colored boys" until Jaworski reminded him he was speaking about "Negro soldiers." Eventually, Jaworski's questions reached the point when Lomax first approached Olivotto's body.

"Was he dead or alive?"

"Sir, he was dead."

"And what did you say was around his neck?"

"A rope, sir."

"Can you give us some description of that rope?"

"Something like a tent rope."

"I will ask you to take a look at this rope, Private Lomax, and state to the Court whether or not it was that type of rope."

"Sir, it was one something like this. I wouldn't say definitely whether this was the rope or not because it has been a pretty good while since that happened."

Both Jaworski and Beeks knew it was not the actual hanging rope, so when Jaworski offered it as Prosecution Exhibit 40, Beeks objected that it was irrelevant, immaterial, and prejudicial. As was his pattern, O'Connor overruled the objection, and the look-alike rope was admitted.

The daily newspapers made no mention of the astonishing fact that the real rope was missing. Instead, they made much of Lomax's breathless recollection of what he said was the first salvo of the riot. The headline in the *Post-Intelligencer* read COURT-MARTIAL WITNESS DECLARES NEGRO SOLDIERS RALLIED TO CALL FOR ASSISTANCE. "'They've got one of our boys and we're going to mob them!' Pvt. Clyde V. Lomax, a veteran of Attu and the Marshalls, declared yesterday. That was the cry which was raised by Negro soldiers at Fort Lawton on the night of August 14 after one of them, Willie Montgomery, had been knocked out in a fight with a former Italian prisoner of war. His testimony provided a fitting climax for the second week of the general court-martial trial."

IF ANY OF THE nine judges had been carefully filling in the blanks of the notebooks Jaworski had provided him, he would have noticed that the page beneath the name of one defendant was still empty. Not one of Jaworski's witnesses had mentioned Milton Bratton, a thirty-two-year-old private first class from Excelsior Springs, Missouri, just outside Kansas City. Having reached the end of his witness list, Jaworski now had no choice but ask the court to let Bratton go. As Bratton made his way happily out the door, Jaworski stood at the prosecution table, confident he had made a strong case against the remaining forty-one. "May it please the Court, the Prosecution rests."

Beeks, the ball now in his court, wasted no time. He knew that Jaworski had not offered a single bit of evidence tying Larkin, Hurks, or Jones to Olivotto's death. He also felt it appropriate to make a motion that is standard for most criminal defense attorneys at the end of the prosecution's case: "At this time, may it please the Court, the Defense moves for a finding of Not Guilty as to each of the accused."

Beeks then asked for a three-day recess, reminding the court that he had barely had a chance to speak with most of the men he'd been defending. Jaworski protested, telling the court that one day should be sufficient, two at the most. He did not, of course, mention how much he wanted to get home to Waco. In a rare ruling for Beeks, Dewitt agreed to three days. After the break, he would rule on the motion for a finding of not guilty.

With a bit of time on his hands, Jaworski caught up on his reading, particularly the nonstop trial coverage in the daily papers. The reporters had treated him well, and he had no doubt that favorable press clippings might help his effort to land a war crimes assignment. Duly satisfied, he sat down to write a letter:

Editor, the Seattle Post-Intelligencer:

As trial judge advocate in the case at Fort Lawton, Wash., and as one who appreciates the task assigned to newspaper men in such cases, I want to thank you for the able men that you have designated to cover the trial.

Permit me to express to you my appreciation of the sketches that Mr. Roth has so admirably done. His ability to sense and sketch with preciseness the exact scene that climaxes a particularly dramatic moment is uncanny.

Mr. Bermann's reporting has been accurate and fair. I know at times he must feel that the interest of the case lags, still he always maintains an interesting and accurate account of the proceedings day by day. From his reporting your readers are given an excellent resume of each day's proceedings.

Thanking you again, I am,

Leon Jaworski (Lt. Col.)

Trial Judge Advocate, Seattle

REPORTS ABOUT THE Fort Lawton trial were delivered weekly to the White House. The State Department continued to raise concerns that Italy's new government might react poorly if Olivotto's death went unpunished. At the same time, the Federal Bureau of Investigation warned White House officials that the trial might be exploited by Communists or their sympathizers. The FBI, at the insistence of its director, J. Edgar Hoover, analyzed comments of "agitators" in the Negro press. Those news accounts, wrote the FBI, portrayed the trial as an example of government's persecution of blacks.

Back in September 1943, Hoover had delivered a lengthy confidential report to the White House called "Survey of Racial Conditions in the United States." The report began with a seemingly ominous alarm: "For a period in excess of two years the Federal Bureau of Investigation has received reports and allegations of forces with foreign influence and with anti-American ideology working among the Negro people of this country as well as exploiting them. Based thereon, inquiries and investigations have been undertaken to determine why particular Negroes or Negro organizations have evidenced sentiments for other 'dark races' (mainly Japanese) or by what forces they were influenced to adopt in certain instances un-American ideologies."

Hoover's unnamed sources and secret agents purported to disclose pockets of Communist influence among blacks in every part of the country. The FBI was particularly concerned, he said, about the Negro press and allegedly subversive organizations like the National Association for the Advancement of Colored People and the Worker's Defense League. The report quoted unfavorably from a popular WDL pamphlet called "The War's Greatest Scandal: The Story of Jim Crow in Uniform":

Every one of the half million Negroes now serving in the armed forces is doing so on a jimcrow basis. Every regiment, every ship, every battery, every flying squadron and medical staff and jeep company is either all white or all colored. The most ingenious planning, the most complicated and voluminous quantities of paperwork, the tireless efforts of thousands of officers are devoted to the great task of keeping apart the two races. The instant he puts on the uniform of his country, the Negro becomes a deadly plague carrier, to be quarantined, isolated at all costs from his white comrades in arms.

By December 1944, the FBI's weekly intelligence reports included the names of alleged Communists attending the Fort Lawton trial. In particular, a Negro columnist for the *Northwest Herald* was singled out for observing that "when the enemy can get better treatment than the citizens of the country who captured him, something is bound to happen. Court-martial the authorities who allowed this to happen."

FBI field agents reported that racial tension was high throughout the Northwest. In Seattle, a reported rape of a white woman by four black men was later found to be erroneous. In Bremerton, across the Puget Sound, informants reported incidents of "pushing among whites and Negroes on buses." In the Seattle-area suburb of Renton, police had to be called when the Boeing Aircraft Company assigned ten newly recruited Negro employees to live in an otherwise all-white housing project. Boeing's own industrial relations department pleaded with company officials to reconsider, suggesting they instead place the incoming employees in segregated housing.

A December 1944 intelligence report mentioned an incident on an army installation in Vancouver, Washington, just north of the Oregon border. The episode gave an indication just how much black soldiers' expectations were changing:

> A white Lieutenant singing "Old Man River" at a local talent show staged at Vancouver Barracks on 13 December substituted the word "Nigger" for "Negro" in the song. There were 1,200 persons in attendance, including some 500 Negro servicemen and women, and when the substitution of words occurred, three Negro enlisted men rose, one of them stating "That will be enough of that, Lieutenant." The Lieutenant apologized, declaring he had no intention of offending the Negro troops. With the exception of three or four, however, all Negro personnel left the building, gathered outside in groups, apparently grumbling, but took no action.

WILLIAM BEEKS UNDERSTOOD that his defense of forty-one black men had implications well beyond their guilt or innocence. But, like any good trial lawyer, he focused only on the task at hand. He was convinced that Jaworski had completely failed to make a case against at least one third of his clients, resorting to hearsay and innuendo and guilt by association. Only one or two witnesses said they actually saw any of the defendants strike a blow; many of the accused were merely seen in the area, standing around or holding a fence picket. And, of course, no one had placed any of the three men on trial for their lives anywhere near the hanging scene.

Beeks and Noyd decided that both common sense and the law re-

quired that at least two credible witnesses identify each of the accused. The nine identifications made by Thomas Battle should be entirely disregarded, they thought, considering how spectacularly Battle
had crumbled under cross-examination. They also believed that the
rather miraculous, if not improbable, ability of the Italian Augusto
Todde to single out so many men in the darkness and confusion ought
to be treated, at best, with skepticism.

When court resumed Friday morning, December 8, Beeks renewed
his motion that all his clients be found not guilty. In any criminal trial,
a defense attorney has a right to insist that charges be dropped if a
prosecutor rests after failing to allege—or failing to offer substantial
evidence for—each essential element of a crime. If, for example, a
prosecutor charges a defendant with armed robbery but never offers
evidence he used a weapon, then the defense is entitled to request a
verdict of not guilty of armed robbery.

Beeks continued by reading the legal definition of a riot from the
Manual for Courts-Martial: "A riot is a tumultuous disturbance of the
peace by three or more persons assembled together of their own authority, with the intent mutually to assist one another against anyone
who shall oppose them in the execution of some enterprise of a private
nature, and who afterwards actually executes the same in a violent and
turbulent manner, to the terror of the people, whether the act intended was of itself lawful or unlawful."

The defendants had all been specifically charged with a violation
of Article 89 of the Articles of War, titled "Good Order to Be Maintained." According to this article, "All persons subject to military law
are to behave themselves orderly in quarters, garrison, camp, and on
the march; and any person subject to military law who commits any
waste or spoil, or willfully destroys any property whatsoever (unless by
order of his commanding officer), or commits any kind of depredation
or riot, shall be punished as a court-martial may direct."

It was Beeks's position—citing case law and legislative history—
that Article 89 had always been applied to protect *private citizens* from
riotous soldiers and therefore was an inappropriate charge in this case.

And even if it wasn't, he continued, then certainly Jaworski had offered inadequate evidence of the participation of at least nine men: Riley Buckner, Lee Dixon, Emanuel Ford, Arthur Williams, Sylvester Campbell, James Coverson, Sammy Snow, Ernest Graham, and Freddie Umblance. In each case, Beeks told the court, the only testimony against these men was an overheard conversation or fleeting glimpse. Riley Buckner, for goodness sake, was the man who helped carry the wounded Alvin Clarke, while Sammy Snow was knocked out before he could do any mischief. Each of these men, he said, deserved to have the case continue without them.

The murder charges against Larkin, Jones, and Hurks, Beeks contended, were even less justified. At best, Jaworski had offered ambiguous evidence that someone—Olivotto, perhaps—had jumped from a window, then been chased or carried as far as the edge of the woods. Nothing in the prosecution's case explained how Olivotto ended up at the bottom of the bluffs with barely a scratch on his body.

It was important, Beeks insisted, to remember that Jaworski had charged the three defendants with actual murder, not felony murder, and that even if he had, rioting was a misdemeanor, not a felony. The charges of actual murder, he said, required Jaworski to offer proof—physical, circumstantial, or eyewitness—of premeditation, malice, and intent. The court could see that whoever killed Olivotto had gone to the extraordinary trouble of bringing a carefully prespliced rope to a remote area, then somehow subdued the Italian without leaving so much as a bruise on his body. Contrast that with the rioters, whose rather blunt weapons of choice had been knives, axes, and clubs and who had otherwise confined all their damage to a small area in and around three buildings.

In rebuttal, Jaworski disputed each of Beeks's contentions, even as he conceded that "Thomas Battle didn't make the best witness." Any black soldier who was in the Italian Area, he said, for whatever reason, and however momentarily, helped contribute to the riot, because such a soldier—by his mere presence—effectively empowered those who did the actual damage. "They did it because they knew there were scores and scores of others standing around behind them ready to come to their assistance, cheering them on, so to speak, and they were back of them and ready to assist them if they needed it."

Jaworski tried to tap dance around the fact that rioting was not an Articles of War felony. He emphasized that rioting "is a very, very serious Military offense," punishable, in a few instances, by life in prison. And even though he had not charged anyone with felony assault, he asked the court to concede that many of the men were armed with "dangerous weapons." "Is there any doubt in anyone's mind—in the mind of any member of the Court—but what these men went down there for the purpose of doing grievous bodily injury to those Italians?" he demanded.

If there was no doubt, Jaworski argued, then those men clearly acted with premeditation and malice. And if that was true, he said, then they were responsible for the consequences of each and every direct result of their illegal activity, including the death of one of the Italians they had attacked. Technically, he pointed out, all forty-one of them could have been charged with murder. And, yes, he would now concede that he had not been able to show that Larkin, Hurks, or Jones "did actually place the rope around [Olivotto's] neck and pull him up on the cable. The Prosecution has not done that, and we are not seeking to do that at this time." But, he contended, he *had* proved that those three defendants had led their fellow soldiers into the Italian Area and, because of that, ought to be held responsible for any resulting consequences, including murder. True, he hadn't alleged felony murder and he couldn't meet the felony murder standard, but, he said, he didn't need to. Their premeditated and malicious decision to lead other men into an area to cause harm, resulting in Olivotto's death, amounted to actual murder.

Jaworski sat down. The court, without discussion or elaboration, denied each of Beeks's motions. The case would continue in full, and it was the defense's turn to proceed.

AT 3 P.M., FRIDAY, December 8—twenty-two calendar days since the gavel first fell—Beeks finally called his first witness. Louis Cabral, brought back from New Guinea to testify at trial, had been the first sergeant for defendants Ernest Graham and Sylvester Campbell. Cabral vouched that the two soldiers, both of them company cooks for the 651st, had stayed near him the night of the riot and that neither had gone down to the Italian Area. By coincidence, all three men had been called upon back in July to help quell the uprising of Fascist Italians headed for Hawaii. Beeks, realizing that that incident may have helped color attitudes toward Italians, tried to slip it in while examining Cabral.

> *Beeks:* Sergeant, at any time prior to August 14, 1944, was your Company ever called out to assist in suppressing a riot or rebellion of Italian soldiers?
>
> *Cabral:* Yes, sir.
>
> *Beeks:* Will you tell the Court the circumstances?
>
> *O'Connor:* Wait a minute—
>
> *Jaworski:* Just a moment! I don't think that is at all admissible in this proceeding, and I ask the Court to strike the answer, and I object to any testimony along the line that is being attempted to be given here.
>
> *O'Connor:* The motion is granted.

Minutes later, Beeks suffered a much bigger defeat, arguably the biggest of the trial. He had called another company cook, Herman Redley, to further bolster the alibis for Graham and Campbell. On cross-examination, Jaworski pulled out a thick report and began to quote from sworn statements Redley had made to Colonel Williams during General Cooke's investigation. Until that moment, Beeks had always been told the contents of Cooke's report were top secret, and were not available to either attorney. Visibly upset, he stood and addressed O'Connor: "It appears for the first time, now, that the Inspector General's investigation has been made available to counsel! And as the court will recall, there are several occasions when I have asked for these reports, and it has been told to me they were so confidential and highly secret that [Colonel Jaworski] has not even been allowed to see it!"

Beeks turned toward Jaworski and demanded a copy of Cooke's investigation and report. Jaworski smiled and shook his head.

Jaworski: The only thing you can do is ask the same authority that I did, and that made it available to me, Major. And if you can get the same authority, you can get this, but don't ask me. I have no authority to turn it over to you.

Beeks: I did not ask you. I asked the Court.

O'Connor: I don't have that authority, Major. The authority for that must come from the Secretary of War.

Beeks, tired of being constantly overruled, did not hide his anger.

Beeks: Oh, no! It does NOT have to come from the Secretary of War. It has lost its confidential nature once it is made available to HIM to use in this courtroom. There is only one thing he can do now, if he uses it for impeachment purposes, and that is to bring it in here and make it available to us.

Jaworski: No!

O'Connor knew what Beeks did not: that the request encompassed more than fifteen hundred pages of transcripts from more than 160 witnesses, plus General Cooke's incendiary criticisms of Branson, Orem, and Lomax. O'Connor was not going to go down that road if he could help it; it could take days or weeks to review all the documents. At most, he might require Jaworski to share whatever snippets of testimony he used whenever he tried to impeach a witness. But nothing more. Beeks was beside himself.

Beeks: I mean, Counsel is not on a different plane than I am. I am representing these men, and I have as much right to see the government records as Counsel has!

Jaworski: No, that is where you are wrong, Major. That is not a correct statement. We are not in the same situation. I am a government agent and you are not, and I have access and am supposed to know things that you are not. As far as examining anything in court, as I told you, I will treat you very fairly, and better than you did when I asked you for your record, and let you see anything that I use. But, whoever you get authority from to use this, and however you get it, or wherever you get it, you will have to get it from the Secretary of War, or whoever can give it to you. But I cannot give you that authority nor can I let you have this.

O'Connor: Do I understand you will turn over to the Major the statement *en toto* on any statement you use?

Jaworski: No, sir, I cannot turn over *en toto* any statement. All I can do is let him see whatever I use and read, and that portion only. I will have no objection to that. There are matters in here, however, that he is not privileged to see, I am convinced of that. They are matters that don't pertain to the issues in this case . . . but he can come and look over my shoulder while I am examining the witness, and see that portion. He can do that, but that is as far as I can go.

Beeks: Well, I am not interested in that. And, as fond as I am of Counsel, I don't wish to stand there looking over his shoulder. When he told me he had not asked for this, and when he told me it was not made available, I was not going to ask for it. But now, when certain parts of this testimony have been made available to this Court, it is no longer confidential and it loses its confidential and secret nature, and it certainly looks to me as though I should be able to use it, also.

Throughout the trial, O'Connor had deferred to Jaworski's judgment on almost every difficult issue. Seeing indecision on the law member's face, Jaworski once again took charge.

Jaworski: While I might have some right to turn over something to you that I have taken, it is all the more reason that I cannot turn over to you what someone else has taken.

Beeks: Well, I think the Court has the authority to make that available.

Jaworski: Oh, no they don't! But, as I tell you, whatever I use, Counsel can see. Now that THAT is over with, where do we stand?

Beeks: I don't know that it is over with!

Colonel Dewitt, sensing O'Connor's impotence and embarrassed by the whole scene, decided to step in. If possible, he said, the court would try to get authorization to allow Beeks to see Cooke's report and the voluminous transcripts. Beeks, unaware of the explosive material in the report, told Dewitt he'd be plenty satisfied with just the transcript. Jaworski wasn't through, though, erupting to a boil and hissing what sounded like a threat.

Jaworski: Oh, no, that is ENTIRELY improper! Whatever I may be using is a different matter, but certainly not WHATEVER testimony has been taken in connection with this matter!

Dewitt had heard enough. Court was adjourned.

Sitting among his fellow defendants, Roy Montgomery was startled with delight. He'd grown used to seeing his court-appointed lawyer knocked around, even though it seemed obvious the little man with the large head and permanent scowl was trying his best. Montgomery figured it had plenty to do with the army's preoccupation with rank; Jaworski, a lieutenant colonel, outranked Beeks, a major, and in Roy's experience, officers with the most hardware on their chest always prevailed, even if they were wrong. Now, in a rare moment, the major seemed to have truly aggravated the lieutenant colonel, who wasn't likely to be singing songs on the drive back to the hotel that night.

Years later, Jaworski would write with pride about his years as an army prosecutor. In particular, he bragged about his fair treatment of defendants, particularly his noble responsibility to share confidential information with the defense, even when it might hurt the government's case. "Soon I was reassigned to a number of sensitive trials," he wrote. "I traveled across the country to other commands, at their request, to serve as trial judge advocate. In the Army, at that time, this position compared to that of a prosecutor, except that the trial judge advocate was sworn to divulge all the facts in his possession, no matter which side was helped."

The next morning, Saturday, December 9, Jaworski approached Beeks before trial. If Beeks would withdraw his motion to request all the inspector general transcripts and report, Jaworski would promise to give Beeks copies of select relevant excerpts from the Cooke/Williams interrogations whenever Jaworski decided to use that particular testimony during his cross-examination. Jaworski, of course, understood just how damaging the entire inspector general records could be. Beeks had no idea, and accepted Jaworski's offer. As trial opened, Beeks had the floor.

> *Beeks:* "At the close of the evening yesterday the Defense made a demand that the records of the Inspector General pertaining to the investigation of this riot be made available to this Defense. And I want the record to show the Court informed of the fact that the matter has been satisfactorily adjusted—as far as the Defense is concerned—with the Trial Judge Advocate, who has agreed to make statements that he uses available to the Defense."
>
> *O'Connor:* "Then your demand is specifically withdrawn?"
>
> *Beeks:* "Yes, I specifically withdraw that request and Counsel has very kindly cooperated with me in giving me what I asked for."

Unfortunately for forty-one men, Beeks's surrender would turn out to be a devastating mistake. Jaworski's contention that he was a "government agent"—and that Beeks was not—might have been true only if General Cooke's report had contained unrelated state secrets or items of national security, which it did not. Since much of the sworn testimony in Cooke's investigation went directly to the guilt or innocence of the defendants, O'Connor should have been compelled to require Jaworski to hand them over, even if it meant the trial might have stretched even longer. Beeks's capitulation, however, let O'Connor off the hook, and Jaworski never brought up the Cooke report again.

By now, it was clear to Beeks and Noyd that any witness who faced Leon Jaworski on cross-examination did so at considerable risk. Each defendant had a right to take the stand, of course, but they weren't *compelled* to do so. "You're going to have to expect that the prosecutor is going to ask a lot of questions," Howard Noyd told them, "and you're going to get mixed up. And so you have to be careful about how you answer. Tell the truth, but it's up to you what the truth is." As far as the defense lawyers were concerned, most of their clients were better off simply keeping their mouths shut.

Twenty-four men agreed, but seventeen insisted on telling their side of the story, chief among them Luther Larkin. Larkin may have been the defendant with the most to lose, but he approached the witness chair with the confidence of a man with everything to gain. Beeks began by leading him through a description of his time in the service, including his many months studying to be a medic, his good conduct medal, and his disappointment when told the quota for Negro medics had been filled. Larkin carefully explained how he had helped the injured Willie Montgomery and Sammy Snow, even as he had been vaguely aware of the rising anger around him. It was Sergeant Gresham, he said—the same Gresham who had earlier testified against Larkin and Hurks and Barber and eight other defendants—who actually sounded the fatal alarm.

"You could hear whispers in the crowd, the fellows was talking like, 'We'll teach them not to come up here and jump on our men.' So I gave him artificial respiration for maybe ten minutes or longer, or maybe a little less. Sergeant Gresham, he came up to me and asked me how bad was he hurt, and I said, 'Oh, he'll be all right.' And he said—he stated these words: 'I should blow the Company out.'"

"What were his words again?"

"He said in these words, 'I should blow the Company out.' And I spoke these words, I said, 'You ain't lying,' just like that. Well, from that point on, he was as close to me as I was to the floor.

And he blew the whistle. He blew the whistle there, and he walked to 719 . . . He stood up on the steps in the doorway of 719 and from the little light that was shining out of the barracks—there was a little light shining through the door from upstairs—I could see him, he blew it again, and from that point on, I don't know where he went."

Larkin said that after reviving Willie, he was exhausted and went into the barracks to get a drink of water. Moments later, Robert Sanders brought in Sammy Snow, blood pouring down his face. "As soon as I got back where Snow was," Larkin went on, "another whistle blew outside. I don't know who blew the whistle nor where it came from."

Beeks pointed out that several men, including Sims, Clarke, and Addison George, had sworn they either heard Larkin ask for a whistle or actually saw him blow it. But Larkin insisted otherwise: "I did not, sir. I was in no position to ask anyone for a whistle. There was a man hurt, and I knew how to render first aid, and I gave the man first aid, and when I got through working on these two men, the fight was over."

With uncharacteristic swagger, Beeks turned to Jaworski and challenged him to ask Larkin anything he wanted about August 14. Jaworski, unruffled, brandished the transcript of his interrogation with Larkin taken the day after Luther returned from the Pacific.

"You remember Major Manchester, Captain Branand, and I talking with you?"

"Quite well, sir."

"In fact, we talked with you some two or three times, didn't we?"

"Twice, sir."

"Twice?"

"Yes, sir."

"And those conversations were longer than just a few minutes, were they not?"

"Well, not with them, but you and I, sir. We talked from eight o'clock till 12:30."

"Weren't they present, too?"

"Part of the time."

"It was not from eight to 12:30, was it?"

"Eight-thirty to twelve, I believe."

"Was it that long?"

"Well, I was taken out of the guardhouse at 8:30."

"Then you were brought to the Port?"

"No, sir; I was brought just across the street."

"Oh, yes, you are talking about the first conversation?"

"Yes, sir."

And so it went. Each time Jaworski asked a question, Larkin responded by fine-tuning the facts or confidently correcting him. Jaworski, perhaps, had hoped to trip him on simple preliminary matters; if so, the strategy backfired. Early on, Larkin spoke like a man who he knew what he was talking about. Soon enough, Jaworski turned up the heat.

"Did you ever tell Captain Branand or Major Manchester or me — or any of us — any solitary thing about Sergeant Gresham blowing a whistle that night?"

"I did not, sir."

Jaworski pulled out the one-paragraph statement Larkin had written after his interrogation.

"Is that statement the truth?"

"It was the truth as far as it went. I was not implicating anybody."

"Didn't you tell us when you gave it to us, it was the whole truth?"

"No, sir."

"You didn't?"

"I told you that was a true statement as far as it goes, every word of it, as I told you."

"What part was left out of that statement?"

"That Sergeant Gresham blew the whistle."

During pretrial investigations, Larkin said, no one had bothered to ask him if he or Gresham or anyone else had blown a whistle. If they had, he would have told them. But it never came up and he had never lied. Jaworski reminded Larkin that he had given him the opportunity back in October to confront Daymond, Sims, and Clarke, his three main accusers. Yet again, he had never mentioned Sergeant Gresham. Larkin would not flinch.

> "You connected Sergeant Gresham with me in no way, sir. You never mentioned his name while I was in there."
> "Did you connect his name or mention his name in any way to me?"
> "I did not, sir."

A good cross-examiner can often rattle a witness by asking dozens of rapid-fire questions about the smallest of details, boring in at the first sign that the witness feels frustrated or confused. Jaworski demanded to know names, places, faces, and times, feigning surprise whenever Larkin seemed the least bit hesitant. But each time Jaworski tried to tighten his grip, Larkin calmly slipped through, matching the lawyer's incredulous questions with common sense responses.

> "You DON'T know the name of a SINGLE one who helped you carry Willie Montgomery from across the street to in front of Barracks 719?"
> "No, sir, I do not. Sir, it was dark. And during excitement like that, you don't have time to pay any attention to anybody."

Years later, Jaworski wrote about the pressure of cross-examining a German prisoner of war charged with murder in a different case: "There is a point in every trial where the case has gone beyond tricks and fancy rhetoric. You can't hold the attention of the jury by pulling out your pocket comb and playing 'The Star-Spangled Banner' on it. So I spoke softly and clearly, pacing each sentence the way a runner puts one foot in front of the other."

Leon Jaworski, a brilliant lawyer, kept his comb in his pocket and lowered his voice. Why, he asked, would so many other men want to finger him as the one who blew a whistle?

"Had you ever had any difficulty with [Dan] Roy Daymond?"
"I don't think so, sir."
"Have you ever had any difficulty or trouble with Jesse Sims?"
"Well, sir, he is just a troublemaker."
"I didn't ask you that. I will ask that that answer be stricken . . . Did you at any time have any trouble with Alvin Clarke?"
"Only a few times . . . only in getting him to work, sir."
"Did you ever have any trouble with Sergeant Gresham?"
"Never; nothing in my life."
"Each of these men told falsehoods, in your opinion?"
"Yes, sir."

Jaworski held the thought, hoping Larkin's eyes might betray some doubt or that his conscience would compel him to fill the silence. Larkin refused to take the bait. Jaworski sat down without asking a single question about Olivotto or a rope or the obstacle course or anything at all to do with the hanging. In the end, it was Jaworski who was left twisting in the wind. Beeks hoped the members of the court took notice.

When Richard Barber took his turn in the witness chair, he had more to say about Sergeant Gresham. After raising his right hand and swearing to tell the truth, he caught the eye of his wife, Jeanne and, as he did every day of the trial, he winked. Beeks noticed it and decided to take advantage.

"How old are you?"
"Twenty-two."
"Are you married?"
"Yes, sir."
"That is your wife, the little lady sitting in the courtroom back there, isn't it?"
"Yes, sir."

Jeanne blushed. Beeks turned back to Barber and asked him to recount the night of August 14. He had been to Sergeant Tanner's party but headed back to his barracks just before eleven.

"What did you do after you got in your barracks?"

"I started to packing my clothes first, then I thought I didn't write to my wife that day, and so I got out my writing material and I went to a table and I started writing a letter to my wife."

"Did you finish it?"

"No, sir, I didn't."

"Why didn't you?"

"Because I was interrupted by Sergeant Gresham. He came up and asked me how come I didn't fall out to that whistle that was blown. And I told him I didn't hear any whistle, and he told me, he said, he said that the fellow had went down there and scared those Italians, and some of those Italians were messed up."

Barber said he stayed at the table to finish his letter, which made Gresham impatient. "He walked back and talked to me directly, and he said, 'I know you aren't scared, Barber, because you are from Chicago, I know you aren't scared.' And he said, 'Hurry up,' just like that, and I said, 'O.K.' and he went on out."

Once Sergeant Gresham left, said Barber, he did hear a whistle, so he ran out of the barracks. Beeks asked Barber to explain the significance of hearing a formation whistle, what soldiers were supposed to do when they heard it. Jaworski jumped, though, when Barber began to talk about the July incident with Italian Fascists. Beeks pleaded with O'Connor to let it in.

"I think the record should be clear, and it should be shown, that these men were sent down—and told to go down there once before and quiet another disturbance, and were told how to fall out, and in what manner to act."

"Now, you don't want the Court to believe that every time a whistle blew they were to go down in the Italian Area, do you?"

"No, but to show why a lot of them went out of their barracks and acted in the manner they did."

"Well, I will hear the testimony that he thought he was being ordered out when he heard this whistle blown. As far as any previous incident between Italian prisoners of war and Negro soldiers, or between Italians and American soldiers, I am not going to admit that."

Beeks, however, refused to let it go. When his next question also made reference to the previous incident, O'Connor erupted, and demanded Beeks approach the bench. In whispered tones, he warned Beeks he would not tolerate any more insubordination. Beeks had no choice but to change the subject.

On cross-examination, Jaworski confronted Barber much the same way he went after Larkin, asking why Barber hadn't mentioned Sergeant Gresham during earlier interrogations. Unlike Larkin, Barber stumbled, especially when Jaworski suggested that the only reason Barber was implicating Gresham was because the sergeant had earlier testified against him. As Barber became more rattled, he admitted arming himself with a metal bedpost, despite his earlier written statement that he had grabbed a wooden fence picket. Jaworski skewered him for the inconsistency until Barber was reduced to stammers. Beeks was visibly perturbed as Barber left the stand. Barber had just demonstrated why it was a good idea for most defendants to keep their mouths shut instead of facing Leon Jaworski.

Even so, fifteen others took a turn on the stand, with mixed results. Willie Basden, a short, quiet thirty-four-year-old private from Miami, insisted he had stayed in bed all night. Private Jefferson Green of San Antonio, previously identified by Battle and Todde, told the court he had never entered the Italian Area. Nineteen-year-old Arthur Williams of Cairo, Illinois, the company barber, swore he had spent the night cutting hair (charging thirty-five cents a head) despite being singled out by Todde and Sergeant Gresham. Gresham, he pointed out, owed him money.

Loary Moore, a twenty-three-year-old private, testified that Wallace

Wooden shook him from a sound sleep to warn that their barracks might be burned down by marauding Italians. The former truck driver from Ellinger, Texas, had earlier been implicated by Sims and Sergeant Gresham, but claimed he brushed aside Wooden and went back to sleep. Herman Johnson, accused by many fellow defendants during pretrial investigations as the man who entered Barracks 708 with a flashlight and shovel to pummel cowering Italians, decided to take the stand nonetheless. He claimed he spent the night ironing clothes for the men in his barracks and repeated his story that he had no idea how a pack shovel with his initials ended up in 708. To Beeks's chagrin, Jaworski shredded the shovel story, and Beeks wasn't surprised that Jaworski convincingly connected Johnson to the violence inside the Italian barrack. This, Beeks told Noyd, was another man who should have kept quiet.

THE FOURTH FULL week of the trial began Monday, December 11. Nine more defendants took the stand and Jaworski had his way with most of them. Time and again, he pointed to contradictions between their courtroom testimony and earlier sworn statements. Russell Ellis, age thirty-two, had a bachelor's degree from Langston College in Oklahoma, a rarity for an enlisted soldier and a near miracle for a Southern black man in 1944. Ellis's story, however, was that he simply sat in his barracks doorway and watched as dozens of other soldiers took up arms against the Italians, an idea that Jaworski scorned—and the newspapers agreed—as highly unlikely.

One of the oldest defendants, thirty-seven-year-old Henry Jupiter, also of Detroit, was the only witness to trip up Jaworski that day. Jupiter was in the same craps game as Jesse Sims and gave unwavering testimony about Sims's foul mood as the dice failed to roll his way. Many defendants had been identified by only two witnesses, and Sims was often one of the two. Jaworski unwittingly helped Jupiter cast further doubt on Sims's credibility.

The final defendant to take the stand was Arthur Hurks. If there was one man whom Beeks felt sure had been wrongly charged, it was

Hurks. Two of his accusers, Sims and Ellis, likely held grudges, and the third, Sergeant Gresham, was probably trying to cover his own involvement. Hurks, like Larkin, was an exception to Beeks's rule about men voluntarily taking the witness chair against Leon Jaworski.

Arthur Hurks had been among those sent to New Guinea after none of the Italians thought he looked familiar. While overseas, he was recommended for a good conduct medal. When he got word he was being returned to Fort Lawton, he assumed they wanted him as a witness. "When I returned," he said, "I was never under guard. I came all the way back to California; from there I was given my transportation to Seattle, and upon my arrival in Seattle, I caught the bus and came out to Fort Lawton . . . It just seemed very funny. Coming all the way back from overseas without escort or guard of any kind and then being put in the guard house and charged with something which I tried to stop."

In the witness chair, Hurks charmed the audience like no one else before him. R. B. Bermann of the *Post-Intelligencer* could barely restrain his admiration: "Hurks, a young man with a singularly open face and a resonant voice which filled the courtroom, proved one of the toughest customers that Colonel Jaworski has yet tackled. During a cross-examination which lasted three hours, Colonel Jaworski failed to shake his story in any way."

Arthur Hurks had helped John Hamilton guide Grant Farr to safety. He had followed the MPs orders to help keep any more men from entering the Italian Area. Although Jaworski caught a few discrepancies between Hurks's courtroom testimony and his lengthy written statement, all the differences were minor. One portion of that written statement made a few of the judges fidget in their chairs:

I looked down the streets and saw John Hamilton coming up the street with a white American soldier. When Hamilton got up to my barrack, I ran out to see what was up. Hamilton told me to take this man to safety so no one would hurt him. While I carried him up the hill he told me that there were white soldiers living down in the Italian Area also. Right there I knew it would be trouble between the whites and the Colored. I know what trouble mean between the whites and Colored—that's why I was willing to hold back the crowd for the MPs. I came from the South and have seen too many things happen; at the end of it the Colored man gets the worst end.

After Hurks sat down, each of the twenty-four defendants who chose not to testify stood before the court one at a time to acknowledge he was freely giving up his right to speak on his own behalf. Five men—John Hamilton, Robert Sanders, James Chandler, Roy Montgomery, and Walter Jackson—submitted unsworn statements. Noteworthy among those who remained silent were Slick Curry, Sammy Snow, Willie Prevost, Les Stewart, and murder defendant William Jones. Jones, who had tried to implicate both Larkin and Hurks during pretrial interrogations, had in turn been fingered during the investigation by nearly everyone else who was in the Italian Area that night. He agreed with Beeks that it was probably best to keep his mouth shut.

After eighteen trial days spread across four weeks, Beeks and Noyd felt fairly confident the murder charges wouldn't stick. Jaworski had presented scant evidence about Olivotto's death, all of it circumstantial, most of it a stretch. Both Larkin and Hurks had been sensational witnesses, and, despite Jones's unpopularity, the bulk of the trial testimony against him came from two discredited soldiers, Sims and Ellis.

Still, Beeks was bothered by the sheer number of important rulings that had gone against him. A smart lawyer, he knew, never got complacent, especially when men's lives were at stake. Before resting his case, he decided to try to plant the possibility that Olivotto wasn't murdered at all. He introduced a stipulation about the Italian captain, Ernesto Cellentani, who couldn't come to court because he was still hospitalized. Cellentani, he said, would testify, if he could, that Olivotto harbored "an abnormal fear of Negroes, which was due to mistreatment of him by

French Moroccan Colored troops." He would have also testified that Olivotto was a loner and expressed unreasonable fears about being quartered so close to American Negro troops. Finally, he stipulated, Cellentani would have reported that he had asked Captain Beckman, commanding officer of the Twenty-eighth ISU, to have Olivotto subjected to a complete mental and physical examination. While Beeks couldn't prove it, he hoped the court might entertain the possibility that Olivotto had killed himself. With that, the defense rested.

Colonel Jaworski, entitled to produce witnesses to rebut anything Major Beeks had introduced, wasted no time calling Charles Sturdevant. The army psychiatrist told how Olivotto had been referred to him for a brief one-hour consultation, aided by an interpreter. He said he had assured the reclusive Italian that American Negro troops posed no threat, then sent him back to his unit and never saw him again. Jaworski asked whether a man with an unreasonable anxiety about black soldiers might, if suddenly confronted with a violent attack by Negroes, be likely to kill himself. Sturdevant thought he would not, that he would be more inclined to become immobilized by fear, unable to run away, much less kill himself.

On cross-examination, Beeks tried to get the doctor to agree that Olivotto might be schizophrenic, with thoughts of suicide. Sturdevant wouldn't bite; as far as he could tell, Olivotto was neurotic, not psychotic or delusional—he didn't actually think, for example, that the members of the 650th and 651st were French Moroccans; rather, his experiences in Africa had made him fearful of blacks in general. Beeks pressed other theories. In June, Olivotto had refused surgery when his tonsils became infected; could that have had some sort of toxic effect? Was it possible Olivotto had syphilis? What about the scar on his head? Sturdevant refused to go along with any of it; Olivotto was strange, maybe, but not crazy.

Jaworski's final witness was John Pinkney, the black soldier who had voluntarily taken up MP duty when he realized a riot was unfolding. Despite his central role in the entire affair—including discovering Olivotto's dead body—neither side had seen fit to include Pinkney in their case. Jaworski, however, decided to use him to buttress the allegations against Wooden, Hughes, and Barber, since Pinkney said he had seen all three in the orderly room. Beeks, however, seized an opportunity to further weaken Jaworski's case against Arthur Hurks. Pinkney was sure that Sergeant Hurks had stayed out of the Italian Area and said he had been a big help keeping other troops at bay. As Jaworski rested his case, it seemed Beeks had won the last little skirmish.

His victory was short-lived. Now that both Jaworski and Beeks were through calling witnesses, the nine members of the court were entitled to keep asking questions of whomever they wished. Wilmar Dewitt brought Grant Farr back to the stand and asked whether it was possible that three men—John Hamilton, Johnnie Ceaser, and Arthur Hurks—had all helped him escape the melee. Farr remembered that a mulatto had stopped others from attacking him and that two or three men had led him out of the orderly room. But, to Beeks's dismay, Farr was "positive" his rescuers had never turned him over to the care of another man once they left the Italian Area. In other words, Farr, though dazed from his injuries, did not agree that Hurks had ever helped him once Hamilton brought him up the road.

There were no more witnesses. Two weeks earlier, Beeks had requested that the army return eight more men from New Guinea to provide testimony on behalf of Hurks, John S. Brown, Herman Johnson, and Booker Townsell. The witnesses had not yet arrived; no one could say for sure where they were, and Christmas was just ten days away. During a long recess, Beeks and Jaworski agreed to stipulate what each of the men would testify if they had been before the court. That afternoon, Jaworski read those stipulations into the court record. Three sergeants from the 650th—First Sergeant Robert Aubry, Staff Sergeant Spencer Martin, and Sergeant Wilbur Jenkins—all agreed that they had talked with Arthur Hurks as he prevented men from entering the Italian Area. Corporal Earl Lallis of the 578th saw John S. Brown in his own barracks that night. Two more corporals—Jacob Person and Freeman Pierce—saw Herman Johnson ironing clothes, although Corporal Person couldn't account for Johnson's whereabouts during the riot itself. Finally, Corporals William Wilson and John Terrell of the 650th swore that Booker Townsell stayed with them in the barracks throughout the night.

And with that, both sides rested. It was now Friday afternoon, and all that remained were closing arguments. The largest army court-martial of World War II was now also the longest: one full calendar month and still counting. Just as Beeks and Jaworski were gathering their files to head home and hone their final arguments, O'Connor dropped a small bombshell: one of the defendants was seriously ill, and under military law the trial could not continue without him. The defendant was Roy Montgomery; for the past three days, he had attended the trial wrapped in blankets, growing ever more gaunt and dehydrated. On this day, hospital orderlies had rolled Roy in with a wheelchair. Post doctors told O'Connor that Roy had pneumonia, and one more day in court might kill him.

No one wanted another delay, and there was no telling how long Montgomery might be in the hospital. Jaworski proposed, and Beeks agreed, that the closing arguments go on without him. O'Connor scanned the courtroom and asked where the "Mulatto Montgomery" was seated. "Will somebody wheel Montgomery over here closer?"

O'Connor's mulatto comment was not meant for everyone to hear, but it was loud enough for Roy. Sick as he was, the remark made him bristle; to Montgomery, it was it wasn't a whole lot different than calling him a nigger.

"Montgomery, the doctor has informed the Court that you are a sick boy."

"Yes, sir."

And so, he was a "boy" too, not a man or even a soldier. Montgomery had little choice but to listen as O'Connor spelled out his rights, explaining there would be no more witnesses called against him and that Jaworski would not mention his name in court as long as he was absent.

"And what are your wishes?"

"I wish just to let the Court go on, and I'll just go on to the hospital."

The court adjourned.

When Jaworski returned to the Olympic Hotel that night, a small, square envelope was waiting at the front desk. It was addressed—in meticulous block letters that would make an English teacher proud—to Lt. Col. Leon Jaworski, Olympic Hotel, Seattle, Wash. Inside was a card, printed with an image of candles, holly and elaborate lace, with the words *Thinking of You at Christmas* on the front. Inside, a pre-printed message read *One of the charms of Christmas lies in the thought that we live in the memory of our friends.* Written beneath, in the same, neat block letters was one word: Willie. Jaworski recognized the handwriting and knew just who it was: Private Willie Basden, one of the forty-one men he hoped to send to prison the next day.

CHAPTER TWELVE

VERDICT
Late December 1944

DECEMBER 16 DAWNED CLEAR but cold—several degrees below freezing. The Olympic Mountains, fresh with snow, glowed in the long, low yellow light of one of the shortest days of the year, making them look nearer and softer than they really were. With patches of ice hiding in the shadows, the staff car chauffeur drove more slowly than usual. Jaworski didn't mind; he'd have a few more minutes to rehearse his remarks.

The gavel fell at precisely nine; Gerald O'Connor directed a theatrical nod toward the prosecution table. "Colonel Jaworski, the case is with you." It was the kind of moment Jaworski lived for. In just twenty years, the self-described muffin-faced small-town outsider with a funny German accent had transformed himself into an imposing litigator, commanding the respect of powerful people and the worldwide attention of would-be lawbreakers. With all eyes cast his way, he could sense the anticipation. Like any great orator, he began by being gracious:

> I want to beg the indulgence of the Court while I pause to pay
> tribute to the work of Defense counsel in this case. It has been
> my privilege and pleasure to serve as Government's attorney in a
> few cases of some importance more or less, but I don't recall any-
> where there has been such a strong devotion to duty, such ex-
> treme diligence, such determination, and I might say, ability, as

has been exhibited by the Defense counsel in this case. Whether the accused be convicted, or whether they be acquitted, it is certain that they must each say to himself, 'I have been served well, and I have been served faithfully.'"

But, he might have added, it was devotion, diligence, and determination in a lost cause. The facts were clear: the confrontation between Willie Montgomery and Giuseppe Belle had prompted American soldiers to grab weapons and storm the Italian Area. The court could plainly see, said Jaworski, that the assault was not random—it was inspired, directed, and organized by three soldiers, men who now bore the responsibility for the destruction that followed:

What a picture of brutality! What a picture of savagery! So intent on carrying out the mischievous, the malicious, the vicious purpose that they had in mind that they didn't even stop in the presence of American non-commissioned officers!

The thought is inescapable to me—and it has occurred not once, but many, many times—of what a wonder and what a miracle—and it WAS a miracle—that there was found to be only one victim, only one deceased, instead of eight or ten. It is one of the things that is most difficult for me to understand.

We know what went on there in that area that night was shockingly shameful. We know that it was a disgraceful thing. We know that it was something that placed a blight on one of the pages of the annals of our Army during this present war. Tragic. And unfortunate.

Many who had participated in the riot, he conceded, had never been caught. The court could be sure, however, that only those who had been clearly identified by at least one credible witness had been brought to trial. And just one witness—if he was the right witness—was enough to justify a conviction. To keep track of those witnesses, he hoped the court had made use of the notebooks he had distributed back on the first day of trial. Those notebooks should now be full, an unambiguous record of the guilt of each of the forty-one defendants, conveniently in alphabetical order. *Nelson Alston . . . seen by Alvin Clarke . . . overheard by Harvey Banks; Richard Barber . . . seen by Roy Daymond, Willie Ellis, Jesse Sims, Augusto Todde, Sergeant Gresham, and John Pinkney; Willie Basden . . . seen by Edward Haskell . . .* And so on.

The prosecution's witnesses were all fine men, Jaworski said, upholding their sworn duty to tell the truth and defend the honor of the United States army, whatever the risk. The court should ignore the attacks on the integrity of soldiers like Sergeant Gresham, who, after all, had not been granted immunity to testify and had obviously been implicated by others only because he had been brave enough to come forward. Willie Ellis? "If the court doesn't believe every bit of testimony Willie Ellis gave, then I am not going to ask you to believe ANY testimony. I have never seen a witness that spoke with more frankness or candor than Willie Ellis." Sure, Thomas Battle became a little confused under the hammering of cross-examination, but many of the men he identified were also identified by others, including Jesse Sims, who told the court everything he knew. And Augusto Todde was calm, collected, and a careful observer, a man able to take meticulous note of faces even as his life was in danger.

And so it continued for almost three hours. *John Hamilton . . . seen by Ellis and Todde . . . overheard by Sims and Chapman . . . left his dog tags in the orderly room; Frank Hughes . . . seen by Daymond, Sims, and Addison George . . .* How could anyone believe the testimony of Herman Johnson, who told several different tales about how and why he had lost a shovel that was later found in one of the Italian barracks? C. W. Spencer? Sims had no doubt that he saw Spencer chunking: "If the Court please, I trust you won't mind my use of that expression 'chunking.' That is an old favorite expression down where I come from in Texas, and I know it means the same to these witnesses as it means to me: If we say someone is doing some chunking, that means he is throwing rocks or bricks. If I am using a colloquialism, I hope I will be forgiven."

Three men, of course, faced the death penalty. Jaworski acknowledged that proof of their guilt must be beyond a reasonable doubt. Was there any doubt, he wondered, that Luther Larkin repeatedly blew a whistle? Daymond, Sims, Clarke, and George all said he did. "No, Luther Larkin didn't admit that he blew the whistle and led those men down there," Jaworski began. "We didn't expect him to admit it because, after all, he is charged with murder. But what DID he admit? He said he heard somebody say, 'Somebody ought to blow the boys out.' And he said himself on the witness stand that he had said, 'You ain't a lying, that's the thing to do.' Now, let's see: here is a man who admits the workings of his mind at the moment—that he wanted to do the very thing we say he did!"

Because Larkin's leadership was well established, Jaworski further argued, he must shoulder the responsibility for all that came to pass that evening, including the hanging of Guglielmo Olivotto. So should William Jones, who not only led a group into the orderly room but, according to the Italian Pisciottano, was also the first man through the door after it was chopped down with an ax. And Arthur Hurks—Jesse Sims admitted going into the Italian Area, following Hurks all the way. "One of two things are true," Jaworski continued. "Either Sims went down with that group led by Arthur Hurks, as he said, or Jesse Sims is just a colossal liar."

Jaworski conceded that Arthur Hurks was nobody's fool and that he was unquestionably the most impressive defendant to take the stand. That said, Hurks was simply using his "rather clever mind" to circumvent the prosecution's questions. Sure, Hurks had helped keep other men from entering the Italian Area, but only *after* he had led a group of men during one of the initial surges. Testimony from Sims and Ellis confirmed it:

Arthur Hurks was down there, but he left in a hurry. And why did he leave in a hurry? He left because Arthur Hurks knew—clever and smart as he is—he knew that the devil was going to break loose in that orderly room. Yes, when he saw what was going on in there, and when he saw that American non-commissioned officers were being cut, yes—oh, yes—I don't doubt but what there ran through his mind what he told you about in another connection: that he knew what trouble meant between Negroes and whites, because he came from the South. That was the time Arthur Hurks deserted his men he had led down there.

And what of the victim, Guglielmo Olivotto? Here was a poor, unfortunate boy who, struck with terror, became "putty in the hands of these Negro boys." The detective work by Major Orem, Jaworski reminded the court, eliminated any chance that the hanging was a suicide. "You know they had a hold of him, and you know they did something with him, and if they didn't knife him and if they didn't club him, what did they do with him? Well, I'll say I don't believe there is a member of this Court that would believe that they had hold of him and then voluntarily turned him loose." The only conclusion, Jaworski maintained, was that Olivotto was ruthlessly murdered on the night in question. Larkin, Jones, and Hurks deserved to die.

With that, it was time for lunch. The defendants marched, as they did each day, past a gauntlet of white military policemen and into a heavily guarded mess hall. Before August 14, many of these men filling their tin plates barely knew one another. Some had just joined the company, others were little more than passing acquaintances. The men from Chicago didn't mix much with those from Texas; the soldiers in their late thirties had little in common with those who were still teenagers. Some drank, gambled, swore, and chased women; others were shy and deeply religious.

Jaworski's accusations rang in their ears. After weeks of often disjointed testimony, the prosecutor had summarized evidence in a way guaranteed to feature each man in the worst possible light. Most of those seated at the long wooden chow tables knew much more, of course, about what really happened that night than Jaworski ever could. They understood better than anyone which defendants had been unfairly accused and which had done far more damage than the prosecutor realized. Almost all of them despised the black soldiers who had saved their own skins by agreeing to help Jaworski sell his case.

Although Beeks had been duly impressed with Jaworski's flair for words, he was no oratorical slouch himself. His opportunity to redefine the evidence in his clients' favor came right after lunch. He, too, knew the importance of leading with charitable remarks. "I say in all sincerity and all candor that had I been permitted to pick this Court myself, I could not have done a better job. I also want to thank counsel for his courtesy and for his fairness, for his cooperation and the very fine compliment he paid to me this morning. Coming from such a brilliant and capable lawyer as he is, I consider it a high tribute."

That said, Beeks minced no words characterizing Jaworski's choice of witnesses:

> I think personally that the lowest form of individual who exists is an individual who will try to save himself at the expense of others. If I were formulating or devising a scale of human degradation, I think without any question that I would place the type of individual who attempts to save himself at the expense of others at the bottom—at the very bottom—of that scale. There is no type of an individual who, in my opinion, is more vile or degraded, and I refer, of course, to Roy Daymond, Alvin Clarke, Willie Ellis, Jesse Sims and Thomas Battle.

The members of the court, Beeks hoped, would see through the strategy of these five men. They had all, he said, figured to curry favor with investigators by implicating men who had already gone overseas, each on the assumption the army was unlikely to bring those suspects back to the States. Clarke fingered six men, half of whom had already left for New Guinea. Seventy-five percent of the twelve soldiers picked out by Ellis were gone; for Daymond, the figure was 80 percent. Nothing topped Sims, however: thirteen of the fifteen men he named were no longer around when he cut his immunity deal. Clearly, argued Beeks, the prosecution's key witnesses had primarily incriminated men that they thought they'd never have to face again.

Beeks argued that each of these "stool pigeons" had at least one serious flaw. Daymond told the court he had gone into the Italian Area but, during his pretrial interrogation with Beeks, had sworn he had never left his barracks. Willie Ellis claimed he was simply an innocent bystander; if true, why was it necessary to grant him immunity? Alvin Clarke claimed to see several men in the Italian Area but was unable to say exactly where any of them were standing when he saw them. Jesse Sims? At best, he was an illiterate drunk and a disgruntled gambler. Beeks went on the attack: "And another thing: Jesse Sims is the man who refused before trial to talk with me about this case. He refused to say a word about it. Is that the attitude of a man who has nothing to hide? Of a man who is willing to tell the truth and of a man who is telling the truth and particularly, when people of his own race and color were involved? I say it is not."

The fifth man, Thomas Battle, was beneath Beeks's contempt. Dismissively, he said, "If ever a man so clearly demonstrated that he was nothing but a prevaricator and perjurer, I think that man did, and I am not going to take another single moment of this Court's time discussing Thomas Battle."

He did, however, discuss the testimony of Augusto Todde. More than two dozen white MPs eventually responded to the melee, but none could pick out a single suspect—not one! Collectively, the white soldiers assigned to the Twenty-eighth ISU—Grant Farr, Edward Haskell, Fred Perata, and Mason Gould—had been able to identify a total of just four men. Eighteen Italians took the stand, and seventeen of them, as a group, could also identify just four men. Yet Augusto Todde—the eighteenth Italian—in the midst of noise and bloodshed and chaos, had confidently named twelve men, including some no one else had reported seeing. It was highly unlikely. It was downright suspicious.

Even if the court were to consider the testimony from each of the prosecution's flawed witnesses, said Beeks, at least a dozen of the defendants had been identified by no more than one accuser. Beeks told the court he couldn't imagine locking up a man without the testimony of at least several credible and trustworthy witnesses. "Counsel made one statement this morning—I had to pinch myself for a moment to tell where we were. I couldn't tell, from what he said, whether we were over in Nazi Germany or here in the United States! He wants you to convict men upon the testimony of a single witness!"

As far as Beeks was concerned, the accusations just didn't add up. As Jaworski had earlier done, he put his own spin on the case against each of his forty-one clients, in reverse order of the weight of evidence against them. *Riley Buckner? All he did was rescue Alvin Clarke . . . Lee Dixon? The only man who said he saw him said Dixon was just standing around . . . Emanuel Ford? The guy fought overseas for three years, and all they have is Sims saying he was somewhere in the area . . .*

The court, argued Beeks, could not ignore the fact that many men were little more than curious bystanders. We all do it, he said—we are all drawn to watch firemen fight a fire or to gather around for two men squaring up for a fistfight. Does that mean we are all guilty of arson? Does merely watching a fight imply that a spectator will rush to assist whoever is getting the worst of it? Of course not! And even those who *did* take up arms: could you really blame them? "The memories of these American soldiers who fought in the Italian campaign—who are walking around without arms, and without legs, badly maimed—is still too fresh in our memories," he said. "You just can't teach men to hate and to kill and then, without anything further, throw them together and expect them to be buddies with those same men they were but a short time ago taught to hate and kill."

The army, Beeks contended, must share a large part of the blame: "It was a terrible and tragic mistake, if this Court please, to send these prisoners of war out here to Fort Lawton, where they were to be mixed with our own soldiers and to set them down side by side where they must, of necessity, intermingle without proper prior training."

To top it all, what had happened to the one soldier who unquestionably *started* the entire affair? Why on Earth, Beeks demanded, did the government choose not to bring charges against the very man who drunkenly launched an assault against an Italian prisoner? Where, he wanted to know, was Willie Montgomery? What was the prosecutor hiding?

The three murder defendants had been singled out as leaders, but none was ever seen actually doing damage, and no one claimed either Larkin or Hurks even had a weapon. Larkin and Hurks had both taken the stand, and neither showed any weakness, even after hours of cross-examination. Colonel Jaworski's theory that Arthur Hurks had led men down to the orderly room, only to desert them when the going got rough was never supported by any testimony—it was nothing more than a desperate last-minute invention during Jaworski's closing argument. And Farr's failure to identify Hurks as one of his rescuers could be easily explained. "Farr was without a doubt," Beeks insisted, "a very badly frightened and upset boy, in a state of shock that evening. He might not have realized it, but—under the circumstances—he couldn't have been otherwise."

As far as Beeks was concerned, the prosecution had utterly failed to make a case for murder. Despite his earlier kind words for Jaworski, Beeks's disgust at the decision to charge Larkin, Jones, and Hurks with Olivotto's death was palpable. "In all the years that I have practiced law," he seethed, "I want to say that I have never known of a case that was prosecuted on more flimsy evidence, on more inadequate evidence, than [the murder] charge in this case."

If one or more defendants wanted to kill Olivotto, why wouldn't they use a club or knife? Why would they take him down a steep, slippery, pitch-black embankment? And if that's what they did, why was Olivotto's body free of cuts and bruises? Why weren't pictures taken of the body? Why weren't casts taken of the footprints? Why had the hanging rope mysteriously disappeared? How was it, for that matter, that the prosecution has somehow "lost" the original list of the black soldiers identified as suspects at Camp George Jordan? "I want to say to this Court, in all sincerity: If you find any of these boys guilty of murder, you will regret it and your conscience will bother you the rest of your life," Beeks warned.

Beeks was not required to offer his own opinion about who might have killed Guglielmo Olivotto. It may not have occurred to him that Private Clyde Lomax had the means, the motive, and the opportunity to commit the crime. Lomax, who was openly racist, was present at virtually every key moment, from the incident at the PX to the aftermath of the fight between Willie Montgomery and Guiseppe Bell to the vicious beatings inside Barracks 708 to the "discovery" of Olivotto's body the next morning. He had lied or been evasive about his whereabouts and was soon to be court-martialed for leaving his post at the precise time that Olivotto disappeared. Perhaps he had come across Olivotto during the riot and offered him a ride in his jeep. That might explain why Olivotto's body had no bruises and almost no scratches. Lomax had purposely delayed reporting the brewing trouble between the blacks and Italians, perhaps enjoying the possibility that two groups he disliked would bring each other misery. If Lomax lynched Olivotto, he may have done it in the hope that black soldiers would get the blame.

But Beeks did not engage in any such speculation, at least in open court. With his limited time and resources, the best he could do was try to show that his clients were not guilty; he could not reasonably hope to uncover evidence of someone else's guilt. The Negro soldier, Beeks told the court, had a long, proud history in America. Many of the men on trial were veterans of overseas campaigns. The color of their skin could not be overlooked. "There is more on trial here today than these accused. The whole Army system of justice is on trial. It has been charged time and time again that a Negro cannot receive a fair and just trial before a military court. This case—as you all know—has received nationwide publicity. The eyes of the Nation are upon this Court."

Beeks was done. Jaworski, as prosecutor, was entitled to one final shot. He could barely restrain himself.

The *army* made a mistake? The *army* erred when it placed POWs next to colored soldiers? What an embarrassing, untimely, out-of-place, and an unjustifiable criticism of higher authority! If we're going to blame the *army* for sewing seeds of hatred, "we might just as well declare open season on prisoners of war—we might just as well scrap the Geneva Convention!" Jaworski was steaming. "We might just as

well forget about our Service Units—those Italian Service Units—
and the pledges these boys have made . . . and we might just as well
forget the noble work they have done and are doing in helping our
Government maintain and obtain the equipment so badly needed that
helps us in our war effort! Yes, if THAT is the attitude, let's just forget
about the whole thing! Let's just forget it all."

Weeks of nonstop work, two months of single-minded focus, feelings of guilt about being away from home, anxiety about the future . . .
all of Jaworski's pent-up emotions were coming to the surface. Here
was the preacher's son, grasping the courtroom pulpit, with the laws
of God in his heart and of man on his table, hurling thunderbolts of
righteous indignation at his courtroom congregation. "I care NOT
whether a human being be a Negro soldier, or whether he be a white
soldier, or whether he be an Italian soldier. If his life is taken under
the circumstances that Olivotto's life was taken, it is murder! Just
plain murder! And it is murder under the laws of this land. We CAN-
NOT forget—we must NOT overlook—that, after all, it is a human being, a body, in which God Almighty breathed a soul, and no one—NO
ONE—has the right to take that life. And when that life is taken, it is
murder!"

If Beeks's version of events was accepted, Jaworski intoned, then
each of the soldiers sitting in the defendants' section was guilty of
nothing more than being a spectator on the night of the riot. If so, who
was wielding the clubs? Who was slashing with knives? Who caused
all the bloodshed? Most of all, who hanged poor Olivotto? "Oh, I am
so disappointed in one thing. I thought surely that among all the witnesses I brought here to this Court, that counsel could at least find
ONE that would tell this Court the truth! Isn't it singularly strange
that—out of the five Negro soldiers' testimony that General Denson
granted immunity to—isn't it singularly strange that we didn't find a
SINGLE truthful one? Isn't it strange that ALL of them are liars?"

And how upsetting, he continued, that Beeks dared impinge the integrity of army investigators, with his thinly veiled suggestion that it
was no accident that the rope had been misplaced and that the list of

suspects identified at Camp George Jordan had gone missing. "What an indictment! What a charge to make! And if any member of this Court for a moment believes that higher authority is seeking to conduct this case in that way, then, I say, make the most of it! The very idea!"

And the very idea that the failure to charge Willie Montgomery had some sort of sinister purpose! Willie was knocked out cold! He couldn't riot or murder if he wanted to! Clearly, the defense was grasping straws. And, Jaworski fumed, there was no better evidence of the sheer desperation of Beeks's arguments than when he dared warn the nine judges about regret. "Why, the idea of talking to this Court about the fact that the Court would be carrying something on its conscience the rest of its lives! Why, that is just an indirect threat to this court! Why, this Court has sworn to perform a duty, and no one has a right to doubt that this Court is going to perform it in a fair and honorable and impartial manner."

It was quarter past five; the winter sun had set long before Jaworski finally sat down. The case was now with the judges. The defendants and attorneys were ordered to remain nearby for as long as the deliberations might last.

THERE WAS NO reason to expect the process would go quickly. The court was permitted to take but one closed-door vote on each of the charges against each defendant, so the judges were likely to spend plenty of time reviewing all the evidence before casting any ballots. If six of the nine judges thought a defendant was guilty, he could later be sentenced to a term not to exceed ten years. If seven judges agreed, the term could be as long as life in prison. It took the unanimous concurrence of all nine judges for someone charged with murder be sentenced to death.

After dinner, the members of the court deliberated from 6:25 to 11:15 P.M. before retiring for the night. They reconvened Sunday morning for a three-hour session, continuing once again at 1:15 P.M. At 5:25 P.M., forty minutes after sunset, Gerald O'Connor ordered courtroom guards to notify the lawyers and reporters that verdicts had been reached. The judges had deliberated almost exactly twelve total hours, an average of less than eighteen minutes per defendant. Military policemen were dispatched to bring the defendants out of the small waiting room where they had been cloistered for most of the previous twenty-four hours. The only civilian spectators in the courtroom were Sadie Hughes and Jeanne Barber.

The defendants stood at parade rest; the lawyers stood at their tables. The smallest sounds echoed in the silence: the clearing of a throat, the shuffling of a shoe, a sniffle, a sneeze. At 5:45 P.M., a door handle turned and— *Ah-ten-SHUN!*—the sergeant at arms shattered the stillness. Forty men snapped to attention, right hands cocked in stiff salute, arteries throbbing at the collar. Nine judges filed in, none making eye contact with anyone in the courtroom.

"This court is in session. Colonel Jaworski?"
"Does the court wish to have a roll call?"
"I believe the roll call is in order, that's right."

For the thirty-ninth time since November 16, the name of each defendant was barked in alphabetical order, from Alston to Wooden. With each call came the echo, "Present, sir!" until all but Roy Montgomery—still in the hospital—were accounted for. Wilmar Dewitt turned to address the forty soldiers.

"The court has found certain accused not guilty, and will proceed to acquit them. As each man's name is read, he will come forward. Afterward, he will return to the guardhouse with the rest of the accused, and the trial judge advocate will take steps to notify the convening authority so that he can be restored to duty."
"Technician Fifth Grade Nelson L. Alston!"

His face impassive but his knees quivering, Alston squeezed down the row, past muttered congratulations of "Uh-huh" and "Yessir, Alston!" Joined at row's end by a burly MP sergeant, Alston stepped over to the space next to the empty witness chair, clicked his heels, and sent a smart salute toward the fatherly face of Colonel Dewitt. "The court, by secret written ballot, has found you—of the specification and charge under which you were tried—not guilty, and therefore acquits you."

Another salute, and Alston spun around; he barely knew where to look. The sergeant grabbed the sleeve of his jacket and directed him toward the back of the courtroom.

"Private Willie C. Basden!" Basden's heart leaped. At the same moment, Richard Barber's heart sunk. The alphabetical chant had been ingrained in his mind, and—until now—Barber always followed Alston. As Basden wriggled his way past quiet kudos, Barber glanced toward his wife, Jeanne. Her expression stayed calm, even as Sadie Hughes began to dab her eyes.

"Private First Class Sylvester Campbell . . . Technician Fifth Grade James Coverson . . . Technician Fifth Grade Lee A. Dixon . . . Sergeant Emanuel Ford . . ." With the announcement of each name, Beeks silently squeezed the table top in front of him, his only outlet for the sense of elation he felt at the mounting victories. Conversely, each saluting soldier represented a defeat for Jaworski, who fought to keep a neutral visage with each chink in the armor of his legal reputation.

"Staff Sergeant Ernest Graham . . . Private Walter Jackson . . . Technician Fifth Grade Herman Johnson . . ." Herman Johnson? The first real surprise; a man who, by numerous accounts, had been handed a flashlight by a white MP and led a charge inside Barracks 708, where he brutalized Italians with impunity. Those who had been in 708 with him, like Slick Curry, had already been passed over in the alphabetical roulette. Several others remembered how Johnson desperately tried to replace the shovel he had left in the Italian barracks. Buckner, Ceaser, Hamilton—they had all helped rescue others, yet they had to stay seated while Johnson bulled past them.

"Technician Fifth Grade Henry Jupiter . . . Sergeant C. W. Spencer . . . Private Freddie Umblance . . . Private First Class Arthur Williams . . ." Thirteen men so far, each one leaving another two or so skipped over in their wake. The only man left with an alphabetically available name was Wallace Wooden. From the bench, Wilmar Dewitt gave the answer.

"That is all. Colonel Jaworski, the Court will hear any further evidence that the Prosecution has to offer on reconvening tomorrow morning."

"I assume the Court has reference to evidence of previous convictions and data as to service?"

"Yes, evidence of previous convictions and records of military service. Court is adjourned."

"Ah-ten-SHUN!"

The judges filed out, and the MPs rose to escort all but the lucky thirteen directly to the convoy trucks. The acquitted left through the main doors at the back of the room. As Jaworski extended his hand to Beeks and Noyd, he could hear whoops and hollers outside; reporters rushed out to see for themselves. When MPs blocked the newsmen's exit, they sought out the attorneys for comment. Beeks was fairly glowing. "General Denson has been at all times most anxious that all of the accused receive a fair and impartial trial. He has given me every assistance and cooperation in their defense, and the result is a tribute not only to his care in the selection of the members of the court, but also to the army's system of justice." Jaworski smiled but declined comment.

Beeks made his way to the holding area where the remaining twenty-seven defendants were still waiting to be loaded onto the trucks. He saw a sea of empty eyes, men struggling to understand what had just happened. He could only imagine what was going through their minds. *Does this mean the rest of us are all headed to prison? Could we be locked up the rest of our lives? Had Larkin, Jones, and Hurks been convicted of murder? Are we entitled to an appeal?* Beeks assured them, yes, all general court-martial verdicts are automatically appealed; not to worry, the process was not yet over. Try to get some sleep, try to stay positive. We'll know more in the morning. "Sorry, Major," said the burly MP, but it was time to go.

As Beeks walked back into the courtroom, it was all but deserted. Still sitting in the same wooden folding chairs they had claimed each of the twenty-three days of trial were the two women from Chicago. Jeanne Barber stared ahead as she cradled Sadie Hughes, who was softly sobbing on her shoulder.

Back in his Magnolia home, Beeks had a tough time falling asleep. His partial victory would seem hollow if any of his clients were sent to the gallows. Yet the court had sent an unequivocal signal: most of the men found not guilty had but one accuser. The acquittal for Herman Johnson was a bit of a mystery, but one of the central witnesses against him had been Thomas Battle, and more of the freed men had been fingered by Battle than anyone else. Other patterns were tougher to detect. Of the seventeen men who took the stand in their own defense, just five had been acquitted. Of the twenty-one men brought back from overseas, only eight had escaped conviction. Just two men—Nelson Alston and Arthur Williams—fell into both categories. All in all, Beeks knew, the initial results could have been far worse.

BEFORE IMPOSING A SENTENCE, a military court considers a defendant's service record, including any previous military convictions. Monday morning—with Roy Montgomery still absent—the remaining twenty-seven men stepped forward one at a time, once again in alphabetical order. Richard Barber was first.

> "Has the Prosecution any evidence of any previous convictions to offer, and will the Prosecution read the personal data from the charge sheets as concerning Private Barber."
>
> "The Prosecution has no further evidence to offer concerning Private Barber or any evidence on any previous convictions. The Prosecution will read the personal data as concerning Richard H. Barber, Serial Number 36945532, Private, Headquarters, Headquarters Detachment number 2, Camp George Jordan, Seattle, Washington; formerly a member of the 650th Port Company,

Transportation Corps. Age, twenty-two and two-twelfths. Pay, fifty dollars per month. Allotment to dependants, twenty-seven dollars per month. Class F deduction, government insurance deduction, six dollars and sixty cents per month. As to service, prior service, none. Current enlistment, inducted 3 January 1944, to serve the duration of the war, plus six months."

And so it continued, twenty-six more times. Only three soldiers had previous military convictions: Jefferson Green and Loary Moore had each been briefly AWOL, and Arthur Stone had been disciplined for disobeying orders of a superior officer.

The judges headed back behind closed doors. Nine hours later—at seven o'clock—they notified Jaworski and Beeks that their deliberations were finished. Instead of bringing all the defendants back as a group, they were to be escorted into the courtroom one at a time. Once again, Richard Barber led the way. He and his MP guard approached the bench and saluted. Colonel Dewitt read the verdict and sentence: "Upon secret written ballot, two-thirds of the members present at the time the vote was taken concurred in the sentence of the accused, Private Richard H. Barber: Guilty of rioting. To be dishonorably discharged the Service, to forfeit all pay and allowances due and to become due, and to be confined at hard labor at such place as the Reviewing Authority may direct for a period of ten years."

A cry went up from the back of the courtroom. Richard's wife, Jeanne, fought to hold back tears as her friend and neighbor Sadie Hughes wept openly at her side. Richard Barber's head was spinning as he saluted, pivoted, and caught his wife's eye. As Barber's MP led him brusquely back out of the room, another MP brought the next man in.

"John Brown . . . ten years hard labor . . ."
"Riley Buckner . . . six months hard labor . . ."
"Johnnie Ceaser . . . five years hard labor . . ."
"James Chandler . . . four years hard labor . . ."

The sentences ranged from six months to ten years. John Hamilton, Farr's rescuer, got eight years. Roy Montgomery, who had stopped the fighting, got two years. R. B. Bermann of the *Post-Intelligencer* had never witnessed such a scene. "All the prisoners received their sentences with stoic courage," he wrote, "and most of them saluted Colonel Dewitt as smartly after hearing the judgment as they had when they first marched into court."

By the time Robert Sanders appeared, his mother was wrung dry. With Jeanne's arm around her, Sadie stared at her hands as Dewitt sentenced her boy to eight years at hard labor and a dishonorable discharge.

Last in line were the three murder defendants, again in alphabetical order. Arthur Hurks stood soldier-straight as Dewitt met his eyes. "The Court, upon secret written ballot, three-fourths of the members present at the time the vote was taken, concurred on the sentence of the accused, Sergeant Arthur J. Hurks . . ."

The moment Beeks heard the phrase "three-fourths of the members present," he shut his eyes. The death penalty required a unanimous vote; it meant at least one defendant would not have to hang. ". . . Guilty as charged of rioting under Charge One, and Not Guilty of the charges under Charge Two, murder in the first degree."

Hurks could not concentrate on the rest, as Dewitt continued talking about dishonorable discharge . . . reduced to rank of private . . . loss of all pay . . . twelve years at hard labor. The words "not guilty" played over and over in his mind as he left the courtroom in a fog. Jaworski raised his chin and kept his expression unchanged as Jones was the next to step forward. "The Court, upon secret written ballot, three-fourths of the members present at the time the vote was taken, concurred on the sentence of the accused, Private William G. Jones . . ." Beeks clenched his fist, trying hard to contain his elation. ". . . Guilty as charged of rioting under Charge One, and Guilty of the lesser included charge of Manslaughter under Charge Two . . ." Manslaughter! The same as murder—someone died—but without a finding of intent to kill. It all added up yet again to no death penalty. ". . . To be dishonorably discharged the Service, to forfeit all pay and allowances due and to become due, and to be confined at hard labor at such place as the Reviewing Authority may direct for a period of fifteen years."

Fifteen years! It was a stiff penalty, but certainly better than hanging. Only Luther Larkin remained. "The Court, upon secret written ballot, three-fourths . . ." Dear God, thought Beeks, we've done it.

". . . of the members present at the time the vote was taken, concurred on the sentence of the accused, Corporal Luther L. Larkin: Guilty as charged of rioting under Charge One, and Guilty of the lesser included charge of Manslaughter under Charge Two. To be reduced to the grade of private, to be dishonorably discharged the Service, to forfeit all pay and allowances due and to become due, and to be confined at hard labor at such place as the Reviewing Authority may direct for a period of twenty-five years."

Luther was twenty-three years old. Twenty-five years was more than a lifetime; it meant 1945 to 1970, a forty-eight-year-old man walking out of prison without family or friends, a future tossed away because somebody killed a man he never met. He tried to salute; his hand felt heavy. On either side, an MP stepped in to grab each arm and lead him out the door. Colonel Dewitt's voice echoed behind him.

"Is there any further business to come before the court?"
"There is no further business, if it please the Court."
"The Defense has nothing futher."
"The court then, at 7:44 P.M., 18 December 1944, is adjourned."

The gavel slammed. R. B. Bermann grabbed his reporter's notebook and slipped outside, around the side of the building. Invisible in the shadows, he could overhear the convicted men bemoaning the severity of their sentences. Some grumbled that a dishonorable discharge made no difference; it was the time behind bars or barbed wire they dreaded. Arthur Stone, who had been sentenced to ten years, disagreed. "I want an HONORABLE discharge!" he protested. "And I'm willing to go overseas and FIGHT for ten years to prove I'm a good soldier!"

All told, eight soldiers were given ten years each at hard labor: Barber, Brown, Green, Hughes, Prevost, Stone, Sutliff, and Wooden. The common thread between those men was that at least one witness—other than Battle—had seen each of them inside the orderly room. Six men drew eight-year sentences: Curry, Hamilton, Sanders, Stewart, Townsell, and Walton; each had been spotted near the orderly room, though not necessarily inside. Hamilton, perhaps, might have been given ten years, except for the testimony that he helped extricate Farr. Ceaser, Moore, and Thornton all got five years; Chandler, Russell Ellis, Shelton, and Simmons each got four years; Nathanial Spencer, three, Roy Montgomery, two, Snow, one, and Riley Buckner, six months. In general, the descending order seemed to reflect how close the members of the court determined that a man had come to the action in the orderly room, although both Ceasar and Roy Montgomery likely had their sentences mitigated for intervening as peacekeepers. All told, the combined sentences added up to more than two hundred years.

The verdicts warranted banner headlines the next day, and the news quickly spread around the world. The editorial board of the *Post-Intelligencer* called the riot "one of the most delicate problems that has confronted the community in years," and complimented General Densen for overseeing "as fair and impartial a trial as they could have before any tribunal in the world." *Time* magazine called it "a trial whose fairness drew praise even from the Negro press," even as the accompanying article incorrectly attributed the riot to "Negroes provoked by special privileges shown the Italians."

The Negro press, however, did not speak with one voice. Writing in the *Northwest Herald*, M. C. Honeysuckle pointed out that all nine judges were white, and suggested that the inclusion of even one Negro judge "would have boosted the morale of the Colored women and men in the armed forces a thousand fold." Other black papers complained about O'Connor's refusal to allow evidence about either the

July uprising by Italian Fascists or the confrontations between white soldiers and Italian in the Fort Lawton PX.

On December 21—the first day of winter—secret proceedings were initiated to determine whether Colonel Harry Branson should be disciplined and reduced in rank. Four days later—Christmas Day—similar proceedings began against Major William Orem. None of it made the papers. That same day, Leon Jaworski received a telephone call at his home in Waco, telling him to stand by for orders to go overseas.

Sadie Hughes and Jeanne Barber spent Christmas Day on an eastbound train, during an interminably long and cold trip back to Chicago. Sadie was beside herself with heartache. She had listened to every word of the trial. She had even walked around the post to test the claims of eyewitness identifications. "I have been all over Fort Lawton, and at night, and you can't tell if a person are white or colored until they get right up on you." In her opinion, the court had permitted way too much questionable testimony, while excluding other evidence that might have saved her son.

Sadie was a widow. Robert was her only child. On December 30, as one of the coldest storms in memory blew off Lake Michigan, she pulled out a pen and her pad of stationery and sat at her kitchen table on Wabash Avenue.

> Dear President Roosevelt:
>
> I am writing you, and I pray to God that you will try to be patient with me, although I may not spell my words right and may forget to put my periods and commas in, but I am writing with all my heart and soul so please try to understand what I am trying to say.

She poured it all out on paper: how she got a letter from her boy saying he had been pulled back from overseas; how the Red Cross had helped her get to Seattle; how she and Jeanne Barber attended trial every day.

I pray to God that you will try to bear with me as I will try with all of my heart to explain; pray to God that He will teach me and help me. He has placed you as our great commanding chief over this great country of ours.

Page after handwritten page, Sadie transcribed all she remembered about the trial: the Fascist disturbance in July . . . the confrontations between white and Italian soldiers in the PX . . . how her son had carried the wounded Sammy Snow to safety:

Robert Sanders, my boy, hasn't never told me a lie. I have always taught him that there isn't anything too bad to tell me. For when he is in trouble, I am too, and he must always let me know the truth about everything. For it is only he and I; I am all he have to stand by him.

It was just a mistake putting the Italian Prisoners of War with any American soldiers. As it has been so often spoken to me while I was at Fort Lawton, by white soldiers and colored, and also, Major Beeks so truly brought out in court, how can you teach a soldier to hate his enemies and to kill them, then bring them and put them right next door to them?

Sadie summarized the sentences imposed on each soldier, explaining to the president that they'd all be dishonorably discharged:

And that hurts them more than anything, for they love their country more than anything. They love their country with all their hearts and souls and everything that is within them all. So do their mothers and families, as I do. And it hurt more than anyone will ever be able to know.

You are our earthly father of our great country—I call you that, and many more like me would call you that—for you have been that to us all. Although they say in history that Washington is the father our country, that may be true, but that was before our times, and I am speaking of what I really know and have experienced. I pray that God will let you find favor in these poor kids and help them to be reinstated back in their country's service so they will not have given up everything in life so young in vain, only to be dishonorably discharged in the country they love so much. They asked me to please write to you and try to explain for them just how they feel, for there are some that I am sure didn't get into the fight, as they said they didn't.

May God's face shine upon you and may He endow you with His greatest wisdom that you may bring our country everlasting peace.

A mother who offered all she had, her only son, with all her heart, to her country, —Mrs. Sadie Hughes

Thank you so much for reading this. I have kept my promise with the boys, as they asked me to write you, the best I know how.

The letter, mailed to the White House, was received by FDR's personal secretary, William D. Harrett. There is no record of how, or even if, the president responded.

EPILOGUE

On January 1, 1945, another court-martial convened at Fort Lawton. The trial was held in a modest room; there was no need to accommodate crowds or reporters since the newspapers knew nothing about it. Staff Sergeant Charles Robinson and Private Clyde Lomax stood accused of two military crimes each: "[n]eglect to give, without delay, information of a threatening disturbance to proper authority, and failure to use reasonable efforts to prevent destruction of certain government property (a fence)." In addition, Lomax alone was charged with two counts of "Failure to use reasonable efforts to quell a riot and failure to repair at a fixed time and place for duty."

On January 4, Robinson was acquitted on all charges, but Lomax was found guilty of both counts of failure to repair at a fixed time and place for duty. He was shipped to Camp Shelby, Mississippi, where on January 16 he was discharged from the army. Because he was prosecuted by a special court-martial and not a general court-martial, army procedures required that the transcripts of his trial and conviction be sealed or destroyed. There is no record of whether the court found that "his failure to repair at a fixed time" included the time between when Guglielmo Olivotto was last seen alive by Imo Nolgi, and when Lomax began his 3 A.M. jeep patrol with Private Pinkney.

The Seattle Port of Embarkation had its own staff judge advocate, a lieutenant colonel named Dolph Barnett. The massive record of the Fort Lawton trial was dumped on Barnett's desk; it was his job to prepare the automatic appeal of the verdicts and sentences for the army's Board of Review in Washington, D.C. Barnett would also have the initial say about where each man should be incarcerated.

Riley Buckner, sentenced to just six months, would automatically serve his brief term in the Fort Lawton stockade. Like all the guilty defendants, he would be busted back to the rank of private, but Buckner was the only convicted soldier not issued a dishonorable discharge by the court. He would serve his brief time, then get back to soldiering.

Ten men, including Roy Montgomery, Sammy Snow, and Johnnie Ceaser, were sentenced to terms of between one and five years. These men were allowed to serve their time at an army rehabilitation center, where, if they kept their noses clean, they'd be entitled to rejoin the army after their sentence was complete and eventually return to civilian life with an honorable discharge.

The remaining seventeen, those with sentences greater than five years, would have to be locked away in army disciplinary barracks. Because of the notoriety of the case, Barnett figured the army would probably want them sent to Fort Leavenworth, the infamous military prison, located near the Leavenworth federal penitentiary in Kansas. Soldiers in the disciplinary barracks system generally served their sentences, then left the military with dishonorable discharges.

Barnett, a conscientious lawyer who later in life became a civilian judge, was in no position to weigh the credibility of the various witnesses—that job had already been done by the court. In preparing his summary, then, Barnett had to assume the testimony of Battle or Sims was as valid as that of Haskell or Perata or anyone else. As long as someone—anyone—had said he'd seen a defendant in the wrong place at the wrong time, Barnett had no choice but to conclude that it was true, because the court, apparently, believed it to be so. Jefferson Green, for example, had been identified only by Todde, the presumed Fascist, and by Battle, the discredited turncoat, and took the stand in his own defense to deny it. Nonetheless, Barnett would have to recommend the Board of Review uphold Green's ten-year sentence.

Colonel Barnett spent extra time reviewing the cases against the three men accused of murder. The case against William Jones was strong, he thought, but Arthur Hurks was a different matter. Ellis, Sims, and Gresham had each identified Hurks, with Sims's testimony the most damaging. Hurks, in turn, had implicated Gresham. Several other witnesses had come to Hurks's defense, and Jaworski's three-hour cross-examination had been a clear defeat for the prosecutor. Jaworski's unsubstantiated theory that Hurks had gone into the Italian Area, then deserted his men, was raised for the first and only time during Jaworski's closing argument. While the court had found Hurks not guilty of either murder or manslaughter, they still saddled him with a twelve-year sentence. Barnett decided to recommend that the Board of Review reduce the sentence to ten years.

Luther Larkin's case bothered Barnett even more. Under what theory could the court have found him responsible for Olivotto's death, even as manslaughter? By his own admission, Jaworski had not a produced a single shred of evidence linking any one individual to the hanging; culpability was based solely on the legal theory that someone can be held responsible for the unintended consequences of their intentional actions. If Jaworski had shown that Larkin had intended to do great bodily harm to Olivotto, and as a result Olivotto died, then a manslaughter conviction would have made sense. Alternately, if Jaworski had charged Larkin with felony murder and aggravated assault, and proven the assault, then, perhaps, a murder conviction might stick. In that case, however, manslaughter would not be an option.

On February 19, Barnett placed a call to the Pentagon. Seattle was a fairly small player in a sweeping global war, yet Barnett knew reports about the Fort Lawton case continued to circulate in military intelligence briefings around the world. He was loathe to make a recommendation that might have political ramifications beyond his understanding. On the other end of the line was the man in charge of all lawyers in the U.S. military, Major General Myron Cramer, the Pentagon's judge advocate general. During the telephone call—tape-recorded and transcribed by Cramer's assistant—Barnett outlined his dilemma, explaining the problems with the misapplication of what he called the "orthodox" forms of murder and manslaughter, and with the apparent effort to shoehorn manslaughter into felony murder.

Barnett: Now, in my opinion, General, it was either murder or nothing. It doesn't come within the purview of the definition of manslaughter because the assaults were aggravated assaults. Now, the question is, what should the policy be? To pass it, and let the Board of Review bring up that point if they want to? Or bust it here?

Cramer: Well, it's entirely up to you that way. If you conscientiously feel you should bust it, I wouldn't hesitate to bust it. On the other hand, if you've got some doubt in your mind, probably the best way to do it would be to pass it and let the Board of Review pick it up.

Barnett: Perhaps—I wouldn't say anything about it—but the thing's so full of dynamite. That is, there's so many different reasons involved—

Cramer: Well, I don't know enough about the facts to tell whether I agree with you or not, off hand. But, as I say, if you are in doubt about it, why, I think probably the best way to do would be to pass it and let the Board of Review pick it up—

Barnett: Not say anything about it—

Cramer: If you are firmly convinced that that's wrong, why I'd do just what I wanted to do: I'd bust it, if you think that's the right thing to do.

Barnett *was* convinced it was wrong. But he was even more convinced that the case was "full of dynamite." In the end, he chose not to highlight his concerns in his report to the Board of Review. Instead, he wrote: "The evidence shows that accused Larkin and Jones were leaders in the riot. Although charged with murder, by appropriate exceptions and substitutions, the Court found them guilty of manslaughter."

Even so, he knew he was taking a cowardly approach and that Larkin had been handed a raw deal. He concluded his thirty-nine page report with the recommendation that the board knock ten years off Larkin's sentence, reducing it to fifteen years, the same as Jones.

A few weeks later, the nation mourned the death of President Roosevelt. On April 19, four days after FDR was buried, a three-member panel of the Board of Review rejected Barnett's suggestion to reduce the sentences for Hurks and Larkin and issued, without further comment, a one-sentence ruling: "The record of trial in the case of the soldiers named above has been examined and is held by the Board of Review to be legally sufficient to support the sentences."

By extension, that ruling also meant the Board rejected every single objection made by Beeks during the month-long trial, including Gerald O'Connor's decisions to exclude testimony about Fascists and the PX. One member of the review board, Abner E. Lipscomb, was the former dean of the Baylor Law School, Leon Jaworski's alma mater.

The Board of Review's ruling was sent to General Cramer, whose assistant, Colonel W. A. Rounds, recommended that both Larkin and Jones be sent to a federal penitentiary instead of the disciplinary barracks, as Barnett had suggested. Frank Dugan, another assistant, agreed, noting that "this case has already received a great deal of publicity." But General Cramer, as he had during his phone conversation with Barnett, thought the decision about incarceration should be made in Seattle. The "convening authority" for the court-martial had been General Denson, so General Cramer agreed to pass the buck back to Seattle. He also sent along a letter he'd received from Luther Larkin, dated April 20:

> I am Cpl. Luther L. Larkin, one of the twenty-eight Negro Soldiers who was convicted of rioting on December 18, 1944, here at Fort Lawton, Washington. Since that time, I have asked for overseas duty, and I have yet to receive any consideration. I know you can help me, sir, if you will be so kind as to look into my case. I have been a good Soldier and I haven't changed since I been under confinement. Please give me a chance. Thank you for an awful lot, Sir. —Corporal Luther Larkin

Denson's chief lawyer was still Dolph Barnett, and Denson saw no reason not to adopt Barnett's initial recommendations. Larkin's sentence was therefore reduced to fifteen years and Hurks's to ten. None of the convicted soldiers would be sent to a penitentiary. Those sentenced to less than five years would be retrained and allowed back in the army. All the rest would be dishonorably discharged, effective May 4, 1945, and continue serving the remainder of their sentences.

The men who qualified for retraining were sent to the U.S. Army Rehabilitation Center in Turlock, California. They settled into barracks that, for most of the war, had been occupied by relocated Japanese-Americans, interred amid hysteria that they might pose a threat to U.S. security. The rehab program at Turlock was glorified basic training, including hours of mind-numbing films and lectures about proper military behavior and decorum. Inmates also sat through brutally graphic films about proper sexual hygiene, a huge issue for the army since U.S. military hospitals around the world were reporting near epidemics of syphilis and gonorrhea. As part of their incarceration, the prisoners shouldered heavy packs on eight-mile marches each Tuesday and on twenty-five mile treks each Friday, hiking back and forth through neighboring vineyards.

August 14, 1945, marked the one-year anniversary of the Fort Lawton riot, but that fact paled next to the stupendous news that day: the war was over. On V-J Day (Victory over Japan Day), the world celebrated the end of the most brutal conflict in human history. As soldiers and sailors danced in the streets, the twenty-seven remaining Fort Lawton convicts—Riley Buckner had completed his six-month term—counted the days in their compounds.

It was all too much for Sammy Snow. His one-year sentence was set to expire in October, counting time served before, during, and after the trial, and then he'd be back in the army. The only way not to head back to duty was to accept a dishonorable discharge. Snow decided that in his achingly poor community in Leesburg, Florida, no one would care one way or another if his discharge was honorable or otherwise. He told his commanding officer that he had no interest in being a soldier and asked for his release. He argued his case for weeks, until the full year of his sentence was served. The army let him go, without an honorable designation.

Back in Chicago, Sadie Hughes and Jeanne Barber took the opposite approach. With the help of neighbors and members of their church congregations, they sent letters to pastors and politicians around the country, seeking a more thorough review of the convictions and sentencing. Requests for clemency poured into the White House and Pentagon, and Thurgood Marshall of the NAACP Legal Defense Fund asked to intervene. The army took notice but also took its time.

The seventeen men serving the longest sentences were frequently transferred from one army disciplinary barracks to another. Most started at Camp Haan in Riverside, California, a tent compound that also housed—of all things—hundreds of Italian and German prisoners of war. Soon after, most were transferred to Fort Missoula in Montana, where the winters were brutal. Some were eventually moved to Santa Cruz, California, or Milwaukee or even to Fort Leavenworth.

More than ten million men and women had served in the armed forces during the war, and by V-J Day, 33,519 were still incarcerated for various offenses. President Truman, under pressure to show mercy and to relieve the crowding in military stockades, established a special clemency board in the War Department. With the help of Thurgood Marshall, Larkin, Jones, Hurks, Sanders, Barber, and a dozen others filed petitions and waited their turn.

On July 8, 1946, the clemency board—without issuing a written opinion or offering any explanation—reduced the sentences of all seventeen Fort Lawton defendants with terms longer than five years. Larkin, Jones, and Barber had their sentence cut to five years; most others, including Hurks, were reduced to three. Several jumped at an offer to transfer out of the disciplinary barracks and into rehabilitation centers, where even those who had been originally sentenced to eight or ten years could reenlist in the army at the end of their terms, and eventually exit with honorable discharges.

As the holidays approached, President Truman issued blanket "Christmas clemencies" to the thousands of imprisoned servicemen who still had less than three years remaining on their sentences, freeing them to either continue in the service or go home. As a result, only three Fort Lawton inmates remained. Six months later, on June 1, 1947, Luther Larkin was paroled; his discharge papers took note of his exceptionally good behavior while in prison. Both Richard Barber and William Jones—each convicted of committing another crime while incarcerated—remained behind bars until 1948. Less than four years after the riot and lynching, none of the defendants was still serving time.

Beeks and Jaworski paid little attention to the men they had spent so much time defending and prosecuting. As he had hoped, Jaworski was assigned to help prosecute war crimes in Europe. After frustrating delays, he finally landed in Germany, where he was selected as trial judge advocate for the very first war crimes trial ever conducted under the terms of the Geneva Convention. He was ordered by the U.S. command to seek the death penalty for several private citizens of the town of Rüsselsheim, charged with murdering American prisoners of war just twelve days after Guglielmo Olivotto was lynched in Seattle. Jaworski's reputation soared after the worst of the perpetrators were all found guilty and went to the gallows. His legal team in Germany included two lawyers he'd brought with him from Seattle, men who had impressed him with their brains and bravado: William Beeks and Howard Noyd.

Jaworski collected several more guilty verdicts in Germany, while Beeks was assigned to tour liberated Nazi concentration camps. The work was absorbing, but as the massive Nuremburg trials approached, all three lawyers were feeling the tug of their families and decided to head back home. William Beeks ascended to the federal bench in Seattle, where he was feared by litigators for his impatience and respected by almost everyone for his mastery of the law of the sea. He died in 1988. Howard Noyd, having fallen in love with Seattle, decided to make his home there and became a respected insurance lawyer. Given the scant time he and Beeks were given to prepare their case, he considered the verdicts major victories, because Larkin, Jones, and Hurks were spared the death penalty. Beeks's failure to uncover evidence of the incompetence of the Fort Lawton command was understandable, he believed, considering the single-minded focus to save his clients' lives.

Leon Jaworski became one of the most powerful lawyers in America, serving as confidant and counselor to Lyndon Johnson, and leading the state of Texas's legal team investigating the assassination of President John Kennedy in Dallas. In 1973, in the infamous "Saturday Night Massacre," President Richard Nixon told Solicitor General Robert Bork to fire Archibald Cox as special prosecutor investigating the Watergate scandal. Nixon replaced Cox with Jaworski but came to regret it, as Jaworski won a landmark Supreme Court decision ordering the president to turn over conversations he had recorded in the Oval Office, an event that ultimately led Nixon to become the first U.S. president to resign.

Jaworski, who served a term as president of the American Bar Association, wrote or cowrote four books, all of them reminiscing about his personal life and legal career. The books are full of anecdotes about Jaworski's many legal victories, particularly in high-profile cases. He mentions the Fort Lawton trial only in passing and, even then, mistakenly reports that Olivotto was hung from "a barracks rafter." "It was never established," he wrote, "whether he had been murdered or committed suicide in terror." Leon Jaworski died in 1982, while chopping wood on his Texas ranch.

General Elliott Cooke continued his war against army incompetence. He eventually returned to Central America, where he became commanding general of the Atlantic Sector Headquarters in the Panama Canal Zone, not far from the spot where he had enlisted as a private in World War I. Cooke died in San Antonio, Texas, in 1961.

In June 1947, Luther Larkin returned to Arkansas and opened a fancy restaurant, complete with white linens. He bought a surplus army jeep and used it to get up into the woods, where he and his best friend loved to hunt. On December 9, 1948, Larkin felt a sharp pain in his abdomen that wouldn't go away. He went up the hill to the segregated hospital above his parents' house but was sent home that same day. The next morning at eight, he died on his mother's kitchen table. His family later determined that his appendix had burst; his mother remained convinced for decades that the hospital had refused to give Luther proper treatment because he was black.

On July 26, 1948, President Truman signed Executive Order 9981, stating, "It is hereby declared to be the policy of the President that there shall be equality of treatment and opportunity for all persons in the armed services without regard to race, color, religion, or national origin." Two courts-martial—at Fort Lawton and at Port Chicago— were cited by White House staff as compelling evidence that the time had come to integrate the military. Almost two years later, Truman signed into law the Uniform Code of Military Justice. The UCMJ replaced the Articles of War and substantially revised the court-martial process. Among other changes, panels of judges would thereafter include both officers and enlisted men.

In November, 1949, Sammy Snow began to have second thoughts about accepting a dishonorable discharge. He applied to the army for reconsideration, but his request was rejected. His discharge made him ineligible for the GI Bill and other veterans' benefits, so he took a job at as a janitor at a whites-only Methodist church, where he was paid to sweep the floors but not allowed to sit in the pews during services. Married in 1950, his two children eventually completed college. In 2002, after a newspaper story mistakenly reported that Snow was "the last surviving witness" to the 1944 riot, the U.S. army flew him to Seattle as a guest of honor. Major General James Collins invited Snow to observe how far the army had come in its attitudes toward racial discrimination.

In August 1950, Robert Sanders, having returned to Chicago, also realized how difficult life could be without an honorable discharge. Like Snow, he filed a formal petition with the Office of the Secretary of the army. Calling the record of trial "one of the most voluminous in Army courts-martial history," the army's expert consultant, L. F. Murphy, reported part of what Sanders had told him:

Willie Ellis, a fellow nobody trusted, got immunity for naming some of them. He and I had an argument, and he did not like me. Why did the court take his word, or the word of Jesse Sims, instead of believing me? I only walked towards the Italian Area to see what the noise was about, and I swear to God I never got there. I met some fellows carrying Sammy Snow, my buddy, who had been knocked out, and I carried him back to our barracks . . . I would not have hurt the Italians, and I had no feelings against them. I knew the MPs didn't like them because they got into lots of trouble.

I couldn't believe it when they found me guilty. I kept begging for a chance to return to active duty, and to earn an honorable discharge. Three times I went through complete basic training, but they never let me back on active service. I tried so hard to please everybody, and I was a trustee at Fort Missoula, at Turlock, California, and Fort Knox, Kentucky. When they asked me again if I wanted to go through training a fourth time in hopes of getting restored to duty, I was so discouraged that I begged only to come home.

All Sanders wanted was a full hearing in front of the Army Board for Correction of Military Records. Murphy concluded that the testimony of Sims and Ellis was "clear and compelling" and rejected Sanders's request. Robert Sanders died in 1992.

On September 26, 1951, the army board refused Willie Curry's request to conduct a review of his sentence. Almost twenty-four years later, in 1975, the same board actually agreed to examine Frank Hughes's conviction but afterward summarily "determined that insufficient evidence has been presented to indicate probably material error or injustice, and the application is denied." Curry died in 1968; Hughes in 1983.

Les Stewart reentered the army, served in Korea, and earned an honorable discharge when his unit returned to its base in California. When it came time to head home to Texas, his train was stopped as it reached the Texas border; Stewart and every other returning black soldier was told to disembark, then ordered to head back to a car reserved for Negroes. Forty years later, Stewart—whose own son eventually joined the army—remained bitter. He was still upset that he had agreed with Beeks's suggestion that he not take the stand in his own defense. And he was incensed by the allegation that black men would use a rope to kill an Italian. Nowhere else in American history had a black mob been found guilty of lynching a white man. "That's just not black people's style," said Stewart. In 1992, he passed away, not long after retiring from his long-time job with the city of Austin.

Arthur Hurks served eighteen months of army duty before earning an honorable discharge. He moved to Los Angeles, where he worked for Hughes Aircraft Company. Hurks raised a son and a daughter, but tragedy struck again when one day he opened a door to discover the body of his daughter, killed by her husband in a murder-suicide. When Hurks learned that he had cancer, he moved to Baton Rouge to be close to his cousins. He died in 1991. His grave in Denham Springs, Louisiana, has no headstone.

John Hamilton also served eighteen months of duty after his release from incarceration, earning an honorable discharge after an assignment in occupied Japan. Hamilton worked for a steel company in Houston and raised two children. He too wished he had decided to have his say in court. But he let his bitterness go, saying, "I have learned from that experience how to hold your poise and be calm and go through whatever. Because, in the ultimate end, you gonna come out. And I did." He was 73 when he died in 1999.

Roy Montgomery served his two years at Turlock, then reentered the army at Fort McClellan in Alabama. He spent the rest of his army hitch doing menial work in the kitchen. With his honorable discharge, Roy went to work for his aunt in a Clarksdale, Mississippi, funeral home. He got married, moved to Chicago, and worked in a casket-making company, before starting his own construction business. One of his grandsons became a star in the National Basketball Association. Fifty-eight years after his trial, he still remembered even the smallest details about August 14, 1944. "I believe the white boys took him down there and hung him, I believe. Now, there's nothing certain, but I believe that."

Harry Branson fought Cooke's efforts to have him disciplined. Several years later, when the Army Reclassification Board reassigned him to a staff position outside the Transportation Corps, he decided instead to retire from the army. He died in San Francisco in 1963. The board decided not to demote William Orem. He died in southern California in 1971.

Grant Farr became a prominent economist, eventually chairing the Economics Department at Penn State University. A lifelong smoker, lung cancer took his life in 1985 at the age of 65.

Fred Perata moved back to his old neighborhood in San Francisco's Portola District and had a long career with the Internal Revenue Service. His daughter, Jean, was an intern for Senator Daniel K. Inouye in 1974 and was in the Senate hearing room as Leon Jaworski testified before the Senate Watergate Committee, of which Inouye was a prominent member. Six decades later, the former interpreter remained certain that Guglielmo Olivotto did not commit suicide.

Edward Haskell stayed with the Twenty-eighth ISU until the war finally ended, bidding his Italian friends a tearful farewell from the dock at Newport News, Virginia, as their transport ship left for Italy in 1945. Haskell returned to San Francisco, eventually becoming a deputy labor commissioner for the California Department of Industrial Relations. He continued to maintain that the army made a huge mistake allowing American soldiers and Italians to mingle in the PX.

Mason Gould's injuries kept him in the hospital for sixteen months, where he underwent excruciating surgeries and rehabilitation to repair his mangled left arm. His dreams of playing professional baseball at an end, he became a journalist and later ran his own public relations firm. In retirement, he became an accomplished tennis player, competing well into his eighties.

Clyde Lomax eventually married, fathered a daughter, divorced, and married again, the second time for forty-nine years. He worked construction and drove trucks and didn't like to talk about his time in the army. He died of cancer in August 1999 and is buried in Independence, Louisiana.

GUGLIELMO OLIVOTTO NEVER left Seattle. His remains are still in the Fort Lawton cemetery, where white marble headstones with arched crests line up in rows that are more or less symmetrical. Most of the graves are confined to four modest quadrants of ragged fescue, dandelions, and moss but just beyond the northeast quadrant, beneath a tall cedar and a wide maple, is a striking solitary marker. At its base is a whitewashed concrete tablet with raised serif letters surrounding a small Latin cross with Maltese points, a memorial that reads:

SOLD. ITAL.

OLIVOTTO GUGLIEAMO [*sic*]

23 OTTOBRE 1911

14 AGOSTO 1944

Rising four feet above the tablet—and much taller than any of the Americans' marble headstones—is a thick column, rippled with convex vertical bands in the Roman style. The top of the column is not level; the anonymous sculptor chiseled a dramatic forty-five-degree angle, leaving the illusion that the column has snapped off—a broken column, if you will, to call attention decades later to a forgotten life cut mysteriously short.

Sixty years after Guglielmo Olivotto's death, most of Fort Lawton was owned by the city of Seattle and was known as Discovery Park. The ravine where Olivotto's body was discovered became part of a city sewage treatment plant at the base of the Magnolia Bluffs. Discovery Park's master plan puts a high priority on erasing most vestiges of the army's presence, particularly in the area where the Italian and colored barracks once stood. Only faint traces of Lawton Road still remain.

NOTES ON SOURCES

Citations to Pretrial Investigation

All sworn pretrial investigative statements were transcribed by court reporters and can be found at the College Park, MD, research room of the National Archives and Records Administration (NARACP) listed under "Investigation of Attack on Italian Service Unit Personnel by American Soldiers at Ft. Lawton Washington," File 333.9: Ft. Lawton, Wash (6), formerly confidential General Correspondence 1939–47, Record Group 159: Records of the Office of the Inspector General, NARACP. This citation is heretofore referred to as "Investigation of Attack," File 333.9, RG 159: Records of the Office of the Inspector General, NARACP.

Citations to Record of Court-Martial

The Fort Lawton court-martial commenced on November 16, 1944, and adjourned December 18, 1944.

The transcript of the entire trial runs 1,809 pages and is bound in four volumes. The included exhibits span another 200 pages.

The transcript of the cout-martial is available through the Court Operations Branch of the Office of the Clerk of Court, United States Army Judiciary in Arlington, VA, and is listed as Court-Martial Number 276-299, Nelson Alston, et al., Fort Lawton, Washington, November–December 1944. This citation is heretofore referred to as CM No. 276-299.

Prologue August 15, 1944

The sworn testimony of Private First Class John H. Pinkney regarding the events of August 15, 1944, is in "Investigation of Attack," File 333.9, RG 159: Records of the Office of the Inspector General, NARACP: 344–46, 650–53, 948; and in CM No. 276-299: 1656–57.

The sworn testimony of Private Clyde Vernon Lomax regarding the events of August 15, 1944, is in "Investigation of Attack," File 333.9, RG 159: Records of the Office of the Inspector General, NARACP: 70–74; and in CM No. 276-299: 1099–1103.

Chapter One Camp Florence: May 1944

The physical description of Camp Florence during World War II is in "Florence Internment Camp," Office of the Provost Marshal General, File 254: Florence, Arizona, RG 389.4.6: Records of Enemy Prisoners of War Information Bureau, NARACP; "Reclamation Building, Camp Florence," Operations Branch, Prisoner of War Operations Division, Correspondence File, RG 389.4.5: Records Relating to Italian Prisoners of War during World War II, Florence, Arizona—Construction, NARACP; "Report of Visit to Camp Florence," Carl Erik Wenngren, YMCA, Administrative Branch, Office of the Provost Marshal General, File 255: Florence, Arizona, RG 3889.4.4: Records of the Prisoner of War Special Projects Branch, NARACP; "Report of Visit to Prisoner of War Camp, Florence," Captain D. L. Schwieger, Administrative Branch, Office of the Provost Marshal General, File 225: Florence, Arizona, February 28–March 2, 1944, RG 389.4.4: Records of the Office of Special Projects, NARACP; "Report on Florence Prisoner of War Camp, June 8–10, 1943," P. W. Herrick, Special War Problems Division, Department of State, File: Florence, Arizona, RG 59: Inspection Reports on Prisoner of War Camps, 1942–46, NARACP; "Report on Visit to Prisoner of War Camp, Coolidge, Arizona," Louis Hortal, YMCA, File 254: Florence, Arizona, Office of the Provost Marshal General, RG 389.4.7: Records of the Enemy Prisoner of War Information Bureau, NARACP; "Visit to Camp Florence, July 29, 1943," Edwin Plitt, Special War Problems Division, Department of State, File: Florence, Arizona, RG 59: Inspection Reports on Prisoner of War Camps, 1942–46, NARACP; and "Visit to Camp Florence, October 27, 1943," Charles Eberhardt, Special War Problems Division, Department of State, File: Florence, Arizona, RG 59: Inspection Reports on Prisoner of War Camps, 1942–46, NARACP.

The description of Italian prisoner-of-war personal effects during World War II is in "Civilian Enemy Aliens and Prisoners of War," Office of the Provost Marshal General, General Correspondence File, 1942–57, RG 389.4.2: Records of the Legal Branch, NARACP; and "Italian Clothing and Equipment Record, Individual," Office of the Provost Marshal General, File: Clothing and Equipment, Miscellaneous Rosters, RG 389.4.7: Records of the Enemy Prisoners of War Information Bureau, NARACP.

The history of POW camps may be found, in part, in "Arrivals and Departures of Italian Prisoners of War in the United States," Office of the Provost Marshal General, File 400.19: Statistics—POWs, RG 389.4.2: Records of the Legal Branch, Miscellaneous Records 1942–57, NARACP; "Historical Background of International Agreements Relating to Prisoners of War," American National Red Cross, Washington, DC, January 1943, Historical Files, Office of the Provost Marshal General, RG 389: 1941–58, NARACP; and "History of Prisoner of War Camp, Utah ASF Depot," Jennie M. Thomas, historian, November 16, 1944, Office of the Provost Marshal General, Correspondence File, RG 389.4.1: Records of the Operations Branch, POW Operations Division, NARACP.

The history of the opposition to the Florence, AZ, POW camp is found in letter,

Fred Gibson, Superior, Arizona Rotary Club, to Honorable Carl Hayden, U.S. Senate, February 17, 1942, Prisoner of War Camps—Florence, RG 389.4.1: Records of the Operations Branch, Technical Services, 1941–45, NARACP; and letter, E. G. Dentzer, Magma Copper Company, to Honorable Carl Hayden, U.S. Senate, February 20, 1942, Prisoner of War Camps—Florence, RG 389.4.1: Records of the Operations Branch, Technical Services, 1941–45, NARACP.

Ferruccio Umek's experience in North Africa is recounted in "Italian WWII Vet Says He's Owed Prisoner Pay," Tom Hundley, *Chicago Tribune,* July 18, 2001: 6. The *speriamo* reference is found in "Interrogation of Captured Italians," G. C. Luntley, Records of the Office War Information, RG 208.21: Records of Historian, 1941–46, NARACP.

The description of conditions for POWs in North Africa is in "Diary of Prisoner of War Richard Smuda," March 1, 1945, File 6.0, RG 389: Records of the Provost Marshal General, POW Operations Division, Legal Branch, 1942–46, NARACP.

Biographical information about Guglielmo Olivotto's childhood may be found, in part, in the sworn testimony of Italian corporal major Bruno Patteri, CM No. 276-299: 1634–36; and Italian second lieutenant Giovanni Lobianco, CM No. 276-299: 1641–42, and Italian lieutenant Vito Melpignano, CM No. 276-299: 1629–33.

Correspondent Ernie Pyle's recollections about the North Africa campaign is from his report filed in the front lines before Mateur, northern Tunisia, on May 2, 1943, for the Scripps-Howard chain of newspapers, also reproduced in *Ernie's War: The Best of Ernie Pyle's World War II Dispatches,* edited by David Nichols (New York: Random House, 1986): 112–13.

The recollections of Italian tank driver John Apice are from an oral interview called "America, My Enemy, My Home," Angelo Boccalini for the New England High Schools Oral History Internet Archive, University of Massachusetts, Boston, http://www.serl.org/oralhistory/Boccalini.

The censored letters written by Italian POWs are in "Florence Internment Center, Coolidge, Arizona," Records of the Special War Problems Division, Subject Files, 1939–54, RG 59: General Records of the Department of State, NARACP.

Questions from the standard interrogation form for captured Italian prisoners are in letter, Richard C. Hottelet, Office of War Information, to Major Thompson, Office of War Information, March 30, 1943, File: Seattle, RG 336: Records of the Office of the Chief of Transportation, Geographic Series, 1941–46, NARACP; and "Questionnaire for the Indirect Interrogation of Italian Prisoner of War on Political Warfare Points," Records of Historian, Office of War Information, Subject File 1941–46, RG 208.2.1: Records of the Office of the Director, NARACP.

Articles by Chester Hanson about conditions at the Florence Camp are in "Arizona Italian War Prisoners Want to Work," Chester G. Hanson, *Los Angeles Times,* September 22, 1943: A; "Arizona Officer Boosts Italian Prisoner Morale," Chester G. Hanson, *Los Angeles Times,* September 23, 1943: 10; "Italian Prisoners 'Overcome' by Food," Chester G. Hanson, *Los Angeles Times,* September 24, 1943: 13; "Italian

Prisoners' Work in Arizona Commended," Chester G. Hanson, *Los Angeles Times*, September 25, 1943: 3; "Humanity Watchword for Italian Prisoners," Chester G. Hanson, *Los Angeles Times*, September 26, 1943: 16; and "Prisoners Devise Own Means of Recreation," Chester G. Hanson, *Los Angeles Times*, September 27, 1943: 10.

The text of the letter from Colonel William A. Holden to incoming Italian prisoners is in "Arizona Officer Boosts Italian Prisoner Morale," Chester G. Hanson, *Los Angeles Times*, September 23, 1943: 10.

Details of daily life for Italian prisoners at Camp Florence are in "History of the 28th Italian Quartermaster Service Company," Captain Arthur H. Hofberg, October 1945, RG 407: Records of Adjutant General's Office, WWII Operations Reports, NARACP; "Memorandum: Films with Italian Captions," Colonel R. T. Arrington, director of training, Office of the Provost Marshal General, File 062.2: Motion Picture Films, RG 389.4.1: Records of the Operations Branch, Prisoner of War Division, 1942–57; "Memo: Request for Sports Equipment," Lieutenant Colonel J. J. Graves, military police, Camp Florence, Office of the Provost Marshal General, Prisoner of War Camps—Florence, Mail and Records Branch Project, Technical Services, 1941–45, RG 389.2.1: Records of the Administrative Division, NARACP; "Memo to War Department: List of Approved Foreign Language Newspapers Published in the United States which May Be Made Available to Prisoners of War in the United States," Lieutenant Colonel A. M. Tollefson, assistant director, Prisoner of War Division, Office of the Provost Marshal General, File 206: Books, Newspapers, Magazines, RG 389.4.2: POW Operations Division, Legal Branch, 1942–46, NARACP; "Report of Visit to Camp Florence," Carl Erik Wenngren, YMCA, Administrative Branch, Office of the Provost Marshal General, File 255: Florence, Arizona, RG 389.4.4: Records of the Prisoner of War Special Projects Branch, NARACP; "Report of Visit to Prisoner of War Camp, Florence," Captain D. L. Schwieger, Administrative Branch, Office of the Provost Marshal General, February 28–March 2, 1944, File 225: Florence, Arizona, RG 389.4.4: Records of the Office of Special Projects, NARACP; "Report on Florence Prisoner of War Camp, June 8–10, 1943," P. W. Herrick, Special War Problems Division, Department of State, File: Florence, Arizona, RG 59: Inspection Reports on Prisoner of War Camps, 1942–46, NARACP; "Report on Visit to Prisoner of War Camp, Coolidge, Arizona," Louis Hortal, YMCA, Office of the Provost Marshal General, File 254: Florence, Arizona, RG 389.4.7: Records of the Enemy Prisoner of War Information Bureau, NARACP; "Visit to Camp Florence, July 29, 1943," Edwin Plitt, Special War Problems Division, Department of State, File: Florence, Arizona, RG 59: Inspection Reports on Prisoner of War Camps, 1942–46, NARACP; and "Visit to Camp Florence, October 27, 1943," Charles Eberhardt, Special War Problems Division, Department of State, File: Florence, Arizona, RG 59: Inspection Reports on Prisoner of War Camps, 1942–46, NARACP.

Details about Italian prisoners chopping cotton are in "Agricultural Work Duties of Italian Prisoners of War at Camp Florence and Side Camps," Security and Intelligence Division, February 29, 1944, Office of the Provost Marshal General, Decimal File 1943–46, File 255: Florence, RG 389.4.4: Prisoner of War Special Program Division, Administrative Branch, NARACP; "Cotton Production Report," Labor Contract and Accounting Department, December 9, 1943, Office of the Provost Marshal General, Decimal File 1943–46, File 255: Florence, RG 389.4.4: Prisoner of War Special Program Division, Administrative Branch, NARACP; "Daily Work Record at Camp Florence," Office of the Provost Marshal General, File 255: Florence, RG 389.4.4: Prisoner of War Special Program Division, Administrative Branch, Decimal File 1943–46, NARACP; and "Visit to Camp Florence, October 27, 1943," Charles Eberhardt, Special War Problems Division, Department of State, File: Florence, Arizona, RG 59: Inspection Reports on Prisoner of War Camps, 1942–46, NARACP.

The history of the formation of Italian Service Units can be found in "Historical Monograph of Italian Service Unit Headquarters," Office of the Provost Marshal General, August 3, 1945, RG 389.4.5: Historical Files, 1941–58, NARACP; "Italian Army of Voluntary Military Work," Colonel Henkle, Camp Como, Mississippi, October 18, 1944, Office of the Provost Marshal General, File 333.9: Forts—Ft. Lawton, RG 159: General Correspondence, 1939–47, NARACP; "Italian Service Units," Headquarters, Army Service Forces, August 28, 1944, File 333.9: Fort Lawton, RG 159: Records of the Office of the Inspector General, General Correspondence, 1939–47, NARACP; "Plan for Organization of Italian Prisoners of War into Service Companies," Major General W. D. Styer, chief of staff, Army Special Forces, War Department, to assistant chief of staff, G-1, War Department General Services, January 6, 1944, File 322/100: ISU—General, RG 389.4.1: Records of the Operations Branch, Italian Service Units, 1944–45, NARACP; "Remarks of Rep. Andrew May of Kentucky," *Congressional Record,* March 5, 1945, Office of the Provost Marshal General, File 014.3: Press Releases and Statements, RG 389.4.1: Records of the Operations Branch, Prisoner of War Division, 1944–45, NARACP; and "Report on Italian Service Forces," memorandum, Brigadier General John M. Eager, commander, to commanding general, Army Service Forces, September 15, 1945, File: Italian Service Units, RG 389.4.7: Records of the Enemy Prisoner of War Information Bureau, NARACP.

Details about the difficulty of getting Italians to join service units are in "Application for Service in Italian Service Unit," Colonel H. M. Pool, Camp Butner, North Carolina, March 20, 1944, File 383.6: Prisoner of War Weekly Reports, RG 389.4.1: Records of the Operations Branch, Prisoner of War Division, Italian Service Units, 1944–45, NARACP; "History of the 28th Italian Quartermaster Service Company," report, Captain Arthur H. Hofberg, October 1945, RG 407, Records of Adjutant General's Office, WWII Operations Reports, NARACP; "Italian Prisoners of War at Camp Florence" (handwritten note), Office of the Provost Marshal General, April 28, 1944, File 370.091, RG 389.4.1: Records of the Operations Branch, Prisoner of War Division, Italian Service Units, 1944–45, NARACP; "Return of Italian Personnel to

Prisoner of War Camps," Office of the Provost Marshal General, File 253.91: Transfer of Prisoners, RG 389.4.1: Records of the Operations Branch, Prisoner of War Division, NARACP; "Segregation of Italian Prisoners of War," memorandum to commanding general, Ninth Service Command, February 26, 1944, Office of the Provost Marshal General, Reporting Branch, Subject File 1942–46: Italian Segregation, RG 389.4.7: Records of the Enemy Prisoner of War Information Branch, NARACP; and "Summary of Procedure in Obtaining Signatures of Prisoners of War for Service in Italian Service Units," Lieutenant Colonel Albert E. Wilfong, Camp Florence, April 20, 1944, File 383.6: Prisoner of War Weekly Reports, RG 389.4.1: Records of the Operations Branch, Prisoner of War Division, Italian Service Units, 1944–45, NARACP.

Chapter Two Fort Lawton: June 1944

Information about the history of the construction of Fort Lawton is in "An Archeological Evaluation of the Fort Lawton Historic District, Seattle," Steve Wilke and Karen James, Report to the City of Seattle Geo-Recon International, Department of Parks and Recreation, Seattle, July 1984; "The Evolution of Intent at Fort Lawton," David Chance, Report to the City of Seattle Geo-Recon International, Department of Parks and Recreation, Seattle, July 1984; *Magnolia Yesterday and Today,* Aleua L. Frare (Seattle: Magnolia Community Club, 1976); and *Seattle and Environs, 1852–1924,* edited by C. H. Hanford (Seattle: Pioneer Historical Publishing Co., 1924).

Information about Luther Larkin's family and childhood came, in part, from author interview with two of Larkin's nieces, Dr. Carletta Boyd and Faye Watson, conducted in Chicago on November 19, 2002, and from author interview with Larkin's nephew, John Fields, conducted in Orlando FL, on November 13, 2002. The history of Larkin's army service is recounted in sworn testimony at CM No. 276-299: 1261–63.

Of the many resources consulted for data about African American soldiers during World War II, the primary reference is *The United States Army in World War II: Special Studies: The Employment of Negro Troops,* Ulysses Lee (Washington, DC: U.S. Army, Center of Military History, 1966). Also helpful were *The African-American Soldier,* Lt. Col. Michael Lee Lanning (New York: Birch Lane Press, 1997); *Democracy's Negroes: A Book of Facts concerning the Activities of Negroes in World War II,* Arthur Furr (Boston: House of Edinboro, 1947); *The Negro Handbook,* Florence Murray (New York: Progressive Press, 1944): 1–27, 128–30, 238–45; "The Negro in the Army," James C. Evans, civilian aide to the secretary of the army, July 31, 1948, File: White House Files, Minorities—Negroes—General, Papers of Philleo Nash, Truman Papers, Truman Library; and *Negro Year Book: A Review of Events Affecting Negro Life, 1941–46,* edited by Jessie P. Guzman (Tuskegee, AL: Tuskegee Institute, 1947): 351–53.

The primary source for information about the structure of the Army Service Forces during World War II was *The United States Army in World War II: The Army Service Forces: The Organization and Role of the Army Service Forces,* John D. Millett (Washington, DC: U.S. Army, Center of Military History, 1954).

The primary source for information about the formation and structure of the Transportation Corps were *United States Army in World War II/The Transportation Corps: Operations Overseas,* Joseph Bykovsky and Harold Larson (Washington, DC: Department of the Army, Office of the Chief of Military History, 1957); and *United States Army in World War II/The Transportation Corps: Responsibilities, Organization, and Operations,* Chester Wardlow (Washington, DC: Department of the Army, Office of the Chief of Military History, 1951).

The observation of a War Department official about white officers assigned to black units is in "Summary of Racial Situation, 10/7/44," memorandum, civilian aide to the assistant secretary of war to Colonel Roamer, File: Reports/Memos/Intelligence Summaries, RG 107: Office of the Secretary of War, October 7, 1944, NARACP.

The list of supposed characteristics of black soldiers is in "Certain Characteristics of the Negro which Affect Command of Negro Troops," File: White House Files, Minorities — Negroes — Leadership, Papers of Philleo Nash, Truman Papers, Truman Library.

The intercepted letter from the black Fort Lewis soldier is in "Racial Situation in the Army, 1944–1946," memorandum, civilian aide to the assistant secretary of war, File: Reports/Memos/Intelligence Summaries, December 20, 1944, RG 107: Office of the Secretary of War, NARACP.

The letters written by American soldiers stationed in Britain are in "Censorship Report for Period 8/16/44 to 8/31/44," memorandum, civilian aide to the assistant secretary of war, File: Reports/Memos/Intelligence Summaries, August 31, 1944, RG 107: Office of the Secretary of War, NARACP.

The history of the African American experience in Seattle during World War II may be found, in part, in *The Forging of a Black Community: Seattle's Central District from 1870 through the Civil Rights Era,* Quintard Taylor (Seattle: University of Washington Press, 1994); and *Jackson Street after Hours,* Paul de Barros (Seattle: Sasquatch Books, 1993): 60–61. Many other materials — including the reference to the International Association of Machinists — are gathered by the Center for the Study of the Pacific Northwest at the University of Washington, particularly in "African Americans in the Modern Northwest," John M. Findlay, professor of history, University of Washington, Seattle, http://www.washington.edu/uwired/outreach/cspn/.

The documentation of Larkin's measles is in "26 Jan 44," Diary AR-40-1005, 1944, Fort Lawton Hospital, AGF and AFF Installations, RG 337: Records of Headquarters Army Ground Forces, NARACP.

The details of the inspection history of the 650th Port Company is in "Basic Military and Personnel Inspections for 650th and 651st Port Companies," Colonel Lloyd

Bunting, director of training, June 9, 1944, File: Training Memoranda, 1944, RG 336: Office of the Chief of Transportation, 1941–50, Seattle Port of Embarkation, National Archives, Seattle; "Minimum Training Requirements for Numbered Army Service Forces Units," Major Joseph Maxwell, Army Service Forces, May 15–16, 1944, File: Training Memoranda, 1944, RG 336: Office of the Chief of Transportation, 1941–50, Seattle Port of Embarkation, National Archives, Seattle; "Results of Basic Military and Unit Inspection, 650th & 651st Port Companies," Colonel Lloyd Bunting, director of training, May 7, 1944, File: Training Memoranda, 1944, RG 336: Office of the Chief of Transportation, 1941–50, Seattle Port of Embarkation, National Archives, Seattle; "Standard Seattle Port of Embarkation Inspection Procedure Guide," Colonel Lloyd Bunting, director of training, June 6, 1944, File: Training Memoranda, 1944, RG 336: Office of the Chief of Transportation, 1941–50, Seattle Port of Embarkation, National Archives, Seattle; and "Temporary Changes in Station, Training, Furlough for the 650th and 651st Port Companies," Colonel Lloyd Bunting, director of training, April 27, 1944, File: Training Memoranda, 1944, RG 336: Office of the Chief of Transportation, 1941–50, Seattle Port of Embarkation, National Archives, Seattle.

Chapter Three Mollycoddling: July 1944

The letter from Corporal Fordyce to Senator Capper is in letter, Corporal George F. Fordyce to U.S. Senator Arthur Capper, August 2, 1944, File 201: Treatment of Prisoners of War in the United States, Capper, RG 389.4.1: Records of the Operations Branch, Italian Service Units, 1944–45, NARACP.

Complaints by American civilians about the alleged preferential treatment of Italian prisoners is found in "Extract: 'Carrying it To [sic] Far,'" *Plainfield Courier-News*, June 21, 1944, File 330.14: Complains and Criticisms, RG 389.4.1: Records of the Operations Branch, Italian Service Units, 1944–45, NARACP; letter, Lieutenant Colonel Earl L. Edwards to Brigadier General John M. Eager, June 26, 1944, with attached letter to editor from "Three Patients, Station Hospital, Fort Devens," File 201: Wigglesworth, RG 389.4.1: Records of the Operations Branch, Italian Service Units, 1944–45, NARACP; letter, Robert J. Miller to Brigadier General Joseph F. Battley, September 22, 1944, File 383.6, RG 389.4.1: Records of the Operations Branch, Italian Service Units, 1944–45, NARACP; letter, M. C. Swope to Brigadier General John M. Eager, July 10, 1944, File: Swope, RG 389.4.1: Records of the Operations Branch, Italian Service Units, 1944–45, NARACP; "Prisoners of War in U.S.," Bill Cunningham, Boston Herald and Mutual Broadcasting Service, June 21, 1944, File: O'Daniel, RG 389.4.1: Records of the Operations Branch, Italian Service Units, 1944–45, NARACP; radio commentary, Leland Stone, August 5, 1944, File 383.6: Weekly Reports, RG 389.4.1: Records of the Operations Branch, Italian Service Units, 1944–45, NARACP; and radio commentary, Walter Winchell, July 16, 1944, File 255: Camps for Prisoners of War, RG 160: Records of the Office of Commanding General, Army Service Forces, Correspondence File, 1943–45, NARACP.

Comments from army officials about the treatment of Italian prisoners are in "Address of Major General Archer L. Lerch, Extension of Remarks of Hon. Andrew J. May of Kentucky in the House of Representatives," Congressional Record—Appendix, March 5, 1945: A1107; and letter, Brigadier General John M. Eager to U.S. senator Arthur Capper, August 17, 1944, File 201: Treatment of Prisoners of War in the United States, Capper, RG 389.4.1: Records of the Operations Branch, Italian Service Units, 1944–45, NARACP.

The history of the army's public relations campaign to solicit support for ISUs may be found, in part, in "Report on Italian Service Units," memorandum, Brigadier General John M. Eager to commanding general, Army Service Forces, September 15, 1945, File: Italian Service Units, RG 389.4.7: Records of the Enemy Prisoner of War Information Bureau: 20–23, NARACP.

News reports in response to the army's public relations campaign are in "Italian Prisoners in Service Units Work for Privileges," Business Week, July 8, 1944: 31; and "Our 'Pampered' War Prisoners," Robert Devore, Colliers, October 14, 1944: 14, 57–60.

News reports about Italian prisoners dating American and British girls are in "Italian Prisoners Vex Yanks by Taking Girls," Washington Post, July 1, 1944: 5; "Britons Demand: 'Save Our Girls From Italian Prisoners of War,'" New York Herald Tribune, September 8, 1944: 1; and "White Plains Girl Announces Her Betrothal to Italian Prisoner of War Held in U.S.," New York Times, January 11, 1945: 25.

War Department concerns about relations between Italian POWs and American girls are in "Conduct of Members of ISU," July 10, 1944, File 322/100: ISU-General, RG 389.4.1, Records of the Operations Branch, Office of the Provost Marshal General, Italian Service Units 1944–45, NARACP.

Correspondence between Congressman Marcantonio and General Eager are in letter, Hon. Vito Marcantonio to Brigadier General John M. Eager, June 26, 1945, File 201: Private Genta, RG 389.4.1: Records of the Operations Branch, ISU, 1944–45, NARACP; and letter, Brigadier General John M. Eager to Hon. Vito Marcantonio, June 29, 1945, File 201: Private Genta, RG 389.4.1: Records of the Operations Branch, ISU, 1944–45, NARACP.

Details about the original mission of Fort Lawton during 1941 and 1942 are in "Origins of the Seattle Port of Embarkation," File: Seattle Port of Embarkation, RG 336: Records of the Office of the Chief of Transportation, Geographic Series, 1941–46, NARACP; memorandum, Captain Howard MacDonald to Technical Information Branch, July 28, 1943, File 000.7: Fort Lawton, RG 336: Records of the Office of the Chief of Transportation, Geographic Series, 1941–46, NARACP; "Reorganization of Fort Lawton," Captain R. D. Hoisington, General Order, July 27, 1942, File 320.12: Fort Lawton, RG 389.2.1: Records of the Administrative Division,

Office of the Provost Marshal General, Technical Services 1941–45, NARACP; and "Use of Fort Lawton, Washington, as an Overseas Discharge and Replacement Depot," memorandum, Brigadier General John C. H. Lee to the adjutant general, May 8, 1941, File 323.3: Fort Lawton, Washington, RG 92: Office of the Quartermaster General, General Correspondence, 1936–45, NARACP.

Details about the reorganization of Fort Lawton in 1944 are in "Revised Table of Organization," General Order No. 52, Fort Lawton Staging Area, File: General Orders 1942–44, RG 336: Records of the Office of the Chief of Transportation, 1941–50, Seattle Port of Embarkation, National Archives, Seattle.

Details about the assignments of black soldiers at Fort Lawton are in "Activation of Port Companies," Colonel John Hood, General Order No. 17, January 19, 1944, File 320.3: General Orders, RG 336: Records of the Office of the Chief of Transportation, Geographic Series, 1941–46, NARACP; "Completion of Overseas Preparation of 650th and 651st Port Companies, Fort Lawton," Colonel Lloyd Bunting, Training Division Special Memorandum No. 120, July 27, 1944, File: Training Memoranda, 1944, RG 336: Records of the Office of the Chief of Transportation, 1941–50, Seattle Port of Embarkation, National Archives, Seattle; "Reorganization of Army Service Forces Units," memorandum to the chief of transportation, April 24, 1944, File 320.3: General Orders, RG 336: Records of the Office of the Chief of Transportation, Geographic Series, 1941–46, NARACP; and "Shortages of Enlisted Men at Seattle Port of Embarkation," report, February 8, 1944, File 320.22, RG 336: Records of the Office of the Chief of Transportation, Geographic Series, 1941–46, NARACP.

The secretary of war's announcement of its nondiscrimination policy may be found in Seattle Port of Embarkation Memorandums, General Eley P. Denson, June 28, 1944, File: SPE Memos 1944, RG 336: Records of the Office of the Chief of Transportation, 1941–50, Seattle Port of Embarkation, National Archives, Seattle.

Details of the uprising of Italian Fascists in July 1944 at Fort Lawton are in memorandum, Italian captain Guglielmo Son et al. to Colonel Harry L. Branson, July 9, 1944, File 383.6: Weekly Reports, RG 389.4.1: Records of the Operations Branch, Office of the Provost Marshal General, Italian Service Units 1944–45, NARACP; memorandum, Italian field major Giovanni Scarpa to Colonel Harry L. Branson, July 9, 1944, File 383.6: Weekly Reports, RG 389.4.1: Records of the Operations Branch, Office of the Provost Marshal General, Italian Service Units 1944–45, NARACP; "Report on the Staging and Shipping of Shipment No. 6541-C (Consisting of 1,000 Italian Prisoners of War)," Colonel Harry L. Branson to Lieutenant Colonel D. E. Farr, July 12, 1944, File 383.6: Weekly Reports, RG 389.4.1: Records of the Operations Branch, Office of the Provost Marshal General, Italian Service Units 1944–45, NARACP; "Shipment of Italian Prisoners of War and Escort Guard Companies to the Central Pacific Area," memorandum, Major General Thomas T. Handy to deputy chief of staff for Service Command, May 19, 1944, RG 389.4.1: Records of the Operations Branch, Office of the Provost Marshal General, Italian Service Units 1944–45,

NARACP; and "Shipment 6541-C," memorandum, Colonel James H. Kuttner to Colonel Harry L. Branson, June 26, 1944, File 383.6: Weekly Reports, RG 389.4.1: Records of the Operations Branch, Office of the Provost Marshal General, Italian Service Units 1944–45, NARACP.

Details of the death of Luigi Canevari are in affidavit, Captain Charles O. Sturdevant, July 11, 1944, File 201: Canevari, Luigi, RG 389.4.1: Records of the Operations Branch, Office of the Provost Marshal General, Italian Service Units 1944–45, NARACP; affidavit, T/5 Robert T. Camozzi, July 13, 1944, File 201: Canevari, Luigi, RG 389.4.1: Records of the Operations Branch, Office of the Provost Marshal General, Italian Service Units 1944–45, NARACP; and "Death of Italian War Prisoner—Luigi Canevari," report, R. K. Gough to Matt McCourt, July 10, 1944, File 201: Canevari, Luigi, RG 389.4.1, Records of the Operations Branch, Office of the Provost Marshal General, Italian Service Units 1944–45, NARACP.

Chapter Four The Life of Reilly: *Early August 1944*

Author interviews with Joyce Langsted Garbe were conducted in Seattle on June 1, 1987, July 16, 1987, and June 30, 2003. Interviews with Joyce's brother, Clyde Langsted, were conducted in Seattle on May 26, 1987, and July 16, 1987.

Author interviews with Fred Perata were conducted in San Francisco on April 26, 2002, May 6, 2002, and December 8, 2002.

Author interviews with Mason Gould were conducted in West End, NC, on July 29, 2002, and February 8, 2003.

Author interviews with Fred Haskell were conducted in Concord, CA, on March 20, 2003.

Author interviews with Grant Farr's son, Grant Farr Jr., were conducted in Industry, PA, on May 22, 2002.

A floor plan of the Italian orderly room (Building 713) is in "Investigation of Attack," File 333.9, RG 159: Records of the Office of the Inspector General, Exhibit A, NARACP.

A description of the treatment of Italian POWs by some American soldiers at Fort Lawton is in the sworn testimony of Italian sergeant Angelo Fumarola, NARACP 333.9 "Investigation of Attack," File 333.9, RG 159: Records of the Office of the Inspector General, September 9, 1944: 206, NARACP; and "History of the 28thItalian Quartermaster Service Company," report by Captain Arthur H. Hofberg, October 1945: 7, RG 407: Records of Adjutant General's Office, WWII Operations Reports, NARACP.

A description of the attitudes of enlisted Italian POWs toward their Italian officers is in "Informant's Report on ISU Camp," October 25, 1944, File 383.6: POW to Weekly Reports, May 44, RG 389.4.1: Records of the Operations Branch, Office of the Provost Marshal General, Italian Service Units 1944–45, NARACP.

Chapter Five Riot: August 14, 1944

Details of President Franklin D. Roosevelt's visit to Seattle are in "Log of the President's Inspection Trip to the Pacific," July 13–August 17, 1944, Folder: President's Trip to Pacific, 1944, Papers of Samuel Rosenman, Franklin D. Roosevelt Library, Hyde Park, NY. The president's radio address from the deck of the USS *Cummings* is in "Radio Address from Puget Sound Navy Yard, Bremerton, Washington," Franklin D. Roosevelt, August 12, 1944, Public Papers of the Presidents, Franklin D. Roosevelt, 1944, American Presidency Project, John Woolley and Gerhard Peters, Department of Political Science, University of California, Santa Barbara.

Author interviews with Fred Perata were conducted in San Francisco on April 26, 2002, May 6, 2002, and December 8, 2002.

The sworn testimony of Italian lieutenant Vito Melpignano is at CM No. 276-299: 1629–33.

Information about the laxity of protocol with Italian POWs came from author interviews with Fred Perata, conducted in San Francisco on April 26, 2002, May 6, 2002, and December 8, 2002; author interviews with Mason Gould conducted in West End, NC, on July 29, 2002, and February 8, 2003; and author interview with Edward Haskell conducted in Concord, CA, on March 20, 2003.

The sworn testimony about the August 14, 1944 riot may be found as follows: Italian Sergeant Antonio Licciardelli, "Investigation of Attack," File 333.9, RG 159: Records of the Office of Inspector General: 302–5, NARACP; T/5 Andrew David, "Investigation of Attack," File 333.9, RG 159: Records of the Office of Inspector General: 90–91, 181–84, NARACP; Italian private Nullo Beretta, "Investigation of Attack," File 333.9, RG 159: Records of the Office of Inspector General: 195–99, NARACP; Italian corporal major Guiseppe Belle, "Investigation of Attack," File 333.9, RG 159: Records of the Office of Inspector General: 200–3, NARACP, and CM No. 276–299: 24–48; Italian private Antonio Pisciottano, "Investigation of Attack," File 333.9, RG 159: Records of the Office of Inspector General: 187–95, NARACP, and CM No. 276-299: 458–87; Italian sergeant Angelo Fumarola, "Investigation of Attack," File 333.9, RG 159: Records of the Office of Inspector General: 204–7, NARACP; Italian corporal major Vittorio Bellieni, "Investigation of Attack," File 333.9, RG 159: Records of the Office of Inspector General: 236–41, NARACP, and CM No. 276-299: 491–503; Italian corporal major Luigi Furlanelli, "Investigation of Attack," File 333.9, RG 159: Records of the Office of Inspector General: 258–59, NARACP, and CM No. 276-299: 508–14; Staff Sergeant Fred J. Perata, "Investigation of Attack," File 333.9, RG 159: Records of the Office of Inspector General: 33–39, NARACP, and CM No. 276-299: 168–74; Private First Class Harold Mason Gould, "Investigation of Attack," File 333.9, RG 159: Records of the Office of Inspector General: 40–47, NARACP; Italian private Nicola Corea, "Investigation of Attack," File 333.9, RG 159: Records of the Office of Inspector General: 296–97, 306–10, NARACP, and CM No. 276-299: 365–86; Italian corporal major Rosario

Sidoti, "Investigation of Attack," File 333.9, RG 159: Records of the Office of Inspector General: 216–21, NARACP, and CM No. 276-299: 677–82; Italian private Primo Bernabovi, "Investigation of Attack," File 333.9, RG 159: Records of the Office of Inspector General: 298–301, NARACP; Italian captain Ernesto Cellentani, "Investigation of Attack," File 333.9, RG 159: Records of the Office of Inspector General: 311–13, NARACP, and CM No. 276-299: 1589–90, 1600–2; Italian sergeant Augusto Todde, "Investigation of Attack," File 333.9, RG 159: Records of the Office of Inspector General: 25–32, 796–804, NARACP, and CM No. 276-299: 290–365; Sergeant Grant Noel Farr, "Investigation of Attack," File 333.9, RG 159: Records of the Office of Inspector General: 1–13, 326–28, NARACP, and CM No. 276-299: 96–124, 482, 1676–88; T/5 Edward Stanford Haskell, "Investigation of Attack," File 333.9, RG 159: Records of the Office of Inspector General:14–24, 324–25, NARACP, and CM No. 276-299: 175–200, 485; Italian private Guiseppe Magnasco, "Investigation of Attack," File 333.9, RG 159: Records of the Office of Inspector General: 269–71, NARACP; Italian private Fernando Catenaro, "Investigation of Attack," File 333.9. RG 159: Records of the Office of Inspector General: 319–21, NARACP; Italian private Attilio Vencato, 260–61, NARACP, and CM No. 276-299: 503–8; Italian corporal Livio Petriccione, "Investigation of Attack," File 333.9, RG 159: Records of the Office of Inspector General: 232–35, NARACP; Corporal Roger L. Bradley, "Investigation of Attack," File 333.9, RG 159: Records of the Office of Inspector General: 470–76, NARACP; Sergeant Thurman McCray Jones, "Investigation of Attack," File 333.9, RG 159: Records of the Office of Inspector General: 126–38, NARACP, and CM No. 276-299: 609–15; Private First Class John H. Pinkney, "Investigation of Attack," File 333.9, RG 159: Records of the Office of Inspector General: 329–55, 650–54, 929–50, NARACP, and CM No. 276-299: 1644–67, 1673–74; Sergeant Robert Gresham, CM No. 276-299: 567–609; Corporal Richard King, CM No. 276-299: 535–66; Staff Sergeant Regis A. Callahan, "Investigation of Attack," File 333.9, RG 159: Records of the Office of Inspector General: 98–112, 185–86, 1506–7, NARACP, and CM No. 276-299: 1079–90, 1496–1500; and Private First Class Gasper S. De Vito, "Investigation of Attack," File 333.9, RG 159: Records of the Office of Inspector General: 145–51, NARACP.

Chapter Six Bad Press: Late August 1944

The memorandum from Colonel Nash is in "Incident at Seattle Port of Embarkation," Colonel John Nash, General Staff Corps, Army Service Forces, Washington, DC, August 15, 1944, File 291.2: Miscellaneous Correspondence Files, RG 160: Records of the Army Service Forces, Office of the Commanding General, 1943–45, NARACP.

The initial Seattle Port of Embarkation press release about the riot is contained in "1 Italian Dead, 24 Injured in Attack at Fort Lawton," R. B. Bermann, *Seattle Post-Intelligencer*, August 16, 1944: A1.

The hospital records of the injured soldiers are in "15 Aug 44," Diary AR-40-1005, 1944, Fort Lawton Hospital, AGF and AFF Installations, RG 337: Records of Headquarters Army Ground Forces, NARACP.

The memo from Major Irving Crawford to Major General Mervin Gross is in "Disorder at Fort Lawton Staging Area," Major Irving R. Crawford, director, Intelligence and Security Division, Seattle Port of Embarkation, August 16, 1944, File 291.2: Miscellaneous Correspondence Files, 1943–45, RG 160: Records of the Army Service Forces, Office of the Commanding General, NARACP.

The transcript of the telephone call received by General Lerch is in "Riot between Port Companies at Fort Lawton Staging Area," Lieutenant Colonel John S. Myers, chief, Emergency Protection Branch, Office of the Provost Marshal General, Washington, DC, August 16, 1944, File 291.2: Miscellaneous Correspondence Files, RG 160: Records of the Army Service Forces, Office of the Commanding General, 1943–45, NARACP.

The newspaper report about "the climax of trouble" is at "Italians' Easy Life Cited as Riot Cause," R. B. Bermann, *Seattle Post-Intelligencer*, August 17, 1944: A1. The newspaper report about "there was resentment" is at "White Troops, Italians Clash, Say Lawton Soldiers," *Seattle Times*, August 17, 1944: 1.

The complaint "deploring the existence of conditions" is in letter, N. C. Casciano, director, Italian Central Council, to Henry L. Stimson, secretary of war, August 17, 1944, File 383.6: Weekly Reports, RG 389: Records of the Office of the Provost Marshal General, POW Operations Division, ISU Decimal File, 1944-1945, NARACP. The reply is at letter, Henry L. Stimson, secretary of war, to John A. Danaher, U.S. Senate, August 1944, File 383.6: Weekly Reports, RG 389: Records of the Office of the Provost Marshal General, POW Operations Division, ISU Decimal File, 1944–45, NARACP.

The newsmagazine report about "the worst yet" is in "Prisoners—Worst Yet," *Time*, August 28, 1944. The newsmagazine report about "the Negroes were bitter" is at "Pampered Italians?" *Newsweek*, August 28, 1944: 40.

The newspaper editorial about the "sad, ill-omened incident" is in "A Despicable Crime," *Il Progress Italo-Americano*, New York, August 17, 1944, File 291.2: Miscellaneous Correspondence Files, 1943–45, RG 160: Office of the Commanding General, Army Service Forces, NARACP.

The newspaper editorial about "strictest disciplinary measures" is quoted in "Italian Paper Hits Fort Riot," *Seattle Times*, August 20, 1944: 1.

The formal briefing noting that "white soldiers at Fort Lawton had been antagonistic" is in "Weekly Intelligence Summary No. 34," Ninth Service Command, Army Service Forces, August 19, 1944, RG 107: Office of the Secretary of War, Civilian Aide to Secretary, Racial Situation in the Army, 1944–46, NARACP.

The newspaper editorial about "none are sufficient to justify the end" is in "Race Soldiers Smear Interracial Relations," *Northwest Enterprise*, August 16, 1944: 1.

The second memo from Major Irving Crawford to Major General Mervin Gross is in "Fort Lawton Staging Area Disorder," Major Irving R. Crawford, director, Intelligence and Security Division, Seattle Port of Embarkation, August 18, 1944, File 291.2: Miscellaneous Correspondence Files, 1943–45, RG 160: Records of the Army Service Forces, Office of the Commanding General, NARACP.

The newspaper article about the July 10 uprising is in "Italian War Prisoners, Revolting at Lawton, Are Quelled with Clubs," *Seattle Times*, August 18, 1944: 1.

The press release about the attack "confined to one barracks" is quoted in "More Than 50 Soldiers in Riot, Army Reveals," *Seattle Times*, August 18, 1944: 2.

The newspaper article about "I read in the paper" is at "More Than 50 Soldiers in Riot, Army Reveals," *Seattle Times*, August 18, 1944: 2.

Colonel Arrington's report on his visit to Fort Lawton is in "Visit of Director of Training, Hq. ISU, to Seattle Port of Embarkation," Colonel R. T. Arrington, director of training, Italian Service Units, August 22, 1944, File 291.2: Miscellaneous Correspondence Files, 1943–45, RG 160: Records of the Army Service Forces, Office of the Commanding General, NARACP.

The campaign by the Bureau of Public Relations is in "Report on Italian Service Forces," memorandum, Brigadier General John M. Eager, commander, to commanding general, Army Service Forces, September 15, 1945, File: Italian Service Units, RG 389.4.7: Enemy Prisoner of War Information Bureau, NARACP.

The angry cable from India is in "Transmitting a Press Release Regarding Attack on Italian Prisoners by American Negro Soldiers," George Merrell, Office of Personal Representative of the President of the United States, New Delhi, India, August 21, 1944, File: Deaths and Escapes, RG 389: Office of the Provost Marshal General, POW Operations Division, NARACP.

Pancho Jones's letter is at letter, Nebraska Jones, 651st Port Company, Fort Lawton Staging Area, to George L. P. Weaver, director, National CIO Committee to Abolish Racial Discrimination, August 19, 1944, File: Fort Lawton Subject File 1940–47, RG 107: Records of the Office of the Secretary of War, Truman Gibson, Civil Aide to Secretary of War, NARACP.

Chapter Seven   Cookie: September 1944

Author interview with Richard Cooke, son of Elliot D. Cooke, was conducted in Keyser, WV, on February 9, 2003.

Author interviews with Cybele Lane, granddaughter of Elliot D. Cooke, were conducted in Check, VA, on September 9, 2002, and September 21, 2002, and in Keyser, WV, on February 9, 2003.

General Cooke's reminiscences about his friend "Dunk" Harvey are in "Warfare a la Carte," Major Elliot D. Cooke, *Infantry Journal* 44, no. 5 (September–October, 1937): 419. His exploits during World War I are in *Devil Dogs: Fighting Marines of World War*

I, George B. Clark (Novato, CA: Presidio Press, 1999): 32, 68, 74, 82, 89, 228–29, 236, 238, 264; "We Attack," Elliot D. Cooke, *Infantry Journal* 45, no. 1 (January–February, 1938): 41–47; and "We Can Take It," Elliot D. Cooke, *Infantry Journal* 44, no. 3 (May–June 1937): 205–12.

General Cooke's interrogations are in "Investigation of Attack," File 333.9, RG 159: Records of the Office of the Inspector General: 426–42, 841–46, NARACP (First Sergeant Wilbert F. Tanner, September 16 and 19, 1944); "Investigation of Attack," File 333.9, RG 159: Records of the Office of the Inspector General: 616–36, NARACP (T/5 Addison G. George, September 17, 1944); "Investigation of Attack," File 333.9, RG 159: Records of the Office of the Inspector General: 503–13, 534–37, NARACP (Captain Alan Wayne Christensen, September 16, 1944); "Investigation of Attack," File 333.9, RG 159: Records of the Office of the Inspector General: 517–21, NARACP (Private First Class Glenn Pescatore, September 16, 1944); "Investigation of Attack," File 333.9, RG 159: Records of the Office of the Inspector General: 596–615, NARACP (Captain Milton J. Carter, September 17, 1944); "Investigation of Attack," File 333.9, RG 159: Records of the Office of the Inspector General: 754–71, NARACP (Major William Walter Orem, September 19, 1944); "Investigation of Attack," File 333.9, RG 159: Records of the Office of the Inspector General: 705–19, NARACP (Colonel Harry L. Branson, September 18, 1944); "Investigation of Attack," File 333.9, RG 159: Records of the Office of the Inspector General: 787–95, NARACP (Lieutenant Colonel Henry Jay Kleinhen, September 19, 1944); "Investigation of Attack," File 333.9, RG 159: Records of the Office of the Inspector General: 781–86, NARACP (Colonel Frederick Welden Teague, September 19, 1944); "Investigation of Attack," File 333.9, RG 159: Records of the Office of the Inspector General: 665–74, NARACP (T/4 Carl A. Johnsen, September 17, 1944); "Investigation of Attack," File 333.9, RG 159: Records of the Office of the Inspector General: 740–43, 775–79, NARACP (Colonel Alfred L. Baylies, September 18 and 19, 1944); "Investigation of Attack," File 333.9, RG 159: Records of the Office of the Inspector General: 824–31, NARACP (Major Robert Howard Manchester, September 19, 1944); "Investigation of Attack," File 333.9, RG 159: Records of the Office of the Inspector General: 655–64, NARACP (Private First Class George E. Durel, September 17, 1944); and "Investigation of Attack," File 333.9, RG 159: Records of the Office of the Inspector General: RG 159: 734–39, NARACP (Captain John Hunt Walker, September 18, 1944).

Author interview with Nils Christensen, son of Alan Wayne Christensen, was conducted in Baker, OR, on December 15, 2003.

Colonel Williams's interrogations are in "Investigation of Attack," File 333.9, RG 159: Records of the Office of the Inspector General: 48–75, NARACP (Private Clyde Vernon Lomax, September 5, 1944); "Investigation of Attack," File 333.9, RG 159: Records of the Office of the Inspector General: 76–89, NARACP (Staff Sergeant Charles Mack Robinson, September 5, 1944); "Investigation of Attack," File 333.9,

RG 159: Records of the Office of the Inspector General: 90–97, 181–84, NARACP (T/5 Andrew David, September 5 and 8, 1944); "Investigation of Attack," File 333.9, RG 159: Records of the Office of the Inspector General: 126–38, NARACP (Sergeant Thurman McCray Jones, September 6, 1944); "Investigation of Attack," File 333.9, RG 159: Records of the Office of the Inspector General: 98–112, 185–86, 1506–7, NARACP (Staff Sergeant Regis A. Callahan, September 6 and 8, 1944, and October 4, 1944); "Investigation of Attack," File 333.9, RG 159: Records of the Office of the Inspector General: 200–03, NARACP (Corporal Major Guiseppe Belle, September 9, 1944); and "Investigation of Attack," File 333.9, RG 159: Records of the Office of the Inspector General: 164–70, 1303–4, NARACP (T/4 Carl A. Johnsen, September 6, 1944, and October 2, 1944).

Author interviews with Nathalie Lomax, widow of Clyde Vernon Lomax, were conducted in Independence, LA, on December 19, 2002, and January 20, 2003. Author interviews with Frank Lomax, brother of Clyde Vernon Lomax, were conducted in Pass Christian, MI, on December 20, 2002, and January 9, 2003.

General Cooke's reports about the Fort Lawton incident are in "Investigation of Attack on Italian Service Unit Personnel by American Soldiers at Ft. Lawton Washington," Brigadier General Elliot D. Cooke, October 5, 1944 (preliminary) and October 28, 1944 (final), File 333.9, RG 159: Records of the Office of the Inspector General, NARACP.

Chapter Eight Jaworski: October 1944

Letters written in 1944–45 by Leon Jaworski to his wife, Jeannette, and to his in-laws, Wilma and "Boots" Trautschold, are in the Leon Jaworski Papers, Texas Collection, Baylor University, Waco, TX.

Details of Leon Jaworski's childhood, education, prewar employment, and JAG prosecutions are in *After Fifteen Years*, Leon Jaworski (Houston: Gulf Publishing Co., Houston, 1961); *Confession and Avoidance: A Memoir*, Leon Jaworski with Mickey Herskowitz (Garden City, NY: Anchor Press/Doubleday, 1979); *Crossroads*, Leon Jaworski with Dick Schneider (Elgin, IL: David C. Cook Publishing Co., 1981); and "Oral Memoirs of Leon Jaworski, March 4, 1976–November 11, 1978" Baylor University Program for Oral History, Waco, TX, 1978.

Leon Jaworski's observation "I have no patience with minutiae," is in *Confession and Avoidance: A Memoir*: 3. His description of "Several Klan members" is in *Crossroads*: 42. His recollection "My wife accepted my decision quietly" is in *Confession and Avoidance: A Memoir*: 76. His opinion "No matter how serious the charge" is in *Confession and Avoidance: A Memoir*: 79–80.

Colonel Williams's interrogations, attended by Jaworski, are in "Investigation of Attack," File 333.9, RG 159: Records of the Office of the Inspector General: 25–32, NARACP (Sergeant Augusto Todde, September 3, 1944); "Investigation of Attack,"

File 333.9, RG 159: Records of the Office of the Inspector General: 200–3, NARACP (Corporal Major Guiseppe Belle, September 9, 1944); "Investigation of Attack," File 333.9, RG 159: Records of the Office of the Inspector General: 356–77, NARACP (Private First Class Roy L. Montgomery, September 14, 1944); "Investigation of Attack," File 333.9, RG 159: Records of the Office of the Inspector General: 378–93, 582–87, 1015–20, NARACP (Private Dan Roy Daymond, September 14, 17, and 27, 1944); "Investigation of Attack," File 333.9, RG 159: Records of the Office of the Inspector General: 1093–1121, NARACP (Private Jesse C. B. Sims, September 28, 1944); "Investigation of Attack," File 333.9, RG 159: Records of the Office of the Inspector General: 1040–79, NARACP (Private Thomas Battle, September 27, 1944); "Investigation of Attack," File 333.9, RG 159: Records of the Office of the Inspector General: 951–67, NARACP (Private Alvin E. Clarke, September 26, 1944); "Investigation of Attack," File 333.9, RG 159: Records of the Office of the Inspector General: 883–928, NARACP (T/5 Willie Ellis, September 25, 1944); "Investigation of Attack," File 333.9, RG 159: Records of the Office of the Inspector General: 1122–48, 1164–65, NARACP (T/5 Willie S. Curry, September 28, 1944); "Investigation of Attack," File 333.9, RG 159: Records of the Office of the Inspector General: 1080–90, NARACP (T/5 Herman Johnson, September 27, 1944); "Investigation of Attack," File 333.9, RG 159: Records of the Office of the Inspector General: 1348–55, NARACP (Private Herman L. Gentry, October 2, 1944); and "Investigation of Attack," File 333.9, RG 159: Records of the Office of the Inspector General: 1322–27, NARACP (Private First Class Samuel Thomas, October 2, 1944).

The designation of Augusto Todde on the To Be Watched list and Guiseppe Belle on the To Be Transferred list is in "Alphabetic Listing of Italian Personnel in Continental United States," March 31, 1945, File: 1945, A-Z, RG 389: Office of the Provost Marshal General, POW Operations Division, NARACP.

The return of two "to be watched" prisoners to Monticello is in memorandum, Lieutenant Colonel W. W. Gaines, adjutant general, Army Service Forces, Headquarters, ISU, July 21, 1944, File 253.91: Transfer of Prisoners, RG 389: Records of the Provost Marshal General, POW Operations Division, 1944–45, NARACP.

Author interviews with Roy Montgomery were conducted in Flossmor, IL, on March 21, 2002, and May 29, 2002. Author interview with Dan Roy Daymond was conducted in Houston, TX, on July 27, 1987.

The sternly worded letter to Ambassador Alexander Kirk is in letter, R. Prunas, secretary general, Italian Ministry of Foreign Affairs, September 7, 1944, File 711.4: Prisoners of War, RG 84: Records of the Foreign Service Posts of the Department of State, Rome Embassy and Consulate, General Records, 1944, NARACP. The letter to the Allied Control Commission is in letter, "Incident in the PW Camp—Ft. Lawton, Alaska [sic]," General Pietro Gazzera, Italian high commissioner for prisoners of war, September 30, 1944, File 4.12: Telegrams, TWX, Cables, Memos—Deaths, Shootings, Violence, RG 389: Records of the Provost Marshal General, POW Operations Division, Legal Branch, 1942–46, NARACP.

Leon Jaworski's observation "Career men know that, in wartime, where you serve . . ." is in *Confession and Avoidance: A Memoir*: 99.

Chapter Nine Beeks: Early November 1944

Corporal Luther Larkin's testimony is in CM No. 276-299: 1260–97. His separate written statement is Government Exhibit 42, in the same file.

Author interviews with Howard Noyd were conducted in Bellevue, WA, on July 22, 1987, and May 14, 2002.

Private John R. Brown's alibi is established at "Investigation of Attack," File 333.9, RG 159: Records of the Office of the Inspector General: 1378–84, NARACP.

Author interviews with Dr. Carletta Boyd and Faye Watson, nieces of Sergeant Arthur J. Hurks, were conducted in Chicago on November 19, 2002.

Sergeant Arthur J. Hurks's testimony in CM No. 276-299: 1500–60. His separate written statement is Government Exhibit 46, in the same file.

Author interview with Deborah Ford, daughter of Private William G. Jones, was conducted in Decatur, IL, on November 21, 2002.

Private William G. Jones's testimony is in "Investigation of Attack," File 333.9, RG 159: Records of the Office of the Inspector General: 1222–48, 1499–1505, NARACP.

The army training film *Baptism of Fire* is produced by the Signal Corps for the Commanding General, Army Ground Forces, 1943, File 111 TF-201, NARACP.

The testimony of Private Edward Sanders is in "Investigation of Attack," File 333.9, RG 159: Records of the Office of the Inspector General: 1314–21, NARACP. The testimony of Private Booker W. Townsell is in "Investigation of Attack," File 333.9, RG 159: Records of the Office of the Inspector General: 1282–89, NARACP. The testimony of T/5 Harvey Banks is in "Investigation of Attack," File 333.9, RG 159: Records of the Office of the Inspector General: 1414–22, NARACP.

The testimony of Private First Class John H. Pinkney is in "Investigation of Attack," File 333.9, RG 159: Records of the Office of the Inspector General: 329–55, 650–54, 929–50, NARACP.

The written confessions of Private Samuel Snow (Government Exhibit 37), T/5 Willie Prevost Sr. (Government Exhibit 35), T/5 Nathaniel T. Spencer (Government Exhibit 33), and Private First Class Roy L. Montgomery (Government Exhibit 34) are in CM No. 276-299.

Author interview with Private Samuel Snow was conducted in Seattle on June 6, 2002. Author interview with T/5 Willie Prevost was conducted in Houston on July 27, 1987. Author interviews with Private First Class Roy L. Montgomery were conducted in Flossmor, IL, on March 21, 2002, and May 29, 2002.

The testimony of Private Samuel Snow is in "Investigation of Attack," File 333.9, RG 159: Records of the Office of the Inspector General: 1166–76, NARACP. The testimony of T/5 Willie Prevost Sr. is in "Investigation of Attack," File 333.9, RG 159:

Records of the Office of the Inspector General: 1263–76, 1298, NARACP. The testimony of T/5 Nathaniel T. Spencer is in CM No. 276–99: 761–72, 1446–56. The testimony of Private First Class Roy L. Montgomery is in "Investigation of Attack," File 333.9, RG 159: Records of the Office of the Inspector General: 356–77, NARACP.

Leon Jaworski's reflection about earnest lawyers is in *Confession and Avoidance: A Memoir*, Leon Jaworski with Mickey Herskowitz (Garden City, NY: Anchor Press/Doubleday, 1979): 56.

Luther Larkin's letter to his aunt Minnie Carr is published in "Court Denies Dismissal of 3 Murder Charges," George W. Wood, *The Northwest Enterprise*, December 13, 1944: 4.

Chapter Ten Prosecution: Late November 1944

Sadie Hughes's recollections about the trial are in letter, Sadie Hughes to President Franklin D. Roosevelt, January 4, 1945, CM No. 276-299: addendum.

Author interview with John Caughlan was conducted in Seattle on July 24, 1987.

Details about the conduct of military criminal proceedings during World War II may be found, in part, in "Military Justice," Robert P. Patterson, undersecretary of war, July 8, 1945, File: Press Releases, RG 389.2.5: Records of the Provost Marshal General, Budget and Statistical Section, NARACP.

William Beeks's examination of the court-martial panel is in CM No. 276-299: 7–8. The summary of that examination is in "Raid by Negroes on Italians at Lawton Described," R. B. Bermann, *Seattle Post-Intelligencer*, November 21, 1944: 1.

Beeks's request for a continuance is in CM No. 276-299: 10–11.

Jaworski's notebook distribution is in CM No. 276-299: 21. His dismissal of charges against Private John R. Brown is in CM No. 276-299: 23–24.

Trial testimony of the following witnesses are in CM No. 276-299, at the pages noted: Corporal Major Guiseppe Belle: 24–48; Private Roy Daymond: 49–95; Sergeant Grant Noel Farr: 96–124; T/5 Willie Ellis: 128–68; Private Jesse C. B. Sims: 228–89; Private Alvin E. Clarke: 200–28; Sergeant Augusto Todde: 290–365; Private Nicola Corea: 365–86; Private Thomas Battle: 416–48; T/5 Addison George: 624–31; Corporal Richard King: 535–66; Sergeant Robert Gresham: 567–609; Private Imo Nolgi: 656–61; Sergeant Major Antonio Urbano: 661–71; Private Gennero Iodice: 671–76; Corporal Major Rosario Sidot: 677–82; Sergeant Mario Marcelli: 682–704; Staff Sergeant Charles M. Robinson: 704–19; T/5 Willie Prevost Sr.: 827–48; Sergeant Ralph E. Young: 870–90.

Jaworski's letter to his sister-in-law, Wilma Trautschold, is in the Leon Jaworski Papers, Texas Collection, Baylor University, Waco, TX.

Chapter Eleven Defense: Early December 1944

Author interviews with Howard Noyd were conducted in Bellevue, WA, on July 22, 1987, and May 14, 2002.

Trial testimony of the following witnesses are in CM No. 276-299, at the pages noted: Private Samuel Snow: 993–1024; Major Robert H. Manchester: 1027–39, 1042–51; Private First Class Elby Murray: 1103–16; Private Clyde Vernon Lomax: 1096–1103; First Sergeant Louis Cabral: 1181–95; Corporal Luther Larkin: 1260–97; Private Richard Barber: 1236–54; and Sergeant Arthur J. Hurks: 1500–60.

The FBI report is in "Survey of Racial Conditions in the United States," J. Edgar Hoover, director, Federal Bureau of Investigation; September 24, 1943, File: Department of Justice; RG OF10b: Official Files, Franklin D. Roosevelt Library, Hyde Park, NY.

The columnist's observation about treatment of blacks versus treatment of Italian is in "Weekly Intelligence Summary No. 50," Army Service Forces, Headquarters, Ninth Service Command, December 9, 1944, File: Racial Situation in the Army, 1944–46, RG 107: Records of the Office of the Secretary of War, Civilian Aide to the Secretary, NARACP.

The "Old Man River" incident is in report, "Racial Problems in Washington State," Captain Cecil Berry, director, Intelligence and Security, Portland Port of Embarkation, December 14, 1944, File 291.2: Racial Situation in the United States, Correspondence 1943–45, RG 160: Records of the Office of the Commanding General, Army Service Forces, NARACP.

Leon Jaworski's writings about a prosecutor's duty to divulge all facts is in *Confession and Avoidance: A Memoir,* Leon Jaworski with Mickey Herskowitz (Garden City, NY: Anchor Press/Doubleday, 1979): 80. His comments about playing "The Star-Spangled Banner" on a pocket comb are in *Confession and Avoidance: A Memoir:* 70.

Private Willie C. Basden's Christmas card to Jaworski is in the Leon Jaworski Papers, Texas Collection, Baylor University, Waco, TX.

Chapter Twelve Verdict: Late December 1944

Leon Jaworski's closing argument is in CM No. 276-299: 1701–35.

William Beeks's closing argument is in CM No. 276-299: 1736–71.

Leon Jaworski's rebuttal is in CM No. 276-299: 1772–81.

The court-martial's findings of guilt or innocence is in CM No. 276-299: 1782–86.

The court-martial's reading of charge sheet personal data is in CM No. 276-299: 1787–1806.

The court-martial's sentences are in CM No. 276-299: 1807–10.

The reclassification proceedings against Colonel Harry L. Branson, Major William W. Orem, and Second Lieutenant James B. Sistrunk are in letter, General Eley P. Denson to chief of transportation, Army Service Forces, January 9, 1945, File 333.9: Fort Lawton, RG 159: Records of the Provost Marshal General, General Correspondence 1939–47, NARACP.

Sadie Hughes's recollections about the trial are in letter, Sadie Hughes to President Franklin D. Roosevelt, January 4, 1945, CM No. 276-299: addendum.

Epilogue

The court-martial proceedings against Private Clyde Vernon Lomax and Sergeant Charles M. Robinson are in letter, General Eley P. Denson to chief of transportation, Army Service Forces, January 9, 1945, File 333.9: Fort Lawton, RG 159: Records of the Provost Marshal General, General Correspondence 1939–47, NARACP. (Because these proceedings were not a general court-martial, the records and transcripts are no longer maintained by the U.S. Army).

Lieutenant Colonel Dolph Barnett's recommendations and the transcript of his February 19, 1945, phone call to Major General Myron Cramer are in CM No. 276-299: addendum.

The Board of Review decision of April 19, 1945, is in CM No. 276-299: addendum.

Corporal Luther Larkin's April 20, 1945, letter to Major General Myron Cramer is in CM No. 276-299: addendum.

The history of the incarceration of the Fort Lawton defendants is in CM No. 276-299: addendum.

Leon Jaworski's mistaken recollection that Guglielmo Olivotto had been hung from a barracks rafter is in *Crossroads,* Leon Jaworski with Dick Schneider (Elgin, IL: David C. Cook Publishing Co., 1981): 92.

Robert Sanders's 1950 petition is in CM No. 276-299: addendum.

Author interview with Les Stewart was conducted in Austin, TX, on July 28, 1987. Author interviews with John Hamilton were conducted in Houston on May 18, 1987, July 8, 1987, and July 27, 1987. Author interviews with Roy Montgomery were conducted in Flossmor, IL, on March 21, 2002, and May 29, 2002.

BIBLIOGRAPHY

BOOKS

Atkinson, Rick. *An Army at Dawn: The War in North Africa, 1942–1943*. New York: Henry Holt and Co., 2002.

Badoglio, Pietro. *Italy in the Second World War: Memories and Documents*. Westport, CT: Greenwood Press, 1948.

Barbeau, Arthur E., and Florette Henri. *The Unknown Soldiers: Black American Troops in World War I*. Philadelphia: Temple University Press, 1974.

Bassett, John T. *War Journal of an Innocent Soldier*. Hamden, CT: Archon Books, 1989.

Berner, Richard C. *Seattle Transformed: World War II to Cold War*. Seattle: Charles Press, 1999.

Boring, Edwin G., ed. *Psychology for the Armed Services*. Washington, DC: Infantry Journal Press, 1945.

Buchanan, A. Russell. *Black Americans in World War II*. Santa Barbara, CA: Clio Press, 1977.

Bykovsky, Joseph, and Harold Larson. *United States Army in World War II/The Transportation Corps: Operations Overseas*. Washington, DC: Department of the Army, Office of the Chief of Military History, 1957.

Child, Irvin L, and Marjorie Van de Water, eds., *Psychology for the Returning Serviceman*. Washington, DC: Infantry Journal Press, 1945.

Clark, George B. *Devil Dogs: Fighting Marines of World War I*. Novato, CA: Presidio Press, 1999.

Converse, Elliott V., III, Daniel K. Gibran, John A. Cash, Robert K. Griffith, Jr., and Richard H. Kohn. *The Exclusion of Black Soldiers from the Medal of Honor in World War II*. Jefferson, NC: McFarland and Co., 1997.

Cooke, Elliot D. *All but Me and Thee: Psychiatry at the Foxhole Level*. Washington, DC: Infantry Journal Press, 1946.

David, Jay, and Elaine Crane. *The Black Soldier: From the American Revolution to Vietnam*. New York: William Morrow and Co., 1971.

deBarros, Paul. *Jackson Street after Hours*. Seattle: Sasquatch Books, 1993.

De Bellegarde, Carlo. *African Escape*. London: William Kimber and Co., 1957.

Fitzgerald, Alan. *The Italian Farming Soldiers: Prisoners of War in Australia, 1941–1947*. Melbourne, Australia: Melbourne University Press, 1981.

Frare, Aleua L. *Magnolia Yesterday and Today*. Seattle: Magnolia Community Club, 1976.

Furr, Arthur. *Democracy's Negroes: A Book of Facts concerning the Activities of Negroes in World War II*. Boston: House of Edinboro, 1947.

Gansberg, Judith M. *Stalag: USA: The Remarkable Story of German POWs in America*. New York: Thomas Y. Crowell Co., 1977.

Gardner, Michael R. *Harry Truman and Civil Rights: Moral Courage and Political Risks*. Carbondale: Southern Illinois University Press, 2002.

Gatewood, Willard B., Jr. *"Smoked Yankees" and the Struggle for Empire: Letters from Negro Soldiers, 1898–1902*. Urbana: University of Illinois Press, 1971.

Guareschi, Giovanni. *My Secret Diary: 1943–45*. New York: Farr, Straus and Cudahy, 1958.

Guzman, Jessie P. *Negro Year Book: A Review of Events Affecting Negro Life, 1941–46*. Tuskegee, AL: Tuskegee Institute, 1947.

Hanford, C. H., ed. *Seattle and Environs, 1852–1924*. Seattle: Pioneer Historical Publishing Co., 1924.

Jaworski, Leon. *After Fifteen Years*. Houston: Gulf Publishing Co., 1961.

———. *The Right and the Power: The Prosecution of Watergate*. New York: Reader's Digest Press, 1976.

Jaworski, Leon, with Mickey Herskowitz. *Confession and Avoidance: A Memoir*. Garden City, NY: Anchor Press/Doubleday, 1979.

Jaworski, Leon, with Dick Schneider. *Crossroads*. Elgin, IL: David C. Cook Publishing Co., 1981.

Keefer, Louis E. *Italian Prisoners of War in America, 1942–1946: Captives or Allies?* New York: Praeger, 1992.

Koop, Allen V. *Stark Decency: German Prisoners of War in a New England Village*. Hanover, NH: University Press of New England, 1988.

Kryder, Daniel. *Divided Arsenal: Race and the American State during World War II*. New York: Cambridge University Press, 2000.

Lanning, Lt. Col. Michael Lee. *The African-American Soldier*. New York: Birch Lane Press, 1997.

Lee, Alfred McClung, and Norman Daymond Humphrey. *Race Riot*. New York: Dryden Press, 1943.

Lee, Ulysses. *The United States Army in World War II: Special Studies: The Employment of Negro Troops*. Washington, DC: U.S. Army Center of Military History, 1966.

A Manual for Courts-Martial. Washington, DC: U.S. Government Printing Office, 1943.

McGuire, Phillip. *Taps for a Jim Crow Army: Letters from Black Soldiers in World War II*. Santa Barbara, CA: ABC-Clio, 1983.

Millett, John D. *The United States Army in World War II: The Army Service Forces: The Organization and Role of the Army Service Forces*. Washington, DC: U.S. Army, Center of Military History, 1954.

Morehouse, Maggie M. *Fighting in the Jim Crow Army: Black Men and Women Remember World War II*. Boston: Rowman and Littlefield, 2000.

Motley, Mary Penick. *The Invisible Soldier: The Experience of the Black Soldier, World War II*. Detroit: Wayne State University Press, 1975.

Murray, Florence. *The Negro Handbook*. New York: Progressive Press, 1944.

Nichols, David, ed. *Ernie's War: The Best of Ernie Pyle's World War II Dispatches*. New York: Random House, 1986.

Osur, Alan M. *Blacks in the Army Air Forces in World War II*. Washington, DC: Office of Air Force History, 1977.

Putney, Martha S. *When the Nation Was in Need: Blacks in the Women's Army Corps During World War II*. Metuchen, NJ: Scarecrow Press, 1992.

Robin, Ron Theodore. *The Barbed-Wire College: Reeducating German POWs in the United States during World War II*. Princeton, NJ: Princeton University Press, 1995.

Silvera, John D. *The Negro in World War II*. New York: Arno Press, 1969.

Stillman, Richard J., II. *Integration of the Negro in the U.S. Armed Forces*. New York: Praeger, 1968.

Taylor, Quintard. *The Forging of a Black Community: Seattle's Central District from 1870 through the Civil Rights Era*. Seattle: University of Washington Press, 1994.

Tillotson, Lee S. *The Articles of War, Annotated*. Harrisburg, PA: Military Service Publishing Company, 1944.

Wardlow, Chester. *United States Army in World War II/The Transportation Corps: Responsibilities, Organization, and Operations*. Washington, DC: Department of the Army, Office of the Chief of Military History, 1951.

White, Walter. *A Man Called White*. New York: Viking Press, 1948.

Wynn, Neil. *The Afro-American and the Second World War*. New York: Holmes and Meier, 1975.

———. *Office of the Provost Marshal General, World War II: A Brief History*. Washington, DC: Headquarters of the Army Service Forces, Office of the Provost Marshall General, 1946.

PERIODICALS

Cocklin, Robert F. "Report on the Negro Soldier." *Infantry Journal* 59, no. 6 (December 1946): 1+.

Cooke, Elliot D. "We Can Take It." *Infantry Journal* 44, no. 3 (May–June 1937): 205–12.

———. "Warfare a la Carte." *Infantry Journal* 44, no. 5 (September–October 1937): 419–27.

———. "We Attack." *Infantry Journal* 45, no. 1 (January–February 1938): 41–47.

Devore, Robert. "Our 'Pampered' War Prisoners." *Collier's* (October 14, 1944): 14+.

"Italian Prisoners in Service Units Work for Privileges." *Business Week* (July 8, 1944): 31.

"Pampered Italians?" *Newsweek* (August 28, 1944): 40.

"The Pattern of Race Riots Involving Negro Soldiers." *A Monthly Summary of Events and Trends in Race Relations* 2, nos. 1–2 (August–September 1944): 15–18.

"Prisoners—Worst Yet." *Time* (August 28, 1944): 68.

Reynolds, Grant. "What the Negro Soldier Thinks." *The Crisis: Magazine of the NAACP* (November 1944): 353+.

Smith, Beverly. "The Afrika Korps Comes to America." *American* 136, no. 2 (August 1944): 28+.

Sturdevant, Charles O."Residuals of Combat Induced Anxiety." *American Journal of Psychiatry* 102, no. 7 (July 1946): 55–59.

"Summer Madness." *A Monthly Summary of Events and Trends in Race Relations* 1, no. 1 (August 1943): 3+.

"Uncle Sam's Unhappy Soldiers." *Time* (July 10, 1944): 65–68.

White, Walter. "Why I Remain a Negro." *Saturday Review of Literature* (October 11, 1947).

REPORTS AND PAPERS

"A Brief History, Office of the Provost Marshal General, World War II." Army Service Forces, Washington, DC, January 15, 1946.

Chance, David. "The Evolution of Intent at Fort Lawton." Report to the City of Seattle Geo-Recon International. Department of Parks and Recreation, Seattle, July 1984.

Evans, James C. "The Negro in the Army: Policy and Practice." Public Information Division, Department of the Army, Washington, DC, September 3, 1948.

Grunsfeld, Mary-Jane. "Negroes in Chicago." Mayor's Committee on Race Relations, Chicago, October 1944.

Hamilton, West A. "The Negroes' Historical and Contemporary Role in National Defense." Paper presented at the Hampton Conference on National Defense, Section on Military and Naval Defense, November 1940.

Hoover, J. Edgar. "Summary of Racial Conditions in the United States." Federal Bureau of Investigation, Washington, DC, September 24, 1943.

Mormino, Gary R. "Little Italy Goes to War: Italian Americans and World War II." Paper presented at the international conference Italy and America 1943-44: Italian, American and Italian American Experiences of the Liberation of the Italian Mezzogiorno, University of Connecticut, Farmington, April 1995.

Wilke, Steve, and Karen James. "An Archeological Evaluation of the Fort Lawton Historic District." Report to the City of Seattle Geo-Recon International. Department of Parks and Recreation, Seattle, July 1984.

ORAL HISTORIES

Boccalini, Angelo. "America, My Enemy, My Home." New England High Schools Oral History Internet Archive, University of Massachusetts, Boston, http://www.serl.org/oralhistory/Boccalini

Jaworski, Leon. "Oral Memoirs of Leon Jaworski, March 4, 1976–November 11, 1978." Baylor University Program for Oral History, Waco, TX, 1978.

PAMPHLETS

Grunsfeld, Mary-Jane. "Negroes in Chicago." Mayor's Committee on Race Relations, Chicago, October 1944.

Lewis, George G., and John Mewha. "History of Prisoner of War Utilization by the United States Army 1776–1945." Department of the Army Pamphlet No. 20-213, June 1955.

Raushenbush, Winifred. "How to Prevent a Race Riot in Your Home Town." Committee on Race Discrimination, American Civil Liberties Union, New York, October 1943.

NEWSPAPERS

"3 Deny Guilt at Ft. Lawton Trial." Seattle Times, November 16, 1944.

"28 Convicted by Army Court." San Bernardino Sun, December 18, 1944.

"40 Others Are Charged in Raid Fight." Seattle Times, November 6, 1944.

"43 Negroes in Court Martial." Seattle Times, November 16, 1944.

"43 Soldiers Deny Charges at Riot Trial." Los Angeles Daily News, November 17, 1944.

"43 Soldiers Will Be Tried Here for Rioting, Murder." Tacoma Times, November 7, 1944.

"Accused Rioters Charge 3rd Degree Used." Northwest Herald, December 5, 1944.

"Army Death Penalty Must Be Unanimous." Seattle Times, December 14, 1944.

"Army Defense Counsel Grills Italian on Riot Testimony." Seattle Times, November 23, 1944.

"Army Defense Granted Stay." Seattle Times, December 5, 1944.

"Army Justice." Seattle Post-Intelligencer, December 20, 1944.

"Army to Ask Death in 3 Cases." Los Angeles Sentinel, November 16, 1944.

Berger, Meyer. "American Soldier—One Year After." New York Times, November 23, 1941.

———. "Observed at Fort Dix." New York Times, January 31, 1943.

———. "World's Biggest Retail Business." New York Times, October 24, 1943.

———. "Captive Italians Enjoy Life Here." New York Times, December 10, 1943.

Bermann, R. B. "1 Italian Dead, 24 Injured in Attack at Fort Lawton." Seattle Post-Intelligencer, August 16, 1944.

———. "Italians' Easy Life Cited as Riot Cause." *Seattle Post-Intelligencer*, August 17, 1944.

———. "Court-Martial Ordered for 43 in Lawton Riot." *Seattle Post-Intelligencer*, November 7, 1944.

———. "43 Negroes Go on Trial in Lawton Riot Death." *Seattle Post-Intelligencer*, November 18, 1944.

———. "Pvt. J. R. Brown Dismissed from Lawton Rioters Trial." *Seattle Post-Intelligencer*, November 21, 1944.

———. "Raid By Negroes on Italians at Lawton Described." *Seattle Post-Intelligencer*, November 21, 1944.

———. "Negro Soldier Identifies 3 Riot Leaders." *Seattle Post-Intelligencer*, November 22, 1944.

———. "Italian Soldier Identifies 12 in Lawton Riot." *Seattle Post-Intelligencer*, November 23, 1944.

———. "Story of Rioting Told before Court-Martial." *Seattle Post-Intelligencer*, November 24, 1944.

———. "Soldiers Tell of Riot at Ft. Lawton." *Seattle Post-Intelligencer*, November 28, 1944.

———. "Footprint Clue in Fort Riot Destroyed." *Seattle Post-Intelligencer*, November 29, 1944.

———. "Negro Charges Coercion of Story of Riot." *Seattle Post-Intelligencer*, November 30, 1944.

———. "Officers Cross-Quizzed in Soldier Riot Trial." *Seattle Post-Intelligencer*, December 1, 1944.

———. "Second Soldier at Riot Trial Says Questioner Coerced Him." *Seattle Post-Intelligencer*, December 2, 1944.

———. "Start of Riot Laid to Fight With Prisoner." *Seattle Post-Intelligencer*, December 3, 1944.

———. "Court-Martial Opens 3d Week." *Seattle Post-Intelligencer*, December 4, 1944.

———. "Riot Trial Adjourns as Prosecution Rests." *Seattle Post-Intelligencer*, December 5, 1944.

———. "Two Riot Defendants Given Alibis." *Seattle Post-Intelligencer*, December 9, 1944.

———. "7 Defendants Deny Italian Post Raid." *Seattle Post-Intelligencer*, December 10, 1944.

———. "9 Defendants Deny Any Part in Riots." *Seattle Post-Intelligencer*, December 12, 1944.

———. "Three Soldiers Admit Presence in Riot Area." *Seattle Post-Intelligencer*, December 13, 1944.

———. "Defense Says Hanged Italian Was Suicide." *Seattle Post-Intelligencer,* December 14, 1944.

———. "Witness Failure Slows Lawton Court-Martial." *Seattle Post-Intelligencer,* December 15, 1944.

———. "Court-Martial Testimony In." *Seattle Post-Intelligencer,* December 16, 1944.

———. "Testimony Concluded in Court-Martial Case." *Seattle Post-Intelligencer,* December 16, 1944.

———. "Defense Chief Scores 'Policy' in Lawton Riot." *Seattle Post-Intelligencer,* December 17, 1944.

———. "Court-Martial Convicts 28 in Rioting Case." *Seattle Post-Intelligencer,* December 18, 1944.

———. "27 Ft. Lawton Soldiers Get Prison Terms." *Seattle Post-Intelligencer,* December 19, 1944.

"Bride Watches for Mate at Court-Martial." *Seattle Times,* December 2, 1944.

"British Ease Captive Life." *New York Times,* August 19, 1944.

"Bull-Headed Calabrese Tries to Run Fort Lawton Trial." *Seattle Times,* November 28, 1944.

"Carrying It Too Far." *Plainsfield Courier-News,* June 21, 1944.

"Command Change Gives Col. Parker Fort Lawton Post." *Seattle Post-Intelligencer,* November 21, 1944.

Copeland, Sidney. "Lawton Riot Area Toured by Court." *Seattle Post-Intelligencer,* November 26, 1944.

"Courtmartial of 42 Negroes Nearing End." *Los Angeles Daily News,* December 4, 1944.

"Court Retains Riot Count." *Salt Lake Tribune,* December 9, 1944.

"Defense Secret in Riot Trial." *Seattle Times,* December 5, 1944.

"A Despicable Crime." *Il Progresso Italo-Americano,* August 17, 1944.

Duncan, Don. "Fort Lawton Night of Horror Recalled." *Seattle Times,* August 14, 1990.

"End Army Court-Martial in Seattle Riot Case." *Pittsburgh Courier,* December 23, 1944.

"Eye Witness Story Telling of Camp Riot." *Los Angeles Sentinel,* August 24, 1944.

"Former Italian War Prisoners in Service Unit." *Seattle Times,* June 18, 1944.

"Fort Lawton Fair, but Firm with Germans." *Seattle Times,* April 29, 1945.

"Fort Lawton Riot Trial to Resume after Recess." *Seattle Post-Intelligencer,* December 8, 1944.

"Get at Root of Evil." *Los Angeles Sentinel,* November 16, 1944.

Golden, Bill. "Droll Witness Amuses Court." *Tacoma Times,* December 11, 1944.

———. "Riot Defendant's Alibi Is Refuted by White Soldier." *Tacoma Times,* December 15, 1944.

———. "Court Ponders Riot Sentences." *Tacoma Times*, December 17, 1944.

———. "Stiff Penalties Given 27 in Ft. Lawton Riot Trial." *Tacoma Times*, December 18, 1944.

Hahn, Jon. "Ugly Incidents Can't Remain Buried in Fort Lawton Cemetery." *Seattle Post-Intelligencer*, August 2, 1997.

Hanson, Chester G. "Arizona Italian War Prisoners Want to Work." *Los Angeles Times*, September 22, 1943.

———. "Arizona Officer Boosts Italian Prisoner Morale." *Los Angeles Times*, September 23, 1943.

———. "Italian Prisoners 'Overcome' by Food." *Los Angeles Times*, September 24, 1943.

———. "Italian Prisoners' Work in Arizona Commended." *Los Angeles Times*, September 25, 1943.

———. "Humanity Watchword for Italian Prisoners." *Los Angeles Times*, September 26, 1943.

———. "Prisoners Devise Own Means of Recreation." *Los Angeles Times*, September 27, 1943.

"He Who Sows Wind Reaps Storm." *La Notizia*, August 17, 1944.

"Horrifying Deeds." *La Parola*, August 26, 1944.

Hundley, Tom. "Italian WWII Vet Says He's Owed Prisoner Pay." *Chicago Tribune*, July 18, 2001.

"I Fioretti (Choice Pieces)." *Gazzetta Italiana*, August 25, 1944.

"Is Horse Stealing Called a Crime?" *Seattle Post-Intelligencer*, December 18, 1944.

"Italian Flyer Tells of Riot at Ft. Lawton." *Seattle Post-Intelligencer*, November 25, 1944.

"Italian Names Lawton Rioter." *Tacoma Times*, November 25, 1944.

"Italian Paper Hits Fort Riot." *Seattle Times*, August 20, 1944.

"Italian Prisoners, Negro Soldiers, Victims of Hate Campaign." *L'Unità del Popolo*, August 26, 1944.

"Italian Prisoners Vex Yanks by Taking Girls." *Washington Post*, July 1, 1944.

"Italian Said to Be Crazy." *Los Angeles Sentinel*, December 14, 1944.

"Italian War Prisoners, Revolting at Lawton, Are Quelled with Clubs." *Seattle Times*, August 18, 1944.

"Italians Moved From Lawton." *Seattle Times*, October 3, 1944.

Jaworski, Leon. "Fort Lawton Trial" [Letter to the Editor]. *Seattle Post-Intelligencer*, December, 1944.

"Lawton Riot Toll Now 32." *Seattle Post-Intelligencer*, August 19, 1944.

"Lawton Trial Nearing Close." *Tacoma Times*, December 16, 1944.

Lentz, Florence K. "Fort Lawton: Gem on the Bluff from the Turn of the Century." *Seattle Times*, March 12, 1989.

Love, Gilbert. "Italian Service Units Work Hard, and Willingly, and Would Like a Chance to Fight Nazis." *Pittsburgh Press*, February 5, 1945.

Mahaffay, Robert. "Italian Describes Fight before Fort Lawton Riot." *Seattle Times*, November 20, 1944.

———. "Jeep Driver Tried to Smash Tent, Ft. Lawton Court Told." *Seattle Times*, November 21, 1944.

———. "Mud on Soldiers' Uniforms May Be Court-Martial Clue." *Seattle Times*, November 22, 1944.

———. "Italian, Stabbed in Riot at Lawton, Remembers Nothing." *Seattle Times*, November 24, 1944.

———. "Defendants to Visit Scene of Ft. Lawton's Fatal Riot." *Seattle Times*, November 25, 1944.

———. "Rioters Tossed Him over Bank, Italian Asserts." *Seattle Times*, November 25, 1944.

———. "Defendants and Trial Officials Visit Riot Scene." *Seattle Times*, November 26, 1944.

———. "Negro Corporal Tells of Aiding Injured Italians." *Seattle Times*, November 27, 1944.

———. "Soldier's Signed Confession to Part in Rioting Is Read." *Seattle Times*, November 29, 1944.

———. "Use of Third-Degree on Riot Suspect Denied by Witness." *Seattle Times*, November 30, 1944.

———. "Army Court Clears Probers and Accepts Disputed Confession." *Seattle Times*, December 1, 1944.

———. "Riot Suspects Not Coerced, Say More Army Witnesses." *Seattle Times*, December 2, 1944.

———. "Witnesses Overseas May Fly Here for Lawton Trial." *Seattle Times*, December 2, 1944.

———. "Italian Hanged about Midnight, Says Captain." *Seattle Times*, December 3, 1944.

———. "Army May Drop Once Riot Charge." *Seattle Times*, December 4, 1944.

———. "Acquittal of 41 Soldiers Asked." *Seattle Times*, December 8, 1944.

———. "Defense's Acquittal Motion Starts Court-Martial Clash." *Seattle Times*, December 8, 1944.

———. "First Riot Defense Witness Denies Any Part in Fight." *Seattle Times*, December 9, 1944.

———. "Soldier, Held for Murder, Denies Calling Fort Rioters." *Seattle Times*, December 9, 1944.

———. "Testimony of Riot Suspect Is Challenged." *Seattle Times*, December 10, 1944.

———. "Crap Game Offered as Alibi in Fort Lawton Riot Trial." *Seattle Times*, December 11, 1944.

———. "Italian's Mental Condition Discussed at Lawton Trial." *Seattle Times*, December 12, 1944.

———. "Lawton Riot Trial Recessed; Overseas Witnesses Awaited." *Seattle Times*, December 13, 1944.

———. "'Come and Find Me,' Said M.P. Entering Riot Area." *Seattle Times*, December 14, 1944.

———. "Murder Suspect's Testimony Contradicted at Riot Trial." *Seattle Times*, December 15, 1944.

———. "Riot at Lawton Blot on Army's Proud Record." *Seattle Times*, December 16, 1944.

———. "Court-Martial Defense Raps Testimony of Five Soldiers." *Seattle Times*, December 17, 1944.

———. "Fort Rioting Verdict Near." *Seattle Times*, December 18, 1944.

———. "Soldiers, Guilty in Hanging, Given 25- and 15-Year Terms." *Seattle Times*, December 19, 1944.

"Making It Easy for Soldiers to Go Out." *Gazzetta Italiana*, August 25, 1944.

"Mood Solemn at Court Martial of 42 Negroes." *New York Times*, November 25, 1944.

"More Than 50 Soldiers in Riot." *Seattle Times*, August 18, 1944.

"'Mother, Help Me!' Shouted Italian Who Was Hanged." *Seattle Times*, November 28, 1944.

"Murder Laid to 3 in Fort Lawton Riot." *Seattle Times*, November 16, 1944.

"Negro Attack upon Italians Is Described." *Nevada State Journal*, November 22, 1944.

"Negro Council to Ask F.D.R.'s Aid for 28 Men." *Seattle Times*, December 20, 1944.

"Negro-Italian Rioting at Fort Described at Army Trial." *Salt Lake Tribune*, November 22, 1944.

"Negroes Denied Defense Motion." *Bend Bulletin*, December 9, 1944.

"New Charges Arise at Court Martial." *Idaho Daily News*, December 2, 1944.

"New Edict Given Italy on Captives." *Los Angeles Times*, August 14, 1943.

"One Found Hanged." *Washington Post*, August 16, 1944.

"One Gets 25 Years in Prison." *Los Angeles Sentinel*, December 21, 1944.

"One Soldier in Riot Carried Rifle, Says Italian Witness." *Seattle Times*, November 23, 1944.

"Press Blamed for Fort Riot." *Seattle Post-Intelligencer*, August 20, 1944.

"Prisoner Tells Riot Story." *Salt Lake Tribune*, November 23, 1944.

"Quarrels with Italians Told." *Tacoma Times*, November 27, 1944.

"Race Soldiers Smear Interracial Relations." *Northwest Enterprise*, August 16, 1944.

"Riot-Trail Officers." *Seattle Times*, November 21, 1944.

Roth, Henry. "At Fort Lawton Trial." *Seattle Post-Intelligencer*, November 21, 1944.

————. "Defendants at Lawton Trial." *Seattle Post-Intelligencer*, November 22, 1944.

————. "Riot Trial Scene." *Seattle Post-Intelligencer*, November 23, 1944.

————. "Trial Scenes." *Seattle Post-Intelligencer*, November 25, 1944.

————. "Artist Depicts Drama in Riot Court-Martial." *Seattle Post-Intelligencer*, November 28, 1944.

————. "Key Witness." *Seattle Post-Intelligencer*, November 30, 1944.

————. "Accused Arrive at Fort Lawton Trial." *Seattle Post-Intelligencer*, December 1, 1944.

————. "Tense Moment Sketched in Riot Trial." *Seattle Post-Intelligencer*, December 3, 1944.

————. "Spectators at Court-Martial." *Seattle Post-Intelligencer*, December 5, 1944.

————. "General Court-Martial." *Seattle Post-Intelligencer*, December 9, 1944.

————. "Defendants Guarded at Court Martial." *Seattle Post-Intelligencer*, December 12, 1944.

————. "Acquittal at Fort Lawton." *Seattle Post-Intelligencer*, December 18, 1944.

————. "'The Sentence of the Court . . .'" *Seattle Post-Intelligencer*, December 19, 1944.

"Sentry-System Probe Follows Riot at Lawton." *Seattle Times*, August 16, 1944.

"S. F. Soldiers Tell Army Court of Seattle Camp Riot." *Associated Press*, November 22, 1944.

"Sidelights on Court-Martial." *Seattle Post-Intelligencer*, December 14, 1944.

"Sketch of Military Trial." *Seattle Times*, November 16, 1944.

"Soldier Exonerated in Fort Lawton Riot Case." *Los Angeles Sentinel*, December 7, 1944.

"Soldier Names 3 Leaders." *Los Angeles Sentinel*, November 30, 1944.

"Soldiers Convicted of Killing Italian." *Los Angeles Times*, December 18, 1944.

"Soldiers' Riot Trial Begins." *Los Angeles Sentinel*, November 23, 1944.

Tait, Jack. "Britons Demand: 'Save Our Girls from Italian Prisoners of War'" *New York Herald Tribune*, September 8, 1944.

"Trial Officials Best in Army." *Seattle Times*, November 28, 1944.

"What about the Fort Lawton Tragedy?" *Gazzetta Italiana*, September 1, 1944.

Whitehouse, Stuart. "Court-Martial Delay Given Until Monday." *Tacoma Times*, November 16, 1944.

————. "Army Summons Riot Witnesses." *Tacoma Times*, November 20, 1944.

————. "Bilingual Trial Drags as Army Men Tell of Rioting." *Tacoma Times*, November 21, 1944.

————. "Soldier, Victim of Riot Attack, Tells of Battle." *Tacoma Times*, November 21, 1944.

————. "Contradictions in Army Case Probed by Defense." *Tacoma Times*, November 24, 1944.

————. "Riot Victim's Last Cry Told." *Tacoma Times*, November 28, 1944.

———. "Riot Defense Protest Fails." *Tacoma Times*, November 29, 1944.

"White Plains Girl Announces Her Betrothal to Italian Prisoner of War Held in U.S." *New York Times*, January 11, 1945.

"White Troops, Italians Clash." *Seattle Times*, August 17, 1944.

"Witnesses Testify at Seattle in Trial of 43 Negro Soldiers." *Idaho Statesman*, November 22, 1944.

Wood, George. "Judge Advocate Frees Another Prisoner—Rest." *Northwest Enterprise*, December 6, 1944.

ACKNOWLEDGMENTS

THANKSGIVING IS MY FAVORITE holiday, and one of my favorite Thanksgivings came on a chilly afternoon in Baton Rouge. We were guests in the home of Vera Baker, matriarch of an extended family numbering more than sixty, all comfortably squeezed elbow-to-elbow in Vera's cozy kitchen and living room for a holiday feast. Amid plates piled high with poultry, ham, and wild game, Vera and her siblings—Mary Brown and Berlin Lockhart—dished up rich stories about the full life lived by the late Arthur Hurks, their beloved cousin. When I think of all the people who so generously contributed to this book, I realize it would take a week's worth of Thanksgivings to express all my gratitude. I'll try my best to be brief.

By my side that November day in Louisiana was Leslie Hamann, my wife, partner, and inspiration. Though her name does not appear on the cover of this book, her heart, soul, sweat, and tears are the watermark of every page. It was Leslie who, after weeks of dogged research, uncovered General Elliot Cooke's damning report, providing what proved to be the "smoking gun" of the Fort Lawton tragedy. It was Leslie who spent many more months tracking down the whereabouts of almost four hundred men and women—dead or alive—connected to the case. Nothing stopped her; she even managed to locate the families of men with such ubiquitous names as Bill Jones and John Brown using scraps of information more than six decades old. Leslie read every single page of the thousands of primary documents we gathered in our research, then organized all that disparate information so efficiently that the truth fairly dripped from those stacks of bureaucratic mish-mash. This book is every bit as much Leslie's as it is mine, and I never could have written it without her.

Of all the family members of the Fort Lawton characters that we were able to contact, Cybele Cooke Lane deserves special thanks. The granddaughter of General Elliot Cooke, Cybele has been a thoughtful, thorough, and reliable resource, willing to trust two strangers with an important part of her family's proud legacy. We are also grateful to Cybele's father, Richard Cooke; to Luther Larkin's gracious relatives, Dr. Carletta Boyd, Faye Watson, John Fields, and Beverly Evans; to William Jones's stepdaughter, Deborah Ford; and to William T. Beeks, who entrusted us with his father's memories for more than fifteen years. Thanks, too, to Elizabeth Braithwhite, Milton Bratton Jr., Barbara Broitman, Joe Carter, Nils Christensen, Eley Denson Jr., Grant J. Farr, Kirk Haskell, Pamela Haskell, Eric Langsted, Frank Lomax, Nathalie Lomax, Chris Orem, Ray L. Snow, and Michael Stewart.

When I first began researching this story in 1987, four men central to the story were still alive and living in Texas. When I met with them in Houston and in Austin, John Hamilton, Les Stewart, Willie Prevost, and Dan Roy Daymond were all clear-eyed and candid; I only wish they were still around to share even more. Among others who were invaluable back in 1987 were Clyde Langsted, John Caughlan, Al Martiniello, Ethyl Martiniello, and Bill Oakes.

As I write this, several other central figures are still very much alive. Howard Noyd, a true gentleman, provided many hours of insight and wisdom. Fred Perata, Edward Haskell, and Mason Gould still have the spunk that I imagine carried them through some difficult times, and all three made us welcome in their homes (special thanks to Fritzie Stevens). Dr. John Hunt Walker impressed us with his modesty and his grace; Sammy Snow with his wit and humor. Joyce Garbe filled in details of remembrances she first shared in 1987. Roy Montgomery proved to be a rock of reliability; his memory is sharper than those of men half his age, and the integrity he displayed back in 1944 is still evident today.

We come away from this experience impressed with the brains and dedication of a host of archivists, librarians, and historians. We are particularly indebted to Wilbert Mahoney at the National Archives, who saw through a maze of oddly classified files and helped clear the way to the unearthing of the Cooke report. At the United States Army Judiciary archives, Mary Dennis opened doors where others might have shut them. Ellen Kuniyuki Brown at the Texas Collection of Baylor University was adept at both pointing the way to important documents and finding a great eatery in Waco. At the Seattle branch of the National Archives, John Fitzgerald was an early and enthusiastic ally in the search for missing documents; he never stopped caring about our project. We also thank Paul McKissick and John Taylor of the National Archives, Robert de Ocampo of the Army Inspector General office, Dan Lavering of the Judge Advocate General's School, Gail Lilley of the U.S. Army Judiciary, and Linda Mastin of the United States Military Academy. Dr. Donald T. Reay, one of the world's best criminal forensic scientists, provided astonishing expertise about the pathology of lynchings. Dr. Connie Lester of Mississippi State University helped us understand the culture of the Delta, and both Pat Aitken and Wes Uhlmann helped steer the way around an important issue of military law. We owe thanks to librarians at the University of Washington, UCLA, the University of Chicago, Northwestern University, the University of Texas, Baylor University, and the Tuskegee Institute.

We appreciate the early cooperation of the Army Reserve at Fort Lawton, especially Major General James Collins, Bud Ray, and Scott Handley.

My first stab at uncovering the mystery of the Fort Lawton court-martial began in 1987 while I was a reporter for NBC affiliate KING-TV in Seattle. Our hour-long special program was truly a group effort, led by photographers/co-producers Diana Wilmar and Brian Huotari, with a mighty collective assist from Jan Boyd, Richard DePartee, Steve Dowd, Bonnie Ernst, Bill Fenster, Bill Gingerich, Ken Jones, Laddy Kite, Don Metcalf, Lucy Mohl, Norm Ohashi, and the irrepressible George Stark.

The decision to write a book got a big boost from the encouragement and support of Steve Ross and Giuseppe Leporace. Fellow journalists who influenced my decision include John de Graaf, Bruce Burkhardt, Bob Brienza, Laurel Spellman, Carlene

Cross, and Kathy Mack. Great chunks of the manuscript were written in splendid isolation, thanks to the friendship and generosity of Catherine Walker, David Fuqua, and Jan and Jamie Koutsky, and to the love of Sharon Buck. Crucial assists came from Cleven Ticeson, Raimonda Modiano, Jennifer Wilkin, Brett Lalonde, and Linda Brill. And whenever my sanity was slipping, I could always look forward to another Boys' Night Out with Steve Moriarty, Phil Irwin, and the always-dapper Rolf Gruen, whose turn it is to buy the next round.

Decades after she was no longer a schoolgirl, my mother continued to correspond with teachers who had influenced her career. I never followed her lead, so I'd like to tell the family of the late Alta Faye Crook that she made a huge difference in at least one boy's life. The same goes for Gloria L. Jones, who taught so many of us to accept responsibility and to think for ourselves. Others who made me a better writer include Rebecca Force, Bob Kerns ("Just write, dammit!"), Bob Simmons, and, especially, Teya Ryan, who gave me more opportunities and cut me more slack than I ever deserved.

My pilot through the turbulent waters of publishing has been my agent, Michelle Tessler, who believed in this book from the very start. Michelle considered my proposal with both her head and her heart, ensuring it would someday come to life. I am deeply indebted.

My editor at Algonquin, Antonia Fusco, is a writer's dream. She sees the big picture; she appreciates the small details. She values accuracy and clarity, and works with me the way editors are supposed to work with authors: side-by-side. This is a much better book than it would have been without her deft touch.

I've spent many Thanksgivings sharing a table with Brett and Lauren Hamann. Brett, my son, has a huge heart and the guts to be different, two gifts that make him a talented writer and that inspire me to stay eternally young. Lauren, my daughter, never met a challenge she couldn't conquer. Nothing intimidates her, and her supreme self-confidence reminds me to keep going when the going gets tough. Of course, there are a lot of other things I could say about both of them, but then they could pull out all those embarrassing things about their dear old dad, so . . .

This book is dedicated to Gerry and Julianna. My father, Gerry Hamann, is the most unpretentious man I know. He works hard, quietly helps the less fortunate, and finds solutions to problems that most people would never even attempt to tackle. Dad gives me strength, courage, and the conviction to speak my mind, all indispensable gifts for a journalist.

My mother, Julianna Hamann, touches more lives than she'll ever imagine. A lifelong teacher and mentor, she dives into each day as if it were the only one that mattered, and finds something good in everyone she meets. Mom inspires me to dream, to explore, to take risks, and to have faith in the basic goodness of nearly everyone. When I put words on paper, I hear her voice. Every writer should be so lucky.